Liberty Kovacs is the most inspiring person I have ever known. The wife and mother of two infamously, recklessly self-centered and self-destructive writers (I'm the son), her life—as teacher, therapist and writer—is an embodiment of self-sacrifice, triumph over adversity, and the never-ending quest to lessen rather than contribute to the suffering of other human beings. It is a religious life, in the truest and most literal sense, and this book is the history of that life. I know it will provide serenity, courage and inspiration to anyone in need of them.

— **Franz Wright,** the author's first-born son
Poetry Pulitzer Prize Winner for his 2003 poetry
collection, ***Walking to Martha's Vineyard***
and author of ***The Beforelife, God's Silence,*** and
The Night World and the Word Night and others

With generous candor and charm, Liberty Kovacs shares her remarkable story of a woman and a family facing life's challenges and finding its joys and sense of self. The wife and mother of two Pulitzer Prize winning poets, she reveals her own remarkable life here. As she declares, "I wanted to reveal all the secrets, myths, and superstitions that ran rampant throughout our lives." We travel with her from family roots in Greece to early life in Martins Ferry, Ohio, on to life with poet James Wright in Seattle and Minneapolis, and finally after divorce to San Francisco, remarriage and a career as a family counselor. Taking "the road less traveled," the author gives us a tale of trials, travail, and triumph. It is a joy to the spirit.

— **Larry Smith,** author of ***Milldust and
Roses: Memoirs***

A person's name is often their birthright. This is certainly the case with Libby Kovacs. Her Greek immigrant father named his first-born child, Eleutheria or, in English, Liberty; and his bestowal set the theme for her life. Through a Depression-era childhood on the banks of the often-flooding Ohio River, struggling to be a good Greek daughter while growing up as an American child, to disinheritance by her father for leaving home to attend nursing school, to an early marriage to a brilliant but alcoholic poet, to her long life as a success-ful marriage and family therapist dealing with her own challenges with familial mental illness and discord in her second marriage to a survivor of Nazi and Communist terrorism, Kovacs shows a desire and drive to be free that will astound and inspire any reader.

Kovacs spent her life dedicated to fulfilling a vow she made to herself at seven, to be free, to find the liberty her father promised her at birth. Her journey has been chaotic, dramatic, and marked by tragedy and, in the end, heroic because she achieves what she set out to do at seven, she made her life hers without oversight and she kept her freedom.

I have always found the lives of others an inspiration for living my own life and Kovacs' life is no exception. The challenges Kovacs faced, the obstacles she overcame, and the courageous steps she took to live her life the way she was compelled to, is an inspiration daily as I travel along my own journey to liberty. Her story should be read and mulled by anyone who ever wondered: "Can I do what I have to do to be free?"

— **Amy Rachel Kaplan,** writer, editor, writing coach, author of **Letters to Jimmie**

Liberty Kovacs' life story has all the elements of the American Dream, both its myth and its reality. Breaking free from the patriarchal rule of her Greek immigrant family, she set an uneasy but independent course that led to her becoming a nurse and marrying fellow Ohioan, the poet James Wright. Headed for the fabled Land of Happiness, Life broke in with all its unpredictable misery: living in Minneapolis with their two sons, the marriage was soon riven by alcoholism, angers, unspeakable trauma and eventually bitter divorce. Bereft but courageous, Liberty set a new course and headed west to San Francisco where she had a scholarship to study psychiatric nursing. A single mother, she experienced triumphs in her profession, married again and bore a third son—that household too fell victim to unhappiness and despairs. Yet with each blow, her spirit rose again and again, never giving up on herself or her sons, whom she writes about with disarming openness. Liberty Kovacs has endured, endures, with what can only be called a spiritual, and maybe American, will. Reading this memoir, we experience her life as an epic quest toward wisdom, learning how to live, as she writes, with love, acceptance and generosity.

— **Merrill Leffler,** publisher of Dryad Press, author
of ***Partly Pandemonium,***
Partly Love (poems) and ***Take Hold***

LIBERTY'S QUEST

THE COMPELLING STORY OF THE WIFE AND MOTHER OF
TWO POETRY PULITZER PRIZE WINNERS,
JAMES WRIGHT AND FRANZ WRIGHT

Liberty Kovacs, Ph.D., MFT, MSN

Robert D. Reed Publishers
P.O. Box 1992
Bandon, OR 97411
Phone: (541) 347-9882; Fax: -9883
Email: 4bobreed@msn.com
Website: www.rdrpublishers.com

Editor: Cleone Lyvonne
Cover Design: Cleone Lyvonne
Interior Design: Amy Cole
Photography: From author's private collection
Photo collages: Cleone Lyvonne

ISBN: 978-1-931741-96-5
ISBN 10: 1-931741-96-4

Library of Congress Control Number: 2008922979

Manufactured, typeset, and printed in the United States of America

Important Disclaimer: This book is sold with the understanding that the author, contributors and publisher are not responsible for the results of any action
taken on the basis of information in this work, nor for any errors or omissions.
The publisher and the author and contributors expressly disclaim all and any li-
ability to any person whether a purchaser of this publication or not, in respect of
anything and of the consequences of anything done or omitted to be done by any
such person in reliance, whether whole or partial, upon the whole or any part of
the contents of this publication.

Manufactured under the direction of Double Eagle Industries.
For manufacturing details call 888-824-4344.

Dedication

I dedicate this book to my family past, present, and future and to the past generations that I knew only briefly and to those not even known to me.

To my parents, Paul and Irene Kardules; and to my siblings, Mary, Tony, Ann, and Jack; and to all their children and grandchildren.

To my first husband, Jim Wright, and our dear brave sons, Franz and Marshall.

And to my second husband, Miklos, and our blessed son, Andy; and to Kaye, Andy's wife, and to our granddaughter, Amanda, and our grandson, Andy, Jr. (AJ).

Acknowledgments

In the most recent past, I am grateful to the clergy and lay people of Trinity Cathedral in Sacramento who are my family now, and to Joan Stock, my spiritual director.

To my writing teachers, Amy Kaplan and Zoe Keithley, and to my editor, Cleone Lyvonne, I want to express my deep gratitude for your expert guidance and your support and friendship.

To my friends, past and present who walked with me on this arduous journey and the good laughs we shared along the way; I thank you as well as the therapists (most recently, Kristie Ellis, Tara Stiles, Karen Vartanian, Robert Robinson) who were so kind and who worked patiently with me over many years to help me find my way out of the underbrush of my life and who assisted me in the life-giving work of integrating body, mind, and soul.

I thank God everyday that all of you have been a part of my life.

ๅ Note From the Editor

This is a deep and profound psychological autobiography of Liberty (Kardules, Wright) Kovacs, a self-actualized Greek-American octogenarian growing up and living between cultures. As her editor and myself a former mental health therapist, my experience working with Libby's manuscript and photos was a gripping experience, often hard to put down until fatigue won out.

In spite of the drama and challenges, Libby led a life of admirable perseverance and courage to be all she could be. She not only changed generational patterns and went to college at the price of being disowned by her father, but she went all the way to earn a Ph.D. and worked as a marriage and family therapist into her late seventies. On top of this, she raised three sons, sometimes single parenting, sometimes being caught in the middle with stepparent issues. This empowering, educational, and enlightening book would be an outstanding text in universities worldwide—in women's studies, cultural studies, cultural anthropology, marriage and family studies—as well as an inspirational read for anyone looking for a really good read.

Meeting her in person, staying in her home, and going through photos in every room of her house, I experienced Libby to be such an easy person to be with. Fun, accepting, easy to talk to, I anticipate the readers will mirror (at least parts of) her story and feel themselves "heard by her," wishing they could have had her for their therapist to guide them through some of their challenges in life.

Now here she is, ready to officially release her book on her eightieth birthday, May 28, 2008.

Libby, may your eighties bring you an abundance of joy as you share your story and bring light and love to your audiences.

– **Cleone Lyvonne,** MSE
Editor/photo collage and
cover designer

Table of Contents

Foreword

In striving for truthfulness and authenticity, Liberty (Eleutheria) Kovacs tells her story with uncompromising and often startling honesty. The structure of her extensive narrative is shaped by paradigms from psychotherapy. But the mainly introspective nature of her material is balanced by a wealth of evocative details from the world she, family, and neighbors inhabited.

Kovacs herself is a clinical therapist who practiced marriage counseling successfully for thirty-five years. Her story tells what happens to families in trouble and why, especially to second generation immigrant youth when they are caught between the language, culture, religion and politics of the parent generation and the promises, customs and mores of the new civilization in the U.S. Liberty's people came from the Dodekanese in Greece. They brought with them an almost Homeric doctrine of honor as the value above values. Liberty, victimized by it, fought this doctrine all her life. Ironically, it also contributed to what is best in her. No wonder her accounts read like parts of a novel from Tolstoy or scenes from a Greek tragedy.

On the surface, all immigrant stories are the same, exuding optimism and happiness: Move to the U.S., get a good job, find a mate, marry, buy a house, and construct a new identity. If we are lucky, we prosper and send our children to college or help them to get a start in business. When we dig below the surface, matters are more complicated and ambiguous because immigrants often bring with them psychic and genetic histories full of incendiary material ready to explode when it comes into friction with the values of the new environment in school, church, work, and community. As Liberty Kovacs shows, the life of many of the people trapped between the Old Country and the American Dream is decidedly unhappy and often has destructive consequences. But her autobiography is not all dark. Her account of white-water rafting on the rivers of the West and Southwest, including the Colorado, is poetic and inspiring. The rivers helped Liberty, as the Irish would say, make her soul. The fight for freedom, integrity and balance was worth it.

Although this book will never furnish the libretto for a Broadway musical, I highly recommend it. It is a must read for all who have struggled and are struggling with adapting to the stages of life. But I hope it will also be read and discussed by immigrant groups, members of the medical profession, therapists and their clients, as well as practicing and aspiring writers. I would have added "politicians" to this list, but most of them are not interested in the stark facts of immigrant realities and would rather build fences to keep the rabble out.

— **Franz Schneider, Ph.D., LL.D.** Professor Emeritus,
Gonzaga University, Spokane, WA
English and Comparative Literature

INTRODUCTION

FROM "THE BOTTOM" TO BRILLIANCE

In 1978 when I reached my fiftieth year, I felt I was mature enough to go back to Greece for the first time. Yes, I know I said, "Go back to Greece." I had never actually gone to Greece before, but all through my childhood I heard my family and the Greek people in my community who had immigrated to this country in the 1920s talk about going back to Hellas—the Greek word for Greece. So, whenever I talked about going to Greece, I would say, "When I go back to Greece," even though I had never been there.

Finally, my dream came true. I did travel to Greece with my twelve-year-old son, Andy, to celebrate my fiftieth birthday. During the trip, I discovered my living roots. I wanted to learn more and more about my extended family. During the next decade, I collected information, papers, pictures, and stories from relatives and family members living in Greece and in the United States. After many more years and two more trips to Greece, I put all of the material I collected, plus my own memories and stories, into this book.

From the very beginning I was determined to write *THE TRUTH* about our family. I wanted to reveal all the secrets, myths, and superstitions that ran rampant throughout our lives. I also wanted to report others' memories and perceptions as they were told to me. I realized that we all (siblings, cousins, aunts, and uncles) had our own recollections and stories to tell and "the truth" was in the eye, ear, and memory of the beholder.

Writing my family story was often painful. I wanted to be completely open about my story, and this required an honest examination of how I had lived my life. Quite unexpectedly, I realized that by accepting the others' views of the events in our lives and how they evolved and influenced our family, the richness of the differing points of view made the writing of this story even more exciting and intriguing than I anticipated.

Exploring my family history was a humbling experience. Life is seldom easy for immigrants coming to this country. The Greek immigrants in our small community were intent on building a new life of work and establishing a family in a foreign land, while at the same time they struggled to maintain their own customs, language, and religion. Many of the immigrants of my parents' generation did all this with the full intent of someday returning to their homelands.

Nor was life easy for the children of immigrants who lived in two worlds—the Greek and the American. They often got caught between these two colliding cultures, and they constantly had to maneuver between two vastly different worlds. Ultimately, our parents expected us to choose their traditional ways and many did.

Every child born of immigrant parents has a unique story to tell. The impact of the parents' past has an enormous influence on the child's development and her perceptions of the world. I will be writing about that influence and the ways I attempted from a young age to cope, adapt, and struggle with the effects of growing up in an immigrant family during the Great Depression and the Second World War.

I was determined to walk through these two worlds and to learn as much as possible. I did as the poet Robert Frost described, I chose "the road less traveled, and that has made all the difference."

Why do I want to write my family story? What purpose will it serve? I remember reading a comment a long time ago by the American philosopher-historian Santayana that stayed with me over the years. He said, "If we don't learn from history, we are doomed to repeat it." And I knew, even as a small child, I did not want to repeat my parents' lives.

As a family therapist who has studied and worked with families for over four decades, I learned that one's family history was essential in understanding marriage and family dynamics in the present. Married couples brought their family histories, culture, structures, and process with them and replayed the family drama in their marriage. Beliefs and behavior patterns in relationships have deep roots in the previous generations. With clients I have traced a pattern of behavior in a family or a marriage through the previous three or four generations. I have observed that couples frequently re-enact scenes from their parents' marriages, and that individuals are emotionally affected by wounds and traumas suffered in previous generations.

My own behavior and our family's patterns were evident to me in relatives whom I met in Greece when I visited them at age fifty. I returned to Greece in 1994 and 1995, and I recognized behavior problems as well as medical and mental health problems that were common in our family on both sides of the Atlantic. So the family's health history was one more important reason I wanted to learn as much as I could about my family.

Genetically linked diseases are of particular interest to me as a mental health professional. I believe it's important for families to know their health histories as a way of taking preventative measures, particularly for the younger generations who may not be as aware of what the older generations have experienced. For example, diabetes, cancer, heart disease, and strokes are prevalent on both sides of our families, in addition to affective disorders, such as depression, anxiety, panic, and bipolar conditions along with alcohol, drug, and tobacco addictions.

In our family the first line of attack of any illnesses were various traditional cultural treatments: chamomile tea, mustard plasters, and *vendouzas*, which consisted of a suction-cup treatment applied to the back for colds, influenza, and pneumonia. The women were in charge of finding cures for everything from warts to the "evil eye."

Another, more personal and significant, reason I wanted to learn more about my family background was the matter of *roots and identity.* Where did I come from? Who am I? As a child I wondered whether I really belonged in my family. Was it possible that I was an orphan and left on my parents' doorstep? I know every child wonders this at times, but I questioned my place in the family most of my childhood. Even later, as a young adult, I felt I did not belong in my family. I wanted more than I was destined to expect. I wanted more than being the obedient daughter who would be "married off" in an arranged marriage at fifteen or sixteen to someone I didn't know. I wanted an education. I wanted to complete high school. The utterly impossible aspects of my dreams were college, and/or a job, and to leave home before marriage. These ideas were unheard of in our community: "A Greek girl does not leave her home to work. Do you want to dishonor your parents? Where did you get such a thought? Just wait. You will want to get married like every other *good* girl."

Even I wondered where my ideas and my desires came from. Getting an education or choosing my own partner in life *was not* meant

20

for me. Yet, that's what I wanted. I did not want my life mapped out for me. Did I have a choice? During my childhood years, I had few models of women working and living independent, productive lives. Of course, there were teachers, librarians, and nurses, and women who worked as clerks in banks and grocery stores, and a couple of women in our neighborhood worked in factories; but a job for its own sake or just to make money did not interest me.

I knew someday I would marry and have children. More than anything else, I wanted to work and have a meaningful life of my own. Greek women in my community did not have choices about their lives. They did not have lives outside of the family and their culture, even here in America. The traditional roles of women did not appeal to me. I wanted more.

Even in the 1940s my dream was radical. If women worked (or went to college) in those days, the assumption was, "I'll work until I meet someone to marry." No one talked about careers. Teachers and librarians were single women who devoted their entire lives to their work, just like nuns did. I never knew a woman lawyer, doctor, or social worker when I was growing up. My sister, Mary, wanted to become a nurse. I was not interested in the nursing profession until I was in high school when I realized that the nursing profession was a first step before college. As a nurse I could work my way through college!

In spite of few role models and a very traditional, patriarchal, re-strictive environment, my desire to live my life differently was a strong motivating force in my life; and this is the story I want to write.

Although I had strong feelings about living with secrets, scape-goating, superstitions, and oppression, I still wanted to understand my ancestors and my family and the effect that four hundred years of oppression by the Ottoman Turks had on them—and on me! Writing my family story was one way of honoring the memory and the lives of ancestors whom I never knew and our immediate family who survived appalling conditions of oppression, poverty, and illness before they immigrated to this country.

There are aspects of our family that I have wished were differ-ent, but we are who we are—good, bad, or indifferent. Given the historical, social, and economic context in which my parents lived, how different could their lives have been? We live our lives in the best way we know how. For their courage and fortitude, my family has my deepest respect, admiration, and love. In writing my story, I have learned to understand their need for secrecy and my own need to be honest, sometimes brutally so. I am grateful that I have the roots that I do, for there seemed to be built into me the determination to be free, to be myself, and to live my own life. I appreciate that I have had the unique experience of growing up as a child of immigrants in this great country. Where else would I have had the opportunities that were available to me here, and where else would I have had the freedom to achieve and grow beyond my destiny?

Writing this book was an evolving process. The earliest memories seemed to float to the surface of my consciousness in bits and pieces and through veils of space and time. I focused on fragments of stories and started putting them together as pieces of a puzzle. I discovered that I could not write about my family, particularly my father and mother, without first mentioning their ethnic and historical background. I realized that if I were to be true to my family's origins and traditions, I had to place their stories, and mine, within the historical, cultural, and religious context of our ethnic background. Thus, I structured this book to include those elements.

Part I of my memoirs are the memories and stories that I recalled and collected, and they are arranged like an album of snapshots of my family, my childhood, and my adolescent years which were spent in a neighborhood located in the small town of Martins Ferry on the Ohio River.

Part II focuses on my leaving home, being disowned by my father, and becoming a nurse. I married James (Jim) Wright who became a famous poet, writer, and winner of many prestigious awards, including the Pulitzer, and the father of our two sons. Our first son, Franz, born in Vienna on March 18, 1953, became a poet and winner of many prestigious awards, including the Pulitzer. Marshall, our second son, was born on July 30, 1958, during a very chaotic period in our lives when we lived in Minneapolis. Jim and I were divorced in 1962, and I took my sons west to San Francisco to build a new life for us.

Part III begins with our journey westward from Minneapolis to San Francisco where my sons and I lived while I attended Graduate School at the University of California for three years. I was hired as an instructor in the School of Nursing where I taught a year in the basic nursing program, then in the graduate psychiatric/mental health program for the next four years. I was the only single mother with two children in a graduate program of 100 students. My professional career extended over the next forty years.

I married a second time in 1965 to another extraordinary man, Miklos M. Kovacs. We had a son, Andre Michael (Andy) who was born on September 28, 1966.

Miklos, a Hungarian Freedom Fighter, came to this country as a refugee along with over a hundred compatriots in early December 1956 He and the others escaped from Budapest to Austria as the Russian troops invaded their country. The Communist Regime exiled him from his homeland for thirty-two years until he returned in 1989 after the Iron Curtain fell.

Our marriage was a long struggle of attempts to blend two families from two different cultures. His return to Hungary was the beginning of the end of our marriage and a new beginning for me.

PART I

Deep
Roots

My Family Story

Historical
Perspective

For inquire now of bygone generations,
And consider what their ancestors have found;
For we are but of yesterday, and we know nothing,
For our days on earth are but a shadow.
(Job 8:8-9)

Our family roots are sunk deep in the Dodecanese Islands in the Aegean Sea of Greece, off the coast of Asia Minor. Our family originated there on those ancient isles. Kalymnos was the birthplace of my father. Although my mother was born on Leros, originally, her family came from Patmos.

The Dodekanese (meaning twelve islands) is a misnomer because there are actually two hundred islands and isles, most of which are not habitable. Fourteen of the islands are inhabited and have local government status. These are: Rhodes, Kos, Kalymnos, Leros, Lipsos, Patmos, Karpathos, Kastelorizo, Halki, Simi, Tilos, Nisiros, Kasos, and Astypalaia. Apparently, at one time, they were one big continent that sank during geological alterations, leaving only the highest points, the peaks of its mountains on the surface of the sea. As a result of those changes the islands were formed. Settlements have existed on these islands since prehistoric times.

Turkey, the archenemy of the Greeks, lies in the mist on the horizon. Both countries are very aware of each other, and the Greeks are constantly on the alert against another invasion. Kalymnos, a small picturesque island, the sponge capital of the world, was carved out of the side of the mountain covered with sweet-smelling thyme and a variety of other wild herbs and flowers and overlooks the harbor of Pothia. The houses built into the sides of the mountain are brightly painted, mostly white and blue, the colors of the Greek flag. The picture-post-card image is deceptively peaceful at first sight. If one looks closer behind the trees in the courtyard of the church overlooking the town below, net-covered anti-aircraft guns can be seen. The Greeks will not be caught off guard again.

The location of the islands was a blessing and a curse. The blessing was being settled in one of the most beautiful environs in this world—the crystal-clear blue waters of the Aegean Sea blended with the blue sky on the horizon in a breathtaking magnificence. The curse was the geographic site of the islands and the strategic importance of their harbors and ports that made them easy prey of the larger neighboring countries of Asia Minor, Northern Africa, and Italy to the west.

The beauty of the islands and their strategic location was a tragic misfortune for the islanders. Since the dawn of history, their setting brought them wars, pillaging by marauding pirates, invasions and alien rulers for almost two thousand years, including the Romans, Venetians, Genoese, and the Turks from 1453 till 1912. The Italians went to war against Turkey in 1912 and immediately occupied the islands on the pretext of liberating the Greek Islands from the Ottoman Empire. Instead of liberating the islands, the Italians stayed for more than thirty years. During World War II, the Greeks had almost defeated the Italians when the Germans intervened, salvaged the situation, and remained to become one of the most savage occupiers. At the end of that terrible war, the islands were under the administration of the British military until the islands were reunited finally with Greece on March 7, 1947.

I would be remiss if I did not mention the importance of some of these islands in ancient times as well as in the modern era. Each island has a memorable story to tell.

Rhodes, the largest and most popular for tourists, is known as the "Isle of Roses" and the "Bride of the Sun." This island was famous for its Colossus, a bronze statue of Helios Apollo, the Sun God, erected in 290 B.C. and considered one of the seven wonders of the ancient world. The Colossus stood ninety feet tall and straddled the harbor of Rhodes. Helios, the protector of the city of Rhodes, was represented with his head framed in sunrays; in his right hand he held a torch that served as a beacon for mariners. Earthquakes destroyed the great Colossus in 225 B.C.

Rhodes was famous for its school of Oratory where its leaders of Greek democracy were trained, and where after the Roman occupation, great leaders of the Roman Empire (Cicero, Caesar, Brutus, and Cassius) also studied rhetoric.

Kos, another island popular with tourists today was at another time famous for its great Temple of Asclepius, the god of healing. It was here that Hippocrates, the father of medicine, founded his first medical school. With the advent of Christianity, the Dodecanese became one of the cradles of the new faith. Saint Paul was one of the apostles who visited the islands in spreading the Gospel.

The holy isle of **Patmos** became a shrine to Saint John the Evangelist who was exiled there and who wrote the Book of Revelation in a grotto named for the Apocalypse. In addition to serving the Orthodox faith, the monasteries on Patmos and many of the other islands served the very important function of retaining the Greek language throughout the many invasions. With time and acculturation, the Christian religion absorbed many of the pagan practices. Churches and cathedrals were built over ancient temples. Even so, remnants remain of legends of ancient gods, nymphs, and heroes and can be seen on the islands.

On **Kalymnos,** in the center of its capital city, Pothos, sits a statue of Poseidon; appropriately so, for the men of Kalymnos, Simi, and the other island have sailed the seas and fought for their country since the Trojan wars in ancient times. They have dived and died for sponges in the depths of the surrounding seas for hundreds of years. Sponge harvesting was a part of the Kalymnian heritage.

The Kalymnians exude a rough pride in their island and their history. Even the myth of the founding of Kalymnos is told with pride and humor: Kronos, the father of Zeus, was building the island of Kos by sifting sand on Kos and tossing the rocks over his shoulder. The place where the rocks landed became the island of Kalymnos. The surface of this island is mountainous and barren. The shoreline is lined with precipitous cliffs, sharp rocks, and hidden coves. Inland, however, the valley is fertile and produces figs, grapes, and olives.

Leros is the island of natural ports and the location of the remains of the Temple of Artemis (and later the Roman goddess Diana). This small island became a stronghold for the Italian Navy during World War II, and the Germans built bunkers in the hillsides. When I visited Leros in 1995, my cousin, Zaharias Matthioudakis, took me on a tour of the island and showed me where the Germans and English fought to the death on its mountainous shores. A cemetery for the English soldiers is located in Alinda, near my mother's birthplace. Zaharias took me to the port in Lakki, on the west coast of Leros where a Roman Catholic Church has stood vacant since the Italians departed the island. The Italian conquerors had made strong efforts to convert the people of Leros to Roman Catholicism, but to no avail.

The Greeks resisted other efforts toward *Italianization* of the Greek Islands. When the Italians outlawed teaching in Greek in the schools, some Greeks refused to send their children. My mother was one of those children who was taken out of school at the age of eight by her father. My father's youngest sister, Eleutheria, was compelled to learn Italian. Resentment toward the Italians and the Turks runs deep in the Dodecanese.

Yet, despite invasions, occupations, and massive oppression endured by the islanders over the ages, they have maintained their language, religion, and their devotion to Greece as their motherland. They are proud that they fought against all attempts by the invaders to assimilate the islanders whether by Islamic Turks or by the Roman Catholic Italians. Marriage to anyone other than a Greek was an unpardonable disgrace. The Greeks prided themselves on the purity of their blood. They claimed no mixture with any of their oppressors. This is doubtful since many Greeks settled in Turkey, Italy, and throughout the world.

The terrible destruction and the brutal campaign of "ethnic cleansing" that occurred in Yugoslavia in the 1990s speak volumes of the hatred that the Serbian Orthodox Christians maintained for hundreds of years toward the Moslems. I have no doubt that a similar level of hatred exists in the Greeks toward Turkey to this day. The immigrants in our community did not discuss the atrocities committed against the Greeks openly, but the hatred was palpable in their attitudes toward the Turks. I learned at an early age that the conquerors were on the islands for 400 years and fear pervaded the daily lives of the islanders, including my family. This was one area I did not question. I was thankful that they escaped with their lives. Later I wondered, what impact did those long years of oppression have on my grandparents, parents, and even on my generation and me?

Our family roots are sunk deep in the Dodecanese Islands in the Aegean Sea of Greece, off the coast of Asia Minor. Our family originated there on those ancient isles. Kalymnos was the birthplace of my father. Although my mother was born on Leros, originally her family came from Patmos.

Cultural
Perspective

Reality has always been a seamless web of interrelated
systems. Within patriarchy we have simply tried to superimpose
our humanly generated hierarchical paradigms onto that reality in
much the same way that we projected in earlier times
a pre-Copernican astronomy upon the skies.
(E. D. Gray, *Patriarchy as a Conceptual Trap*)

From early childhood onward, I was aware of the differences in the cultures that surrounded me, particularly my parents' Greek world and the external American world. I believe I was very fortunate that I grew up in what today would be called an integrated neighborhood that was multiethnic, multiracial, and multigenerational. On our one-block neighborhood on Carlisle Street lived three Serbian families, one Croatian, one Italian, one French, three Greek families (including ours), and four "American" families, three of whom were Negroes (as they were called in those days). Across the street from our home a three-generation Negro family lived in one house.

For many years I did not consider myself "white" because my skin would get very dark in the summertime. I identified more with the Negroes and the "foreigners" than I did with the "whites" who lived uptown. I felt different from those who spoke only English, and they behaved differently from us. They seemed so carefree and un-burdened by all the rules of behavior that were imposed on us by our culture. We spoke two languages; even the Negroes spoke a strange vernacular that they called "Pig Latin."

I managed to grasp the structure of Pig Latin and understood some of it, just as I picked up phrases and words from the Serbians. We were in and out of each other's homes and shared food, music, and traditions with each other. We all had in common fathers who worked hard in back-breaking jobs in steel mills, mines, and blast furnaces, and mothers who worked hard in their own kitchens cooking, cleaning, washing and ironing clothes with few if any conveniences or appliances. We had a washing machine, a refrigerator, and an electric iron. I noticed that some Negro mothers ironed their clothes with an iron that was heated on a coal-burning stove.

This intermingling of different ethnic and racial groups was the matrix in which my ideas of freedom, independence, equality, and selfhood were grounded. Even though words like "integration/segregation" were not descriptive terms used in the Ohio Valley when I was growing up, our schools were not only integrated, but we were taught the values of individuality, of "pulling ourselves up by our boot straps," and the possibility of achieving whatever we wanted if we worked hard enough. Patriotism and Bible studies (during the third year of my elementary education) were part of our curriculum along with reading, writing, arithmetic, and physical education.

Three evenings a week after "American" school, the Greek children in our community also attended Greek School. Here we learned the language, culture, and religion of our parents. Since there was no Sunday School in those days, Old Testament Bible stories were used as our reading lessons. There was no kindergarten in the public schools in our town until 1935 when I was in the second grade.

When I was four years old, I pleaded with my mother to enroll me in Greek School. I wanted to go to school just like all the older children. She, in turn, convinced the teacher, Kirios (Mister) Andreas, that I was a quiet, well-behaved child who would not be a problem in his multi-age schoolroom. Reluctantly, he conceded. I was anxious to learn, and I was thrilled that I was allowed to sit in the classroom with all the "big kids." I learned to read and write Greek as well as my older classmates.

Kirios Andreas was a big gentle bear of a man who loved children and teaching, but who left our town after a few years, perhaps for a better-paying position, or more likely, because he was not harsh enough in his teaching methods. Unfortunately, after he left, the responsibility of teaching the Greek children fell to the priest of our church. He was a heavy-handed disciplinarian who probably was not trained as a teacher and had little patience for this difficult endeavor. He seemed more intent on teaching us the principles of morality and the virtues of suffering and fear than on reading and writing. His methods seemed more acceptable to the parents because many of them believed that strict discipline was essential in the upbringing of respectful, obedient children. Their rule was "spare the rod and spoil the child." Another rule that was prevalent in our families and in Greek School was "be very stingy with praise, and very generous with criticism." Any teacher or priest who was too gentle, kind, or playful did not last long in our community.

In our neighborhood, my father was the strictest disciplinarian when I compared him with the other Greek fathers I knew. Yet, there were many more similarities among the Greek families than the other ethnic groups. Over the years as I have considered the differences among our neighbors and the uptown American culture, I realized a number of reasons for the differentness.

The Greek families of my childhood were characterized by several principle elements:

- The family structures were based on patriarchal and authoritarian foundations with rigid male and female roles.

- Men prided themselves on their individualism and achievements, and they found it intolerable to work for an employer. This was considered an affront to their pride and an insult to their self-esteem.

- Cultural standards did not allow women to work outside the home or leave home until married. However, they could work with their husbands or fathers in the family business. For a woman to work outside the home implied that the man was not capable of supporting his own family, and this was viewed as an insult to his pride and honor.

My father was the master in the family. My mother submitted to his rule, and she never openly contradicted him, except on two occasions. The first occurred when I was about six months old. My mother never told me the details of what happened. She said only, "You were crying for a long time and your father slapped you so hard you passed out. I was frightened that he had killed you. I screamed at him that he was never to hit you again with his hand."

He never did that I can remember, but he threatened us with his belt. Neither do I remember that he ever took the belt off. My mother quietly defied him when he told her she could not visit her mother and sister. She didn't argue or reason with him. She simply went to see them when he was at work

We children were to be quiet when he came home from work. When he walked in the door, we stopped our noisy interactions and scattered in different directions and played quietly alone or outside. We were taught to be obedient and respectful both inside and out-side of the family. Although my father was short in stature, he was a very powerfully built man. He was very strong and proud—proud of his heritage, his independence, and his achievements. His name, his word, and his honor were his most valuable possessions.

Our behavior was a reflection on him, and we knew we were never to do anything that would bring shame, embarrassment, or dishonor on his name. We were expected to be polite, quiet, and well behaved in public. Any digression was met with a dark look. All he had to do was look at us and that stopped us in our tracks. If we dared to ignore the look, his hand would move quickly to the wide belt around his waist and his fingers would start to undo the buckle. At that moment, children fled in all directions.

Misbehavior by children in public was considered shameful and implied the parents were unable to control them. Any adult in the community who witnessed unacceptable behavior by a Greek child was expected to report it to the parents.

I remember one time when I was in high school and I was seen by a Greek neighbor walking down the street after school with a male classmate. By the time I got home, my parents had been told and I was scolded severely. Greek girls were not permitted to have boyfriends, nor were we allowed to date or be seen in public with a male friend. His daughter's virginity and virtue were the father's responsibility and came under the family and cultural jurisdiction of "philotimo," the love of honor. Any stain on the family's honor due to questionable behavior by a daughter meant a loss of stature in the community and made it very difficult for her to "marry well."

In Greek families, this love of honor was held sacred. Death was not considered too high a price to pay if the family were dishonored. The honor of the family was instilled in children from infancy. Marriage was essential for women; and the father, or oldest son, was responsible for arranging the marriage to a *kalo paidi*, or a decent man. If she did not marry by thirty, she became an object of shame and would be criticized for her spinsterhood. She continued to be the father's responsibility, since *philotimo* did not permit her to leave home, nor work outside the home. If she did so, the implication was that her father was not man enough to support her and the community would consider him a failure.

When a young woman accepted the arranged marriage tradition, she avoided falling in love, or she achieved the illusion of falling in love with the man who pleased her parents. If she did fall in love and the man was Greek, the father coerced them into marriage whether they were prepared or not. The only status a woman had was as a wife and mother, and the more male children she produced the higher her status, prestige, and validation. I was aware of the custom of arranged marriages from a young age. I remember telling my father when I was seven years old: "Don't think you can arrange a marriage for me. I want to graduate from high school."

By the time I graduated from high school, I saw a number of young Greek girls, classmates, friends, and neighbors "married off" and our family attended their weddings. They had chosen to comply with their parents' customs and to marry for financial security and status.

The male was valued more than the female, and the first son stepped into the authority position when the father died, even if he were younger than his sisters. This was the case in my mother's family: her youngest brother Stavros was the only unmarried son when their father died suddenly. He became the head of the household and responsible for providing for his mother and three sisters, and for arranging "good" marriages for them.

I learned very early in life that men had privileges and rights that women did not. Men were free to "sow their wild oats" during their youth. They were usually older than the woman when they married. The culture was accepting of the men's sexual appetites and permitted the double standard for them that were out of the realm of possibility for "decent" women. Men could have mistresses, even when married, as long as they were discrete about the other relationship. A wife maintained her purity by being available for her husband for the purpose of bearing children and perpetuating the family name with honor. He or his family never acknowledged any child born of the husband's mistress. I came to believe that the practice of married men having mistresses served the wives as a means of birth control.

Greek family life is extremely close and children are strictly controlled, especially the females. Although loving parents used teasing and shame as child-rearing tactics, their reasoning was to toughen them in preparation for difficult lives that awaited them. Generally, parents were affectionate until the children reached the age of ten to twelve. Then, the females were expected to be compliant, achieve in school, and help with the housework. Boys worked with their fathers from an early age.

When I was a child, we never had babysitters. Children attended all social activities with their parents, even if it meant they fell asleep on chairs or on adult laps. We attended all the dances, picnics, and parties that adults did. I learned most of the folk dances as soon as I walked and we were encouraged to join the line dances. Children attended church services with their parents and participated in the rituals of marriage, baptisms, funerals, and memorial services. We were not excluded from any family activities, but we were expected to be unobtrusive. I can remember observing dinners and parties that my parents had with their friends from the top of the stairs. When I got tired, I'd quietly go to bed.

Children were not permitted to talk back to adults and questions were discouraged. If you asked why, you would get advice or be told, "Because I (or your father) said so." We were expected to accept things the way they were. If a child challenged the rules or the parents' authority, she could expect punishment, rejection, or worse, getting disowned. Mothers often protected or ran interference for the children with their father. Occasionally, she might be able to persuade him in private to permit the child a special toy or activity, but the usual response in our family was "no."

When I pushed the family rules too far and my Mother was at a loss as to what to say or do, she stepped out of the way and I was free to speak directly to my father. For example, when I was a sophomore in high school, I asked his permission to go into the nursing profession after graduation. I knew college was out of the realm of possibility for me unless I earned my own way. Quite expectedly, his response was, "No. No daughter of mine will ever go into nursing or anywhere else or you're no daughter of mine! Greek women do not leave home without marriage!" I pushed the boundaries as far as I could in my attempts to negotiate and persuade him that I would not disgrace him. But he was adamant and unbending. When I left home at twenty to attend nursing school, I was disowned.

Many years later, on my trip to Greece, I learned again why my request was so outrageous to my father. I met a woman on a ferry, from Piraeus to Kalymnos, who was a schoolteacher. We shared a stateroom and as we became acquainted, I asked her whether she had married. With a tinge of bitterness in her voice, she responded, "School teachers do not usually get married." When I inquired quietly, "What are the reasons they don't marry?" She answered, "Women who are teachers live alone and are independent. For these reasons they are not considered marriageable. They are not acceptable to men." After a few moments, she added, "Change is coming to Greece, but it is coming slowly. Today, women do work as bank clerks and even in department stores. One day things will be different for women here, too." The year was 1978!

The Greek
Orthodox Church

OUR RELIGIOUS PERSPECTIVE

The Greek Orthodox Church was an influential and integral factor in the lives of the people of Greece and for those who immigrated to countries all over the world. The Church, accepted as the conscience and guardian of the Greek peoples' moral and spiritual life, was credited with saving the Greek culture, language, and the religion during the many occupations of the island. Thus, when Greeks emigrated from Greece, the Greek Orthodox Church emigrated with them. The power of the church was steadfast no matter where it was located. The Church was the custodian of religious practices, rituals, and the cultural customs and traditions of her people and the foundation of every community where Greeks settled.

In Kalymnos a huge cross, probably over forty feet tall, stands like a sentinel on top of a hill overlooking the terrain, the sea, the comings and goings of the ships, and the people below. On every island there is at least one large church and small chapels scattered on the mountainsides. Standing on a beach in nearby Lipsos, a relatively small island, I counted thirteen chapels within view of the beach, and a majestic cathedral on the tallest hill. I could not see how many were on the other side of the mountain.

CUSTOMS

When I was in Greece I noticed the custom of women crossing

themselves. This was practiced by older women who walked in the path of a church or if they were riding by on a boat and spotted a chapel on the hillside. Even some of the younger women seemed compelled to cross themselves, but did so more surreptitiously, appearing embarrassed when noticed by tourists. All the chapels were left unlocked. Travelers or picnickers were invited to spend the day in exchange for replacing the olive oil in the *kandelia*, red globes filled with water and olive oil. The wick on the top of the *kandelia* was lighted during services or when praying.

Every home had an *iconostasis*, a nook that held icons of saints and a *kandelia*. Prayers were said every morning and every night, again mostly by the women. The men were more casual about their religious practices. The saying in Kalymnos was: "If you can hear the church bells, you are in church." The chapels were too small for more than a priest, the cantor, and a few nuns who sang in the choir. The congregation gathered in the churchyard to participate in the service or to gossip.

The patriarchal influence was still very evident in the Greek Orthodox Church in Greece when I visited there in 1978, and again in 1994 and 1995. Men assisted the priest during the liturgy as cantors and in administering the church. Male acolytes and the priest were the only ones permitted in the sanctuary. I was told once that if a woman set foot in the sanctuary, the entire church would have to be re-consecrated. This is still true today.

The women had their places and the men, theirs. Even husbands and wives who went together did not sit together in church. This was true when I was a child in Martins Ferry: the men sat in the pews to the right and the women, on the left. When there was a choir of women, they stood in the back of the church. In recent years, when I attended a Greek Orthodox Church, I observed some slight, but remarkable, changes: a woman cantor participated in the service, the choir of men and women stood in the front of the church, and little girls in white dresses were standing in front of the sanctuary.

As a child and adolescent in Martins Ferry, Ohio, I was aware of the hierarchical structure of the church, as well as the mystical quality of the service that was palpable in the atmosphere filled with incense, chanting, and the brightly hued robes of the priest that added a sense of a sacred presence and authority. The mystery was enhanced every time the priest withdrew behind the altar and closed the doors to pray. The life-sized icons of Saints Michael and Gabriel stood guard on each side of the door facing the congregation. I used to fantasize that the priest's whispering was his secret conversation with God.

Since there were no Bibles or printed material that we could read, we were expected to accept the liturgy and the rituals without question. The effect of this lack of information and knowledge seemed to be a strong dependence on rote learning of beliefs and practices intermingled with superstition. Women were fearful of the influence of "The Evil Eye," particularly on infants and children. I wore an amulet that my mother pinned on my petticoat until I was eight years old to ward off any inadvertent evil looks or stares that might cause some kind of misfortune while I was in school. Ignorance and fear contributed to a strong dependence on shame and guilt as control mechanisms in families, especially control of women and children.

Another custom in Greek families was the tradition of passing on names from one generation to another. The first child was usually named after the father's mother or father, and the second child was given the names of the mother's parent. Sometimes traditions and customs had a way of breaking down depending on events and circumstances. When I was born, my father and his mother were upset with each other; and rather than giving me his mother's name (Naomi), I was christened "Eleutheria" which means Liberty, his youngest sister's name. My sister Mary, who was born after me was given both of our grandmothers' names, Maria Naomi.

There was another consideration when naming children. When a child was baptized in the Greek Orthodox Church, the name given to the child at birth had to correspond with a saint's name. Thus, in addition to being named after a grandparent each child was named after a saint. It was not uncommon that a child would have one name on her birth certificate and another name on her baptismal record. For example, a girl who was named Vickie would be baptized Vasiliki—after Saint Basil whose name is pronounced Vasilis in Greek. To make matters even more complicated, there were male and female versions of the same name. A boy called Bill would be christened Vasilis after the same St. Basil. A son of our neighbors, Mihalis and Katina Kotellas (later translated into Michael and Katherine), was named Eleutheris—the male version of my name. Somehow his name was translated to Harry—I suppose from the last syllable of his Greek name.

My father's name, Apostolos, came from the word Apostle, which was not a Saint's name but the title of twelve saints. Interestingly, Apostolos became Americanized into Paul – another Saint's name. My mother's name Ereni (which means peace) became Irene in English. Her oldest brother's name, Christodoulos, means servant of God. The Greeks were very patriotic as well as devoutly Christian. I believe that such names as Liberty and Peace were given to children in protest and defiance toward the many invaders who conquered the Greek Islands.

I discovered another custom when I became twelve. My mother quietly announced one Sunday morning as I prepared for church, "You have now become a woman and on those days you can no longer kiss the icon or the priest's hand when he offers you bread after the church service is over. At other times it's all right."

I was surprised and indignant, "I don't understand. Why not?"

"Because you are unclean during those days," was the answer she gave me. I did not believe such a far-fetched notion, and I was skeptical about the other beliefs about women, but I knew it wouldn't do any good to argue or try to discuss the subject further with my mother. That's what she believed, and that's as far as the subject went.

She was patient with me even when she couldn't or wouldn't answer my questions, but my father was not. Questioning was not tolerated, especially from a female child. The truth was what the priest and your parents told you what was to be done or not, and you were expected to abide by that, no matter how you felt about it. Resentfully, I resigned myself to what I could not change. Slowly my anger simmered and my disillusionment with the church and our culture grew.

PERSONAL EXPERIENCES IN THE CHURCH

A terrible tragedy occurred in 1935 that brought about a change. I remember that year; the winter was stormy and very cold, and the snow was wet and heavy. I shivered as I walked home from Greek School, and my hands felt stiff from the freezing wind. Trudging home through the snow was difficult. The next morning the Greek community awakened to the shocking news that our priest had been murdered in the basement of the church. He had been hit in the head with a hatchet. *Who would do such a terrible thing? To kill a priest must be a dreadful sin.* The murderer was never found. This terrible loss left the Greek community in a state of confusion and turmoil for months. Six months passed before another priest was sent to Martins Ferry.

Finally, the Archdiocese sent Father Lambros. He was a young man, probably just out of seminary and unmarried. The priests in the Orthodox Church may marry before they graduate from seminary. After that they must remain celibate, especially if they had any intentions of becoming Bishop. At the time, I had no idea what celibacy meant. Later, when I learned that a seminarian was seeking an arranged marriage prior to his graduation, I found the search for a wife by a priest (or any other man) very distasteful. I think I preferred the idea of celibacy for myself rather than an arranged marriage.

I knew I liked Father Lambros the moment I saw him. He had a full black beard and a wonderful smile. He obviously loved children because he wanted to start a Sunday School to teach us Bible stories and the scriptures. He announced his plans the first Sunday after his arrival. He asked the parents to send their children to church on the following Saturday so he could get acquainted with us. We were to bring a brownbag lunch so we could picnic together. This request astounded the parents and the children. Imagine a priest having a picnic with children!

All the children were excited about attending Sunday School, even if we had to attend on Saturday morning. The previous priest did not have time to teach Sunday School because the church service lasted about four hours. No one had considered having Sunday School on Saturday before, in addition to Greek School three evenings a week after public school classes.

Papa (Father) Lambros was a kind and gentle teacher and quite enthusiastic about teaching us Bible Stories and the parables of Jesus. My favorite story was about Joseph and his many-colored coat that got him in trouble with his jealous brothers who sold him into slavery. The parable that impressed me the most was the one about the talents: The two slaves who invested their talents were rewarded, and the one who hid his talent was discharged and punished.

For to all those who have, more will be given, and they will have an abundance; but for those who have nothing, even what they have will be taken away (Matt.25:29). I took this lesson to heart and it became a beacon for me. In a culture where women and girls were devalued, I heard Papa Lambros telling me that whatever skill or talent I had was important and useful and that it should not be wasted.

Unfortunately, within six months after his arrival, Papa Lambros was gone. The congregation asked the Archbishop for a replacement. Some parents complained, "He was too easy on the children and he was spoiling them." *He was too kind and gentle!* The parents were concerned that he was not using enough discipline, and, yes, even more harshness was necessary if children were to learn.

The loss of Papa Lambros was a terrible shock to me. I could not understand how the adults could be so insensitive and uncaring to send away such a fine priest and teacher. I was hurt and angry. All the children were. My hope for new possibilities withered into sadness, and I buried my disappointment and disillusion deep within me. Years passed before I realized the unexpressed grief I felt when he left. In my child's mind, Papa Lambros became a live representation of Jesus for me. He was the first, and the last, to tell us that God loved us.

Another year went by before another priest was assigned to our parish. This one fit the criteria for discipline and harshness. He used the ruler more frequently and generously. The parents were more satisfied that their children would not be corrupted with kindness. We never had Sunday School again.

My sister, Mary, and I both had very bad experiences with the priest who replaced Papa Lambros. I was so afraid of being punished for not knowing my assignment that I froze from anxiety. I had more difficulties with assignments than I ever had before. Mary was punished more severely. The priest locked her in the basement "to teach her a lesson in proper behavior" for whatever she had done. This was the same basement where the former priest had been murdered.

My mother was so angry, she refused to send us back for several months. He, too, was eventually replaced. For me the damage was done. After the age of twelve, I did not continue attending Greek School. My education in Greek had become sporadic and fear-laden, and as a result, my knowledge of the language was minimal. I spoke what we called "kitchen Greek." My interest in the church waned significantly. My attendance to church services became irregular. Like many parishioners, I attended mostly the Christmas Eve and Good Friday services. I felt more determined than ever to stay in public school where I was safe and to graduate from high school. I had to find a way out of the harsh environment of home and church.

A PERSONAL DEFINING MOMENT

One warm June afternoon as I was sitting on a grassy bank on the Ohio River, lost in the merging of myself with the fast flowing waters, a gentle clear voice pierced my reverie.

"You can escape. You will be free."

I was startled by the quiet certainty of the words. I sat up straight and looked around me. No one was there. *Escape? How can I escape?* I asked wordlessly.

I savored the words and repeated them over and over in my mind, and I wondered, "How will I escape?" Then slowly the thoughts became: *If there's a way, I will find the way. Now I have my own secret! I will not tell anyone—not my best friend Lillian, certainly not my family. No, not even my favorite second grade teacher, Miss Stark.* Gradually, an escape plan took shape in my mind, and it became a motivating force, the blueprint for my life.

First, I must find a way to stay in school and to finish high school. Yes, I have to finish high school, no matter what I have to do or what I have to give up. This will be very difficult. This will mean that I cannot allow my parents to arrange a marriage for me. I know that's my fate, but how will I stop them? I have no idea—yet. Just a few months ago our family attended the wedding of a young woman in our community whose parents had arranged her marriage to an older man. She was only sixteen, and he must have been twice her age. That was the custom, and that's what happened to all Greek women when they reached the age of fifteen or sixteen. This was our culture's way of dealing with adolescence. The parents did not have to deal with a daughter who might go wild during her sexual awakening and bring dishonor to the family by getting pregnant. Marriage became a logical solution in the prevention of unwanted pregnancies, and probably unwanted sons-in-law.

Was I only seven when I decided to give up everything like dating which Greek girls were not allowed to do anyway? I was willing to make any sacrifice that was necessary to make a different life for myself. My plan became my sustenance and my direction through childhood and adolescence. For the next decade or so it gave me patience and courage to endure whatever my father demanded of me. I knew deep in my soul that his power over me was limited by time.

I was acutely aware of the customs that preceded the wedding celebration. First, the husband-to-be approached the father, the head of the household, and offered a proposal of marriage. If the man was considered suitable in terms of means to support his daughter, then the father accepted the offer. At a party arranged by the groom's family, they were permitted to spend time together where she could be chaperoned by her mother or grandmother. The date of the wedding was usually announced at the engagement party or soon afterwards. The whole affair from meeting to marriage usually took a few weeks or months. The couple would have the rest of their lives to get to know each other.

I knew this was my fate, too. How was I to stop the inevitable? Even at the age of seven, I knew I was not like the "American" girls who were growing up around me. Dating was out of the question. Attending high school was not guaranteed. The common thinking in the Greek Community at that time was that girls did not need to be educated. Getting married and having children did not require a high school diploma. For me, attending high school became more important than dating. In my mind I was willing to sacrifice everything: my friends, my home, and my family, whatever was necessary to change my destiny! This decision grew out of the promise of my escape, which sustained and gave me hope and a sense of direction throughout my childhood. I learned patience, and I endured the restrictions and expectations of my family and culture. I knew deep in my soul that their power over me would not last forever.

Paternal
Roots

THE KARDOULIAS FAMILY

Life was hard for my grandparents, Antonios and Naomi, who were born and raised on Kalymnos. Here the men learned a rough kind of confidence verging on arrogance, and the women learned submission and nurturance. For both, emotions were submerged; yet, when the occasion arose, emotions burst forth in spontaneous combustion. Some relatives said grandfather was a soft, gentle man, especially, Eleutheria, his youngest daughter who cared for her mother and father in their later years. Uncle Savvas remembered his father as a very hard worker who grew and sold tobacco for a living.

"Those were different times. Men were harder," Savvas told me almost apologetically when I asked him about Grandfather as a young man.

My father, Apostolos, the oldest son, remembered his father differently. He remembered growing up hungry. His father was young and strong then and still wild. He hadn't given up his bachelor ways. He struggled to make a living for his family raising and selling tobacco. Grandfather Antonios had a reputation of stubbornly defying the Turks who occupied their island and spending many months in Turkish jails. He supposedly spent so much time in jail that Grandmother had to go there to sew clothes for him.

One family story has Grandfather and Apostolos' godfather walking in the mountains when the godfather spotted a Turk and shot him. Another version of this story was that Grandfather, on his way to church one Good Friday, killed three Turks. I've had doubts about these stories because the Turks were ruthless occupiers, especially when they were defied. I suspect that Grandfather got drunk and took some shots, and fortunately he missed shooting the Turks and was hauled off to jail. And the story grew from there. Greek men are notorious for exaggerating and embellishing their stories, especially when they are sitting in the *kafeneio* (coffee house) trying to outdo each other's stories.

My father was selective about the stories he told us. He never revealed that his youngest brother died at the age of twenty in a sponge-diving accident around 1940, or that he had two younger brothers who died at birth. Uncle Savvas gave me this information. One child who died was named Savvas. I wondered how he felt about being given the dead child's name. The five surviving children of Antonios and Naomi Kardoulias were Apostolos (1904), Maria (1908), Eleni (1910), Savvas (1914), and Eleutheria (1918).

SCENES FROM MY FATHER'S LIFE

Apostolos was a restless, wild, and fierce-tempered young boy—just like his father. He did not like school or his teacher. "An empty stomach is not conducive to learning," he sardonically told my siblings and me, as he related the story of his short school career.

He knew the consequences if he did not recite his lessons correctly. He was beaten by his teacher, and later at home, by his father. The more he got hit, the more defiant he became. By the age of eight, he decided he would not let his teacher hit him again. One morning Apostolos was poorly prepared to recite his lesson. As the teacher approached him with that look of contempt in his eyes, Apostolos reached for the huge clay vase beside the door that was used to collect water. Quickly, he picked up the vase, lifted it over his head, and threw it. The vase grazed his teacher's head. Then, Apostolos ran as fast as he could for the hills. " Now, I've done it," he thought. "Papa will kill me."

As evening turned to night and his stomach growled in hunger, he walked home slowly to face his father's wrath. He knew his mother could not protect him or she would have to face Grandfather's anger herself. Besides, she was pregnant and she did not have the energy to deal with her husband. So, Apostolos faced his father "like a man" and admitted, "I hit the teacher over the head with a vase..." Before he could complete his sentence, fists were pounding his head, shoulders, and back. His thin arms were not strong enough to block his father's strong, quick blows.

At eight years of age, Apostolos was expelled from school. The next day after the beating, his father took him to the harbor and got him a job on a sponge boat where he learned the hazardous work of sponge diving. This was the work performed by the young men of the Dodecanese Islands for hundreds of years.

He was either too small for the diving equipment or they did not have equipment in those days (around 1912), or he just didn't want to use any. With bravado my father told the story of his early days as a sponge diver. "I tied a rope around my waist and on the other end I tied a large rock. I held on to the rock as tight as I could and plunged into the depths where the sponges were located, about two hundred feet."

The stories that my father told us about his childhood were told with the pride of achievement, and with humor and admiration. I hated what Grandfather did, even if my father did not complain. I felt the harshness that he suffered at the hands of his father and, later, the hardships that he endured as a sponge diver and seaman when he was only a child like me. I felt sorry for his early life; at the same time I was relieved that I did not have to grow up in the "old country" where there were so many privations.

Frequently, I compared my life with those of my parents. I loved school and I could not imagine being expelled or taken out of school as my mother was by her father who did not want her to be taught the Italian language by the new conquerors. I did not understand that at all. Learning another language did not seem that bad to me. Another thing that I was grateful for: we didn't have foreign invaders to worry about. Both of my parents' families grew up under the rule of first, the Ottoman Empire, then the Italians.

Apostolos was twelve years old when Grandfather sailed with him from Kalymnos to Marseilles, France, to do some gambling.

After losing all his money, and afraid of being stranded in a foreign country during the first World War, Grandfather offered his son to a sea captain in servitude on a freighter in exchange for return passage to Greece.

I was outraged when I heard this story! How could a father do such a thing to his own son? I looked for any little sign of resentment on my father's face, but I saw none. I never understood my father's compliance and acceptance of being an indentured servant because of his father's irresponsibility. The only complaint I heard from my father was his hatred of gambling which was directed at our Uncle Steve (Aunt Katina's husband) who was a gambler, too. There was a big difference in my mind between Grandfather and Uncle Steve. It's true my uncle was an ardent gambler who gambled with his family's grocery money, but he loved his children and did not mistreat them. He worked very hard in the steel mills until he was 75. Unfortunately, he had declared himself ten years younger when he signed up to work, and he died six months after he retired.

Uncle Savvas told another version of this story to me. Grandfather took Apostolos to Marseilles when he was twelve and put him to work in a steel mill until he was fourteen. It was because Grandmother constantly pleaded with him that Grandfather finally went back to France and brought his son back home. Although Dad never said so, I always suspected that his earnings were sent home. Whether his mother ever saw any of the money is questionable. Perhaps the two stories about my father's servitude and his working in the steel mills as a young boy were really one story.

I put the pieces together like this: Apostolos did work in Marseilles for two years, as his brother related; and on his return trip to Greece, he served on the ship in exchange for his father's passage. Afterwards, he got hired on board as a fireman and traveled around the world several times.

In 1924 the freighter, *Patris*, docked in a New York harbor. Apostolos was getting weary of life on the ship and traveling to foreign ports. He started feeling the urge to settle down. He had heard stories of Greeks immigrating to the states of Ohio, Indiana, and Pennsylvania and finding jobs in the steel mills. He knew he could do the

51

work, for he had done it before. After much thought, Apostolos realized that if he left, he would have to go without his passport. Even though he was uncertain about the consequences of no identity papers, he decided to jump ship. After all this was a free country. He was willing to risk it, and he spoke no English! The worst that could happen was he would be deported back to Greece.

Apostolos packed a small bag with his clothes, waited for nightfall, and slipped quietly off the ship. He wandered around Brooklyn neighborhoods until he spotted some Greek letters on the window of a grocery store. With the help of other recent immigrants, he fled inland to Martins Ferry, Ohio, where he quickly found work in the Laughlin Steel mills, despite being an illegal alien. He found living quarters with several other Greek men and they became close life-long friends. As they each married, they became godfathers for each other's children.

From the stories I heard about Grandfather, he impressed me as an erratic, unpredictable, impulsive man who was a heavy drinker and a gambler who wiled away his time in the kafeneio and brothels, and that he was brutal and cruel toward his oldest son. From his behavior patterns and from the fact that several members of different generations in our family were afflicted with affective disorders (panic, depression, and bipolar), I am almost certain that Grandfather was affected with an agitated depression or a manic-depressive condition.

In modern medicine these ailments are considered genetically-linked; however, I am convinced that people who have suffered from generations of oppression, fear, traumas, and hunger are definitely predisposed to mental and emotional disorders and to a variety of addictions, as is evident from our family's medical and psychological histories.

Despite his father's abusive behavior, Apostolos remained completely loyal to him. I don't remember that he ever said an unkind or critical word about him. The stories that my father told were always related with humor and admiration. He identified strongly with his father and became very much like him, with the one exception that he hated gambling so much that he did not permit us, his children, to have a deck of cards in the house. Although he played cards in coffee houses with his friends, he never played for money. (The candy that he won, he brought home to us in his lunch box.)

Aunt Maria related another story about my father and Grandfather to me. Apostolos was eighteen at that time and was still very much afraid of his father's anger. On the day he was preparing to leave on the *Patris* for a long voyage, his father was antagonized about something he had said or done. As Apostolos climbed up the gangplank, he looked back and saw his father's dark face and panicked. He ran without looking, stumbled, and fell three stories down below in the hold of the ship. He spent the next three months in the hospital recovering from his injuries. As soon as he was completely healed, he was on the ship again headed for the United States and other ports around the world. Apostolos did not return again to Kalymnos until 1960 (when he was fifty-four).

Uncle Savvas, Aunt Eleni, Aunt Eleutheria, and their parents left Kalymnos before the outbreak of the Second World War and settled on the island of Rhodes. Aunt Maria stayed on their home island. They all married and had their families. Years later, I learned that my father had provided the *prika, or dowry,* for his sisters. The *prika* was an exchange of land, money, or other valuables that the woman's family was expected to pay to the bridegroom in order to arrange a "good" marriage. The Greek government outlawed this custom in 1983. I cannot imagine the hardship these dowries must have caused my father and mother during the Great Depression.

MY TRIP TO GREECE BROUGHT FURTHER DISCOVERIES

In 1978 when I went to Greece to discover and visit my relatives, my son and I spent almost a week with Aunt Maria. Andy spent most of his afternoons at the beach playing with several Greek boys his age. Although Andy spoke only English and his new friends spoke Greek, they didn't seem to notice. Their different languages were no obstacle to playing and enjoying new friendships.

I stayed at home with my aunt, a very strong, vigorous, and agile woman of seventy. In her own words, "I climb these steep hills like a mountain goat," and she laughed. She wore the black dress, apron, and a veil over her head that was customary for widows. Her husband had died five years before, and her son was living in Australia. Uncle Savvas had two daughters and several grandchildren who also lived in Australia.

One afternoon she took me on a short tour of the hillsides above her home to the tiny one-room stucco house where my father lived as a child. Then, we climbed up the steep slope to the little church on the top of the hill that overlooked the seaport below. In the courtyard just below the church, I was surprised to see soldiers and anti-aircraft guns, under camouflaged nets, pointed in the direction of the coast of Turkey.

Aunt Maria laughed gleefully as she walked and talked about her memories and experiences. She showed me the place where she and other women on the island barricaded themselves on the hillside overlooking the port and observed the Italians landing on Kalymnos in 1919. The women flung rocks at the soldiers as they came ashore. This was the women's one act of defiance, and when they got tired after twenty-four hours, they all went home.

She told me the story of her wedding day when she married a sea captain. She described the celebration as a happy one with much food, music, and dancing. That night after the festivities were over, her groom took her home and left her. He spent the night with his mistress. She laughed and slapped her thigh as she saw my shocked expression.

"And you are still wearing black for that man after all those years!" I exclaimed.

"Yes," she explained in a serious tone, "because he is the father of my son."

That summer I learned more about the Greek cultural mores and customs that defined the appropriate behaviors of women and widowhood. Women did not walk alone on the street. Even to go to the market or perform errands of any kind, a woman had to be accompanied by another woman or a child. Occasionally, a man accompanied his wife, but this was not common on Kalymnos. The men spent their leisure time at the *kafeneio* where they drank coffee, played cards, talked politics, and told stories. Women were not permitted there. Finally, around the mid-1990s, women could go to a *kafeneio* for coffee or an ice cream if their husbands accompanied them.

In my father's day, a woman sitting alone in a *kafeneio* was in danger of having her throat slit. My father told me the story when I was eight of a woman who did go into a coffee house and ordered a cup of coffee and lit a cigarette while she waited. She was killed by a man who considered himself morally justified for slitting her throat. She had intruded into male territory. Men were not only the protectors of their own wives, daughters, and sisters, but they considered themselves responsible for the moral behavior of women in general. I was not certain why he told me this story. I knew there was a lesson to be learned—and a warning.

By the time a woman reached the age of fifty, she was expected to wear black clothes whether she was widowed or not. Once her children were grown and married, her life was over. She and her husband may have grown increasingly distant over the years, or perhaps there was not much closeness throughout the marriage. The purpose of the relationship was for procreation of legitimate children, not necessarily companionship and intimacy. When the husband died, the wife went into deep mourning for the rest of her life. Her sole interest, then, was her religion, her children, and her grandchildren.

My aunt Maria was a living example of Greek widowhood. When I invited her to dinner to show my gratitude for her kindness and hospitality, she graciously refused. Since she was still in mourning, she said it would be "unseemly" to be seen in public. So a few days before I left, I made arrangements with the seamstress who lived next door to sew a dress and an apron for my aunt as my gift to her. The material was black. I had been informed that any other color was inappropriate for her station in life.

Maternal Roots

The Zaharias/Matthioudakis/Kostantinos Family

Zaharias Matthioudakis, a carpenter and mason, (also known as Kostantinos and "Oongaras"—meaning one who grows cucumbers) was from the island of Patmos where he married Maria Casidi. Her parents arranged the marriage when she was an infant. My mother did not tell me how old Zaharias was when the marriage was planned. They had seven children—(Christodoulos, Anna, Katerina, Kostantinos, Stephanos, Antonios, and Stavros) before moving to Leros in the early 1900s. The reason for the move was never explained to me. Ironically, their home in Patmos was sold to the grandparents of Steve Provezis who would marry Katerina, in Martins Ferry, Ohio, years later. Grandfather built a small stone and stucco house on a hilltop overlooking Alinda Bay, and later my mother, Ereni, was born in that house. The family lived there until 1924 when the family dispersed to different countries after grandfather's death.

Grandfather traveled from island to island building and repairing homes. Frequently he took one or two of his sons to assist him with the heavy work and, occasionally, he took his oldest daughter, Anna, to cook for them. Katerina, his second daughter, became an accomplished seamstress, and she traveled with her father so she could find work. For a period of time, she lived and worked in Kalymnos.

Ereni, the youngest, was born on March 15, 1904, in that small white-washed stone and stucco house that her father built on top of a picturesque hill overlooking windswept Alinda Bay on one of the most beautiful mountainous islands on the Aegean Sea. She arrived into a paradoxical world of ecological splendor, strong patriarchal traditions, and foreign oppression that existed alongside a deep yearning for freedom and independence, the burning themes in the minds of islanders.

Someone wrote the date of her birth on the back of a calendar. None of her five brothers and two sisters knew their birth dates. There were at least two reasons for this occurrence: first, the date of one's birth was not considered as significant in Greek families as the name day which was a saint's day, the real cause for celebration. The other reason was that the Greek people were very secretive and extremely protective of their privacy. They kept few, if any, records because they not only did not want the Turks, and later the Italians —the enemy—to know their affairs; they did not want even their neighbors to know what was going on in their homes. If any records were kept, the church maintained them—particularly baptisms, marriages and deaths.

In 1912, Italy went to war against the Turks on the pretext of freeing the islands. Instead of liberating them the Italians moved in and stayed there for thirty years. That year Ereni was in her third year of school. The Italians mandated that all classes would be taught in the Italian language, but Grandfather would not have his daughter learning Italian instead of her native Greek. In protest, he took her out of school and put her to work shepherding the sheep and the goats on the hillsides, and she learned to sew and crochet. I often wondered whether Grandfather, in addition to his objections to the *Italianization of classes,* considered education for a male child more important than it was for a female child.

Suddenly, and mysteriously, Grandfather died in 1922, and the family was left without their provider. At the same time the country was going through a major political upheaval due to the expulsion by the Turks of over a million and a quarter Greeks from Asia Minor. The economic conditions worsened and poverty was rampant.

After Grandfather's death, the entire family dispersed. The oldest son Christodoulos was married and his wife had given birth to their only son, Zacharias, that year. Christodoulos decided to take his family to Egypt where work was more readily available. He and his family left their home and island when Zaharias was six months old. Soon afterwards, Stephanos and Antonios left for Marseilles. France. In time, they both married. Antonios married a French woman, and they had no children. Stephanos met and married a Greek woman and they had five children. After they went their separate ways, my mother corresponded with Antonios and Stephanos for years, until the Second World War broke out.

Stavros and Katerina sailed to the United States and settled in Martins Ferry, Ohio. Stavros worked in the Laughlin Steel Mill and Katerina worked as a seamstress for two years. They worked very hard, lived frugally, and saved enough money to pay for passage for Anna, Ereni, and their mother to travel to America. There was no information about or ever a mention about Kostantinos and what happened to him. Nor did anyone mention why Grandfather used the name Kostantinos on occasion. I was puzzled about another way my mother's family used different names. When my grandmother and her two daughters came to the United States, they used Grandfather first name, Zaharias, as their last name. However, the men in the family used the name Matthioudakis. That always seemed strange to me, but I never had any explanations from my mother or anyone in her family.

Because Leros was under Italian rule, the three women were required to go to Naples and await sailing permits and immigration papers. They waited there for three months. My mother described Naples as an extremely dirty, noisy city. "… and it smelled terrible. People threw their garbage and pots of urine out of windows and on to the street. You had to be careful where you walked," my mother suggested with a smile. "We didn't have much money, so we couldn't do very much. I spent time with our landlady and she taught me Italian. I liked learning and she enjoyed teaching me." This was as much as she would say. I thought about the irony of her situation, and how sad it was, too. Her father took her out of school so she would not learn Italian, and there she was in Italy, learning the language her father hated.

They left Naples on September 7, 1924, on the *SS Dante Alighieri* and disembarked in New York two weeks later. Her only comment about that sea voyage was, "We were packed like cattle on that ship."

Over the years as I tried to recall some fragment of a story I may have forgotten, I was struck by the overwhelming sense of passivity and resignation that I perceived in my mother. Finally, I concluded that she was grieving the enormous losses of her father, her three brothers whom she never saw again, and her beautiful homeland. I can't imagine how homesick she must have been for her home and her friends when I was growing up.

When I was in the third grade, she told me the story of having to quit school. I was outraged that her father would do that. She did say she was sorry that she had to quit school, but she never complained. I remember my mother as a very shy, quiet, gentle woman, "Too gentle for her own good," I thought, and even as a small child, I felt compelled to take care of her.

Over the years, I have come to see her as very strong, much stronger than I realized when I was young, and she was attractive with her black hair and hazel eyes. All who knew her loved her for her gentleness and kindness.

I have snapshots of her in my memory; but, for the most part, she is ethereal and quickly vanishes as I try to focus on her, just as she disappeared into her inner world when she sat in the kitchen crocheting her life into the tablecloths that she made for my two sisters and me. Her personality, her identity, seemed submerged under the rubric of her ethnicity, her history, and her family. I cannot find her as a whole person. I can grab a snatch of remembrance of her for a moment, and then she's gone. Yes, she was very shy and very quiet—reticence and humility described her perfectly. She could not or would not say what she thought or felt about her life. She was tight-lipped, absorbed in her inner world that was not to be shared with me. Yet, this was not always true.

Frequently and urgently, she talked and whispered with her sister, Aunt Katerina. But afterwards, she would not say what they talked about. I think I was jealous that she shared so much with her sister and not with me. I remember moments when she appeared more vital, excited, and even happy. One morning in particular stood out for me. My mother and father came home early that morning after an all-night party with friends. Her face was flushed, and her eyes were alive and shining, and she was laughing, or more like giggling. I remember the warmth and pleasure that came over me as I watched the two of them being playful with each other.

Later, this memory of my parents together would stimulate more questions: "How did you and dad meet?" Or "Tell me about the time you and daddy ran away and got married." And she would tell the story of their courtship, and their forbidden love. They were the only Greek couple I ever knew who did not have their marriage arranged.

Meeting Across the World

MY PARENTS' MARRIAGE AND THE FAMILY THEY CREATED

Although Apostolos Kardoulias and Ereni Zaharias came from neighboring islands in the Aegean Sea, they met in the little town of Martins Ferry, Ohio, early in 1927. Ironically, if they had stayed on their islands, custom and mutual antagonism between islanders would have prevented such an encounter. However, the Greek community in Martins Ferry was small and the people from different islands lived close by the steel mills where the men worked. Their loneliness and fears, associated with this new land and its incomprehensible language and customs, pulled the Greek families together.

All the Greek people within a radius of ten to fifteen miles gathered in the one Greek Orthodox Church in Martins Ferry for the liturgy on Sunday and holy days. In the summers, they gathered together for picnics, where they roasted whole lambs and danced to the *Zembetiko* music that they brought with them along with their other customs and traditions. During the winter months, they all gathered in rented halls for dances that lasted all night.

The church and the social events served as a meeting place for young men interested in marriage. At these events, custom permitted them to look at young women and decide which one they wanted to marry. The subject of marriage was then broached with the head of the household, usually the woman's father. The woman herself was never approached directly until the arrangements were made between the men. Usually, she met her husband-to-be at their engagement party.

Apostolos first saw Ereni in the small Greek grocery store on Main Street. He was immediately attracted to the shy, dark-haired young woman with the gentle smile. He quickly learned her name from one of the neighbors, and that her older brother, Stavros, was the head of the family since their father died.

A few days later, Apostolos approached Stavros, and in his usual direct way announced, "I am interested in Ereni and I want her for my wife. I'm a hard worker and I'll take care of her."

"Are you crazy?" Stavros retorted angrily. "Ereni is the youngest in our family. Anna, the eldest is not married. Ereni will have to wait. Besides what makes you think you are good enough for her? Everybody knows your reputation. You're wild and you drink too much. You argue with everyone and ride around like a crazy man on that motorcycle of yours. My sister is a good girl. I don't want her marrying someone like you!" and he walked away before Paul could answer.

Apostolos was not one to take "no" for an answer. He went to the corner *kafeneio*, ordered a cup of strong Greek coffee and sat alone at the corner table defiantly thinking of his next move. "I'll show him!"

He was not only rejected, but Ereni was forbidden to speak to him if they ever met on the street. Needless to say, Ereni was excited with the prospects of being courted by this young handsome man. She was pleased to be the center of so much attention. Secretly, she enjoyed making her oldest sister jealous. For years afterward, the story of my father's determination to marry mother was the talk of the town.

One night late in June 1927, Apostolos took a ladder and placed it against the house where Ereni and her family lived. Waiting until the house was dark and everyone was asleep, he climbed up the ladder and quietly "stole" his beloved from her family. With Ereni in the sidecar of his Harley-Davidson, Apostolos sped off for Wellsburg, West Virginia, where Rev. H. L. Wiggins of the Methodist Church married them.

The minister gave them a little Bible with the following inscription: *"We know that all things work together for good to them that love God, to them who are called according to his purpose."* I still have that little Bible with a piece of my mother's veil between the yellowed pages. My sister, Mary, sent it to me as her contribution to my book.

On the contrary, instead of good coming to the young lovers, they were assaulted by the outrage of both sides of the family. Ereni's family never accepted Apostolos; and his family in Kalymnos, in turn, did not accept her. In fact his mother wrote, "You can have any girl in Kalymnos if you will come back here and get married." Thereafter, my mother was referred to as "the bride," as in, "give our regards to the bride." In twenty-five years of marriage, never once was my mother called by her name by her distant mother-in-law.

Another difficulty presented itself almost immediately after their marriage "outside of the church." The Greek Orthodox Church and the community did not consider the marriage legitimate. Apostolos resisted their demands until Ereni discovered she was pregnant and told her mother and sisters. Then, the pressure was on for them to marry in the church. She was three months pregnant with me when they were married again late that autumn, but Apostolos and Ereni always celebrated their true anniversary on June 25th.

I have no difficulty imagining my father stubbornly refusing to be coerced into the "real" marriage because he did the same thing with his second wife after my mother died. They were married in a civil ceremony. And again, Paul refused to marry in the Greek Orthodox Church—this time until he was on his deathbed. He finally consented to marry his second wife of twenty-five years in the Church. The priest came to their home a week before he died on July 11, 1979 and performed the ceremony.

My Birth

Six months after my parents were married again in the church, on May 28, 1928, I was born after a long, difficult, and excruciating labor, and a breech delivery. I weighed ten pounds. Stories were told that I screamed louder than any of my other three siblings who were also breech babies. The first four of us were all delivered at home. Zaharias (Jack) was born in 1943, eleven years after my youngest sister, in the Ohio Valley Hospital, Wheeling, West Virginia. Dr. Phillips attended my mother in all her deliveries and my grandmother was always present helping her daughter with her difficult deliveries.

Almost fifty years later, on a weekend in February 1978, in an EST Workshop, I unexpectedly re-experienced the original birth process during a guided exercise late in the evening of the second day. Early that morning an ache started in my upper right arm and shoulder. As the day progressed, the ache intensified into a sharp pain. I was puzzled, because I had neither injured my arm nor did I resort to physical symptoms under stress.

As the exercise continued, I focused all my attention on the pain. "Where will this take me?" I wondered. The pain became excruciating and encompassed my whole being. My right arm was behind my head and felt caught there. I turned on my right side, and I felt pulling sensation of my feet and experienced sliding along a narrow, smooth passageway. As I felt those sensations and pain, I remembered being told that I had been born breech. Despite my surprise at this realization, I persisted with the rebirthing process.

In my memory, I came out of the passageway coughing, choking, and crying. Gradually, the pain in my shoulder subsided and I was in a lighted room. My memory propelled me back to a statement that haunted my childhood: "It's a girl! Send her back! No, better still, toss her out the window!" My father's voice and laughter resounded in my ears again. This memory of my birth burst forth into my consciousness at the age of fifty as I was giving birth to my adult self. I had come to the EST Workshop to decide what to do with my future. Soon afterwards, I decided to make the trip to Greece and to go for a Ph.D. in marriage and family therapy.

This "greeting" was repeated many times throughout my childhood with a great deal of laughter and joking, but it was not funny for me. Sometimes I felt hurt and insulted by such a mocking welcome. Sometimes I tried to see and feel the underlying affection that might be there. Sometimes I just felt confused and uneasy by my father's joking, especially as I got older and became aware of traditional attitudes toward women and female children.

Those early days after my birth were painful for another reason: according to Greek custom at that time, a newborn was bound tightly, supposedly to help the child grow straight. I was bound for the first three months of my life, until Dr. Phillips discovered this practice and scolded my mother. She did as she was told and removed the binding.

Although the cloth bindings were removed, they were reinforced by cultural and traditional expectations and practices that, in addition to being valued less than males, the female children were under tighter control, scrutiny, and restrictiveness, especially as they approached preadolescence. She was not encouraged to think, to question, or to plan for her future. Her future was decided the day she was born.

Consciously or unconsciously, my father gave me the gift of my name, Eleutheria (Liberty). He instilled in me—and I know this was not intentional—his love and need of freedom. Freedom and independence were strong forces in the Greek mentality that drove the men from their beloved islands to this foreign country where they found freedom as well as more hardships. I've often wondered whether Papa would have given me that name if he knew I would take it to heart and make it a driving force in my life.

I was told that at three months, my father gave me a beautiful dark brown German Shepherd puppy with soft, gentle brown eyes. We grew up together side by side. She was my constant companion. Many stories were told about Lottie, like the time she nursed a kitten that was abandoned by its mother at the same time that she nursed her own puppies. Mama once told me she sent Lottie to the grocery store with a basket around her neck and a list of groceries in it, and she would bring back everything, including meat. Her shopping days stopped after the time Lottie sneaked into the back of the store where the butcher was cutting up a lamb, and she grabbed the lamb's head off the table. She sped off with the butcher chasing her, but he never caught her and she feasted on lamb that day.

When I was five, some kids were teasing me as I walked with Lottie. She growled and snapped at one of the boys who was closest to me. He went off yelling that she bit him. Frightened, I ran home with Lottie, and I told my mother to hide her. I knew when a dog bit a child or an adult, she would be taken away and shot. I did not want her killed.

I don't remember how Lottie was hurt a couple years later. Her hip was injured. Dad thought a car hit her. We didn't have a veterinarian in our town, so she was never treated. Over the next few weeks, her hip became so painful she couldn't walk. She groaned whenever she moved. Sadly and reluctantly, my father made arrangements to have her taken away and "put to sleep." That morning I was out on the sidewalk jumping rope. Suddenly, I saw a car go by on First Street with Lottie in the back seat. She had pushed her head and nose out of the right rear window and looked steadily at me as the car went by.

"Lottie! Lottie!" I screamed at the car. I turned and ran back home, sobbing. "Someone is taking my dog! Where is she going?" I cried to my mother who was standing by the stove stirring something in a pot. She looked very sad, and she spoke softly and slowly as she tried to comfort me with an explanation, "You know Lottie's been hurting because her back leg was broken. You know how much pain she had dragging it behind her. She can't stand or walk anymore. Your dad and I couldn't stand to see her suffer so much…" Her voice trailed off and I saw tears in her eyes."

I ran out of the kitchen and fled upstairs to my room crying, "I don't want to hear all that. I know he's going to put her to sleep. I want Lottie," I wailed. I curled up on my bed and grieved for my companion and friend of seven years.

Now, after all those years, as I recall that day when Lottie was taken away, I feel that distant grief again and tears well up in my eyes. "That was so long ago," I muse to myself. Yet, the pain is still there. I see her again, with her head and nose out of the window of that car, saying "good bye" to me. This time I say "goodbye" to her and, "You were a good friend, Lottie."

MY SISTER MARY AND GODFATHER MIHALIS

On October 25, 1929, my sister Mary was born. My position with my mother was usurped by this newcomer and, much to my chagrin, she became my father's favorite. Fortunately, my godfather, Mihalis, was available to attend to my needs and take me for walks around the neighborhood and to the little beach at the river where he taught me to swim. When he was laid off from his job in the steel mill, my father invited him to come and live with us and help rebuild the old house he had bought. Mihalis not only helped rebuild our home, he became godfather ("Nonos") to four children who were born in quick succession between 1928 and 1932. Needless to say, my mother also needed his help. He helped her with the cooking, cleaning, and the nurturance and care of my sisters and brother and me.

When my father arrived in Martins Ferry, Mihalis was one of several Greek men who lived in a rooming house and welcomed my father. He came to Martins Ferry in the early 1920s to find work, make his fortune, and return to his homeland, Simi, another island in the Aegean Sea. He had left behind his wife and two small children, a son and daughter. As it turned out, thirty years passed before he made the return voyage to Simi. His plans were interrupted by the Great Depression and by World War II.

He was always there for us. He was gentle and patient. He sang Greek folk songs, taught me to sing the Greek National Anthem, and he told us stories of his adventures as a seaman before landing on the shores of the United States where he decided to stay awhile. Sometimes he talked about his daughter and son who were older than I was, and who were growing up without their father. I sensed his unspoken sadness, and I wondered how his children felt about their absent father. He was my guardian angel.

One of his most generous acts was to provide me with a young tutor when I started the first grade. Her name was Katherine Johnson, the youngest of the three daughters in the Negro family next door, and she was twelve years old. She came every evening after dinner to help me with my reading lessons. Since neither Nonos nor my parents spoke or read English, he wanted me to get all the help I needed to learn to read. He paid Katherine a quarter a week for her tutoring me. A quarter was a lot of money in those days if you consider that our family of seven got fed on a dollar a day. I was very aware of the value of even a penny, and I was deeply grateful not only for the money that he paid for my tutoring, but for the meaning of his generosity. He *wanted me to learn and this was his gift to me!* His gentle encouragement has been with me all my life. I hope he realized how much his gesture meant to me.

After my lessons were over, Katherine told my siblings and me great scary ghost stories that had us shrieking in fear. I had never heard ghost stories before, and I found the horror stories thrilling. "One more story," I begged. "Please tell us one more story before you go." I particularly liked the one about the headless man creeping upstairs searching for the terrified children waiting helplessly in their beds.

Sometimes Katherine taught me to speak "pig latin," a dialect the Negroes spoke with each other when they didn't want the white folks to know what they were saying. When I went over to her house to play with her, her mother fed me biscuits and gravy and pieces of ground hog that tasted like fried chicken. Mr. Johnson hunted the ground hogs in the hills north of town. The Johnsons introduced me to jazz and blues that have remained one of my most favorite forms of music.

Another memory that I have treasured occurred early one summer morning before anyone else in the family was up. I heard Nonos sweeping the front porch and yard. I slipped out of bed, quietly went downstairs, and sat on the swing. I simply sat there and watched him as he worked silently, absorbed in his own thoughts. When he finished sweeping, he took the hose and washed down the porch and watered the plants in the two little plots of earth that were our garden. He loved growing flowers and tomatoes. He planted four grapevines and built a trellis that the vines draped over. They provided my mother with enough grape leaves for *dolmathes (stuffed grape leaves)* during the winter months.

I didn't realize for a long time that it was my godfather's silence and serenity that touched me so deeply and made him such a special person in my early life. He accepted what life and God gave him without questions and doubts. He believed that someday he would go home again, even when he had been away for thirty years. And he did. This meant he would have to leave us someday. During the war years and afterwards, he moved to Detroit where he worked and saved enough money to return to his own family and homeland in 1952. Although I missed him, I knew he had to complete the journey he started so many years before.

MY BROTHER TONY AND SISTER ANNA

Antonios (Tony) was born on July 13, 1931. He was smaller than my sister and me and rather sickly. As a toddler, he placed his hands on the hot oven door and burned them severely. His hands were bandaged for several weeks. Earlier when Mary was learning to walk and climb, she had a terrible accident. She fell down the steps at the grocery store while holding her bottle of milk, and her face was cut very badly. I still remember Papa carrying her with her face bandaged. Only her eyes and mouth were uncovered. I felt scared and sad for both my brother and sister.

Anastasia (Anna) arrived on the hot summer morning of August 9, 1932. My mother's cries were frightening. I remember Yiayia (Grandmother) scurrying up and down the stairs assisting the doctor. My father sat at the kitchen table with a cup of coffee. He looked very stern and worried.

As soon as Yiayia carried the infant down to the kitchen and very gently laid her in the bassinet, I went over and looked down at her. I was awed by the beautiful miniature child with the black curly hair and tiny fingers. I gently touched her face and hand. She clasped my finger and I felt very happy as she held my finger. I called her "Anna" and reached over to lift her out of the bassinet. I wanted to hold her. Suddenly, my father in a loud, angry voice, shouted, "Leave her alone! Don't touch her!" Surprised and frightened, I moved away from her. I did not understand my father's anger at that moment when I thought he was pleased, too. He gave no explanation for his outburst, as was his way.

My other early memory of Tasia, as we called her until she went to school, was chasing her as she ran naked down the street when she was about two. She seemed averse to wearing clothes when the days were hot. I'd run after her, carry her home and dress her again. Our Negro neighbor, Katherine, called her "you-you" because Tasia would walk up to our neighbors, point her finger, and say "you-you" when she could not pronounce their names.

She was a very active, outgoing child, and I was to keep watch over her. Even so, she was badly injured about the age of three. One of the Kotellas boys told her to put her hand on the ground. Then he ran a lawn mower over her hand cutting off the first joint of her right ring finger. She screamed with pain and went running home with her hand covered in blood. I was horrified by what I saw, and

I ran with her to tell my mother what happened. My father must have been home that day because he took her to the hospital emergency room to have her treated. I felt so bad for her and for myself. I didn't watch her closely enough and I felt responsible, but I never dreamed anyone would do such a terrible thing to a small child. After that we stayed away from those boys. I learned early in life that there were mean-spirited people in the world and bad things happen when you're not alert and careful.

Our First Home and Other Memories

My father's voice was reassuring and persuasive as he tried to convince my mother that buying this ramshackle house was a good idea. We were in the back yard surrounded by dilapidation that was spilling broken doors and old furniture like sewage into the river. The shack behind us, which must have been a garage at one time, seemed to be crumbling before our eyes.

"Can't you see what I can do with it?" Papa pleaded with her. "It's very cheap and I can rebuild the walls and the floor. The foundation is solid and the house is brick. It won't burn like the clapboard house did" (when I was an infant).

My mother sat on an old cane chair, and tears flowed down her cheeks. She held my sleeping infant sister, Mary, who was six months old. I was almost two and clinging to her cotton print dress, merging into her legs. Mama was not reassured and still crying, "But it's dirty and it smells like chickens lived in it," she said, nodding her head toward the kitchen door that was hanging on one hinge. "Look at that garage. The roof is falling and the walls are rotten. It looks dangerous."

"Don't worry, Ereni. I can clean it up and Mihalis will help me. We're both strong and we know how to work hard. We'll have it fixed up and have it ready for you and the babies in no time." Then in an earnest tone, he appealed to her one more time, "You know how much I want to own my own house, and you do, too."

Mama nodded her head slowly. Mary squirmed, stretched, and woke up. Mama shifted her to the other arm and gently rocked the baby. She looked at me and I pleaded with her wordlessly, "Don't cry.

Please don't cry." Finally, she agreed to my father's request. "We do want our own house," she sighed, and with disappointment added, "But I didn't know it was going to be so much work."

My father got his house. He wanted one for a long time. If he could have afforded something better, he would have bought it. He was not stingy when he wanted something. Although the Depression hit the Ohio Valley and many men lost their jobs, Papa was still working at the Laughlin Steel Mill. He was ambitious and driven to start his own business. He purchased a small trailer (by breaking into my piggy bank—I had $21—my godparents were generous with me) that he hooked up to his Ford, and he hauled coal to homes after working in the mill all day. With the money he earned from hauling coal, he was able to save enough to pay cash for the house; and a year later, he saved enough to buy his first truck—an International!

His business plan included the purchase of a big truck, an International Harvester that could carry two or three tons of coal in one load! He wanted the best and the biggest truck on the market. Then, he would be able to haul truckloads of coal to the big houses uptown, instead of the few bushels the trailer held. More importantly, he intended to quit his backbreaking job at the mill *and make more money to boot!*

After Papa bought the house he invited our Nonos Mihalis to come and live with us. He worked in the same mill with Papa, and in the evening he prepared the house for rebuilding. While Papa worked at his second job, Nonos gutted the inside of the house, and later Papa hauled the debris to the dump yard.

On the weekends, he and Papa rebuilt the house from the inside out. They plastered walls, and Mama painted them with oil-based enamel because it washed better than water-based paint. They put down sweet pine-smelling floors, and my mother varnished them. The steps to the upstairs loft became more solid, and there was a rail to hold on to. The loft was transformed into two bedrooms, one for my parents and one for Mary and me.

In time we graduated from cribs to a double bed. We each had our own side of the bed, and we did not allow the other to come over the imaginary line we had marked off in the middle of the bed.

In the next two years, Tony and Anastasia (nicknamed Anna, then, Tasia, and finally Ann) were added to our family. We all slept in one room until Tony was old enough to have his own room. Then he was moved into our parents' room, and they moved their bed downstairs to the living room.

There were no decorations on the walls of our bedrooms. Mama arranged several icons on a small table in the north corner of their bedroom. This sacred space was called an *iconostasion* on which she placed an icon of Saint George and one of the *Theotokos*, the Mother of Jesus. In front of the icons stood a *kandili*, a red globe containing water with olive oil floating on the surface with a wick in the middle. Mama lit the wick in the evening, said her prayers, and crossed herself in front of the icons before going to bed. In the morning she usually extinguished it.

There's a story that I always remember when I think of that special little sacred space in our house. One morning my father came home after working the midnight shift at the steel mill and started to undress for bed. He noticed the *kandili* was still lighted; he swore under his breath, and irreverently blew it out. He fell asleep; shortly afterwards, he screamed and went flying down the stairs in his underwear, and out the back door. My concerned mother asked, "What happened!" He answered in a quaking voice: "St. George came and sat on my chest and told me to light the *kandili* or he would kill me! Go! Light it so I can go back to bed." She did as he asked. We never heard from St. George again.

Meanwhile, the transformation of the house continued. In the kitchen was a coal-burning stove that served to keep us warm when we children dressed on winter mornings. The stove was used for heating water for the dishes and baths, and it kept the coffee warm throughout the day. In the middle room against the southern wall, stood a pot-bellied stove which not only warmed the room, but generated enough heat to dry the weekly wash that my mother hung in there to dry when it was raining or too cold to hang clothes in the back yard. Eventually, this room became a dining room furnished with a long walnut table and matching chairs. When I was eight my father had a telephone installed for his business, and a few years later we got our first radio, a Philco. The coal-burning stoves were later replaced with a coal-burning furnace in the basement.

As time passed, the icebox that required a lump of ice every day to keep the food cold was succeeded by a Kelvinator electric refrigerator. A heavy mahogany and leather chair and couch stood majestically in the parlor. The west wall was covered with pictures of our mustachioed grandfather and stern grandmother, aunts and uncles standing stiffly with unsmiling faces, and one picture of our parents' wedding group, all framed in heavy cherry wood and thick glass.

Every Saturday morning Mama and I polished the furniture with Old English furniture oil, including the narrow table in the middle of the room with the curled legs. When the oil dried and the room smelled of that peculiar pungent oil odor, we replaced the doilies that Mama had crocheted on the backs of the chair and the couch and on the table. Then we closed the door which was only opened when company came or on the next Saturday when the cleaning routine was repeated.

The last bit of remodeling was the building of a bathroom. In those days, we all took baths in one of the products of the steel mills: a square, steel tub of about a yard in diameter which stood about two feet high; the insignia "Wheeling Steel" was stamped in large letters on the bottom. These tubs were used by all the local families for rinsing the clothes that were washed in their Maytag wringer washing machines.

Since there was not enough space in our house for a bathroom, Nonos Mihalis ingeniously decided to place it just off the kitchen and outside along the side of the porch. We may have been the first family on Carlisle Street to have a bathroom in our house with an actual bathtub in it. When we were small children, Mama would put all four of us in the bathtub together. One day she left us to splash and play for a few minutes, and we became so rowdy sliding down the back end of the bathtub that the floor collapsed. After that we bathed separately, and Nonos replaced the wooden floor with a cement one.

In time the house was completed, and Mama and Papa purchased all the necessary furniture from Rudner's Furniture Store. Mama got her own special Singer sewing machine, and she sewed all our dresses for us. I remember walking up Hanover Street with my mother every Saturday afternoon to pay the $2 that was due on the furniture. I think I was six years old before that furniture was all paid off. My friend Lillian, who lived two houses down from ours, did not have a bathtub. They had a laundry room where they washed clothes and where they bathed in a large steel tub that had *Wheeling Steel* stamped on it. Saturdays were bath days.

As fate or life would have it, within a year or two after completing all the work that made our home quite comfortable, the winter storms of 1936 overwhelmed the banks of the Ohio River. The water gushed over the flood plains, poured onto the streets, and covered the Bottom where we lived. Our parents and Nonos moved all the furniture upstairs, and we were all taken in by relatives and friends who lived out of the range of the flood. The water rose to record levels, and the first floor of our house was completely inundated. If the water had risen one additional foot, the waters would have been upstairs where our furniture was stored.

I can still see myself as a little eight-year-old girl standing forlornly on the hill overlooking the Bottom and watching the waters rising and covering our homes. I remember what an awesome and frightening sight that was. When the water receded, we gathered in the front yard to see what damage was done. The mud left imprints on the walls and lay thick on the floor. With shovels and hoses, Papa and Nonos did the backbreaking work of removing the mud and grime. Later on, Mama again painted the walls, and the floors were scrubbed clean and waxed. A week or so later, we were all back home, until the next flood. This was the first of three major floods that we endured in the next decade.

The second time the floodwaters pulled the plaster off the walls and they were repaired again. Each time the waters rose, they took their toll on the house, on my parents' relationship, and on my mother's health. Mama wanted to move uptown, but my father stubbornly held on to *his* house. I was twenty years old and out of the home before Papa consented to sell *his house* and move uptown to 731 Pearl Street.

"A man may work from daylight to dusk, but a woman's work is never done."

I can't tell you how many times I heard women quoting this little ditty when they were tired, frustrated, disappointed, or angry. Our fathers worked very hard at backbreaking jobs, as I've said before. The women worked very hard, too. They were well organized and efficient with every day scheduled for certain activities: Monday was washing-clothes day and it was an all-day chore. In fact, everything —washing, ironing, cooking, and cleaning—were all-day chores. Even though they had wringer washing machines, the women boiled clothes, washed them twice, rinsed them well; and finally the clothes, sparkling white or colored, were hung out to dry on lines of rope in their backyards.

We had no vacuum cleaners, and Saturday was house-cleaning day. Rugs were swept with a broom. Floors were scrubbed with mops or on hands and knees, and furniture was polished with Old English furniture oil. Two or three times a year, rugs were dragged out to the backyard, hung on rope lines and pounded with a rug cleaner made of circular steel rings on a short wooden handle until all the dust was removed. In addition to the rugs, the walls inside the house had to be cleaned two or three times a year.

I remember all these cleaning chores because I became my mother's helper from the time I could stand on an orange crate and pass clothes through the wringer. My mother told me that I had my arm though that wringer three times in my third year. I was sent to the grocery store for small items at four, and I cleaned house with my mother from the age of five and ever after. After I started school I was allowed to help with the ironing.

Cooking was a time-consuming task done primarily by women, although my godfather was an excellent cook, too. Before cooking could start, someone had to go to the grocery store and buy the necessities for that day's meal. When I wasn't in school, shopping was my responsibility. I can remember shopping with a dollar for one day's groceries for our family of seven. As I went out the door with the grocery list, my mother always said, "Keep the change."

Sometimes the change amounted to two or three cents, and sometimes more, as much as seven cents! With that much money I could get an ice cream cone and two pieces of candy or gum. You must remember, in those days, earnings were about a hundred dollars a month. Movies were a dime, and for a quarter you could get a box of popcorn and a candy bar.

My mother cooked every day. Our meals were always hot, which meant Mom spent the entire morning preparing it. Our lunches and suppers were the same, because a big pot of soup or stew, or pasta was enough for the next meal. In fact, a second or a third cooking made the dish taste better.

On Wednesdays, my mother baked her own bread. When we got home from school on those afternoons, we had a special treat —hot rolls and butter! For holidays like Christmas and Easter, my mother spent days preparing sweet bread, cakes, and cookies. Their exotic names still make my mouth salivate. There were the *kouloura- kia* covered with sesame seeds, *halva* and *diples* smothered in sweet honey syrup and sprinkled with cinnamon, and *kourambiedes* rolled in powdered sugar with a whole clove *in the* middle.

My favorites dishes were *fassolada* (bean soup) and *dolmathes* (stuffed grape leaves). On special occasions, we had *pastitso*, baked pasta with thick rich cream sauce to which she added about a dozen eggs and cinnamon. Mom sprinkled lots of grated Parmesan cheese on top of the macaroni. She always cooked with olive oil and home-canned tomatoes or tomato paste. Everything was "made from scratch"—the only way that cooking was done.

On Sundays the meals consisted of roasted lamb, beef, or chicken with potatoes or rice, and a huge Greek salad with lettuce, tomatoes, cucumbers, onions, olives, and feta cheese. Occasionally, small crabs from Baltimore were shipped inland. Then we spent the whole evening around the kitchen table eating freshly cooked crabs in the shell right out of the boiling pot.

During the summer months, I helped my mother with the canning. She canned tomatoes, tomato paste, and catsup that she learned to make from a recipe given to her by Mrs. Johnson. In addition, she canned peaches, pears, and made quince marmalade. Every mother in the neighborhood cooked up a storm during the summer months. They not only cooked fruits and vegetables, but they boiled and sterilized the jars in which the food was stored.

The Hazel-Atlas jars that were popular in those days were manufactured across the river in Wheeling. My friend's sister, "Sissy" Dadasovich and my future father-in-law, Dudley Wright, worked in the Hazel-Atlas plant for fifty years. The fruits and vegetables that we ate and canned were grown on farms in the neighboring hills surrounding our town. The farmers loaded their trucks with bushel baskets of freshly picked fruits and vegetables in season and drove slowly through the neighborhoods calling out, "Corn! Tomatoes! Peaches! Pears! Apples! Plums! They rang a large bell that brought all the women out of their kitchens to select the foods that they would be preparing for the next few weeks. The butchers sometimes sold freshly butchered lambs, beef, and chickens by driving through neighborhoods. We had fresh bread delivered by the Greek baker, Mr. Makris, in Yorksville (the little town five miles to the north). [His youngest daughter, Cally, married my brother Tony in the early 1950s.] In the autumn, my mother ordered several five-gallon cans of milk from one of the dairy farms and made yogurt and a soft cream cheese that was spread on bread.

As time passed, I became the one in our family who introduced "American" foods to our diet: hot dogs, potato salad, and canned baked beans! One of our favorite treats was a baloney sandwich made with Wonder Bread. Of course, we only got this for lunch when Mom was certain Dad was not coming home for the noon meal. He absolutely had no tolerance for such "disgusting" food on his table.

By the time I was in the third grade, I learned about the American Thanksgiving tradition and having turkey with all "the fixings." My mother had no idea what I was talking about, and she made a big pot of bean soup that Thanksgiving Day. I was thoroughly disappointed but, as I was wont to do, I talked with the other kids in the neighborhood and their parents and learned the kinds of foods that were cooked for that holiday. I collected recipes and the next year on Thanksgiving Day, we had a turkey, stuffing, mashed potatoes, and creamed peas. I think I was twelve before I learned to make a pumpkin pie.

For several decades after I left home, married, and had my own children, I continued to cook some of the Greek traditional dishes for special occasions. During the holidays, I continued the tradition of baking for holidays just as my mother did. Nowadays, when I get hungry for a Greek meal, I will go with a friend to the Village Inn and have a Greek salad and a bowl of lemon-rice soup or a *spanokopita*. As for sweets, I make a yearly pilgrimage to the Greek Festival where I purchase *baklava* and an assortment of other delicacies that seem to fill a yearning for the "Good Old Days."

* * * * *

By the time I was ten years old, I observed my mother sinking deeper into herself. She would sit in the kitchen for hours crocheting doilies, tablecloths—anything that would keep her hands and her mind occupied. The realities of her life seemed to be overwhelming her capacities to cope: two floods, the on-going family feud, her sister's health was deteriorating, the weight of all her losses over the years—and, of course, my father was not an easy man with whom to live and to mediate between him and her children.

My father was a moody, angry, and aggressive man at times, but with a few drinks "under his belt" he became quite charming and fun like an extrovert. He laughed and talked loudly, and he danced the Greek folk dances gracefully and beautifully. I liked my father when he drank a little. He was like a totally different man.

Even though my mother was depressed, she still went through the routine chores: washing on Monday, cooking every day, ironing on Tuesday, and baking bread on Wednesday. Thursday and Friday, she would sit and crochet all day. Sometimes we would go and visit her sister, Katerina, and her mother in the Clarks Addition. Then, she would talk in whispers to her sister, not wanting me to hear her complaints or her pain.

One of my regular activities during the summer months was a regular trip to the library. Every week I would go to the Martins Ferry Library on Fifth Street and come home with an armload of books to read during the week. On one of my explorations of the shelves, I discovered a few shelves with books in foreign languages. There were even a few books written in Greek. I would take two or three to my mother and ask her to read them. Reading was becoming a very important pastime for me, and I wanted her to find some pleasure in reading, too. But the books were too heavy for her. "I've only gone to school for three years. I can't understand these books." Disappointed, I would try to find something less difficult for her, but the library was not equipped with a wide range of Greek books.

Next, I tried encouraging her to go visit some of our Greek friends—the Kaikises or our godparents in Yorksville; but she could not bring herself to do anything more than what she was doing. Besides she didn't have the energy to walk uptown nor the inclination to be sociable. I felt frustrated and helpless to move her out of her depressed state. I would even scold her that her dresses were getting old and she needed to go buy some new ones. Occasionally, she would get tired of hearing me nag her, and she would change and walk uptown to Woolworths or to the park. Sometimes I would go with her, or my own restlessness would propel me out of doors to the river bank where I would stare at the muddy water, throw stones, and watch the waves grow in bigger and bigger circles. I would count the number of circles that each stone would make. On the other side of the river were the gray hills of West Virginia blocking my view. I wished I could see what there was on the other side.

After working in the mental health field for over forty years, I can see so clearly now that my mother was suffering from a major clinical depression. Unfortunately, there were no treatments available for the general public at that time. Gradually, my mother's depression would lift for a time and cycle back again. At the age of sixty-five, my father called me to ask me what he could do about his insomnia. By that time, I knew exactly what he needed. I suggested that he make an appointment to see a doctor who could prescribe an anti-depressant for him. I told him, "Dad you've suffered from depression all your life. It's time that you get treated." He followed my suggestion. For the first time in years, he could sleep through the night.

Depression was one of the main illnesses in our family since my grandparents; I've experienced depressive episodes myself, and I have observed the signs and symptoms in members of our extended family. Since the late 1950s medical treatment and psychotherapy have successfully relieved the symptoms of this type of depression.

Family Feuds
and Secrets

Life in the Ohio Valley in 1930s was very difficult for many reasons: hard physical labor, if you were lucky enough to have a job; then, there were the floods, the contaminated air and river, and the industrial accidents. The worst of the difficulties were the family grudges or "feuds" that went on for several generations and divided the family into adversarial camps.

The feud between my father and my mother's family continued throughout their life together. Fortunately, my father's family lived in Kalymnos and Rhodes, so they were not physically there to get entangled in the family mess. Although they were so far away, their resentments were transported over thousands of miles by mail. The mutual antagonisms escalated over the years and, at times, disintegrated into verbal disputes and actual physical fights between my father and my uncles (my mother's brother and brothers-in-law). My father retaliated and forbade my mother from visiting her extended family. Mother, in turn, was unable to tolerate being cut off from Yiayia (grandmother) and Thea (aunt) Katina, so she secretly went to their home to visit them while my father worked.

Now, from my present position of distance and a more objective stance, I can see that dad was probably very hurt by the rejection of my mother's brother and her family. His honor as a man was insulted, and perhaps he was wounded deeply—reoccurrences of the insults and injuries he suffered at the hands of his own father. Yet, he could not display his sensitivity and, once again, he had to reinforce the armor to protect his fragile self-esteem and *filotimo* (honor, which is highly valued by Greek men). In Greece *filotimo* was maintained by attributing failures and problems to outside circumstances or fate, which are not completely under anyone's control; but my father's need for self-aggrandizement became excessive and essential for his survival.

The "false" self had to become even tougher: he had to prove his strength by fighting, and later he exhibited his strength and power within the family as well through intimidation and fear. No doubt, he knew my mother was visiting her family against his wishes; yet, he participated in the family collusion by not confronting her. This might have been too disruptive for our family to overcome; the collusion served the purpose of stabilizing the marriage. My mother got to see her family and my father could maintain his honor and self-esteem. He became almost a stereotype of the *pallikari*—the Greek ideal of a man: fearless, inflexible, implacable, virile, handsome, and proud.

With time, however, stakes would escalate and neither my mother nor my father could extricate themselves from the web of secrets, lies, and deceptions that the whole family had woven—even the children became active participants and inextricably involved in the family mythology: dad was the ogre, the "bad guy"—the tough guy —and my mother, the quiet, submissive, self-sacrificing one who had to tolerate my father's moods and bad temper.

Fear of my father pervaded my childhood years. His quick temper and his complete intolerance of frivolity or playfulness conditioned our watchfulness and vigilance for his arrival. Absolute silence reigned when he walked in the door. No matter how noisy we had been the moment before, we all scattered. By this time there were four of us children: Mary, Tony and Anna (short for Anastasia), and myself (Eleutheria). We all had our "quiet places" where we hid or played silently and alone. I don't remember that we joined each other in our solitudes or offered solace or understanding to each other. We went our own ways: I buried myself in books and at the library; Mary played endlessly with her dolls; and I have no idea where Tony and Anna went. Not until years later did it occur to me to ask them what they did at those times when dad came home angry. "Scatter," was Tony's straightforward response.

Now, I can let myself remember the very early, gentler years when my father would come home after working long hours and mother would massage his back to ease the pain. He would bring us *loukoumia* or Turkish delight, a sweet covered in powdered sugar in his lunch pail; or he would leave us one of his sandwiches that was just as much a treat as the candy. My earliest memory (I couldn't have been more than two years old) was getting a bath in the kitchen sink and recalling the tentative, gentle touch as my father washed my back. The most memorable event was seeing my mother and father coming home after an all-night party laughing and faces flushed with wine and dancing. They seemed so happy and full of joy that I wanted to hold on to that picture my whole life—and I have. Whatever happy events happened earlier, as time went by, they seemed to grow scarcer and occurred less and less frequently as we got older.

All of the children on both sides of the family were swept up in the maelstrom when we were old enough to be inducted into the family secret. I was three when Mama confided the secret to me. "We will visit Thea Katina, and Yiayia while Papa is working, but we must not tell Papa where we went. This will be our little secret. Do you understand?" I nodded enthusiastically. I wanted to do everything I could to please her. She was much easier to please than Papa who teased me and then made fun of me when I cried.

Like two naughty children we waited until the middle of the morning hours to make our secret little jaunt across town. Yiayia and I went into the garden in the back yard, and I helped her pull weeds that grew around the lettuce, onions, and tomatoes. Sometimes she pulled a ripe tomato off the vine, and she and I sat on the porch swing and ate the wedges of the sweet fruit.

In the kitchen Mama and Thea sat close together around the table and whispered to each other as they drank cups of thick black coffee and ate feta cheese and slices of homemade bread. Yiayia was partially deaf, so I wondered what they were talking about that they didn't want me to hear. The frowns and serious expressions on their faces aroused my wordless concern. Sometimes I walked into the kitchen and stood close to Mama, but they quickly straightened up, smiled at me, or patted my head, and offered me something to eat. "What would you like?" Thea would ask me. "Some fruit or cookies?" I shook my head "no". Even if I had words, which I didn't, I knew better than to ask about their conversation. I felt uneasy and uncertain, even ashamed, but I didn't know what I had done wrong. I climbed on Mama's lap until she sent me outside to help Yiayia, and they continued to whisper.

I felt more at ease with my grandmother. She was clear, pleasant, and honest with me. I didn't have to wonder what she was thinking or saying. She must have been all of five feet tall and weighed about a hundred pounds. Like other Greek widows, she was dressed in black from head to toes. She wore a black triangular veil-like covering on her head that she wrapped around her neck, and then tucked the end piece behind her left ear. Her long-sleeved blouse was black as well, and had a high collar, and hung close around her waist. Her black-layered skirt came down to her ankles, covered her black-stockinged legs, and only showed the tips of her black shoes. Regardless of the weather, this was her style from morning to night, from Sunday through Saturday, whether in church, the kitchen or the garden.

Grandma had three changes of clothes: one for church, one for the house and garden, and one complete outfit locked up in her trunk in the attic. "This is the one I will be buried in when my time comes," she told me with a small smile on her lips as she patted the unworn dress in the trunk and closed the lid quietly and reverently. She did not know the exact day she was widowed because she did not think dates significant. The only words spoken were, "Papou died." I did not know until much later when my sister, Mary, told me that Yiayia prepared herself for her own death every morning. She would have a small glass of wine and a piece of bread that she dipped in the wine and said a prayer—this was in case the priest did not arrive in time before she died. Then, she would go about her chores and activities.

She lived with Katina, her second oldest daughter, her son-in-law, Steve, and their three sons and daughter. There was always plenty of work to be done, and she kept herself busy cooking, cleaning, or out in the garden weeding and cultivating. She was an experienced midwife, and she attended her three daughters when they had their children. She helped them deliver ten grandchildren.

One of my fondest memories was standing next to her in the Greek Orthodox Church when I was four. I was completely awed by the mysterious sounds, the burning candles and incense, and the priest dressed in red and gold robes. Unknown emotions and wordless wonder were stirred in me as I watched Yaiyai crossing herself and bowing reverently. I knew I was in a special place. I moved close to her and clung to the folds of her skirt. She was a very important influence in my life. She taught me the value of quiet and silence; and she (like my Nonos) was a very special person in my life.

Our silent relationship continued until the autumn of 1943. I was a sophomore in high school and in the first period class of World History when I was called to the office and told to go to my aunt's house. "You're grandmother is very ill and your family wants you to go there right away," the principal, Mr. Hart, told me in a very sympathetic tone. I was frightened by the urgency. I grabbed my books and coat and walked as fast as I could to the North end of town where my grandmother lived.

As soon as I walked in the door, I felt tension in the quiet stillness of the house. Everyone (except my father who was at work) was there: my cousins, aunt and uncle, and my mother. Someone, I think it was my older cousin Jack, whispered, "Yiayia had a stroke. She was mending the back fence. She got very tired and came in to lie down. She's in a coma, like she's sleeping, but she can't wake up. The doctor was here earlier. There's nothing he can do." Everyone looked very serious and very anxious. They sat around her watching her shallow breathing, and they waited.

I went to look at my sweet grandmother who was lying so still on the couch in the middle room. Her face was serene, and I thought I saw a small smile in the corners of her mouth. "How peaceful she looks," I thought to myself, and I went out in the kitchen and sat at the table with a book. I don't think I read very much, but the book was a comfort for me. My mother and aunt seemed totally absorbed in their grief, and I tried to be as quiet as I could. Oddly, I didn't feel like crying. Yiayia had prepared herself for this day. She did not seem afraid of dying when she showed me her burial dress, and she probably had her morning communion, even though the priest was there right after the doctor. He spoke her name, "Maria," and said the special words for the dying; she opened her eyes, took the communion that was offered and lapsed back into the deep sleep. She was not suffering, and I was thankful for that.

I went back to my book and started to read again. After a few minutes, Aunt Katina came out to the kitchen, looked at me with a severe look and in a disapproving tone of voice said very loudly, "What kind of a person are you?" I looked up at her startled. I was trying to be as quiet as possible, and she was shouting at me.

"You haven't shed one tear for your grandmother all day. You are so cold-hearted..." She didn't finish her statement and stormed back into the middle room. I could not believe what she had just said to me, and I knew better than to try to explain. She didn't know how I felt, and she didn't care. I wasn't grieving in *her way so I was bad/wrong/unacceptable!* That's how things were in our family.

Late that afternoon, Aunt Anna arrived from McKeesport, Pennsylvania. She was a big buxom woman whom I had not seen before. I was surprised how much her eyes crinkled around the edges when she smiled, just like Mama's, I thought, even though tears were streaming down her face. I liked the warm hug she gave me; then she went into the room with the others, and I returned to my book.

An hour or so passed. All at once I was shaken out of my reverie by the shrillest, most horrifying sounds I had ever heard, and I went running into the room where Yiayia lay to see my mother and her sisters weeping and wailing, "My God, My God. She's gone!" The shrill keening and lamentations continued for what seemed a long, long time. I could not believe that such a sound could come out of my mother's throat, and I prayed I would never hear that sound again. (I learned about another custom that day.)

I looked at my grandmother and she appeared as peaceful as she had been earlier. Her hands lay folded on her chest and she had breathed her last. Her silence was in sharp contrast to the moans and groans of her daughters. The males stood by quietly with downcast eyes, and I stood near them, thinking, "Yiayia died a good, peaceful death. She did not suffer. I hope I die as well as she did." And I still do.

* * * * *

In the other parts of our lives, the secrets and the feuds spread like an invisible, malignant tumor that ate away at the fabric of the family. My siblings and I learned that there were things going on in our family that no one talked about, and we all colluded with the secret-bearers. If my father suspected what was going on, he never let on. The collusive behavior, and the disapproval of my father by my aunts and uncles, conveyed to me that this man, my father, was too dangerous and frightening to oppose. If adults were afraid of him, how could I confront him? By the time I was in late adolescence, I was terrified of him.

One secret grew into another and another and another. When I was five Uncle Stavros became very ill and was taken away to a hospital far away. My mother explained sadly, "Stavros went to a hospital to get better." Again the impenetrable veil of silence and sadness fell over my mother and Thea's family. I knew I was not to ask, "What happened to Uncle Stavros?"

At about that same time, I noticed something strange happening to Thea Katina. Her fingers were turning into hard discolored knobs. She lost the feeling in her hands, and she burned herself frequently when she cooked. I heard my mother gently scolding her, "You must be more careful Katina. The burns are terrible." Before long, she could no longer stand or walk.

I was seven years old when my mother received word that her brother, Stavros, was dead. He died in the hospital in Louisiana. She was grief-stricken. Of course, she never mentioned how he died. I felt helpless. I didn't know what to do to make her feel better.

Later that afternoon, Mama wanted me to take a tray of glasses of wine around to the neighbors to honor her brother and to share her grief. This was a tradition on the islands, but I had not seen it practiced before. I was too shy and embarrassed to do as my mother asked. Here was something I could have done for her, and I couldn't bring myself to do it. Mama became irritated by my lack of understanding and cooperation. She took the tray and served the neighbors herself. I went along and translated for her as she told them that her brother died, and this was our customary way of respecting the dead.

Our neighbors were very sympathetic, and they honored Uncle

Stavros by drinking the wine with great solemnity. I was grateful that they were so kind and understanding when I couldn't respond. My mother mourned quietly and privately, most likely with her mother and sister. Uncle Stavros was never mentioned again.

My mother revealed to my sister, Mary, (who told me this story years later) her memories of the day that Stavros was taken away by the public health authorities. She and Katina fled from the house and hid in the tall grass that surrounded the steel mills in that part of town. They were afraid that Katina would be seen and diagnosed with the same symptoms as their brother. Then she, too, would be removed from the family and never seen again.

Years later in 1949, as a first-year nursing student in a class on Skin Diseases, I learned the name of the horrible disease that had ravaged my Uncle Stavros and Aunt Katina. Leprosy! So, this was the deep dark family secret, that unspeakable disease and its dreadful aftermath. This was the reason that Uncle Stavros was removed from the family, and Aunt Katina remained isolated and imprisoned in her own home.

In that nursing class, I came to the sudden realization that when my aunt and uncle emigrated from Greece, they carried in their bodies the incubating bacteria of Hanson's Disease, better known as Leprosy. For thousands of years this dreaded disease, which caused horrible debilitating deformities, was feared; and the afflicted were stigmatized and ostracized. In Biblical times, people with leprosy were considered unclean. It was no wonder that my mother and other relatives hid Aunt Katina from the view of the neighbors as well as doctors. Although my mother very quietly cautioned me, "Don't get too close" and "Don't let Thea Katina kiss you," the terrible word was never mentioned. These words seemed to come out of mother's mouth with so much pain and sadness that I knew not to ask, "What's wrong?" Finally, I understood why all the adults were afraid she would be taken away to die in the hospital in Louisiana, the only Leprosarium in the country at that time, where Uncle Stavros died.

Since I discovered the truth about my aunt's condition, I decided it was my responsibility to tell my cousins the name of the disease that afflicted their mother. More importantly, I had to tell them that there was treatment available.

I tried to persuade them. "But this is 1949. There are treatments and medications available. It's no longer necessary for your mother to stay hidden. She can get help, and she will not be taken away like Uncle Stavros," I argued passionately. "Don't you want your mother to get better?" But it was all to no avail. My cousins did not want to hear what I had to say. I had mentioned the unmentionable. Instead of seeking help for their mother, my cousins, as well as my aunt and uncle, everyone became enraged with me for daring to reveal her illness. I had broken the family rule of secrecy, and I had to be ostracized. Even my mother could not comprehend what I had done.

More years passed before she was treated, but it was too late. Even after she died in 1976 of a heart disorder, the family never acknowledged her true condition. The depth of fear and the stigma associated with this disease for thousands of years had penetrated our parents' generation and were transmitted to the next. I understood that the denial was for the sake of protecting my aunt and keeping her in the family. That was their way of coping with a dreadful disease that had afflicted several family members.

The coping mechanism of denial was most difficult for me because I could not live with the expectation that I was to ignore, not comment, or pretend to not notice the deteriorating changes that were taking place gradually on Aunt Katina's extremities and skin. Her fingers eventually became short knobs, her legs became swollen and covered with sores, and they were wrapped in bandages, and over them she wore heavy cotton stockings. Slowly, her feet and toes shriveled and her lower legs became stubs that could not sustain her weight in an upright position. She could no longer walk, so she crawled about the house doing her chores, and she cooked as she sat in a chair.

I wondered whether this was the reason my father had forbidden my mother to visit her sister, but this was one time my mother quietly defied him. My mother would not abandon her sister or her mother. We continued to visit them several times a week during the daytime hours. Thus, the secrets were perpetuated, and the younger children unknowingly were inducted into the family collusion. Even my father participated in the conspiracy; he pretended he did not know that we were visiting our relatives.

My response to the secrecy, collusion, denial, and pretense, at first was to refuse to participate. I was given looks that filled me with shame and guilt when I said the "wrong thing again." Or I would get the silent treatment from my mother or aunt, and I would wither inside. The worst of all was being called "loud mouth," because this made me a caricature of who I was. I wanted to be honest and tell the truth. I needed some kind of validation that what I was seeing and what was happening to my aunt was real. Instead I was punished.

Gradually, I withdrew from the family and felt that I did not belong. A deep desire to escape developed. Slowly and unobtrusively, I became the outcast because I refused to doubt my own observations. As I grew into adolescence, I increasingly became sullen, defiant, and angry—sometimes explosive. I could not pretend. I saw what was happening, and I refused to lie to myself.

As I write about these events that occurred so many decades ago, I still reel from the impact that the secrets and feuds had on me. Although I understood the motives of the family members who concealed the dreadful truth, I was (and am) convinced that concealing the truth was more damaging than knowing ever could have been. The secrets became enormous barriers among the immediate family members. My trust in others and even myself eroded. They all went about their lives laughing, playing, working as if everything was just normal, and I felt crazy inside. What was real? Who was I? My senses and intuition told me something was wrong. I could not understand what I saw and heard.

Since no one acknowledged my feelings and observations, I became the troublemaker in our family. I questioned everything. The atmosphere that surrounded me at home oppressed me and I wanted to run away. I was prone to temper tantrums. I remember my first tantrum at four. I pounded my foot on the floor and screamed, "I don't care! I don't care! I don't care!" The tantrums continued into childhood and sporadically into adolescence.

"I hate the lies, and I hate all the pretending," screamed my mind. In the outside world, I played games, visited the neighbors, and went to school where I found solace and comfort, but inside I was alone and separate. I lived on the edge of chaos and destruction where the unspoken was powerfully present. I was afraid, and I felt ashamed, and I didn't know why until the secrets were uncovered and dispelled.

In school I learned to read, write, and think. Eventually, I learned to do research, and I used this skill to discover my own answers and to learn as much as I could about the unspeakable disease of our family. The information indicated that Leprosy, or Hanson's Disease, resulted from the microorganism called Mycobacterium Leprae, or Hanson's Bacillus, named after the Norwegian doctor who described it in 1784.

How the bacterium was spread was uncertain, but most likely by droplet infection. No age was exempt for the disease. Since leprosy was endemic in Southern Europe and in Africa, many were exposed to the infection but not everyone succumbed to the disease. This is a very complex condition, and nothing was known with certainty about healthy carriers or whether immunity or genetics determine how the individual deals with the bacillus once it enters the human tissue. Interestingly, the incubation period was very long—anywhere from two to four years and as long as ten years. Onset was insidious and unnoticed.

The long incubation period explained how Stavros and Katerina got past immigration inspections. They probably showed no signs of the disease when they arrived in this country. The symptoms did not become manifest for several years. I found it very interesting that several members of the family developed the illness and the others, who were exposed, did not. I learned in 1994 another brother, Stephanos, who immigrated to France, also developed the disease. Both Katina and Stephanos married and had children. Neither spouse nor children acquired the disease.

Leprosy, a common disease in Mediterranean countries, contributed to the ostracism and the stigmatization of the family. The resulting shame that they experienced certainly was reason enough to account for the dispersal of the family from Greece.

Except for very rare occasions, neither my maternal grandfather, nor three of the brothers—Stavros, after his death, Christodoulos, nor Kostantinos—were mentioned in our family. My mother did stay in touch with Antonios and Stephanos until the outbreak of World War II. They both survived the war, but Antonios died soon after the war ended and Stephanos died in the late 1960s.

Another family secret was uncovered in the early 1990s by my cousin Mary (Aunt Anna's youngest daughter) who had traveled to Leros to visit her mother's home. Talking with one of the elders in Alinda, she learned that an unknown cousin was living in our Grandfather's house. His name was Zaharias Matthioudakis, and he was the only son of Christodoulos who had immigrated to Egypt. He was unknown by our generation because his father was cast out of the family and his son was rejected, especially by Katina. I met him in September 1994, in Athens where he lived most of the year. In the summers, he and his wife, Eleni stayed at the homestead in Leros.

Zaharias was a tall, handsome man in his early 70s who was just as thrilled as I was to meet an unknown family member. I was very pleasantly surprised to realize that we had one common interest, our family history. He, too, had struggled to discover what happened to Grandfather and why the whole family dispersed all over the world. He searched the records of the administrative offices on Leros as well as those of the monastery and churches and learned nothing. Nor did he find any reason for the two family names.

We shared our stories and explored all the questions that no one had answered to our satisfaction. We even speculated that perhaps Grandfather was part of some underground movement and was conspiring against the Turks, and later, against the Italians. Our speculations seemed a little fantastic and did not fit the image of Grandfather we had heard about from our parents.

I confided in him the two stories I had heard from my mother and my Aunt Katina, that he was killed when he became confused and fell off a cliff and that he died of pneumonia. He found no records of his death or of his burial. Zaharias searched the island's burial sites and found none for Grandfather.

"I think he committed suicide," whispered Zaharias.

I was startled by his comment. "I've had the same thought," I acknowledged just as quietly.

"What other possibility is there?" he asked. If he died of pneumonia, he would have been buried in the church cemetery. He is not there, because I have looked there and in several other graveyards." "Why do you think he committed suicide?" I asked. He looked at me for some moments uncertain how much he should tell me. His wife Eleni was very sensitive and did not like to talk about these matters. Still, he wanted to shake these terrible thoughts out of his head.

"Please tell me what you think. I really want to know; I'll tell you what I believe happened," I said encouragingly.

Quietly he continued. "Before my father died here on Leros in 1960, he told me that his brother, Stavros, had killed himself in the Leprosarium in Louisiana. Well, I suspect that Grandpa must have acquired Leprosy during his trips around the island, and when he discovered what was occurring to him, he committed suicide. The Church would not bury him on consecrated ground under those circumstances."

Zaharias shared with me that he had sailed to Marseilles, France in 1961, to visit our Uncle Stephanos, and discovered that he had leprosy, too. I then told him about our Aunt Katina who had been ill with the same disease for many years. Together we had uncovered the family's secret nightmare. After a long silence we sighed with relief.

Finally, the pieces of our family puzzle were falling into place. After Grandfather's death, the family dispersed joining thousands of other Greeks of the Diaspora who scattered all over the world. There was so much shame and disgrace associated with leprosy and with suicide that the rest of the family could no longer stay on Leros. Their grief was too deep to stay where they were no longer accepted.

Later, he told me his own story – the hardships he and his mother endured after his father, a brutal, abusive man, deserted his wife and abandoned his son. With the help of his maternal grandparents, they managed to survive. He was an excellent student and learned four languages: Egyptian, Greek, English, and Italian. For twenty years, he worked in a General Motors Plant building Buick cars.

After Nassar became President of Egypt (1956-1960), all foreigners were threatened with deportation or prison. Zaharias was considered an Italian citizen, and he had to demonstrate that he was born in Greece in order to get a visa to enter Greece. His father had his birth certificate. This was the first time he saw his father since childhood. After asking Zaharias to wait for two days, his father retrieved the document for him. They said nothing else to each other. In 1960 when Zaharias returned to Leros, he was surprised to discover his father was there living in the family homestead. They spent a few days together getting reacquainted when he realized his father was dying of a heart condition. Before he died, Christodoulos asked his son to forgive him for his bad behavior.

Innocence
Revisited

I Can Get There All By Myself

I was a toddler about three or so, and Mama and I were walking along First Street to Yiayia's house. Mama was pushing the baby carriage with my baby sister, Mary, who was asleep. I was absorbed in watching the huge steam engines pulling long lines of cars filled with coal. The red caboose at the end of the line amused me. It looked like a little house on wheels. I waved to the man standing outside on the platform. As the train passed, I focused my attention in the direction of Clark's Addition where Yiayia lived.

All of a sudden a thought crossed my mind, "I know the way to Yiayia's house! I can get there all by myself!" This realization was so intense and powerful that, without a word to Mama, I took off and ran as fast as I could in the direction of my grandmother's house. If I had had words to describe what I was experiencing, I may have thought, "Mama will be so surprised and pleased when she realizes I know the way."

I was so intent on running that I didn't hear my Mother's panicked voice screaming my name, "E-leu-the-ria! Stop! Wait for me!" I only wanted to show her I could find my way alone. I was thrilled with my new discovery.

A few minutes later, I arrived at Yiayia's house breathless and laughing with pleasure. I did know where the house was! I sat on the porch step waiting for Mama and savoring the pleasure of my flight. "I can't wait to see the look on her face," I thought, just as she came in the gate pushing the carriage ahead of her. She was breathless, too, and her face was flushed. Little beads of perspiration formed on her forehead. The look in her hazel eyes was one of fear and anger. I saw no pleasure or surprise as I had anticipated.

The sting of the spanking that followed immediately after her arrival was not nearly as painful as the disappointment I felt. She didn't understand at all what I experienced, and I did not know how to tell her.

I Know the Way!

A year later, on a beautiful spring day, I had a strong desire to go outside and take a walk. The rain had stopped, the sun was shining, and the air smelled fresh. Mama was lying down. She was sick again. She said the baby inside her was making her feel bad.

"I think I'll take Mary and Tony for a walk," I decided. They were my younger sister who was two and a half years old and my brother who was almost one. Tony was better now. He had burned his hands on the oven door. They were wrapped in bandages for a long time. Mary was the "pretty one." That's what Papa called her. She had curly hair. Mine was straight.

I took them each by the hand, and we walked out on our L-shaped porch, past the swing and the rose bush in our little square garden in front of our house. I pushed the latch on the gate and it opened. We turned right on the sidewalk and headed toward Second Street. Our house was in the middle of Carlisle Street, and I decided I wanted to walk all the way to the corner. "Then," I thought, "I'll take us down to the next street—"I'm not sure what that street is called—and we will come back by way of First Street."

I did not tell Mama of my plan. I didn't want to bother her. As the oldest of the children, I felt confident. "We'll be all right. I know the way!" I told myself. I felt tall beside Mary and Tony. They were tiny beside me. I held their hands firmly in mine, and I guided the two little ones along. I walked slowly so they could keep up with me. "When I'm on my own, I can go much faster," I thought feeling very pleased with my accomplishment.

As we moved past our house, I pointed out to them the homes of the other Greek families. "The Petsoes live in this yellow house next door to us. Anna Petso is my age, and she has an older brother. His name is Tommy." When we reached the two-story brick house, I told Mary and Tony, "This is where the Kotellas family lives. Mrs. Kotellas has four boys. Her baby is called Tony too, just like you are." I looked at our Tony and smiled.

Slowly, ever so slowly, we continued our walk. We stopped to examine house doors, front yards, and flowers growing there. The building on the corner of Carlisle and Second Street was empty—it looked abandoned—the windows were cracked and dirty. I felt scared; maybe someone was hiding there. We turned right onto Second Street. Next to the empty building was a huge junkyard, and for a while we stood silently near the entrance where the large wooden gate was swung back against the fence, and we observed the men in their sweaty blue work shirts tossing pieces of iron on piles in the yard.

When we tired of watching the men work, we continued our walk. We crossed the alley and passed a couple of clapboard houses. Now we were at the corner of Second and the street whose name I didn't know. Up to that point, I was familiar with the area because Mama walked that way with us on our way to Yiayia's house.

I had not been down this street before. As we turned right, we saw the monstrous blast furnace at the far end of this unknown street and across the railroad tracks. The huge furnace looked like a giant spewing fire out of his gaping mouth. I was not allowed to go across the railroad tracks unless Mama or Nonos was with us. The river was down there. Sometimes Nonos took us to the little beach that was way down there off First Street in the other direction.

We continued walking slowly. Still holding Mary and Tony's hands, we gazed at closed doors and shaded windows. We were beginning to feel tired. In the middle of the block, a tall, thin, white-haired woman stood in her doorway. "Where are you going, children?" she asked.

Very quietly and shyly, I answered, "For a walk." Her next question intrigued me. "Would you like some cookies and milk?" Without another word, we followed her.

We were in a warm, pleasant kitchen filled with the sweet smells of cinnamon and chocolate. The old lady placed a plate of cookies on the table and three small glasses of milk. I helped Mary and Tony climb on the chairs, and I climbed on one, too. She gave us each a cookie, and she joined us at the table. I had no idea how long we sat at the kitchen table eating cookies and drinking milk with the little old woman who had become one of us. Unexpectedly, I was awakened from the reverie of sweet smells and soft talk, and I heard Mama's frantic voice calling our names.

I ran to the front window and looked out. I saw my Uncle Steve running down First Street. I stepped out of the door and waved to my mother. She was running toward me. Her face was red and sweaty, a strand of hair falling over her cheek. I called out, "Mama, we're here." Tony and Mary joined me on the doorstep. I looked around and to my surprise, I saw my three older cousins, Gusty, Jack, and Nick, running toward us.

"What are they doing here?" I wondered. Then, I saw the fear and anger in mother's face, and I knew immediately I was in trouble. I dropped the hands of Mary and Tony and ran as fast as my short legs would take me back to the house. I slid under my bed trembling. I knew what was coming.

That spanking hurt even more that the first one when I left Mama and ran to Yiayia's house. She was afraid that I had taken us to the river. I was never able to explain to her that I knew where I was going and I knew how to find my way home. Her fear puzzled me. *I knew better than to go to the river without her.*

* * * * *

As time passed, I realized that my mother was overwhelmed by her life: four children in four years, all born breach. When I took that walk with my sister and brother, my mother was pregnant with my youngest sister Anna. Now, I know she must have been exhausted as well as fearful. She was an immigrant in a strange country; she did not speak the language, and she was frightened by the violence that surrounded us—drunken brawls, mining and mill accidents, and burning crosses.

From her conversations with Aunt Katina and my father, I gathered little bits of information that did not make sense to me but troubled her. Earlier she had seen a cross burning on the hillside overlooking our town and this confused her even more. In her culture, the cross was a revered and sacred object. She was horrified that anyone would burn a cross. That seemed like a very sinful thing to do. In 1932 when I was four, the Lindberg baby had been kidnapped from its bed and was later found dead. I heard the words, "baby stolen, and killed," as my mother whispered to her sister.

Later, as I put these tidbits of information together, a more coherent picture evolved. To my mother, the world here was an evil and dangerous place, but for me the world was a challenge and a place to explore. Those little escapades of mine became metaphors for my attempts to achieve more autonomy and independence. Every time I made an effort to try my wings, I was yanked back into the constricted boundaries of my family, which with time strengthened my desires and yearnings to pull away. Many years would pass before I understood that the cultural and religious customs were built into our family structure to frustrate and prevent such desires from reaching fulfillment, especially for the female children. Unbeknown to me, these were only the beginnings of the identity struggles that were to come.

Innocence
Lost

HIDE AND SEEK

My seventh year was a momentous one for me. I felt as if I had come out of a cocoon and had suddenly awakened from a deep sleep. I was aware and I could remember and wonder about the world around me. I could think and plan and I had my own secret! Some of my experiences were awesome, like the one with the still, small voice that told me I could escape. I still felt the sadness, the deep grief, and disappointment of losing Papa Lambros, our priest. The loss of my dog, my friend, Lottie was heart-breaking for me, too, but the worst incident happened on a sunny autumn afternoon, and I was so scared.

I never told anyone what happened on that day. It must have been a Saturday because I was not in school. Mama and Papa were going on an errand and they wanted to take me, but I wanted to play with my new friend, Mary. They allowed me to go to her house until they returned. Her family had moved recently into the corner building on Second Street next to the railroad tracks. Her father opened a *kafeneio* in the front of the building, and the family had their living quarters in the back.

Mary was my age, seven years old, and she had dark eyes and black hair just like mine. She was very shy and reticent. Her father was Greek and her mother, American. She had an older sister and two older brothers. Rosie was about ten, Michael was twelve, and Tony the oldest was fifteen and very muscular like a football player. I felt uncomfortable around him. I didn't like the way he looked at me; I felt embarrassed and like I wanted to melt away, so I stayed away from him.

This particular afternoon, Michael said, "Let's play hide-and-seek." Some of our other friends from the neighborhood had joined us, and we all ran off to hide. Rosie, with her eyes closed was counting slowly, "…30, 35, 40, 45, 50…." I ran and hid under the old wooden platform that ran along the railroad tracks. I could stand under there without bumping my head on the wooden slats above me. I could hear Rosie counting "…80, 85, 90, 95, and 100. Here I come!"

In an instant, Tony was there. He wasn't playing with us when the game started. I didn't know where he came from. He bent over and sat down on the floor with his back against the wooden slats. He was too tall to stand up like I could.

"Come over here," he said softly.

"No," I shook my head. I felt afraid. I wanted to run out of there, even if Rosie caught me.

"Don't be scared. I won't hurt you. I want to play a game with you. O.K?" he said as he patted the floor beside him.

My curiosity was somewhat aroused until he said, "Take your pants down, and I will do the same. It's only a game."

Suddenly I could see my dad's face, and I started to cry. I was terrified of what would happen if my father found out…what? I didn't know what was happening, and I was confused and afraid. I turned and ran out of there as fast as I could, sobbing all the way home.

When my parents returned later, I was still crying and holding tightly to the gate in front of our house. "What's the matter?" asked my mother. "Nothing," I muttered. "I was afraid being alone." They didn't let me stay home alone after that, even though they did not know what had happened. I never told them. I avoided Tony, and I wouldn't look at him when he was nearby. A couple of years later, Tony left home for the Conservation Corps and I never saw him again.

Mary and I remained friends through the eighth grade. To my distress and unhappiness, Mary and her family moved away after that school year ended, and I didn't see her again until we were adults. Her father removed her from high school. He bought a house out in the country and Mary worked on the farm. I was very sad to lose my friend, and I could not believe or understand why she was not allowed to continue her schooling. School buses brought children from the country to our high school every day. I tried to make sense out of incidents that happened in my own life as well as those of others. Perhaps her family had secrets like ours, or different ones, which meant I would never know the reasons or ever understand. I felt just as sorry for Mary as I did for my mother, and that made me more determined to go on for them as well as for myself. I was sad to lose my friend and horrified that she was not allowed to continue her schooling in high school.

Childhood Memories of "The Bottom"

I lived on Carlisle Street until I was twenty years old. Even though our neighborhood on the Bottom no longer exists, I can still see our homes built on the flood plains of the Ohio River near the steel mills and blast furnaces.

In a flicker of a memory, I can revive the whole scene. There's Carlisle Street, a strip of dirt one block long situated between the tracks of the Baltimore and Ohio Railroad alongside First Street and the Pennsylvania Railroad tracks next to Second Street. To the East, across the river I see the gray-green hills of the Allegheny foothills in West Virginia surrounding our valley. This point on the river, where parts of Ohio, West Virginia, and Pennsylvania meet, is known as the Tri-State area, the heart of our universe where industry is king.

I feel proud of the history of Martins Ferry before and after the Civil War. Our town became famous, or infamous, depending on one's point of view, for its underground railroad. Thousand of slaves escaped across the river from West Virginia and found refuge in Martins Ferry before moving further north.

Most of the Negroes who settled in Martins Ferry lived in the southern part of town, and the majority of European immigrants lived in the Clarks Addition in the north. Our neighborhood was in the middle of the Bottom and the only section that was a multi-ethnic and multi-racial mix of European immigrants and Negroes living together.

The Johnson family from Georgia lived next door to us, and on their other side was the Serbian Dadasovich family who had newly remodeled their brick house. Katherine Johnson was the youngest of three daughters. She was my friend and my tutor when I started elementary school. With her and her family I learned about ghost stories, jazz and blues, and about eating ground hog that tasted like chicken. I learned something new from each family in our neighborhood.

Three generations of the Jackson family lived in the clapboard house across the street, and next to them dwelled the Martins who had two sons, Melvin and Jimmy. Mr. and Mrs. Dadasovich had emigrated from Serbia as did the Visnics and the Mirics who lived across the street. The Presley family lived on the corner next to the Visnics and they were Croatian. In their own country the Serbians and the Croats had been bitter enemies for generations, but here in Martins Ferry there was no animosity that I could detect between neighbors. The immigrants from Europe and the Negroes from the South gathered on that dirt street and lived side by side.

To the west of our house, was a yellow and green house where the Petsos family lived. Anna their daughter was about my age, and her brother Tom was in the Conservation Corps where many young men went during the Depression when jobs (other than mill work) were difficult to find. Beside them, in a big red brick house lived the other Greek family, Katina and Mihalis Kotellas and their four sons: Mike, John, Harry, and Tony. The Edens, the one white family, lived across the street from the Kotellas. As I said before, I did not consider myself "white" for many years because I turned as dark skinned as our neighbors in the summertime. Besides, I felt different from the whites who spoke only English and had very different customs from ours. Most of them lived uptown and were considered middle class. We were working class.

The Mirics, an elderly couple, spoke very little English. Mary and Mike, their adult children, lived at home, worked and provided for their parents as many young people did in those days when there was no welfare or social security. The living arrangement of the elder Mirics seemed very odd to me. Mrs. Miric, a tall thin stern woman, lived in the house with Mary and Mike, and her husband lived in a shed in the backyard. I remember the shock and sadness that I felt when I saw the shed where he lived. It did not look comfortable or warm. The winters in Ohio were damp and cold.

When Mr. Miric died a few years later, the casket containing his body was shown in their living room of the house. "How strange," I thought, "the husband and father of the family was relegated to the shed in the backyard until he died; then he was allowed back into the house for a couple of days before he was buried." Rumors were whispered that he drank a lot, but that did not seem reason enough to me to banish him to a place appropriate for chickens or pigeons rather than a decent living space for a sickly old man. If drinking were the only reason for such banishment, then most of the men in our neighborhood should have suffered the same fate.

Across the railroad tracks on First Street lived Lillie Williams, a majestically tall Negro woman who had come from the Deep South to Martins Ferry to raise her four children. I was fascinated by her two youngest sons who were twins and very tall and thin. Their names were Esau and Jacob. They were extremely polite, and they spoke with a Southern drawl. Every time I saw them, alone or together, I would struggle to figure out which one was Jacob and which, Esau. I don't think I ever did tell them apart. Years later I learned that Lillie's husband had been lynched in Alabama, and her father and brother were brutally murdered. Jacob wrote a book about his mother's life and called it *Lillie*. He portrayed her very honestly, I thought. He obviously had a deep respect and love for her, and his book honored her life. I felt very touched by it, and I felt proud that on Carlisle Street, we accepted each other and, generally, had a "Live and let live" attitude about each other.

On the corner of Carlisle and Second Street, on the north side was an abandoned brick building next to a junkyard, and on the opposite side was another brick building that housed the transient population as well as "the homeless drunks." They seemed quiet and harmless enough, but when we played we stayed closer to the other end of the street.

Lillian Dadasovich was the youngest of seven and was two years older than I was, and we were very good friends. When I wasn't home, I was at her house. She had four older brothers and two older sisters. Her brothers and father all worked in the Laughlin Steel Mill;

and her older sister, Mary (who was always called "Sissy") worked at the Hazel-Atlas Glass Company in Wheeling, West Virginia. Ann, a high school senior when the Second World War was declared, went to Detroit, Michigan, to work in a defense factory after her brothers were drafted into the Army.

The Dadasovich family was very warm and cordial, and I enjoyed sitting in their kitchen while Mrs. Dadasovich cooked pots of sauerkraut or chili—foods that we never ate at our house. She was very adept at making large loaves of nut bread. She rolled out the dough on the large square table in the kitchen, and very methodically spread the walnut mixture of ground walnuts, sugar, cinnamon, and raisins evenly on the dough. Then she would roll the dough and mixture over and over until she had one large nut bread roll that she gracefully slipped into the oven.

Everyday during the week, she put thick slices of nut bread in her husband's and son's lunch pails. And I would sit there quietly observing her movements as she prepared meals for her family and as she readied the lunch pails for the men in her family who worked the afternoon shift at the mill.

On Saturday evenings during the winter months, I was there with the Dadasovich women putting jigsaw puzzles together on the kitchen table, or playing Gin Rummy as we listened to Frank Sinatra on the "Hit Parade" and "Grand Central Station" with Helen Hayes.

From the end of May when school was over, we barefooted brown-skinned children played in the backyards or on the dirt street and alleyways. Some of our favorite games were hide-and-seek, run-sheep-run, and "Shinny," a game that required a can, two sticks and two players; the point of the game was to hit a goal. This was a game we either made up or someone adapted from hockey; I'm not certain how it came about. We played baseball and football. The boys and girls all played together.

Mary Visnic and I were ardent Chinese-checker players and we played for hours sitting on the ground in front of her kitchen door. Mary won most of the games, and I, determined to improve my skill, persisted in playing with her for hours despite my frequent losses. When we got tired of playing checkers, we wandered around and explored the neighborhood. I liked gathering pieces of colored glass and white agate stones in the alleyway parallel to Carlisle Street. I can see us still, as small barefoot girls in print cotton dresses, standing on the corner of First Street waving to the railroad engineers and watching the trains as they went north carrying their loads of iron ore and coal to the mills and blast furnaces.

If we wanted to play on swings and seesaws or go swimming, we had to go uptown, past the Central School, and down a short hill to the City Park. The W.P.A. (Work Projects Administration) built the swimming pool late in the 1930s after the big flood and it is still there today.

Most of us from the Bottom had few if any toys and very few of us had radios. We got our first radio in 1940. During the summer months everyone with a radio turned them up full blast as we sat on our porches and listened to the Joe Louis fights and to President Roosevelt when he spoke to us during his "fireside chats." We all cheered Joe Louis when he won, as he usually did, and we listened reverently when the President spoke.

* * * * *

There was another side to the Ohio Valley. When I remember that aspect of my hometown and neighborhood, the primary color that I see is gray; and I recall that the basic tone was violence and death. These were the ever-present specters that hovered over our valley and our lives. Not only did the Ohio River rise out of its muddy depths, wreaking its own kind of destruction on the Bottom, but also we witnessed the most hideous and insidious violence that man inflicted against nature. There were unnamed and unknown industrialists who, in the name of progress, destroyed the river with chemicals and waste products from their mills and furnaces. By 1938 the river was so polluted and full of holes that we were not allowed to swim there. The Sand and Gravel Company dug the holes and claimed whatever was left of any worth at the bottom of the river. Every summer a child or two drowned, pulled down by the suck hole, lost to the deep, dark waters. The river became a malignant symbol of what would become of you if you were not careful and aware.

The strip miners burrowed into the hills and farmlands, stripped the surface layers of coal, and left gaping wounds as their mark of economic success. The green fragrant hillsides where cattle once grazed were now covered with smoke and iron ore particles that turned everything into a monochromatic shade of gray. The air we breathed turned our lungs black by the time we reached adolescence. Sometimes the air was so thick with smoke the sun could not penetrate its screen, even in the summer.

As a child I was very aware of the dirt and smoke, because I had "high-water marks" (a coating of coal dust that remains on the skin of the forearm after washing our hands) up to my elbows everyday by the time I came home from school. We were all familiar with the other effects of the bituminous soot that covered the valley, seeped into our homes, and coated the walls with gray-brown film. My mother and I scrubbed our walls two or three times a year.

Violence and chaos were our constant companions, and in a warped sort of way, we learned to accept whatever outrage broke out on the weekends as our "Saturday night entertainment." The men worked hard all week in backbreaking jobs to eke out a living of sorts for worn-out exhausted wives and hungry children. Then, on Friday nights, they started their hard drinking that lasted through Sunday. [All the tensions that had accumulated during the week— the strains of work and the relentless poverty and deprivations added desperation to already overburdened homesick lives—exploded in their minds.] Inevitably, a fight broke out in a home, in a beer joint, or on the street. One man attacked another; a husband beat his wife; or a son beat up his father for beating his mother.

One of the bloodiest fights I ever saw happened between Mr. Martin, a short, thin man and his fifteen-year-old stepson, Melvin, who lived across the street from us. Mr. Martin, in a drunken rage, beat up his wife, and Melvin slashed him with a knife. Both bloodied and bruised fell out of the house and onto the street where they continued punching and wrestling with each other before the horrified children who had gathered to watch. Eventually, several men in the neighborhood pulled them apart, and they went off in different directions with each one and helped them nurse their wounds.

Bootlegging violence thrived through the years of Prohibition. Early one wintry night when I was about four, several husky policemen kicked a hole in our front door and routed us out of bed and searched our house and basement for illegal whiskey. They found only a few bottles of homebrew. Their apology was a warning. "Don't you Greeks think you're getting away with nothing. We'll catch you sooner or later, so watch you ass." Then they slammed our splintered door and left.

Mr. Miller, who lived across the alley, was the "real" bootlegger. I remember one Saturday morning while my siblings and I were eating breakfast; we suddenly heard glass smashing behind our garage. We ran out to see dozens of policemen carrying armloads of bottles that they dropped and shattered spilling strong-smelling whiskey into the dirt alley. Ironically, after Prohibition was repealed, Mr. Miller became an upstanding citizen and an officer of the Martins Ferry police force.

My father was another one who settled matters with his fists in family disputes, as he did once with Uncle Chris (Aunt Anna's husband). I never knew what they were fighting about in that notorious alley behind our house. My mother was too distraught to do anything but cry. This was the second time I saw her cry. I guessed it was about the rejection and the blame that was heaped on my father for marrying my mother, but I was not privy to any explanations from adults. The violence inside and outside my family was always terrifying whether I witnessed it or not.

I have never forgotten that beautiful Sunday morning, May 12, 1940, to be exact, when Mr. Stavros, the owner of the Greek coffee house on Main Street, quietly went berserk and methodically shot and killed six men as they played cards or leisurely read the paper while drinking their thick black Greek Coffee. He wounded six others. My Uncle Steve was one of the wounded. The bullet lodged in his neck too close to the spine to be removed. Fortunately, my father stayed home that morning. Some said that Mr. Stavros had called his name.

A year or so later, George Doty, a taxi driver, raped and killed a young woman in his cab. Both Mr. Stavros and George Doty were tried in St. Clairsville, the township seat, and within a year of the murders each man was executed in the electric chair at the Ohio State Prison in Columbus. There were no lengthy appeals in those days, only "sweet" justice.

The mills sounded shrill long whistles when an accident occurred. The people knew the meaning of that signal. That night around the kitchen tables and coffee houses, the story was told about the laborer who lost a hand to the belts, an eye to the sparks, or a life to the engines, the furnaces, or the train. Down the river in Powhattan a terrible mine disaster took sixty-six lives. I can still see *The Daily Times'* pictures of the women hovering outside the mine shaft waiting to hear whether a husband, a father, a brother, or a son was dead or alive.

Death and destruction were as much a part of our lives as school, church, and the high school football games on Friday nights at the stadium in autumn. The children were not shielded from the dark events that played themselves out in our environment. No matter how terrible the event, the excitement would die down gradually; and each family sank into its ordinary, unobtrusive, routine day-to-day lives.

School and
Other Memories

After a long, hot humid summer, September finally arrived. The day after Labor Day, schools opened their doors and welcomed us back. We put our shoes back on our feet and walked excitedly up Hanover Street and over to Fourth Street to the Central School that I attended for eight years. I loved the excitement of the first day of school and seeing classmates and the teachers again, and the smell of those old wooden floors and the echoes of feet running up and down stairs as children lined up to enter their classrooms. I was always happiest when school started. Having my own desk where I kept my notebook paper, pencils, and crayons was very special. I never had a place for my own things before.

School became my safety zone, my escape, and my sanctuary. I felt safe and I did what I loved most—learning! I wanted to learn everything: Arithmetic, English, and History—whatever was taught was new and exciting and I soaked up classes like a sponge. Needless to say, my motivation and enthusiasm made me a model student, well behaved and polite. Most of the children that I went to school with in those days were well behaved. Of course, we were reprimanded and scolded when a student whispered while the teacher was talking or when one of us got caught with chewing gum in his/her mouth.

I was reprimanded once in the third grade when classes were changing. Miss Smith had warned us that we were to be quiet during the change. I saw a friend coming into our room, and I very excitedly motioned to her to come and sit with me. Miss Smith noticed what was happening and immediately sent me to the cloakroom (a space in the back of the room that was used to hang our coats and place our boots in the winter time). I was in tears, mortified, that I was punished. Of course, that was the first and the last time for me. Nothing like that ever happened again.

The years in elementary school merged one into the other. I was always at the top of my class. Getting good grades was very important to me. I had to prove to my father I was a "good" girl. I had to demonstrate that I was responsible, dependable, and most importantly, trustworthy. My father's threat, "Be good if you want to finish school," was very real to me. I knew if I gave him any reason, he would pull me out of school and bury me in the house. I knew that "be good" meant "stay away from boys."

Being a good student made school more difficult for my sisters and brother who followed me through the years. So, almost weekly for the first months of Mary's first year, Miss Moore, the principal and the first grade teacher, called me into her office to tell me to go home and bring my sister to her class. I did so, but I was angry and embarrassed about being taken out of class. I walked rapidly back home because I didn't want to miss part of the class. When I got home, I told her she was coming to school with me, but she resisted. I took Mary's hand firmly in mine and forcibly led her to school. That probably did nothing to entice her to attend classes, but I knew of no other way at that time; and I never understood why she didn't want to go to school. We knew nothing about school phobic children in those days.

A RETURN HOME

Life in the Ohio Valley was grim enough during the years I was growing up. By the end of the 1930s, the peoples' hopes and spirits were rising. More and more jobs were available, and my father's business was growing. By 1939, he had three International Harvester trucks, and he had to hire two drivers to haul coal to the homes uptown and to the businesses in the area and to the hospital.

In 1938, my father sank into one of his dark moods, despite the fact that his business was doing very well. Whether he was discouraged or homesick was not clear. There was no word that described what ailed him at that particular time. On the surface, he was achieving his dreams. He had his own home and business. He was making more money, but he became restless and angry and started talking about taking all of us back to Greece. Perhaps he had some bad news from his mother and father in Kalymnos. I once heard my mother say, "He gets really upset when he hears from his family." At one point, he actually went shopping and bought a trunk and the clothes that we would take with us.

I was very afraid. I did not want to go to Greece. I saw that my mother was reluctant, and I realized that if we went to Greece, I would be lost there. There was no escaping the destiny that the culture had mandated for its women. At least, in this country, I could dream and hope for something different.

The rumbling of war in Europe was sounding louder and louder, and as dreadful as it sounds, I breathed a sigh of relief. There was no way we were going back there if a war broke out. I followed the news of the events in Germany with great interest. I felt I had a personal stake in the outcome of the war that, ironically, saved me from a life of oppression in a foreign land. No one knew the extent of the horror that was to befall Europe in the very near future. Certainly, I didn't.

HOPE

Even though hopefulness infused our town, there still were remnants of unmet needs in our community. Homeless transients came to our homes begging for food and work. We lived close enough to the riverbank, and we saw the poor people who lived in ramshackle shacks. One woman who lived in one of those shacks made fudge and an assortment of other candies that she sold for a few pennies to make a living. My friends and I were regular customers.

I listened to adults talking about the possibilities that were developing. "If you work hard in this country, you can do better than anywhere else in the world." In school we learned that through education one could achieve a better life. These ideas and thoughts were prayers that I said every night before falling asleep. "Yes, even a woman can make it if she works hard enough and goes to school long enough—that was the key! An education! I had no specific job in mind. Career was not even in our vocabularies. In my mind, the primary purpose of an education was *Freedom, the ability to choose what I wanted to do, no matter what that was.*

I realized at some point in my early childhood that if I wanted something, I had to find a way to get it for myself, not only because my parents did not have money for frivolous things like toys and dolls, but because they weren't even aware that those things were important for children. My father, in particular, seemed to dislike and disapprove of the idea that children needed to play. He was impatient with our playfulness in the house and insisted on "Quiet!" when he was home. He once told my third grade teacher, Miss Smith, "I am not sending my daughter to school to play. She is there to learn." He did not believe that crayons and art lessons were essential activities in school. In her quiet and unobtrusive way, Mama provided our school supplies, and I was grateful that she understood. The message was very clear: children were to be seen and not heard. If I wanted to play, I went outside the house. Mary played quietly upstairs in the bedroom with her collection of dolls that I helped get for her. At Christmas I became Santa's helper. I went shopping with my mother and told her the kind of toys my sisters and brother liked.

I didn't have a doll until I was eight. By selling "chances" to the neighbors, I had an opportunity to win a Shirley Temple Doll if I sold all the chances on the card: about twenty-five of them. The chances cost a nickel, and each buyer won a small prize with each one. I was required to submit the money and the list for prizes to the company that circulated the chances. A few weeks later, I received a box of prizes for the customers and my prize—a Shirley Temple doll that stood about three feet high. I was absolutely thrilled.

Even though I was excited about having a doll of my own, I don't remember playing with her very much—not like Mary who played with her dolls for hours. I looked at my doll and held her for short periods of time, and then I returned her to her box and placed it on the top shelf in the closet in the parlor. Every few months, I took her down, bathed her, washed and ironed her clothes, and put her back on the shelf alongside the set of dishes that Uncle Steve gave me for Christmas. If the dishes were dusty, I washed them and put them away, too. Years later, when I was too old to play with the doll and the dishes, I gave them to my little stepsister after her mother and my father married (following my mother's death).

MY VISION

As I recall my early years, I see the activities that I participated in as metaphors for the shape of my life to come: separate, serious, and independent. Mary surrounded herself with dolls as a child. When she married, she devoted her life to her adopted son and daughter, and later to her grand children. I was always restless at home. As soon as my chores were done, I was out—at a neighbor's home, on the street playing all sorts of games, and wandering off by the river and dreaming about the future.

One summer morning as I walked along the riverbank, I started throwing stones in the river and counting the circles absentmindedly. The circles expanded and grew bigger and bigger. I was fascinated by the ever-growing circles that were perfectly round and blending into each other. I stared at the circles within circles until I felt myself blending with them. I made a connection!

Ten circles...one decade.... I am in the first decade of life! Ten decades equaled a hundred years. Would I live that long? The year was 1938, and in fifty years it would be 1988. Where would I be then? Twelve years later, I'll be 72 and the year will be 2000! Imagine living that long. Now, the women look so old at 50. Maybe I won't live that long.

My young mind could not grasp that there might be a time when I would not be alive. Quickly, I went to another thought. I discovered time—its limitations and its possibilities—and I felt excited and anxious. There was an urgency about time I had not experienced before. That image of the ever-expanding circles was imprinted on my mind and became symbols of expanding and contracting time. I could not imagine the enormous possibilities that life had in store for me. Those circles within circles became mandalas of inner peace and tranquility, which were rare and precious states when I was growing up.

READING AND LEARNING

When I discovered the library, I brought home armloads of books and read for hours on the front porch in the summer time. I'd start reading with my chair leaning against the wall of the house, on the east end of the porch; and by four o'clock in the afternoon, I was at the west end of the porch. I moved with the sun from one end to the other. I played a game with myself. I wanted to see how many books I could read by the time school started in the fall. One summer I read a hundred books. I wrote the titles of each book in a notebook as a record of my accomplishment.

In school I learned enthusiastically, and I soaked in everything the teachers had to teach. Whatever I learned in school, I practiced at home and outside on the street. At times, this worked against me, because the other children thought I was "showing off" or I was teased for being the teacher's "pet." That didn't matter to me because I realized that I was developing skills and tools I never had before.

When I wanted or needed something, I'd figure out a way to get it for myself—like the doll. Another time, I saved my pennies for three months in order to purchase a bathing suit that was in Woolworth's window. It was a multicolored and one of the most beautiful things I ever saw. I was so proud when I wore it to the swimming pool that summer. It was mine. I had saved and bought it for myself, and I felt so good. I learned the lessons and rewards of self-sufficiency and the value of independence very young in life.

Inadvertently, my parents reinforced these lessons and rewards. Since I was the oldest child in the family, I was given, and I accepted, responsibilities for helping them. From an early age, I helped my mother with the washing, ironing, shopping, and housework. I became the family interpreter for my mother when she could not understand what the neighbors were saying to her, and I ran errands for my father. I even purchased parts for his truck; I paid bills; and I went to the bank and made deposits for him. I read the mail as well as the paper to him.

By the time I was twelve, and fast approaching womanhood, all the street games were over. I was reading most of my spare time. On Sundays during the autumn, winter, and spring months, we went to the movies after the noon meal. In the summer, we were permitted to go swimming several times a week in the pool uptown. However, riding bicycles or sledding were not permitted. "I am not raising you to get yourselves killed," my father firmly and clearly laid down the law for us.

Still, I had to try learning how to ride a bicycle or go sledding. Of course, every time I tried to do something that was forbidden, I got hurt. Inevitably, I became so frightened of "getting caught" that I made mistakes that resulted in accidents and minor injuries. Like the time I talked John Kotellas into letting me ride his bicycle. I did fine until I saw a car coming toward me; then I panicked. I froze and couldn't think how to put the brakes on. I swerved and slammed into a low wall. I went flying over the wall into someone's backyard, and I landed on my face. I was bruised, shaken up, and terrified my father would find out how I got hurt. I went home and hid in my bedroom for two days. I avoided my father for a week until my wounds were healed, but he knew. I could tell by the disapproving looks that he gave me later. My mother must have talked to him because he did nothing else, as I was afraid he would do. As for sledding, none of us in the neighborhood had sleds, so we took boxes, flattened them, and slid down slopes that way. I didn't want to miss anything, even if it meant punishment later.

The War Years and After

On December 7, 1941, the Japanese bombed Pearl Harbor. It was Sunday afternoon, and I was at the home of my friend, Lillian, listening to the radio when the announcement came over the air. Shock waves went through all of us. Frightened I ran home to tell my parents.

The next day we listened to President Roosevelt as he declared war on Japan. I followed the terrible events of that war in *The Daily Times,* our local afternoon newspaper, and reported the news to my parents. My father read the Greek newspaper that was published in New York, but it was always about a week late in arriving. I found it very painful to read about all the losses we suffered during the first two years of the war. The Bataan March was dreadful, and the news from Africa and Europe was not much better.

We kept our hopes high as we planted our "Victory Garden" in the little plot of ground in the front yard, and we collected cans for recycling. At school, we purchased U.S. Savings Stamps and Bonds every Monday morning as our contribution toward the war effort. Some foods were rationed, such as sugar and coffee, as well as gasoline and silk stockings.

Since my father was in the trucking business and was hauling coal to the blast furnace, power plants, and other industrial factories, his work was considered essential to the National Defense. His supply of gasoline for his trucks was not controlled. He implanted a five-hundred-gallon tank underground in front of our house and was guaranteed his own supply of gas on demand. By that time, he owned three trucks in addition to those that he sublet from other truckers when he needed additional trucks to haul coal. His business was going full steam—from morning to night, six days a week. He was making more money than he ever dreamed of making, but our lifestyle changed only slightly. Mama had more money to spend on food, but otherwise, everything was as it had been.

The one hardship my father had to confront was an inability to keep a good bookkeeper. He had two women for a period of time, but they got better paying jobs in the Defense industries. I saw his inability to hire a steady bookkeeper as an opportunity to prove my worth and gain some recognition for my abilities from my father. One of the bookkeepers showed me the basic fundamentals of her bookkeeping system before she left, and I asked Mama to find out whether Dad would let me do the bookkeeping for him. He was reluctant because I was only thirteen, but he had no other choice. He watched me like a hawk as I entered the loads that his drivers hauled each week, and I wrote out the checks for their payment on Saturday mornings. I did this work until I was twenty.

Unbeknown to my father, I developed a method of self-payment. He was unwilling to pay me a regular salary, so whenever I deposited a check in my father's business account, I cashed the change and deposited it in my own account. I rationalized that I was not stealing, that it was money I had earned, and it was much less than the amount he paid the bookkeepers.

In the seven years that I worked for my father, I saved seventy-five dollars. My father didn't believe in paying his children for working for him (or having money of there own, i.e., when he took my money from my piggy bank to buy a trailer)—he considered all the money his. When he found out I had saved seventy-five dollars by taking the change on the checks I deposited for him, he went to the bank president and demanded "his" money back.

[In 1946 my father and other illegal aliens were given amnesty and citizenship by President Truman for their contribution to the defense effort during World War II.]

In September 1942, I entered the Martins Ferry High School. This was the exciting adventure that I had waited for throughout my entire childhood! Every day of the school year was special. I was thrilled with the study of algebra, even though I did not understand its application. I enjoyed learning the formulas and getting the correct answers. Mr. Hart, our teacher and principal, made algebra an intriguing game. English was easy for me, and my background in Greek made Spanish undemanding.

In my sophomore year, Miss Morris, an elderly, white-haired autocratic teacher, taught Geometry. She had a tendency to shout very loudly at students who did not understand. I was so frightened of her that, after a couple of weeks, I dropped the class and signed up for World History. I knew I would freeze if she yelled at me, and I was afraid I would fail if I continued in her class. I did very well in the history class, and I liked it so much that I did the assignments and all the extra credit work as well.

That year Miss Willerton was my English teacher. She had taught us Bible study in elementary school, and I had looked forward to having her in high school. One day she asked me to see her after class. I was surprised and pleased that she encouraged me to write an essay on the subject, "I Am An American," for a contest that was sponsored by the American Legion. To my utter amazement, I won honorable mention! This was, indeed, an honor for a child of immigrants.

The joy of learning in high school was marred by my apprehension about graduating. Then – what? What would I do? My father had become more controlling with my enrollment in high school. The reality of his restrictiveness, and his adamant refusal to hear any discussion to the contrary, sent a cold chill through my spirit. His opposition to any form of advanced education for women was unbending. "I am not going to spend my hard-earned money to send you to college. What do you need college for? Certainly not for raising children. I agreed to let you go to high school. Now you want more!" And he waved his hand, closing the subject.

I felt trapped. Everything that I had done to demonstrate my trustworthiness was to no avail. I had obeyed his command, "Stay away from boys." Most of the boys who knew my father did not even ask for a date. They knew better and I did, too. Dating had always been out of the question. My focus was completely on my studies, not on extracurricular activities.

There were several boys who were interested in me at different times, but my constant refusal to consider meeting them at a movie or elsewhere discouraged them, and they stopped asking. One boy, Joe Gallagher, did not know my father and asked me to go to the prom dance with him when we were juniors. Somehow the invitation was retracted. I didn't know how he found out, but he would not risk taking me to the dance. I knew it was impossible when he asked me, but I wanted to think about it and fantasize about the possibility of going to a dance and wearing a long dress. I was relieved when he did not mention it again, and I didn't either.

At home my siblings and I avoided Dad as much as possible. Fortunately, he worked long hours, so he was only at home late in the evenings. When he was home, I went to one of my friend's homes. Mary was upstairs playing with her dolls, and I had no idea where Tony and Ann were. Mama sat in the kitchen and crocheted or went about her tasks as he ranted about whatever was wrong that day—something was always wrong for him. If it wasn't us, it was something out in society or the world that bothered him. He worked very hard, and he did not let us forget who "put the food on the table, clothes on your backs, and a roof over your head." He did not let us forget that he worked as a child to support his mother, sisters, and brother. He did not tell us that his father was a gambler, a heavy drinker, and a womanizer who took out his frustrations on him as a child and his wife (our grandmother). I learned about my grandfather's habits many years later. I can see that Dad perceived us as having a very easy life compared to his. And it was true. In many ways we did have a much better life than he did, and he was not cruel and brutal like his father. With all his shortcomings, I give him a lot of credit for his hard work and honesty; and he did the best he could do as a parent.

In the outside world, I observed the women who surrounded me, mostly mothers and wives. The working women were teachers, saleswomen, beauticians, and librarians. I knew I needed some kind of job to support myself, and I knew my father's response to that idea: "No daughter of mine is going to work outside the home. Greek women do not leave the home except by marriage or death."

I continued to observe and to ponder my secret dream of graduating from high school, working hard, and going to college. The life I dreamed about was impossible and unreachable, yet the yearning persisted and was compelling and relentless.

One day, on my way to school—sometime in the autumn of 1943, I saw a poster in Rudner's Furniture Store window that brought me to a complete halt. I froze in my tracks. I stared at the poster in disbelief:

YOUNG WOMEN WANTED
TO JOIN THE NURSE CADETS.
AFTER TWO AND A HALF YEARS OF TRAINING
IN A NURSING PROGRAM,
THE GRADUATE WOULD CONTRIBUTE
TWO YEARS OF SERVICE
TO THE ARMY NURSE CORPS.

The most significant aspect of the poster was that no tuition was necessary. In fact the Army would pay each Cadet a stipend each month: fifteen dollars the first year, twenty dollars the second year, and twenty-five dollars the third. I was overjoyed.

Once again, that soft, gentle voice in my ears said, "This is your way out. Go into nursing." Again, I felt the shiver of excitement shoot through my body, and the thrill of the possibility poured over me like cool water on a hot summer day. "A way out! A way out!" The words rang in my ears like a large bell in the church steeple. "A direction, finally!"

As I turned to continue on my way to school, my mind was filled with questions to be answered and information to be gathered. My heart was pounding with hope and enthusiasm. By the time I arrived at school, I was calmer. I went straight to the office to find out what classes were required to enter the Nursing Program. The secretary was very helpful. She told me I was on the right academic track, and the only class I needed that I had not planned for was chemistry. We decided that I could take that course the next year in my junior year. Later that week, I even stopped by the Martins Ferry Hospital to get the necessary application papers.

The other person I confided in was my mother. I needed her to transmit my plans to my father. She looked puzzled and concerned, but I knew she would talk with him: "She is studying very hard. She has been good and no trouble for us. She cleans the house every Saturday; she helps with grocery shopping, ironing, and running errands for your business. And she's been doing your bookkeeping for three years. She's very responsible and we can trust her."

My father's response to my mother's request that he permit me to enter the nursing school was the expected, "No. My daughter will not leave my house without getting married." Even though I anticipated his answer, I had a horrible letdown feeling and a deep sadness. I had convinced myself that if I were "good" and obedient, he would give me his blessing and allow me to follow my inclination. Later, he confronted me, "Where did you get such and idea? I should never have allowed you to go to high school. The next thing you'll want is to go to college." He walked away without waiting for a response from me. The sound in my head was an iron door clanging shut trapping me inside. I can still feel the sickening, nauseous feeling in the pit of my stomach as if I had been punched with a hard fist. My body went numb with shock and terror. "I'll never get out."

That little ever-hopeful voice answered, "You still have two years of school. You will find a way." Sick with disappointment, my inner world shut down and grew dark. This was the first of many journeys into the dark underworld. Like Persephone, I felt betrayed. Hurt and alone I descended into the darkness.

The rest of that year, I lived on two planes. On the surface I went through the motions of doing chores, reading, studying, and doing my father's bookkeeping without revealing what was going on deep inside, in the darkness of my soul. There I felt lost, wounded, and confused. "What more can I do to convince him?" The answer was "Nothing." I held on tenaciously, and he was unshakeable in his determination to keep me in my place. "How can I do better than I have already? I gave up every aspect of a social life to please him and that was not enough." I continued to search the darkness for answers.

There were no answers to be found. Along with my own darkness and hopelessness, I was horrified reading the newspaper about

the American troops captured by the Japanese. Hungry and wounded soldiers were forcibly marched to prison camps in Bataan. Many
of the men died in that march—The Death March. The wars were
dreadful on both fronts. London was being bombed everyday. Our
armed forces were not able to stop the Germans or the Japanese.

The next fall, I returned to school and registered for chemistry
as if nothing were happening at home. School was still my sanctuary, and I focused on my studies. I even included typing and short-
hand classes on my schedule, just in case things did not work out as
I hoped. My father grew more sullen and quiet. He did not speak
except to bark out a command or demand. When he looked at my
report card at the end of the first semester, he asked, "Why are you
taking chemistry?" "I'll need it to go into nursing," I answered quietly. He stormed out of the room.

My intent was not to get into a power struggle with him, but I was
just as stubborn and determined as he was. I preferred persuasion and
negotiation, but I was not skilled in those tactics. I wanted to say to
him, "Let me show you what I can do. I want you to be proud of me.
I don't want to disgrace you. Why can't you see that?" As his position
became impervious, I could feel my heart getting harder. Sometimes
the atmosphere was so tense, "You could cut it with a knife," as Mary
commented. Most of the time we all tried to ignore the undercurrent of tension and anxiety. I continued doing the bookkeeping; we all
went about our activities as usual, attending school, doing chores, and
going to the movies on Sunday. My younger siblings seemed to disappear when either my father or I were on the scene. I had no idea what
they were doing most of the time.

I was absorbed with my own dilemma, and some good news
was coming out of the war zones. By 1943, the tide was turning.
The Allies gained in strength and mobilized themselves to confront
the enemy on two fronts in the Pacific and in Europe. For the next
two years, the Allies declared victories and we were celebrating. The
ending of the wars had their own dark endings.

Unfortunately, our beloved President Franklin Roosevelt died on
April 12, 1944. Later, as the war was turning against the Germans,
the liberation of the Jewish prisoners from the concentration camps

125

was too horrifying to fathom. The newspapers and the newsreels in the movies were filled with pictures of the Allied Forces freeing skeletal victims of the Holocaust.

When I viewed pictures of the thousands of bodies not yet buried, of mounds of jewelry, gold teeth, and other belongings of those who had been exterminated in the furnaces, I was shocked (and wounded unconsciously) to realize that so-called human beings performed such hideous acts. The deliberate destruction of millions of human lives was inconceivable, incomprehensible, and utterly overwhelming. Then the unbelievable occurred: Hiroshima and Nagasaki were destroyed by atomic bombs. I felt traumatized as if I had been there myself. How could we claim victory when such horrors were happening and more upheavals lay waiting for the world?

During the summer of 1944, I worked in the hospital dining room serving meals to nurses and doctors. I wanted to get a sense of what hospital work was like. There were shortages of workers in all areas. Although I was hired primarily to work in the dining room, I helped in the kitchen washing dishes and setting tables; and once I was sent to assist the laundry workers.

In August, the staff shortage on the wards was even more severe than usual. One morning I was told to report to the head nurse on the second floor. Without further ado, I was escorted into a twelve-bed men's ward and told to help the student nurse bathe the patients and make their beds. The student was so overwhelmed with her assignment that she did not have time to instruct me. She simply said, "Do as I'm doing."

For the rest of the month of August, I reported for duty as a Nurses' Aide. I never expected to come so close to patients that summer, but it became an opportunity to observe the work of nurses and to decide whether I really could do the work. I enjoyed most of what I learned in such a short time, and I was invited to return the next summer. This was all the encouragement I needed.

The following summer when I returned to the hospital, I was surprised and very happy to see my old friend Mary again. She was working in the kitchen as I had done the previous summer, and I

126

worked on the medical ward as a nurses' aide. I couldn't believe my eyes when I saw her. She was getting out of her father's truck and seemed lost and afraid, and she couldn't look at me. She had been living "out in the country" for three years and seemed unable to make any kind of friendly gesture. Her father brought her to the hospital and picked her up in the afternoon. We didn't connect at all. She looked like a prisoner. I was so sad for her. I knew what she felt like. I would have died on the inside, too, if my father had taken me out of high school.

First Meeting

In my senior year, fortunately, I was assigned to Miss Willertons's English class. She was an excellent teacher—my favorite—and she motivated us to read American and English Literature and she encouraged self-expression. Her assignment for us that year was to write our autobiographies. They were to be turned in in the spring. This was the first opportunity I ever had to look back on my life and describe it for someone who was truly interested and cared. I knew she cared because she was one of the few teachers who stayed after school and invited students to drop in and talk about literature, poetry, and music.

On the first day of class I noticed a new student was sitting in the middle seat in the last row by the windows, and I was in the third seat in the second row near the door. He told us his name was Jim Wright and he had missed the last year due to illness and would be graduating with our class. He was handsome with a strong build and a shy, gentle smile that quickly turned into an impish, sardonic grin when he responded to Miss Willerton's question about the poet or writer whom we were studying.

I decided that he was a terrible show-off and a know-it-all because he argued with and frequently contradicted Miss Willerton. I'd get irritated with his brash arrogance, until I began to realize he knew the material almost as well as she did, and she encouraged him, as well as the rest of the class to express our thoughts and reactions to the literature we were reading. He not only read the textbook, but he sounded as if he had read every book in the library.

Whispers by classmates hinted that he had missed school the previous year because he had been hospitalized with some kind of nervous problem. I felt uncertain and uncomfortable around Jim. I didn't understand his arrogance in discussions with Miss Willerton. I thought he was trying to shock us with his extensive reading, and he did. I was quite intrigued when I learned he wrote poetry.

As the months passed, I learned more about Jim. He was a winner of the American Legion Essay Contests. Jim was the Editor of the Ferrian, our school yearbook. I also realized we had a common interest in our love of literature and our dreams of escaping the Ohio Valley. Jim was the first person I met who felt as trapped as I did, and we both agreed that the only way out was through education: first, high school, then, college.

I was most impressed when I heard he was writing poetry since junior high school, and, particularly, when I heard him reciting entire poems by Blake, James Whitcomb Riley, Robert Frost, and Walt Whitman. One day he told me his secret: "I have an eidetic memory." I was astonished to learn that this meant he could read a poem once and he'd remember all of it. Of course, I was awed by this unbelievable gift.

The major English assignment of our senior year, writing our autobiographies, was completed in April. During the final English examination, Miss Willerton gave my autobiography to Jim to read. He had finished his examination very quickly, and she did not want him leaving early and disturbing the rest of us who were still writing. Afterwards he came up to me and told me he was very impressed with my writing and my story. I felt awkward and shy and mumbled, "Thank you," and went on my way.

The long years of anticipating my graduation came and passed. I graduated on my eighteenth birthday, and my father allowed me to invite several girl friends for ice cream and cake. I think he was saying to me, "See, I let you graduate as you wanted. Now, it's time to settle down to more important things." I continued to do his bookkeeping. During my senior year, he even gave me permission to go to a few football games. In retrospect, I believe my father was trying very hard to understand and be a little more flexible, and friendlier. Probably my mother had persuaded him to let up a little and relax his tight hold. If so, it lasted a very short time.

After graduation, I saw Jim one more time at Miss Willerton's home, a rambling old farmhouse in Bellaire, about fifteen miles south of Martins Ferry. She had invited three college students, Jim, and me for an evening of conversation, reading poetry, and listening to music. I was quite excited and deeply touched that I was included in such a gathering. That evening ignited the dying embers of my dreams and hopes for college. There was a world out there that I knew nothing about, and I wanted to find out for myself what was out there for me. I had to find a way out. Nursing was one way, and that was the direction I wanted to go. Miss Willerton had always been very kind and encouraging. I knew this was her way of telling me to continue working on fulfilling my dreams.

Soon afterwards, Jim enlisted in the Army and trained in the engineer corps. He was stationed in Japan and served in the Occupational Forces. He loved Japan and the gentle, polite people. He especially loved Kyoto and spent as much time as he could at the temples there. He fell in love with a young Japanese woman, but he only spoke of her once. That was a sad memory that he never approached again.

A Long Two Years

That evening at Miss Willerton's sparked my hopes of going to college. The desire became so intense that I was willing to sacrifice everything, including my family. That evening became an image burned in my memory. My dream was to live in a college town in a small cottage surrounded by students and teachers who would sit in front of the fireplace and talk about poetry and listen to music.

The realistic part of me knew that was not going to happen anytime soon. I came from a different world than the American people who had the option of going to college. Miss Willerton knew how difficult that was going to be for me. She had read my story and knew I was the eldest daughter of Greek immigrant parents. Their culture and traditions required that a marriage was to be arranged for me. I was the only Greek girl in my class. The common practice at that time among the Greek immigrants was for their daughters to marry by the age of sixteen or seventeen rather than attend high school.

My father considered himself very generous for allowing me to go to high school and to graduate. Now, it was time for me to get serious about my obligations to my family and culture. I decided that I would go to nursing school and become a registered nurse in order to work my way through college at some time in the future. I even applied to the Martins Ferry Hospital School of Nursing and was accepted. I was due to start the program on August 1, 1946, but my father would not permit me to leave home. "Greek women leave home by marriage or death," was his only remark.

Unable to start my new life or forget my dreams and hopes, I chose another way: I tried to convince my father I would not disgrace him. For two miserable years, I worked as a file clerk in a collection agency; then I took a job as a grocery clerk. At the same time, I worked for my father as his bookkeeper in his trucking business. I was persistent in my attempts to demonstrate to him that I was not only a competent and responsible employee, but I was worthy of his trust. He was relentless in maintaining his own position.

Deep inside me, I knew he would never understand, nor would he ever consent to sending me to college. After all, he only had two years of school and he could "feed, clothe, and give us a home" so, "What do you need all that education for? All you're going to do is have children. High school is not enough for you?"

"No," I thought to myself, "that is not enough for me."

I rejected the first two young men who approached my father, much to his dismay. He even consulted with the Greek priest who threatened me with ex-communication if I did not obey my parents. I believe my mother intervened on my behalf with the priest, because I was never ex-communicated. However, I knew my father was a man of his word, and he was prepared to disown me if I left home without being married. If that happened family members would be forbidden to communicate with me, and he would impose silence between us. During those two years after graduation, I descended deep within myself, into the darkness of my "underworld," where

I was confronted with my hopelessness, fear, and guilt. I felt an utter failure. My teachers had encouraged me. They taught me about freedom of choice and the rights of the individual, but they did not teach me how to convince my father.

I was imprisoned inside a culture that was unchanging and my efforts to become independent were unprecedented and anchored in 2000 years of patriarchal history. My destiny had been sealed at birth and my father was unrelenting in his demand that I submit to his authority and marry. Between 1946 and 1948 while I worked and lived at home, three young men approached him for my hand in marriage. The first young man had completed his college education and was interested in me as his wife. My father tried to persuade me to accept this young man's offer to marry me. "He will make a good husband. He has a college education." He was surprised and puzzled by my rejection of this seemingly perfect man for me. "He is American-born, he speaks Greek fluently, and he has a college education. What more do you want?" my father demanded.

"I want to go to college myself!" I cried, tears streaming down my cheeks. I knew he would never understand, nor would he ever consent to send me to college.

One day during the summer of 1947, I met a young woman, Rosemary Neal, in the coffee shop on the corner of Fourth Street, across from the police station. She was reading a book by Thomas Wolfe and I recognized the title: *You Can't Go Home Again.* We struck up a conversation and became fast friends. She was an avid reader as I was. I was so pleased to find someone who loved reading books and talking about them. She knew Jim Wright, and she had a friend, Ken, who was attending Ohio State University in Columbus.

Rosemary and I met often and spent hours talking about books we were reading, our lives, and our plans for the future. She worked in Bridgeport as a telephone operator. Sometimes, she called me and asked me to meet her during her dinner hour. I took the bus to Bridgeport and spent an hour with her. I learned that she left home when she was sixteen, and she worked to support herself while completing high school. I admired her courage and her independence.

The following spring, 1948, I met Jim Wright uptown in Martins

Ferry. He had returned from Japan where he had served in the Army Occupation Forces, and he was attending Kenyon College under the G.I. Bill. I was pleased to see him again, and he was in an exuberant mood. We had coffee and talked for a couple of hours. He was very excited that he was given the opportunity to attend such a prestigious school by serving in the Army. He talked almost non-stop about his friends, Eugene Pugatch, Edgar Doctorow, and Frank LeFever, and the fun they had, and his teachers who included John Ransom, Robert Penn Warren, Phillip Timberlake, and Charles Coffin. His dreams were coming true, and I was happy for him. He asked me to write to him, and I was delighted to have another friend with whom I could share my thoughts and concerns. The silence and tension at home were grim. I had withdrawn from childhood friends who were working, having social lives, and getting married. Even though my parents did not want to force me to marry, they were obliged to look for an appropriate husband for me.

I shared my painful situation with Jim in a letter. In his response, he made an observation that was to change my life. He said, "Lib, you can complain about your father all you want, but if you wait for him to give you permission, you may be waiting until hell freezes over. Don't you see? Either you must choose to go to nursing school and face the consequences or you must be content with the life you have." The sensations of shock waves, surprise, and excitement that I experienced when I read his words overwhelmed my senses. He was the first person who ever told me I had a choice! Not even my teachers had dared to be so explicit. "Of course! Why didn't I think about that? My father will never agree to my leaving without marriage. What was I thinking? I do have a choice! I can go into nursing or I can stay home! If I stay home, I will die!"

When I approached my father once again, he shook his head, "No." He sighed and threw up his hands as if to say, "I give up. What can I do with you?" After an interminable silence, he looked at me sternly and said, "You have three choices: first you can stay home and I will take care of you. Second, you can get married like every other normal woman, and third, you can leave. If you leave, you can never come back into the family." I looked at my mother's sad face and I looked into my father's severe face. And I knew instantaneously the choice I had to make.

On the first of August 1948, with all my belongings in two suitcases, I asked my brother, Tony, to drive me to the Martins Ferry Hospital Nurses Home. He was so shaken, he asked me, "My God, Lib are you sure you're doing the right thing? Is this what you really want to do? Do you know what you're doing?"

"Yes, I know what I'm doing. If I don't do this, I will die," I answered him. I knew he was very concerned about me, but I had made my choice. We said nothing else.

With the acceptance letter from 1946, I presented it to Ruth Brant, the superintendent of the hospital and the school of nursing and said to her, "I'm here to start the nursing program. Miss Brant knew my father as the hot-tempered Greek man who hauled coal to the hospital. He had warned her against taking me into the nursing program. Her first action was to call a judge to determine whether legally I could attend.

Numb and in shock, I waited for her to return. "You can't go home again," said the small clear voice in my head. "Do you know what you did? You just pulled up two thousand years of history and roots. You can't expect any help from the family. Dad will not allow the others to come and see you or speak to you. You know the rules!" Yes, I knew the rules, too well. I knew I had to be accepted because I had no place to go.

A quiet calmness spread over me as I waited to hear from Miss Brant. A few minutes later, she came through the door of the dormitory room where I was waiting. She had a slight smile on her lips. "The judge informed me that you are past twenty years of age and you are old enough to make the decision to enter the school of nursing."

I was in!

Apostolos (Paul) Kardoulias (Kardules) & Ereni (Irene) Zaharias
Liberty's parents got married in the church months after
they had eloped and married on June 25, 1927.

Libby's father, Paul Kardules, second from left in front row,
with his fellow workers at the
Laughlin Steel Mill, Martins Ferry, Ohio, 1920s.

Libby's
Mom
and
Dad,
Ereni
and
Paul
Kardules

*In 1946, my father and
other illegal aliens
were given amnesty
and citizenship by
President Truman for
their contribution to
the defense effort
during World War II.*

Eleutheria (Liberty) Kardules
Born May 28, 1928
Martins Ferry, Ohio

First Libby was born to Paul and Irene Kardules, then
Mary, next Tony, then Ann, and last but not least, Jack.

PART II

Escape Over the Green Wall

The Story of My Marriage to James Wright

Second Breech
Birth

Bearing witness in speaking or writing,
in public or just to one significant other....
is a powerful human urge.
(Sophia Freud, *My Three Mothers and Other Passions*)

I was born at home on May 28, 1928, after a long, difficult, and excruciating labor, and a breech delivery. Now, on the morning of August 1, 1948, I left home to give birth to my new life.

NURSING SCHOOL

When I uprooted myself and moved a half a mile from home on that hot August morning, I was in a state of shock and numbness for months afterward. I did what I usually did with traumatic experiences: I locked them up deep inside me in a compartment that contained other fears, pain, and wounds from the past. If I allowed myself to feel that terrible sense of loss, I would be overwhelmed and unable to function. I could not afford to let all that pain interfere with the work that lay ahead of me. I found solace and comfort in learning nursing just as I had done for twelve years in public school. No matter how hurt, sad, or depressed I felt, my ability to think and focus on my studies was intact.

Fortunately for me, the structures of the school of nursing and the hospital were very rigid and familiar and the discipline was almost as strict as I'd had at home. "Out of the frying pan into the fire," I mused to myself. At least I was better prepared for this lifestyle than some of my classmates. I was accustomed to tight controls, and I adapted well. Curfew was 9:00 p.m. on weeknights, and midnight on weekends after the first six months.

The probationary period was a "weeding-out" time. This was when students demonstrated how well they studied and learned, or they flunked out. One young woman was expelled for smoking, which was not permitted. She was observed smoking and blowing the smoke out of her bedroom window by a neighbor who reported her to Miss Brant. Our class lost about ten of the original thirty-two students within the first few months (and two were expelled for getting pregnant just months before graduation). On the positive side, students were permitted to go home on weekends during this period until we were required to work on the wards. I was the only one who stayed in the nurses' home on the weekends.

The first day of class was our orientation to the nursing program and the hospital. We were given the rules of proper behavior; for example, we were expected to attend all classes unless we were sick. Then, you had to see Dr. Carson to get excused from class. Several "Don'ts" were emphasized: "Don't talk about religion, politics, or sex with patients." We were informed that there were two permanent residents in the hospital: Danny and Joe. We met them on our tour of the hospital. Danny was described as more friendly and sociable. Joe was aloof and distant. Somebody cautioned us to, "Leave Joe alone. He's stubborn and aggravating. He insists on doing everything his own way—even his treatments." There were rumors that Joe had been a union organizer and a communist as a young man.

I noticed the two men in wheelchairs in the solarium when I walked to the dining room. Sometimes they were outside in front of the hospital chatting with neighbors or other patients or reading the newspaper. We learned that both, as a result of separate mining accidents, had sustained spinal cord injuries and were paralyzed from the waist down. They were relegated to wheelchairs and were free to move about on the grounds of the hospital when weather permitted. Neither had family to go home to, so the nurses and doctors became their family.

Of course, I was intrigued. I didn't know what a communist was exactly, and since I had time available on the weekends, I became acquainted with both Danny and Joe. When Joe was alone I made the added effort to spend time and to talk with him. I learned that Joe had been a patient and a permanent resident in the hospital for twenty-five years when I met him. As a young man he came to this country from Poland to work in the coal mines in Ohio.

As we got to know each other, this was the story he told me: "My life was very short. I was seventeen, and all my life I had been half-starved. Now I had work in the mines—all the work I could do—twelve hours a day. Six month later, there was an explosion in the mine. My friend was killed, and my back was broken. I've been here ever since. The miners' welfare is paying my room and board here. I had no place to go, and the hospital is as good a place as any. Besides, my life stopped there in the mine, so what difference does it make?"

Over the next three years, I grew to like and respect Joe. He was quite articulate and well read. I enjoyed talking politics with him. He didn't seem all that radical to me. He was friendly enough. He liked to ask questions and to laugh at my naïve approach to politics, and my idealism. I think he learned more about me over time than I did about his beliefs. He was alone without a family, and so was I, so we decided we could be friends.

During the first five months, we were in the classroom in the mornings where we learned the history and the scientific foundations of nursing: anatomy and physiology, chemistry, microbiology, pharmacology, and nutrition. In the afternoons, we were in the laboratory practicing the basic skills, or nursing arts: bathing (dummy) patients, making beds, taking temperatures and blood pressure (on each other), and learning how to give injections (into oranges). As we became proficient in these skills, we were placed on the hospital wards where we worked under the sharp observation and supervision of Miss Gondola, our nursing arts instructor. She watched us like a hawk while we measured and prepared oral and injectable medications, gave baths, and took TPRs (temperatures, pulses, and respirations) of actual patients. In the evenings after dinner, we studied; then we collapsed into bed. The next day we started again and went through the same routine again. One day flowed into the next and slowly our formation as nurses was underway.

My mother, in her quiet and unobtrusive manner, and despite my father's dictum, came to visit me on Saturday afternoons. She always left me a few dollars and some snacks. Otherwise, I studied, walked downtown, or met Rosemary at the coffee shop for a few hours. I became acquainted with her friend, Ken, and his family. Over time, they became my adopted family where I spent weekend evenings and holidays, especially after the Christmas holidays that year.

My mother wanted me home for Christmas. She wanted me to come on the days I had off from my nursing duties. We had baked together during the holidays, and then she asked me to the house; but my presence angered my father so much that, in the middle of dinner, he stood up, pointed toward the door, and demanded that I leave. The devastated look on my mother's face hurt more than being cast out of the family again. I think this was the first time my mother realized that Dad would not back down. When he said, "You can't come home again," he meant it. Again, I buried another layer of pain deep inside. I had a few days alone in the dormitory to grieve and to prepare myself for the return of my classmates.

At the end of the first five months, our probationary period was completed, and my nineteen classmates and I were initiated as first year students with a "Capping" ceremony. We were fitted with uniforms that consisted of a blue dress with a stiffly starched white apron over the dress that we wore at the ceremony. Then, we were presented with our school's cap, white and stiffly starched, and we were required to wear white shoes and white hose.

I was quite startled when I heard my name called and asked to come forward to the platform where Miss Brant presented me with a check for $25.00 and an award as the Outstanding Student in my class. Two other nurses, a junior and a senior, received awards of $50.00 and $100.00, respectively. I was very pleased that my mother and my sister, Mary, were present when I received the award. I knew they were proud of me. Secretly, I hoped they would tell Dad.

CLEVELAND CITY HOSPITAL

In January 1949, I was with the half of our class who were sent to Cleveland City Hospital for six months for training in pediatrics, tuberculosis, and psychiatry. When we returned at the end of June, then the other half of our class went to Cleveland a week later and returned in December. These services were not available in our small hospital, and we were required to study and practice in these specialty areas as prerequisites for licensure. This was my first trip so far away from home—about 125 miles—and to a big city!

My roommate in the large dormitory in Cleveland was Millie, a very attractive blond young woman of Serbian descent whose father and brothers worked in the coal mines of Powhatten. Soon after we arrived in Cleveland, Millie invited me to go on a double date with her. Curfew was 2:00 a.m. on weekends, so we wouldn't have to rush back by midnight. I was hesitant, and she was persuasive, so I agreed to go this one time. I was not comfortable going out with complete strangers, and I did not enjoy myself. My patriarchal background was still deeply entrenched, and I was not yet ready to date.

FALLING IN LOVE

One Sunday afternoon in February, while I studied my pediatric assignment, I received a call from the office, "You have a guest waiting." Puzzled, I went downstairs. I was not expecting anyone. I had no ideas who it might be.

To my great surprise, I saw Jim standing there with a big grin on his face. I wanted to run and hug him, but all I could do was stand on the stair and smile back at him. I was so happy and pleased to see him. I couldn't believe he would take the bus from Gambier to come to Cleveland to see me.

"Hi, Lib, do you want to spend the day with me?" he asked nonchalantly.

"Yes! You know I do. Let me run up and get my things."

Jim was bundled in a heavy, long, dark woolen overcoat that protected him from the chill and snow of the Northern Ohio winter.

I wrapped myself in my own green winter coat, as well as boots, gloves, and a wool cap. We took a bus from the hospital to downtown and wandered around in the snow and wind. I held his left arm as we walked and talked. He, about his classes, papers he was writing, and poetry, of course. I told him about my experiences in pediatrics, the classes we had with specialists, and how wonderful to have lectures by really knowledgeable people. We were completely oblivious to our surroundings until we realized how cold we were. Then, we went into the nearest coffee shop to get warm, and after a while we were off again to a movie.

Afterwards, we took a bus back to the nurses' home where I prepared a light supper for us in the tiny kitchen that was available for the student nurses. I felt happier that evening than I had been in a long, long time, and I felt safe with Jim. I could just be myself without any pretenses or affectations. I felt a kind of electric excitement and energy flowing through me. Jim awakened something completely different in me – an aliveness and a closeness I never knew before. The time together was much more enjoyable than the date with a stranger ever could be. I felt closer to him that wintry day than I ever had before.

Lost in thought, I stirred the soup and made the sandwiches. Jim came up to me and wrapped his arms around my waist and kissed me. Our first kiss! "I love you," he whispered softly. I responded, "I love you, too. I wish you didn't have to go." We held each other close and we kissed again. I was breathless with excitement and the pleasure of being held so closely, feeling loved, and being loving. Our combined emotions were overwhelming.

Reluctantly, I pulled away. "Jim, we must stop. I don't want to, but you must eat something before you go. We kissed again and whispered, "I love you," as we pulled apart and sat quietly at the table. Slowly, we returned to the realities of space and time. We ate without talking, and unwillingly, we said our goodbyes.

Jim left to return to Gambier. I cleaned up and put the dishes away. I felt as though I were floating up the stairwell to my room. The thrill of being kissed and feeling loved·was almost unbearable. In one day, our relationship was transformed from a friendship to a deep loving relationship. How could that happen so quickly and unexpectedly?

We had become good friends in the past year, but mostly by mail. I had no idea he could be so warm and gentle…. and loving!

The next morning, after a restless night, I awakened with a headache and nausea. I felt too sick to report to my assigned ward, so I called to let the head nurse know I would not be there. I was admitted to the medical ward where I was examined and declared, "Not pregnant." I felt insulted that the doctor thought I might be pregnant. We had not been that intimate. After resting a few hours, I was released to return to my room. I thought that I probably got chilled walking around town for several hours, but I did give consideration to the possibility that all the excitement of falling in love completely threw my equilibrium off balance. The next morning I was back on the ward, a little shaky, but functioning. Much, much later, I wondered whether I got sick because I knew my father would not approve of Jim. I could hear him saying, "Yes, he's a poet and an intellectual, but how is he going to support you and a family?"

Jim was the first man I loved. I lived for his letters. I think I fell in love with him through his letters. He was so exuberant about attending Kenyon, having such great classes and teachers, and making such good friends. I would get swept up with his effusiveness and begin to dream again of the possibilities of going to college myself after graduating from nursing. I even allowed myself to fantasize of someday attending Ohio State University in Columbus. I never allowed myself to imagine a life together after he graduated from Kenyon. I didn't let myself dwell or even think of marriage. I was certain that would frighten him away. I remembered the young Japanese woman whom he left. He never talked about her.

Our letter writing continued for the next two years. *I saved all his letters until 1965 when I remarried. Then, I burned them in the fireplace in my flat. I wanted to start my life over again without the encumbrances of the past. I have always regretted that impulsive and foolish act.*

A few weeks later, Millie and I had a rather whimsical and magical evening together at a concert by the Cleveland City Orchestra. We arrived at Severance Hall early in order to purchase tickets. As we walked in through the wide doors, I stood there awed by the sparkling beauty of the gold trimmings and adornments on the walls, and the glistening crystal chandeliers. I couldn't move or speak. Never before had I seen anything as grand and splendid as that hall.

Suddenly, from across the hall a short, puckish man dressed in a tuxedo came running up to me and with a large grin across his mouth, he asked, "Do you have a ticket? I shook my head "No." He took my right hand, placed a ticket in it, and laughing aloud, he ran toward the open door into the symphony hall. Stunned by this unexpected gift, I was finally able to blurt out, "Millie! Did you see that?" She was smiling broadly, too, and said, "I'll go get my ticket now." I was speechless.

A MULTI-FACETED EDUCATION

We spent two months in each of the three services. The work on the wards with children and adults with tuberculosis was fascinating and the treatments were complicated and difficult, but we learned something new everyday. We had lectures by doctors who were specialists in every service, and they encouraged questions. I was particularly intrigued and frightened by the psychiatric units. The locked doors clanged loudly when they were closed by the nurses who carried large metal rings with keys that locked and unlocked heavy doors made of steel bars. The sound of those doors was most distressing to me. The idea that mentally ill people had to be locked up was incomprehensible to me until I saw a woman in her late twenties attack her mother as the older woman walked onto the ward. All of sudden five nurses were pulling the patient off her mother. I stood there watching, horrified by the viciousness of the attack.

The next day the staff psychiatrist lectured on the different types of schizophrenia. We had observed the actions of the young woman who was diagnosed Catatonic Schizophrenic, and he explained to us that the repressed rage contained in the patient's body turned her into a statue. She could stand in one position for hours, and the nurses encouraged her to move around. She had been standing in a frozen posture for about an hour when her mother came on the ward; then something triggered off the rage, and she attacked like a tiger after its prey.

The closing statement made by the psychiatrist at the end of his lecture impressed me very much. He gently admonished us to not give up hope for these unfortunate people. "We don't know yet what happens to the mind to bring about such a dreadful condition. We must be patient and kind."

The only treatments we had in those days were electroshock therapy and insulin shock therapy. As nursing students, we were required to assist with the shock therapies. On the days the treatments were scheduled, we gathered patients first thing in the morning and lined them up in the hallway. Each one in turn was laid on a gurney and strapped down. The doctor placed the electrodes to the temples of the patient; then he pushed the switch in a small machine that contained the electric current, and the patient was thrown into a convulsive state. Our task was to hold the arms and legs of each patient firmly in place. A tongue blade covered with bandages was placed in the patients' mouths so they could not bite their tongues.

The same procedure was followed the next day with patients scheduled for insulin shock. They were given an injection of a large dose of insulin that produced convulsions; then they were gavaged (force-fed) with a bottle of sweetened water solution, and the convulsions subsided. Afterward, the patients of both shock therapies were subdued and confused for several hours.

The doctor could not explain how or why these treatments worked in relieving the symptoms of schizophrenia or severe depression, but "somehow they worked." One theory presented was the placebo effect. The patients' conditions improved because they were selected and received special attention from the staff. Most of the patients were hospitalized for months and even years.

One woman on the ward was a heavy-built Greek woman who did not speak English. Since I spoke Greek, the Head Nurse assigned her to me during the month I was scheduled on that ward. I spent an hour with her each day. She talked quite animatedly about her family, and I listened. Then I translated whatever she told me into English and wrote a summary note in her chart. I only remember that she was very paranoid, depressed, and distressed. She was a recent immigrant to this country, and she believed that members of her family were trying to kill her. No family members visited her while I was there. I felt very sorry for her. She didn't understand what was happening to her. She felt lost and abandoned, and she was very ill. Later, in the 1950s nurses such as Hildegard Peplau of Rutgers University and Marion Kalkman of the University of California, San Francisco, introduced the concept of "talking with patients" on psychiatric wards, and they taught these skills to nurses in graduate programs. This was a revolutionary idea that nurses were skilled enough to work therapeutically with patients, but these changes in nursing practice were the trends of the near future. This was the period of time when medications were being developed that eased the severity of patients' symptoms and helped them to participate and become more involved in their treatments and group activities.

I was one of the nurses who returned to college in the late 1950s to prepare for specialized training as a psychiatric/mental health clinical specialist. Community mental health programs were being established in the 1960s for anyone in crisis or experiencing any kind of emotional or mental distress as well as for patients released from state hospitals. We had open wards for most of the hospitalized patients who were admitted voluntarily. The patients who were admitted involuntarily were considered a danger to themselves or others, or were gravely disabled. These patients were hospitalized in locked wards for limited periods of time, usually seventy-two hours to fourteen days, until they were stabilized on medications and could be released to their homes with follow-up in outpatient clinics. Unfortunately, these programs lasted only about fifteen to twenty years because of federal and state funding cutbacks that resulted in the dismantling of very successful community programs all over the country. Many psychiatric patients were released in the middle 1970s after many years in state hospitals without adequate facilities to provide follow-up services in the communities. Many of the homeless in our cities today are mentally ill persons with little or no community support.

Beside the opportunity to learn about these three medical specialties (pediatrics, tuberculosis, and psychiatry), Cleveland City Hospital was an exciting place for me because we met nurses from different schools of nursing. I was particularly interested in one school that trained nurses in a college program at Northwestern University. That was the first time I'd heard about nurses earning a Bachelors Degree in Nursing.

The general attitude of the staff and students in those days was that nurses trained in hospitals were more skillful and better trained than college-educated nurses. The latter had more book learning but were not as proficient on the wards. In the next decade, this attitude started changing. As medical technology improved, nurses required more complex, theoretical courses as well as technical skills. Eventually, all hospital schools of nursing were closed and nurses were and are being educated in two-year community colleges and in four-year baccalaureate programs.

Cleveland City Hospital accepted Negro nurses from the East Coast who were trained there, and I became good friends with one nurse from New Haven, Connecticut. Her name was Mirvin Taylor, and we enjoyed the same kind of movies. I realized again how much I enjoyed the friendship of these nurses because I grew up with Negroes in my neighborhood, and I missed not having them in my life.

The school of nursing sponsored Friday night dances in the auditorium and invited men from the local colleges. Several of my classmates and I went down to the auditorium to check out what was happening. A band was playing the lively music of the 1940s and the dance floor was packed with dancers. "There are a lot of men here," said Dora with a big smile. The atmosphere was festive and people were laughing and talking and enjoying themselves. When I heard the music, I couldn't keep my feet still, and I did a few dance steps with Millie. A tall slim handsome Negro man came over and asked me to dance. He was a good dancer, and I was happy that I knew how to do the jitterbug. When the dance was over, I thanked him and went back to where our group had been standing. No one was there. They all left. Mirvin was there, and I asked, "Where did they all go?"

"They left when you started dancing with the Negro," she replied with raised eyebrows.

"Really? Why?" The school sponsored these dances and all kinds of college men come here. "Did I do something wrong?"

150

She shrugged and shook her head "no."

None of my classmates said anything to me. "That was fun." I said cheerfully. "Where did you all go?" No one responded. I let the subject drop, and I got ready for bed.

In June we returned to Martins Ferry. A few days later, I was called into the office by one of the instructors, and she queried me about my "troublesome" behavior in Cleveland. I did not understand what she was implying. She was not direct, except to warn me to "be careful about the friends" I chose. Later that week, a senior nurse came up to me and whispered, "Watch your step. There are rumors that you might be expelled because of your communist leanings,"

This warning came as a tremendous shock to me. I had grown up with Negro neighbors, and I felt at home with Negro people. I could not believe, nor accept, that that kind of hidden and unspoken prejudice existed in our hospital. Apparently, one of my classmates must have informed the faculty. This was the first of much disillusionment that I would experience in nursing. I decided to monitor my liberal thoughts and actions more carefully because I wanted to graduate. I had no place to go if I got expelled.

The late 1940s and early 1950s were the days of the House Un-American Activities Hearings in Congress and the McCarthy investigations of communists in government, in the movie industry, and in the universities. For the first time, I realized that the faculty and the administrators of the school of nursing were serious about their conservative politics, and I had to be careful. I never dreamed that dancing with a Negro would be considered un-American. I wondered whether my friendship with Joe was considered threatening. Mirvin and I corresponded for years after we both graduated and went our separate ways. She returned to New Haven, Connecticut, after graduation and later moved to New York. We met again in the middle 1970s when I attended a Conference at Columbia University.

BAPTISM BY FIRE

The second and third years of nursing were difficult years. We had very few classes and we worked full-time shifts on medical, surgical, and obstetrics wards. Those years were called "baptism by fire". In addition, we had a small pediatrics ward that we worked again, and we spent six weeks in surgery learning surgical procedures by assisting in major surgery cases. The nursing students did the majority of the care of the patients. We bathed and fed the patients who were unable to care for themselves, gave them their medications, and did their treatments. The few registered nurses on duty were our supervisors and instructors.

We had no intensive care units or burn units in those days. I remember seeing the first EKG machine in 1950 and observing Dr. Carson who had received special training in using and interpreting the results. At that time the doctors were responsible for the administration of intravenous medications. They finally relinquished this responsibility in the early 1950s, and we were trained to do IV treatments in the last six months of our training period. In my final year in training, I spent about four or five months in obstetrics, the labor and delivery rooms, and in the nursery. I assisted in the delivery of sixty-six babies. Each one was an exciting and miraculous event. Most of those deliveries occurred at night when I was on call.

GRADUATION AND BIG CHANGES

Our class graduated in June of 1951. Two more of our classmates were expelled just months before graduation because they became pregnant. My close friend and roommate during the last two years, Jean, had eloped at the end of the first year, and I was the only one who knew her secret. Just months before graduation, she confided in me that she might be pregnant, and we were both very anxious about that possibility. A few days later, she whispered, "False alarm," on her way to her assigned ward. We both breathed a sigh of relief then and when we received our diplomas.

During those last two years of nursing school, Jim and I corresponded, we saw each other during his vacations and breaks, and we spent as much time together as we could manage around my schedule and his. In one of his letters to me, he described a dream he had of his dead grandmother. He described her presence in his room in such great detail that I thought he had actually seen her. Later he made a poem about his dream, and it was published in his first book.

Whenever I could get away for a day or an occasional weekend, I'd take the bus to Jim's parents' small farm in Warnock. A few times I took the bus to Gambier where Kenyon was located. Our relationship had shifted and changed gradually from friendship to our secret life as lovers. I wasn't sure how our relationship blossomed into love, but our love was warm and nurturing as well as exploratory and experimental. We were both learning about an area of life and loving we, or rather I, had not experienced before.

Jim's family had moved from Martins Ferry to the little farm in the hills nearby in Warnock. It was a sad little farm but something Jim's mom had wanted for a long time. When Jim was home for the summer we walked the green hills. We made love one warm June day in those hills. Soon after he wrote a poem and called it, "Eleutheria," my Greek name, which he included in his first book, *The Green Wall*. He did not include in that poem our little secret: we both developed a rash from poison ivy after our little adventure. "Are you going to tell about the poison ivy in your poem?" I teased him, and we laughed uproariously.

Still, how was a girl to feel receiving this gift? I was deeply touched and more than a little frightened. He told the world about our closeness and love:

Eleutheria

Rubbing her mouth along my mouth she lost
Illusions of the sky, the dream it offered:
The pale cloud walking home to winter, dust
Blown to the shell of sails so far above
That autumn landscape where we lay and suffered
The fruits of summer in the fields of love.

We lay and heard the apples fall for hours,
The stripping twilight plundered trees of boughs,
The land dissolved beneath the rabbit's heels,

And far away I heard a window close,
A haying wagon heave and catch its wheels,
Some water slide and stumble and be still.
The dark began to climb the empty hill.

If dark Eleutheria turned and lay
Forever beside me, who would care for years?
The throat, the supple belly, the warm thigh
Burgeoned against the earth; I lay afraid,
For who could bear such beauty under the sky?
I would have held her loveliness in air,
Away from things that lured me to decay:
The ground's deliberate riches, fallen pears,
Bewildered apples blown to mounds of shade.

Lovers' location is the first to fade.
They wander back in winter, but there is
No comfortable grass to couch a dress.
Musicians of the yellow weeds are dead.
And she, remembering something, turns to hear
Either a milkweed float or a thistle fall.
Bodiless shadow thrown along a wall,
She glides lightly; the pale year follows her.

The moments ride away, the locust flute
Is silvered thin and lost, over and over.
She will return some evening to discover
The tree uplifted to the very root,
The leaves shouldered away, with lichen grown
Among the interlacings of the stone,
October blowing dust, and summer gone
Into a dark bar, like a hiding lover.

I had another secret. I was torn between the emotion of those cherished moments and the fear of losing him to his talent. I remembered the girl he left in Japan, and I feared he would leave me, too. I felt his talent was too great to be confined by marriage, that I was too naïve, a small-town girl, and unprepared for his world of the intellect and academia. We never discussed marriage, and living together was unheard of in those days. Yet I would not consider letting go of him.

This period in our lives brought us great joy and lingering uncertainty. Several times, I took the bus from Bridgeport to Gambier, rolling across Ohio. Kenyon was such a clean and open place, just like the small college towns I had dreamed about. We walked about the campus, darting behind trees to kiss, and Jim would tell me about his professors – John Crowe Ransom, Philip Timberlake, Charles Coffin – men who had exerted a great influence over Jim's mind. He loved Kenyon, and being there the world was opening up for him. He introduced me to his friends, men who would become important writers, poets, and physicians and his very good friends over the years: Edgar Doctorow, Robert Mezey, Roger Hecht, Eugene Pugatch, and Frank LeFever. Jim even had his own little country and western music show on the college radio. He played what he himself called "hillbilly" music. He loved Roy Acuff.

One November weekend Jim and I attended Kenyon's Bacchanalia Festival. Then he and two of his friends drove me to Columbus that Sunday night and dropped me off at the hotel where I was to take the nursing board examinations for the next two days. We had had such a lovely, exciting time that I was not the least bit anxious about the next day. I took the exams and passed with flying colors.

I knew I stood on the circle's edge of this world that I dreamed about. I hoped I somehow would belong through loving Jim. I see now that it was a mistake to surrender myself to my dreams of a life in the literary and academic world, but Jim needed and wanted me with him. I knew I was good for him. I was confident I could take care of all the practical, everyday things in life that he seemed not to notice. So I stayed.

As graduation approached for Jim, we each sensed a decision had to be made. Jim had secured a teaching job (starting in February 1952) through his friend Tom Tenney. Tom's parents were headmaster and headmistress of a boy's boarding school in Center Point, Texas, and they needed an English teacher for one semester. I was still working at the hospital in Martins Ferry, mostly the evening and night shifts. His course work was completed in December as well as his thesis on Thomas Hardy. He had won Kenyon's *Robert Frost Prize* for poetry that year, and he had applied and received a Fulbright Fellowship to the University of Vienna for the fall of 1952.

One cold afternoon in the middle of December, Jim and I walked up to the graveyard overlooking the valley below. Dusk was falling and we could see the fog rising on the river. We could see the fires burning in the Bessemer furnaces in the steel mills that lined the riverfront and the blast furnace spewing fire like a monster. As we stood there quietly observing the scene below, I heard Jim say softly, "Give up hope all ye who enter here."

"Have you ever felt hopeless, Jim?" I asked quietly.

"Yes, I suppose I have. When I was fifteen I felt really bad. One morning I woke and looked in the mirror and I started screaming. I put my fist through that mirror. The next thing I knew I was taken to the hospital in Wheeling."

"Were you there very long?" I wanted him to go on, but I didn't want to pry. He seemed willing to talk, "I was there about four months. The doctor was very nice. He encouraged me to get out of the house and get a job and make more friends. I stayed out of school my junior year and got a job. That was great, earning my own money! I got to know some of the guys in the neighborhood, and we played a lot of sandlot football. That was great, too. You know Harley Lannum, don't you?" (I nodded yes) "We got to be good friends, playing football. Afterwards, when we were sitting around, he'd say to me, 'Jim, say a poem.' And I would." He smiled remembering the good times.

A couple days later, Jim proposed. "We can start our new life together in Texas and get out of this hell hole," he said. I was thrilled and frightened by the proposal. I knew he was determined to leave Ohio after completing his studies at Kenyon. I knew about his mental breakdown when he was fifteen. I had learned at Cleveland City Hospital that for many young people, the breakdown in adolescence was the beginning of a long history of chronic illness.

I had talked about my relationship with a nurse friend who knew him in high school. "Do you have any idea what you're getting into, marrying Jim?" she asked me. I knew she was concerned and so was I. What *was* I getting into? I decided to go to the Wheeling Hospital where Jim had been hospitalized and talk to his psychiatrist.

I was anxious and almost walked away when a very tall man in a white coat approached me. I blurted out that Jim had told me his name. "We're thinking of getting married and I want to know whether he's going to be all right?" I said. I was scared and embarrassed. I felt overwhelmed. He spoke softly and gently, "I'll be glad to talk with you. Would you like to make an appointment?" That really frightened me. I knew I was not ready to look that closely at myself. I don't remember what I said to him and I left.

In late December, I was on duty on the Pediatric Ward on the afternoon shift, and around ten o'clock that night; I had a call from Jim. My heart was pounding as I picked up the telephone. I knew something was wrong. He never called me. "Lib," he said his voice quivering, "I can't go through with it.... I can't get married.... I'm sorry." He hung up, and I stood there trembling. My worst fears had come true. I felt crushed, but I couldn't give up hope of freeing myself and living my own life. I had to start thinking more realistically. I even consulted a psychologist who was a patient. I knew this was not appropriate, but I was desperate. She was not optimistic that our relationship would work. *This* was not what I wanted to hear.

In January, I was working the midnight shift on the medical ward. This was the ward where Joe lived. The nurse going off duty reported that Joe was talking about wanting to die. Medically, his condition was deteriorating. His kidneys were failing. "Don't worry," she said. "He's had these spells before. Give him time. He'll come out of it. He usually does." I checked him several times that night. He seemed to be sleeping peacefully. Early in the morning I went in to take his pulse. I touched him lightly, "Joe," I whispered. He was too still. Suddenly, I felt frightened. I pulled back the covers quickly and reached for his wrist. "Oh, Joe," I moaned. "What have you done?"

For an instant I stood there staring at the cut wrists, the razor blades beside him, and the huge, liver-shaped clots. There was still a pulse, but it was very weak. I ran to the telephone and called the doctor. A sleepy voice answered and in a trembling voice I explained what happened. The doctor gave me orders: "Get a type and cross-match for blood, call surgery and tell them to get ready, and give him a sixth grain of morphine if he seems to be in pain." Mechanically, I followed the orders, and Joe was taken to surgery. At seven that morning in the middle of my report to the staff on the day shifts, I stood there sobbing uncontrollably. Tears were taboo for nurses at that time. I felt disgraced that I was unable to control my emotions better than that. I knew I would not be able to stay there much longer.

Two days later Joe was transferred to the state hospital for the mentally ill where he died several years later. I pondered what Joe had done for years afterward. The only consolation I had was I had been his friend. Perhaps, he decided to die that night because he knew I was on duty and I would take care of him. Years later, I wrote a paper about his suicide attempt, and I dedicated it to the memory of Joe. It was published in a book called *The Nurse as Caregiver for the Terminal Patient and His Family* (1976).

After the dreadful incident with Joe and Jim's rejection, I knew I had to get out of Martins Ferry and start my life over again. This was my chance to go to college as I had dreamed about so many years ago. Ohio State University was just a hundred miles away. I felt confident I could find a job. I turned in my resignation to become effective the end of January. I didn't talk to anyone. I was numb with pain for the loss of my friend, Joe, and for Jim.

Two weeks later, Jim called. I remember taking the call at the nurses' desk after midnight. He said in a trembling voice, "Lib, I panicked. Forgive me. I do love you. Please marry me." I was relieved and ecstatic. My concerns about his mental state were pushed out of my conscious mind, and my plans for college were postponed. Jim panicked once more at the church when the priest expected him to sign an agreement to raise our children in the Greek Orthodox Church. The wedding ceremony started a half hour late and only after I reassured Jim that we would discuss the matter when we did have children. First, we had a ceremony to attend.

As I recall that long-ago wedding day, I can still remember how afraid and brave we both were and the terrible tension between our families. My parents held a small reception for family and friends at their home. My father was there, and without a word spoken, he handed me his white handkerchief and he danced the Greek Sirto with me. That dance meant the world to me, and I was deeply touched. I felt forgiven, loved, and accepted.

Robert Mezey, Tom Tenney, and Jim's beloved Professor Timberlake attended our wedding on February 10, 1952. They gave us a wedding gift of an album of records called Wozzeck, and Edgar Doctorow wrote a lovely little epigram called "Epiphany." Robert Mezey was younger than most of the students at Kenyon, and he was very attached to Jim who became his mentor and friend. Their relationship lasted many years after they graduated from Kenyon, primarily by mail.

After the reception we were given a happy send-off as we were driven to Steubenville. Early the next morning we boarded the train for Texas. Like the winged phoenix, we were clearly flying above the green walls of home to another life.

Jim's Family
Background

Dudley Wright, Jim's father, worked hard his entire life. He worked as a machinist for the Hazel-Atlas Company for fifty years. The capacity for hard work probably was the only characteristic that our two fathers had in common. Otherwise they were very different. My father was aggressive, ambitious, and driven to succeed. Dudley was a gentle, kind, and very sweet man who accepted his "lot in life." He worked mainly to provide for his family. If he had dreams and hopes of his own, he never mentioned them.

Jesse, Jim's mother, came from an impoverished family and was forced to quit school to work in a laundry to help support her family. Jim described his mother as an intelligent woman and a great storyteller as well as an erratic, temperamental, and volatile person. At times, she was vitriolic in her verbal attacks on Dudley. As a mother, Jesse was gentle and loving with her children and grandchildren when they were infants. As the boys grew and became more rambunctious and independent, her inclination was to tighten the reins and restrain them. She, like my father, had little tolerance for the noise of children. Neither my father nor Jesse learned "to accept their lot in life." Their frustration and anger with their lives was more than they could contain. Their childhoods had been sacrificed to survival and work—never-ending work that left them drained, empty, and angry.

Jim grew up in Martins Ferry. His mother was restless and unable to tolerate living so close to other families. She preferred to live out in the country but stayed in town so that Jim could graduate from high school. They lived in seven different houses in Martins Ferry before she insisted that they move to a farm.

MOVE TO WARNOCK

They found a small house with some acreage in Warnock, which was about thirty miles or so from Wheeling where Dudley worked. Since he did not drive, he realized he would have to commute by bus, and commuting everyday was extremely tiring. The bus ride took at least two hours. He and Jesse agreed that he would have to get a room in Wheeling and come home on the weekends. He did find a room easily enough, and he had a hot plate on which he could warm up a can of soup after a long day's work, before falling asleep. On Friday evenings he returned to spend the weekend with his wife and sons. Then, on Sunday evening he would leave for the long tedious bus ride to Wheeling.

FAMILY MEMBERS

Their adopted daughter, Marge, a large cheerful woman, was married to Paul Pyle, a factory worker, and they lived near Warnock, on the outskirts of St. Clairsville. They had a son and daughter, and the whole family was very involved in a fundamentalist church in their small community. Jim's oldest brother, Ted, was married to Penny; they had two children. They lived in Zanesville where he had a photography studio. Dudley and their sons helped Jess (they all called her Jess) with planting hay and alfalfa to feed their animals. However, after a few years, the chores became too much for Jesse to handle alone.

Ted's family was growing and he was very busy with his photography business. Jim was attending Kenyon College and could help only during the summer months. Jack was in high school and a very studious, quiet boy with a sardonic sense of humor much like his mother's. The country school that he attended in St. Clairsville was very small, yet he managed to find teachers who tutored him in Latin, calculus, and trigonometry. I remember how proud the family was when Jack received the highest score in mathematics in a statewide test. Later, he would study astronomy in California after completing his studies at Ohio State University. *Once Jack came to San Francisco from Southern California to see us, and I wrote to him when Jim died. I heard that he married and was working in an astrolab, but we had no further contact.*

MOVE BACK INTO TOWN

Somehow, and I never understood how decisions were made in the Wright family, Jesse was persuaded to sell the farm and move to Zanesville into a large house with a sizable plot of land in the back for a garden. Jesse resumed her sarcasm and verbal jabs, but they were coated with a veneer of joking and teasing. Jim said very little when he was home, and Jesse seemed a little more reserved around Jim, but they both enjoyed telling humorous stories and laughing with each other. He encouraged her to tell some of her funny stories about family members, neighbors, and particularly about ministers, except when Marge or Paul were there. Her humor had a biting quality, almost bitter and anti-social. We all laughed and this encouraged her to tell more stories. She could "spin yarns" all through dinner. Then she would leave to milk the cow and to feed the pigs.

Leopold was Jim's favorite pig when they lived in Warnock, only Leopold was a sow with a dozen piglets. She would root with her snout under the fence around the pen until there was enough space for the piglets to get out. Then, the whole family would spend the rest of the evening rounding up piglets while Leopold watched the commotion she had caused. Jim insisted that Leopold did this deliberately whenever he was home.

Little bits and pieces of information from Jim in those early years of meeting at Warnock told me that his own childhood was not so funny. Jim described his mother as a "nervous" woman, irritable and impatient with three small boys to deal with. Jim's punishment to "sit quietly in a chair and read" was converted over time into one of his greatest strengths.

The other painful event in his early life that he revealed to me was hearing his mother verbally "tear apart" his beloved father. He felt helpless about not being able to "do anything about it," and his father would not defend himself in any way. Dudley would just walk out in the backyard and sit there quietly and alone, just as he did years later when he would withdraw from Jesse's "ranting and raving" and occupy himself with his garden hoeing the weeds and watering the plants.

Jesse's bitterness intensified as the years went by. I understood her anger because school was my salvation and sanctuary as I was growing up, and I don't know what I would have done had I been forced to leave school. Jim and Jack were the first to graduate from college on either side of the family, just as I was the only woman in my family from both sides to complete college and graduate schools. My youngest brother, Jack, also completed college and graduate school and became a social worker. (Jim and I were the only members of our high school class who earned Ph.D.s.)

Jesse was the dominant parent in the Wright family, and my father was definitely the patriarch in our family; and temperamentally Jesse Wright and Paul Kardules were very similar. Jim and I were the ones in our families who got the brunt of our parent's agitation and anger. Jim withdrew from the ugliness of the reality that surrounded his world into books and writing poetry. He started developing his identity as a poet at a young age under very stressful circumstances that today would be considered emotionally abusive.

As a child Jim was constantly being told by his mother to be quiet and sit still. When he learned to read, he was expected to sit quietly and read for long stretches of time. By the age of twelve, Jim decided his role in life and his identity would be that of a poet. Little else mattered. He knew he could not be like his father—a laborer in a factory—and being a husband and a father was not that great either. He concluded that he could not be an ordinary man who worked and supported a wife and children "until he dropped dead." "There must be something better in life for me," he declared emphatically to himself and, later, to me. We both came to this conclusion in our own thoughts and reflections. I, too, could not see myself living out a fate of being "only a wife and mother. There has to be more that I can do with my life." These thoughts reverberated in my head since the age of seven. I only consented (to myself and later to my father) that I would marry if I could choose my own husband.

163

SURVIVAL MECHANISMS

The persona that I developed for my survival was first of all, the helper. I started at the age of two believing that my mother was unable to take care of my baby sister and me, so I "decided" I had to be her helper. As my two sisters and brother came into our family, I became something of a caretaker. When I needed some attention for myself, my godfather was there to take me for walks, and later he taught me to swim in the Ohio River. By six I was cleaning house and shopping. The "good" girl was my strategy for getting the permission I needed to get to high school for the education that was going to be my first step toward freedom and selfhood in a very different world.

Jim built a persona out of his intellect and talent, and with the added gift of an eidetic memory, he presented himself as an outgoing, very personable poet who could quote reams of poetry and who developed a talent for comedy, imitations, as well as that of a hillbilly who enjoyed country music. Yet, underneath the persona existed a fragile, sensitive, and deeply wounded child embedded in layers of anxiety, fear, and rage. Later on I came to view his exuberance and effusiveness as one layer of protective mechanisms that shielded him from the deep-seated anxiety that would rise up whenever his identity as a poet was threatened.

Jim and I grew up in families with one angry, bitter parent and one gentle, kind parent. I know my parents had depressive episodes, and I suspect Jess did, too. I had an episode of depression at the age of fifteen; and afterward, I suffered with depression about once every decade, sometimes for years. Since I was twenty-five, I have been in therapy every decade for several years. I had a series of electroshock treatments in 1959, but not ever again. Medications were not well developed until a decade later. I did try an anti-depressant in my older years, and it worked very well for me. I had learned to bury my depression, and I never let it interfere with nurses' training or my years in college or my professional work. With therapy my depression became more manageable.

NERVOUS BREAKDOWN

Jim suffered a more severe psychotic episode at fifteen and was hospitalized for several months. Jim never revealed what precipitated that episode. He only said that one day as he looked at himself in the mirror, he became so enraged that he smashed his fist through the mirror. Several months later when he was released from the hospital, his psychiatrist advised him to stay out of school the rest of the year, to get a job, and to learn how to have some fun. He told him to stop reading the Bible. Scrupulosity was a common problem for some adolescents who were filled with anxiety and terrified about one's sinfulness and guilt. I know that Jim started attending a church at the age of fifteen, but I don't know how much or whether church activities triggered off the breakdown. My impression was that he enjoyed church attendance. More likely, his mother's bitterness toward religious institutions may have contributed to putting Jim in a conflict with his mother, and he could no longer contain his anxiety and rage. Jim never discussed what happened in any detail after he mentioned the hospitalization.

Obsessive-Compulsiveness is known as one of the anxiety disorders, thus those who suffer with this type of problem do not lose touch with reality and are not psychotic. Their thoughts do involve themes of danger, fear of loss, aggression, and concerns about disorder and symmetry. For a time, the ritualistic compulsive behavior decreases the discomfort of the obsessive thoughts. In Jim's situation, the obsessive-compulsive behaviors became a major safeguard against a much deeper disorder that would break through in his thirties. I came to the conclusion that his ability to remember and quote pages of poetry and prose served the purpose of protecting him from the psychotic core in his psyche.

Jim was genetically vulnerable because there were a mixture of affective disorders (depression and/or manic-depression), anxiety, schizophrenia and alcoholism in Jesse's family of origin. I had no information about Dudley's family. I've mentioned that my family's predisposition was genetically loaded toward anxiety, phobias, major depression, manic-depression, and alcoholism, which made our sons very vulnerable to these conditions and addictions. In the 1950s the psychiatric fields did not know about the genetic factors or the neurological-biochemical theories that we hear about today. In addition there were the environmental factors of deprivation (economic, social, and psychological) as well as abusive relationships in each of our families.

I was aware that the rituals (counting steps) would not hold back the tide of devastation that lay deep in Jim's unconscious. At times when his condition worsened, I'd suggest that he see a psychiatrist, but he scoffed at my suggestion or did not respond at all. Wine would become his medication of choice to ease the troubling thoughts and the depression. The combination of alcohol and depression released the dark angry demons in his soul. Writing poetry had become a large part of his ritual for controlling the inner chaos. I had very serious concerns about his mental and mood problems.

Like our parents before us, Jim and I had neither preparation nor adequate skills to develop a healthy marital relationship or family. We had none of the tools that I teach to couples today in preparing for marriage. Jim responded to every major event in our lives with fear and anxiety: our marriage, pregnancies, trips in this country and in Europe, and the recognition he was receiving. I had to calm him down and reassure him that everything would work out. I became the over-adequate wife who handled everything so he would not worry. He played the under-adequate husband. As I look back over those ten years of our marriage, from the perspective of many years, much questioning and much therapy – the process of healing old wounds—I can say without rancor that our marriage was doomed from the beginning, and I believe I knew it all along. Psychologically, our family dynamics were very similar despite the differences in cultural and ethnic backgrounds. The positive note in all this was that our marriage became the means by which both of us escaped over the green wall of the Ohio Valley, and we started our journeys together on the paths toward our discovering who we were as a couple, then as individuals.

Libby graduated from High School, then went to nurses school.

Libby in college   James Wright at about age 19

Jim's First Teaching Job in Texas

Instead of a honeymoon, we spent three happy days on the train being very close and holding hands all the way to San Antonio where Mrs. Tenney met us and drove us to the school. She was very cordial and pointed out the special sights as we drove the fifty miles to the school in Center Point. When we arrived twenty-five boys, Mr. Tenney, and two teachers met us at the driveway and escorted us to our room in the dormitory where everyone stayed. There was a floor lamp with a ribbon on it in our room—a present from the Tenneys. We were surprised and pleased by the welcome we received, and it was a rather unusual place to spend the rest of our honeymoon. I don't think Jim or I had any thoughts about a honeymoon at the time; only in retrospect did it occur to me that we never discussed that subject.

The two other teachers were both from Yale; the older one had served in the Navy and he seemed confident about handling the boys; the other younger man had just graduated and was inexperienced as a teacher. The boys were harder on him than on us. We all learned and adjusted to our new surroundings.

Although a fairly large wooded area that was pleasant for walks surrounded the school, Jim did not have as much privacy as he needed for his own writing and reading time. The first Friday after we arrived Jim became more distant, and that night he announced that he was going to stay up and do some reading. I was disappointed because I liked that we had slept together all night at the hotel and this was our first week with each other. It was difficult trying to sleep with the light on most of the night, but I did not say anything either. The next day he slept in late. This was his habit at home when he stayed at his parents' home, but I don't recall that he did that again in Texas.

All I remember about Texas and the school was that we all lived together in the dormitory, and we were surrounded by two dozen boys for four solid months. Many of these boys had been expelled from private schools in the East, their parents were unable or unwilling to manage their children, and they were wealthy enough that they could send them away to school for others to deal with them. I thought that two of the boys might be psychotic. I mentioned to Mrs. Tenney they might consider having them evaluated by a psychiatrist, but that was not an acceptable thing to do or to even mention.

We actually found scorpions in the light fixture on the ceiling and once a snake was tossed in our room. One evening a group of eight or ten boys surrounded the dormitory where we were all living and whooped and hollered around the building as if they were getting ready to invade us, and we were uncertain what they were planning to do. Our goal was to get out of there alive.

The one saving grace about the school was the Negro couple that cooked for the school. They were quiet and observant and said very little. I tried to befriend them, but they knew their place, which I didn't; and I learned a little bit about cooking, which they did very well.

On Saturdays the teachers and I escorted the boys to a nearby town that had a couple of movie theaters, and for an afternoon we could relax and talk without interruptions. Sometimes Jim did not go with us. He stayed in our room to work on his poetry. I remember he worked on a long allegory based on the story of the Biblical David. He must have written and rewritten that story until it grew to almost hundred pages. As he worked on it he pared it down to a 73-page dramatic poem that he called, *The Care of Phaltiel: A Tale in Ten Scenes.* Eventually, that long poem became a sonnet and he called it *David.* I don't remember that he ever published it, but Saundra Maley mentioned the long poem in her book (*The Solitary Apprenticeship*).

One time we spent a lovely day exploring Austin, Texas, a beautiful city, almost mid-western in design; and later we went to Dallas where I had my first experience with segregation. There were actually drinking fountains marked for Whites and Negroes, as well as bathrooms in a department store. I was shocked and couldn't believe what I saw. How could they do such a thing? On the bus returning to Center Point and the school, we decided to sit on the large seat in the back of the bus so we could talk. In a few minutes, a Negro man came up to us and said very quietly, "I think you better sit in your own seats," and walked away. Again, we reacted as if we had been slapped in the face. It was true! This segregation thing actually existed!

During spring vacation (1952), Bob Mezey hitchhiked from Kenyon to Texas and arrived at the school to spend a few days with us. He rescued us from the scorpions, snakes, and spoiled children. We were so happy to see him. He was not too much older than the kids in the school, and we felt relieved to have him with us. He invited us to follow him to Philadelphia for the summer, and Jim and I agreed to go there. We did get out of Texas without anything disastrous happening, and we chalked up the whole venture to "a good learning experience."

Philadelphia Sojourn

We took the train back to Ohio, and from there a bus to Philadelphia. I easily found a job at Temple University Hospital that hot, humid summer; and Jim, not so fortunate, labored on the railroad. I don't think he did much writing in Philadelphia. We were waiting to hear about the Fulbright scholarship to study in Vienna. We learned it was approved at the same time I got word that my mother was dying in Ohio. I took the bus from Philadelphia to Martins Ferry as soon as I packed and resigned my position at the hospital. I immediately took my mother to the Cleveland Oncology Clinic for a second opinion about her condition. While we waited for the report, I dozed off and slept, my head on the foot of her bed. I thought I was just tired, but she recognized the early signs of pregnancy. We talked later that day, and I told her I was worried about leaving her again to go to Europe with Jim. She smiled very peacefully and knowingly and said, "You go with your husband and don't worry. Women have been having babies in Europe, too." I was surprised. I was just beginning to wonder whether I was pregnant. How did she know?

The report was not good. The breast cancer had metastasized to her lungs. Nothing more could be done.

My father was not as gracious when he received the report that my mother was dying. His response was an automatic and quick slap across my face. I was startled and fell over on my back. As I picked myself up, I shouted at him, "What is wrong with you?" He went out the back door shaking his head. He dealt with his grief as badly as he did with everything else that he could not control. Shortly afterwards, he turned to another woman for solace and comfort.

Jim had another panic attack when I told him I was pregnant. Wringing his hands and pacing in his parents' home, he cried out desperately, "How can we go to Vienna now if you are pregnant? What are we going to do?" Quietly and patiently, his mother and I reassured him that women have been having babies for centuries. "They have hospitals in Vienna, too. As soon as we get there I'll find an obstetrician. I'll be fine and so will you; besides, I helped deliver babies. I know what to do," I reassured him patiently. He seemed to accept our explanations and reassurance, and we went on to plan our trip.

Onward to Vienna

Jim enrolled at the University of Vienna the first week in September along with all the other students. I did as I had promised Jim. At the Fulbright Office, I received a referral to an obstetrician who spoke English, and I had my first visit with him a week later. He told me I was fine and would see me again in about four months. I was surprised because in our country, women were seen more frequently. He agreed to see me every month if I wished and that was preferable for me.

Two months later, on a beautiful late October day, I received a telegram. My mother had died on the nineteenth. Jim was very supportive when I grieved for her, but mostly I postponed my grief. I tucked it away with the other losses, and ten years later my grief surfaced and I dealt with it when a favorite teacher at the University of California left to take a position at another university. The loss of my teacher triggered off my unexpressed grief for the loss of my mother. Finally, I was able to mourn and accept her death.

That year in Vienna was one of the happiest times in our lives. In the great river of Vienna life, we swam together. Jim immersed himself in the writings of German poets Hölderlin, Heine, and Rilke. He began translating Theodore Storm and stumbled upon the poetry of George Trakl, which he would later translate. He spent hours in coffee shops drinking coffee and writing poems on napkins that he later typed and put in his notebooks. I studied German and learned enough to converse with the shop people and buy the groceries that we needed. I think I learned more of the *Wienerisch* dialect than *hoch deutsch.* I took an evening course in English at the University on Beethoven's Symphonies.

During the day and evenings, there were concerts, the opera, and parties. We went everywhere on foot or by trolley. On Sunday afternoons, we walked alongside the Viennese walkers in the beautiful woods that surrounded the city. We discovered several houses with markers indicating that Beethoven had lived there. We attended an elaborate Thanksgiving dinner at the U.S. Ambassador's palatial home, and we celebrated Christmas in Salzburg. The presidential candidate, Adlai Stevenson, arrived in Vienna, and all the Fulbright scholars and their wives were invited to a cocktail party in his honor at one of the grand hotels.

PREPARING FOR FIRST SON

Life took on a happy glow as our son's birth grew closer. I remember how active Franz was as I carried him. At concerts he would start kicking inside of me as soon as the first notes were played, so Jim and I were certain he would become a musician. As my due date came and went, we were making contingency plans to get to the hospital quickly. Jim had alerted the cab drivers on the corner near our apartment, but my doctor decided to induce labor because I was two weeks past my due date. So we took the trolley to the hospital on St. Patrick's Day. I delivered Franz early the next morning after only six hours of labor. We were both thrilled with our beautiful son. Jim became a loving and attentive father as soon as he held Franz the first time. He wrote a poem on the day Franz was born that he called, *On the Birth of my Son in a Spring Morning.* Not long after Franz' birth, Jim was composing another poem for him:

A Song for the Middle of the Night

By way of explaining to my son the following curse
by Eustace Deschamps.
"Happy is he who has no children
for babies bring nothing but crying and stench."

Now first of all he means the night
You beat the crib and cried
And brought me spinning out of bed
To powder your backside.
I rolled your buttocks over
And I could not complain:

Legs up, la la, legs down, la la,
Back to sleep again...

He wrote a poem about my being pregnant, which he called, *To a Girl Heavy with Child*, which was not published for several years. I was deeply touched by his efforts to try to understand what a pregnancy felt like.

I THE CARETAKER, JIM THE POET

I felt more involved in his work that year. He shared the poets he was studying and his excitement about discovering Hölderlin, Storm, and especially Trakl. He was frequently excited and pleased with the translations he was doing. I was so touched and happy to observe his creativity in action on a daily basis. We were truly in love that first year of marriage. We were very close. I had never experienced such closeness with anyone. We gave and received from each other, sharing our hopes and expectations. We nurtured each other with warmth, affection, and caring we had not experienced in our families. We did almost everything together. We attended parties and dinners with the other scholars and their wives, and we browsed in books stores or we rode the trolley cars and gazed at ancient buildings. Frequently we would get off the trolley and go someplace that looked interesting and we'd explore museums and palaces. I felt more at ease in Vienna than any other place, except Kenyon. I felt accepted there, too. Here we were attempting to learn how to stretch ourselves to explore our new relationship together.

As much as he loved us, however, there were times when Jim became irritable and angrily pulled away and stayed away from us, sometimes for a few hours, at others times, a day or more. At first, his distancing himself from me felt very hurtful, but I soon learned that these were parts of Jim that I would have to learn to live with. I would quickly reassure myself that he only needed to be alone to write. "He's not rejecting you," I reassured myself.

On one level this was an accurate perception. He had learned patterns of denying his emotions, and he found ways to channel them through his writing; but he did not know how to express whatever he was feeling or was troubling him about our relationship, and I did not know how to tell him when I was feeling lonely or felt shut out from him. Neither of us had learned how to communicate in an intimate relationship.

I, on the other hand, had learned all the practical skills for running a household. Since I was the oldest daughter in our family who accepted the role of helper and caretaker, I was quite familiar with the responsibilities of family life. However, neither Jim nor I had healthy models of the marital relationship, and neither of us knew how to design and build a relationship based on mutuality, sharing, and the development of each individual and the relationship. Neither of us had the skills that were necessary to deal with the complex issues of marriage and parenthood.

I was much less skilled in the areas of poetry that Jim was constantly exploring. I would listen when he wrote a new poem and respond in my own personal way which, I suspected, was not enough for Jim. He was accustomed to the intense intellectual discussions with his fellow students at Kenyon and I, of course, could not meet such an expectation. However, if he was totally absorbed in whatever poet or writer was his focus, he spent hours typing his poetry, long letters to friends, and later he could go on for hours talking in great detail about the writer who impressed him. I was intuitive enough to realize he needed time alone, that he could not tolerate too much "togetherness" or intimacy, so I found ways to entertain myself or stay busy, and later I'd take Franz for walks when Jim was not available. I began to realize that this must have been his experience in his own family. His mother had insisted that he sit quietly and read a book and occupy himself alone. I, too, was very content to spend hours with a book.

SIMILAR AND DIFFERENT

Psychologically, Jim and I were similar in some ways and quite opposite in others. I had learned to wait; to be patient; to postpone gratifying my needs, desires, as well as my dreams and my ambitions. When we married I consciously agreed to put off my desire for a college education until Jim completed his studies. I willingly accepted the responsibilities of our life together as long as I knew that my opportunity to study would come later.

Jim, on a psychological level, had converted most of his emotional and mental resources into his persona of The Poet. Almost every other aspect of his Self was repressed and unavailable on a conscious level. A sliver of his Self was permitted to come out briefly as a husband and father. The Poet inevitably intruded; then he would pull away and retreat into himself and reconstitute his boundaries. I was intrigued by Jim's ability to take on the personality of the writer he was studying at particular times.

In a very deep sense, I can say that Jim was obsessed with his identity as a poet: every thought was recorded and later transcribed into a notebook; every draft of a poem was preserved. Every letter was written with the conscious or unconscious intention that it would someday appear in a book. Even his letters to his sons, when they were very young, were composed with the words of The Poet. The poet was his role, his identity, and his defense mechanism. Everything else in his psyche had to be kept out of his awareness, unless it could be transformed into a poem.

In a psychological sense, we were a good match for each other: I was very practical and could hide my talents, even from myself. Jim, on the other hand, developed his talent and hid, or did not develop, the practical side of his life.

Unfortunately, without growth as individuals, this arrangement could not be sustained for long periods of time. In order to continue living this way, we would have had to stagnate and cease growing; and nature has a way of propelling us to our natural development whether we want to or not. We held on to the fragments of our individual selves as long as possible until we got swept away by the flood of needing to grow and become whole, and our life together was shattered.

I learned to share him with his "demanding muse." Although we laughed about his affair with the muse, this was an uneasy, but expected, triangle in our lives. I remember feeling a tinge of jealousy, sometimes, when he wrote about women; and I didn't know whether they were real people or figments of his imagination. This was not a problem for me until later on in our relationship when I was uncertain whether the relationship with the muse became an extra-marital relationship. Then, I was not tolerant or understanding; in fact, I became deeply resentful and angry, and all the feelings, needs, and wants came pouring out in tears and resentful words. Almost instinctively I found it was easier and less painful to simply withdraw into work, housekeeping, or caring for Franz.

A NEW FRIEND

During the year in Vienna, Jim had become very good friends with Herb Lindenberger from the University of Washington, in Seattle. He could talk to Herb about the German poets he was studying, but most of the other Fulbright people were not English majors. They came from a variety of backgrounds and from different parts of the country. From the long talks they had about graduate school, Jim decided to apply for entrance to the graduate program in English. In characteristic self- assurance, he applied to that one graduate school, and of course, he was accepted.

Well stocked with diapers and baby food that were given to us by the Ambassador's wife, we started our journey back home in late May 1953. We stopped over in Germany where we took the Rhine journey to Cologne and stayed there a couple of days. Next, we spent a few days touring around London; then we took a bus out to Dorchester to visit the home of Thomas Hardy and the area Jim wrote about in his thesis at Kenyon. He had a long, wonderful conversation about Hardy with the caretaker of the old home with its thatched roof; and soon afterwards, we headed home feeling complete and fulfilled with our long journey.

Journey Home and Westward

We had enjoyed our cruise on the SS Queen Elizabeth so much that we booked return passage on the SS Mauretania, a smaller ship that took seven days to cross the Atlantic to New York. Unfortunately, the weather in the North Atlantic was much stormier than our trip to France, and I spent the first two days being very seasick. Jim and Franz handled the rough seas like experienced sailors.

We disembarked at New York Harbor and found our way to Richard and William Goldberg's apartment where we were greeted by Roger Hecht and few other friends from Kenyon. In the company of his old school friends, Jim reminisced about and relived the good times they had together. This time I did not feel as comfortable with all the men and their loud laughter and conversation, especially when I was putting Franz to sleep and I was very tired after three weeks of traveling. I realized that Jim was his exuberant self when he was with his Kenyon friends, and he was much more reserved in Vienna where most of the Fulbright scholars were from different fields with the exception of Herb Lindenberger and an English Professor from Rice University and his wife.

We stayed two days in New York City before returning briefly to Ohio. I wanted to visit my mother's gravesite and to get in touch with the reality of her death. My father remarried six months after my mother's death, and I met my stepmother, Irene, and her young daughter, Priscilla. I knew my father could not manage without a wife to take care of his needs. Besides, my youngest brother, Jack, was only ten years old, and he needed a mother figure in his life. She seemed like a very warm, loving woman; and I was pleased that she was there, and not me. I gave Priscilla my Shirley Temple doll that was still in her original box. Perhaps now the doll would get the care of an eight-year old little girl who knew how to play with her, which I never did.

Jim's parents were thrilled with their new grandson, and we had a happy reunion with the Wright clan, Ted and his family, Jack, Marge, and her family. I was happy to be home again for a little while. I realized how much I missed the little things: hearing jazz and blues, hearing American English spoken, especially with an Ohioan twang. I even missed those gray-green hills, and the river. For the first time I understood what it felt like to be a foreigner and to miss one's home. I felt more empathic for all the immigrants, especially my parents who came to this country without any knowledge of the language, frightened by the freedom and the violence, and knowing they would probably never return to their homeland. Still, they dreamed of one day returning. Even though we were only gone for ten months, I, too, had experienced that feeling of being a stranger in a foreign land and yearning for home and its familiar language, music, sounds, and atmosphere.

Seattle and
Getting Settled

The train trip from Ohio to Seattle took three days. Fortunately, Franz was an excellent traveler, and the stroller we bought in Vienna was very sturdy. By the time we arrived in Seattle, he was almost six months old. Our first task was finding an apartment within walking distance of the university. Jim and I were strong walkers, but I found pushing a stroller and carrying groceries up the hilly streets of Seattle a little more strenuous than I enjoyed. So, in addition to getting a job, I felt the urgent need for a car, although I did not know how to drive.

The job was very easy to acquire. The director of nurses at Doctors Hospital hired me on the spot. "If you were wearing a uniform, I'd put you to work right now," she announced with a smile, and I knew she was serious. She was satisfied that I appeared bright and early the next morning. She escorted me to the medical ward and introduced me to the head nurse, a tall handsome male nurse who had been a corpsman in the Navy during the war. He was the first male nurse I had ever met. He was friendly, efficient, and worked very fast. He gave me my assignment of five patients, took me to their ward and introduced me, and then left me to my own devices. No further orientation was considered necessary. The patients where helpful, and I adapted quickly as I had learned to do.

Within six months, I was the head nurse of a newly remodeled medical ward. When I told Mrs. McAllister, the Director, that I planned to be in Seattle at least five years while my husband was in graduate school, she knew she had hired a dependable nurse. Very soon I learned that Seattle was a stopping-off place for Canadian

181

nurses on their way to San Francisco. In the first year and a half as head nurse, I oriented twenty-four nurses. I had established my own orientation program to ease new nurses into their jobs, hoping they would stay longer than the average six months. They didn't. There seemed to be a constant flow of nurses from Canada.

My next vital task was buying a car, and I did that through the newspaper. I saw an advertisement for a 1946 Ford Coupe in excellent condition, and I called and asked the owner to deliver it, "If you don't mind. I don't know how to drive yet." He was very obliging. I think it cost $250.00, and I was absolutely enamored with my first car with a rumble seat in the back!

Jim had never learned to drive because "I'm too easily distracted." A graduate student in the psychology department who lived in our apartment house with his seven-year-old son taught me the basics about the stick shift, and showed me where the brake and the gas peddles were. He was a good and patient teacher. First, he took me for a demonstration ride; then he turned the machine over to me. Every day after work I practiced driving around the neighborhood; then I drove to the grocery store; and within a month or so, I felt confident enough to drive to work. I don't know whether learners' permits were required in those days, but I didn't take the driving test for six months. I passed on the second try.

I not only practiced driving to the grocery store, taking Franz to nursery school and myself to work, but on weekends, we toured the state of Washington and occasionally drove down to the Oregon Coast. As I look at our photo albums from those years, we were forever standing before lakes, rivers, and mountains with Indian-sounding names. We toured most of the Northwest; and our favorite places were Snoqualmie Falls, the Olympic Peninsula, and the Skyhomish River in the snow-capped Cascade Mountains. Those drives were some of the happiest times we had together. Once I got a flat tire on a dark, deserted road, and I cannot recall how we ever got it fixed. Probably, as in many other situations, a stranger would come along and help us. I drove through blizzards and heavy rains and Jim was there beside me encouraging me; we always made it home safely.

We explored all the parks and the zoo in Seattle, and of course

Franz was with us everywhere we went. He rode ponies, small trains, and observed wild animals while eating ice cream cones. These were memorable times for the three of us.

Jim threw himself enthusiastically into his studies and quickly became friends with fellow students: Jerry Enscoe, Franz Schneider, Larry Parks, and poets Carolyn Kizer, Richard Hugo, and David Waggoner. He admired the teaching of poet, Stanley Kunitz, and became a leading poet himself in Theodore Roethke's workshops and seminars.

Jim had a way of becoming completely absorbed in particular poets and writers, and almost taking on their personalities. I saw this when he was studying Hardy. He imitated most of the characters in Hardy's books, but he really outdid himself with Dickens' characters and Chaucer's. His eidetic memory was a great source of verbatim quotations of poets and writers. This ability made him popular at parties. He could so completely lose himself in the works of writers that I was never certain which personality would be home for dinner. Sometimes he was Dickens or Chaucer, or at parties he could suddenly become Jonathan Winters or W. C. Fields. Often, there was no room for us, as his family, to express our own thoughts or concerns when he was "on a roll" as a particular writer, or when he was absorbed in the music of Schumann, Schubert, or Bach.

One of his favorite singers was Kathleen Ferrier who sang German Lieder. I can remember many times when I was preparing dinner or tending to Franz (and later to Marshall) when he wanted me to sit with him and listen to the music. He seemed completely oblivious to the tasks of running a household or caring for small children, or even the possibility that I might have a different interest.

Needless to say, I fell into the traditional role of wife and mother, one of my survival mechanisms. I took care of all the day-to-day details of living plus working full-time, so Jim could study and get through graduate school. Typical of the overly responsible first child, I quite naturally assumed responsibility for everything and began to lose myself in the process. To be fair to Jim, he did help with the care of Franz on weekends when I had to work. He picked him up at the nursery, and they walked home together chatting and exploring the neighborhood. Franz said his first poem when he was three as they walked to the nursery early one unusually sunny Seattle morning:

"I saw the shining wind;
I saw the shining cookie on top of the tree."

Jim was so excited that he quoted the little poem to Ted Roethke who laughingly said, "I wish I had thought of that!"

During the first year in Seattle, we discovered that student housing was not adequate for the three of us. The first one had a leaking roof right over Franz' bed. The second one was a basement apartment with a wood stove; that is, in order to cook, we had to build a fire and keep it stoked all day. This was not possible since we were not at home all day. The third place we found was in a couple's home. We shared the kitchen with the husband who did most of the cooking for his wife and child, a toddler about the same age as Franz. He was named Anthony, and he walked a month earlier than Franz who never crawled. He sat until he was ready to walk; then he stood up and took his first step.

We moved out when we came home one evening and were told that the wife, who was a binge drinker, rented a truck, took most of the furnishings and her son, and left without a word to her husband. Apparently, she had done this before. Despondently, he said, "She will be back when she runs out of money."

Shortly after that distressing incident, I found a two-story clapboard house on Sunnyside Avenue for $40.00 a month. Our furnishings were purchased at St. Vincent de Paul's, and we settled in for the next three years. When we left, we passed the house and everything in it to another married graduate student.

FRIENDS AND PARTIES

Having a house with a combined living room and dining room made Jim even more popular for another reason beside his memory for quotations: we had a home big enough for graduate students' parties. For the most part, these gatherings were fun and a way for me to become better acquainted with Jim's friends and their spouses. Later, those of us who had children got together for picnics and outings at parks and the zoo with our children and spouses. I found these groups and outings very congenial and friendly, and in this environment I felt more a sense of belonging. We wives could identify with and support each other through the struggles of graduate school, work, and family life. In the 1950s, women working and supporting their husbands were considered unconventional.

During a week in the spring of our second year in Seattle, we had a surprise visit from Roger Hecht. I don't remember the occasion. I think he wanted to see Jim again and revisit some of their good times together. I remember it was a day in the middle of the week. We called a number of our friends to come over for a small party and to meet Roger, but everyone was busy that night. I felt somewhat embarrassed, but Jim and Roger had a good time talking and laughing together about old times.

Whenever I saw Jim with his cohorts from Kenyon, I had a distinct feeling they loved and accepted each other as family members. They had been together for four years; they worked hard and found common ground, and with much humor constructed an environment of belonging, closeness, and acceptance. In other words, with excellent teachers who valued individuality and the creative spirit, together they built with their students a happy, healthy family where each could grow a Self of integrity, competence, and confidence. I know Jim loved and valued the relationships he had at Kenyon and many of them lasted till the end of his life.

Pilgrimage to Hell

Jim was something of a celebrity around the English Department and the cultural community of Seattle because he had published poems in a variety of journals as an undergraduate and as a graduate student. After his first book, *The Green Wall*, was selected by W. H. Auden as a winner in the Yale Series of Younger Poets, he was inundated with invitations to read his poetry and to attend parties. On one Saturday evening after this major event, we had a huge party at our house. Jim and I were overwhelmed by the number of people who arrived that night. He got drunk, and of course I was sober. "Someone has to be," I thought sarcastically.

Suddenly, as I came out of the kitchen and into the hallway, there was Rae Tuft, the wife of one of the graduate students in the music department, with her arms wrapped around Jim's neck and kissing him as passionately as any Hollywood star in a movie. I stopped in my tracks. My heart was beating so fast I could hardly breathe. I could feel the blood draining out of my face. My whole body was shaking. I went over to the chair by the window in the living room to sit down and calm myself.

I looked up and she was sitting across from me on the couch asking quietly, "Do you want to talk?" I could not speak. I wanted to scream. I wanted to grab her by the neck and shake her... no... kill her. I wanted to disappear off the face of the earth. I felt ashamed, for God's sake. I was embarrassed and ashamed that my husband was betraying me in my own home. I felt enraged.... furious. I felt wounded; my heart was ripped out, yet I was still alive! I felt as if I were bleeding to death. I don't remember what happened the rest of the evening. Jim disappeared.

I felt as if I had absorbed all the unexpressed anger of every generation of women in my family who had been betrayed. I was supposed to release that burning rage and allow it to burst out of me in order to cleanse all of us of this horrendous betrayal. Not a sound came out of my throat. I stood up, when I finally could stand, like a zombie, frozen, and I walked slowly up the stairs to my room.

Greek men were notorious for having affairs. Even my father said that most men needed at least two women, but they were discrete, not so blatant. This was our first major crisis. I was painfully disappointed, disillusioned, and hurt. I knew Jim had women in his life before me. I believe I met a woman in Philadelphia who had been a former "friend" of Jim's. I learned she was a writer and I could see the sadness in her eyes, and they acted as if they wanted to talk privately. I didn't quite know what to do or where to go, and Jim never discussed her before or after their meeting.

The next morning as I prepared breakfast for my son, my mind was spinning out of control. I was trying to make sense out of what happened, to understand, and to plan my next move. What should I do? Leave? Yes, but where? There's San Francisco. I could easily get a job as a nurse. I'd have to take Franz who was only two, and I knew Jim would be devastated. I didn't care at that moment. I wanted him to hurt as much as he had hurt me.

By the time Jim woke up, I had made up my mind. When he came into the kitchen, still drowsy and hung over, I announced, "I am leaving, and I'm going to take Franz with me. We're going to San Francisco." I was cold, distant, and shoring myself up for excuses. "Lib, I'm sorry. I was drunk. Will you forgive me?" he sobbed.

"Do you think being drunk is an excuse for doing that to me? In my own home in front of all those people? I've got to get away from here. You all make me sick. You think because you're a poet and you're writing a book, you can do anything you want? You can all go to hell!" I screamed at him and went out in the backyard to cool off.

When I returned, he was still sitting there on the couch looking forlorn and pitiful. "Please, Lib, don't leave. I promise it will never happen again."

"It had better not!" I shot back at him. "If I ever see anything like that, I will be out of here so fast it will make your head spin." My anger was a huge fireball in my gut. I still wanted to get out of there. At that moment, I decided, "I am going to take Franz and go back to Ohio to visit my sisters and your parents for a week or so. I have some vacation coming. I'll have to arrange to take some time off at work," I thought aloud as my plan began to take shape.

A week later, Franz and I flew to Ohio. I didn't tell anyone in my family what had happened. I buried the wounds from that event deep inside me. Two days before we were due to return to Seattle, Franz came down with the mumps, and a week later, the measles. My attention turned to my son and to my work. I remember on the first morning back to work, my chest felt heavy with grief and sadness. As I came up to the entrance of the hospital, I said to my self, "You can't go in there with all that pain. Leave it here on the doorstep. You can pick it up on your way out." I did that many times in the next two years.

Jim kept his word. He never did anything overtly to embarrass me again. If and when he did anything of an extramarital nature, it was out of range of my sight or hearing. I did not attend many of the graduate student parties after that incident, or if I did, I always left early. I had the excuse that I had to be at work early the next morning. If he was going to drink, be dishonest and betray me, I didn't want to be exposed to such superficiality. I didn't like what fame was doing to Jim. When he was clearheaded, he admitted that people who were hanging on were only there because he was getting recognized outside in the poetry world. "They wouldn't give me a second look if I hadn't written this book."

Of course, he was flattered. Who wouldn't be flattered with all the adoration and fawning of beautiful young women who wanted to sit for hours and listen to him? After all, I myself had been entranced by his passionate voice and his copious memory. We talked together of the frivolousness that surrounds famous men, and how he could protect himself. Basically, he couldn't. He needed them as much as they needed someone to admire and idolize.

I convinced myself this was only temporary, and in a couple of years we would be gone from Seattle and all this foolishness, and we could settle down to a nice ordinary life in some college town where he would teach and write, and I would work on my degrees. I was wrong, of course. Jim had no such ideas about an ordinary life. His identity as a poet suddenly was validated and seemed to swallow the parts of him that we had shared with each other. I had hoped that he would grow the parts that we needed if we were to become a true family. As his wife I needed him to be a husband, my helpmate, my lover, and my partner. As a father I needed him to help raise his son. I was willing to devote my life to help him gain the recognition as a poet that he had dreamed about all his life. My dream for us was to make and share a life together, to have a family, to have a comfortable home environment where he could write and fulfill his potential not only as a poet but also as a man, a husband and a father. I wanted to fulfill my own dreams for a college education and a professional position.

Although he adored his father, I remembered his comment about not wanting to be a husband or a father. He wanted more out of life, and I did, too. I thought we could fulfill our hopes and dreams together just as we got out of the Valley together. I was beginning to see that Jim's dreams and mine were going in different directions. Jim was becoming the archetypal Poet who had separated from his Self and could not connect on a person-to-person level with his wife, his son, or anyone else for any length of time. He smashed the mirror that reflected back to him who he was; then he spent the rest of his life looking for his true self.

WORK—MY LAST REFUGE

My nursing job was challenging and exhausting. I had been trained well in the practical aspects of bedside care of patients, but I had not had time to learn and fine-tune my skills as an administrator who was responsible not only for patient care but for managing the needs and wants of staff and doctors. I did reasonably well learning and doing by trial and error until I was given the opportunity by Mrs. McAllister, the Director, to attend a workshop at the University of Washington School of Nursing. The topic of the workshop was Team Nursing.

I can still remember the excitement I felt being in a learning environment again. I absorbed the principles and concepts of team nursing and could hardly wait to return to work on the following Monday to try them out. (The concept and process of change were not presented in the workshop.) My enthusiasm for change did not exist in hospitals then. Resistance to change was enormous. I blithely went along believing if only the staff would cooperate and I demonstrated how the new approach to nursing care worked, we would convince all—the other staff and the nursing administrators—of the effectiveness of team nursing. My biggest mistake was assuming that because I was sent to the workshop, the administration expected me to implement what I had learned. I did not realize, until it was too late, that hospital and nursing administrators did not accept new concepts presented by faculties of universities for decades. The process of change in hospitals was extremely slow and tedious.

In any case, I started presenting the idea of team nursing to the staff on my ward to get their reactions, but they were skeptical and too busy to take on any new tasks. The Christmas holidays were on the horizon, and I decided to postpone the discussion of team nursing until after the New Year.

I worked on January 1, 1956, and I came home with a sore throat, chills, and fever. When I took my temperature, it was 104 degrees. I called one of the staff doctors, and he told me to return to the hospital immediately to be admitted. Tests were done and the next day I learned that I had a staphylococcus infection, which proved to be resistant to antibiotics. I was in the hospital for ten days.

Jim came to see me twice. The first time he brought Franz. I visited with them for a few minutes in the waiting room. I was happy to see them, but I did not feel strong enough to stay up very long. A few days later, he returned with his friend, Jerry Enscoe. They were laughing and having an animated conversation about "free love." This was a very popular subject for intellectuals in those days of Ayn Rand's *avant-garde approach to marriage and love*, and Jack Kerouac who preceded the radical movements of the 1960s. As I understood what they were discussing, it was all right to have sexual relations with anyone they desired whether married or not. Later of course, in the next decade, the feminist movement along with the invention of "the pill," open marriages, spouse-exchanges, and multiple partnerships became much more prevalent and almost the norm.

I was so thoroughly disgusted and disappointed that I broke into the middle of their discussion with a shout, "Will the two of you get the hell out of here and let me get some rest? I do not need this!" They were startled by my outburst, and they left. "How could he be so insensitive and uncaring?" I thought. I cried myself to sleep that night.

I recovered slowly and returned to work to resume my crusade for team nursing.

That spring the hospital administrator appeared on my ward. I was surprised by his unexpected visit. He looked around the ward, and I asked him if I could help him in any way. Rather nonchalantly, he said, "I understand that you are trying to revolutionize the hospital."

"What? Revolutionize the hospital? Oh, no, sir!" I replied. Before I thought what I would say next, I blurted out, "I'm only trying to ease the work of the nurses. I think if they work in teams of two with ten patients, instead of each one working alone with five, that the nursing care would be improved." He walked away without a word. In retrospect and after acquiring the strong background in group dynamics that I did in the 1960s, I can see the mistakes I made: in my excitement to make what I thought was a constructive change, I was oblivious to the administrative structure. I did not consult with Mrs. McAllister. I did not know how to present the new ideas to the staff and involve them in the process. I simply made the suggestion and said, "Let's try it." I was completely inexperienced in making changes in hospital systems. If any change in procedures were made, they were presented by the administration.

[In the 1970s I did become a change agent. I had a job and a mandate from the Director of the Mental Health Program to change the roles of psychiatric nurses and prepare them for outpatient and community functioning. I learned again that the main obstacles to any changes in job descriptions and procedures were nursing and hospital administrators and often the nurses themselves.]

WHAT? FIRED!

A month or so later after the administrators visit, Mrs. McAllister called me down to her office, and without much ado, she announced, "You're services are no longer needed. I will call Miss Anderson (my assistant) up on the ward to bring your belongings."

When I asked, "Why? What did I do?" Her answer sounded contrived, "I have had complaints that you are prejudiced against Negroes." I could not respond. I felt shocked and hurt again, this time about my work, which had been my salvation from the isolation I was feeling in my marriage. I could not believe what she said or that I had failed.

When my coat and purse were delivered, I left the hospital in tears. By the time Jim came home that afternoon and I had picked up Franz, I was almost cheerful. "You won't believe what happened today. I got fired!" Before Jim could not say anything, I said, "Let's celebrate! Call Jerry Enscoe and Ann, and tell them to come over for dessert. Don't worry. I'll get another job." And I did. Surprisingly, a week later, I received an evaluation from Mrs. McAllister in the mail. It was one of the best evaluations I had ever received from her.

A few weeks later, I accepted a job in a small medical clinic where I worked as a nurse for Dr. Williams, a general practitioner. Before long, I realized he was an alcoholic who gave himself a Vitamin B-12 injection in the morning (to counter the effects of the alcohol) before he saw patients. I was not pleased with the quality of the care he gave his patients and six weeks later, I resigned.

My next job was in a small minor surgery hospital. With some additional training by the assistant head nurse, I became quite competent as a surgical nurse. However, I don't remember when I felt so bored, restless, and unhappy in my work. I decided I needed some help to get me through the year and a half that remained before Jim completed graduate school. I started seeing Miss Shirley Myers, a social worker, once a week where I cried every hour for the next year and a half.

I was exhausted, confused, and lonely. Jim was so absorbed in his own life, his studies, his teaching, and his writing that he was unaware of the turmoil in my life. Since I had a therapist, I did not discuss my work or my unhappiness with him. I had stopped trying to fit into the circle of Jim's friends, and my depression deepened like the muddy water of the Ohio River. I felt like the outcast again.

OUR RELATIONSHIP BECOMES MORE DISTANT

Whatever closeness we had had in the first two years slipped away from us, and we moved into a rather mechanical, parallel relationship. Jim continued to attend parties and soirees at Carolyn Kizer's and to stay out late on those nights. I was too numb to be upset or jealous that he was seeing someone. I saw them together in the coffee shop once. I didn't recognize her, and I didn't even bother to ask or accuse him again. I was looking forward to leaving Seattle and starting over again in Minneapolis where Jim had applied for and was accepted as an instructor at the University of Minnesota in the English and Humanities Departments.

With the publication of his first book while he was in graduate school, Jim convinced himself that the national recognition he received would be sufficient to change the policy of the University of Washington English Department that prohibited the hiring of their own graduates. At the very least, he was certain an exception would be made for him and he would be hired. Jim was so angry and hurt by the perceived rebuff when he was not hired that he applied only to one school for a teaching position. (Not until we were in Minneapolis did I realize how deeply wounded he really was by the "rejection" of the English Department. He had suffered a severe assault to his identity as a poet, the mainstay of his personality. The blow was almost a mortal wound for Jim. (I did not know until many years later that Jim had attempted suicide in Seattle.)

Oddly, in the midst of all the emotional turmoil that we were both experiencing, I felt the deep stirring of a primal instinct. I felt the urge for another child. No, this is not the right time, I told myself. Let's wait until we get settled again. As the summer of 1957 approached, I began to feel relieved, hopeful, and even a little happier about the possibility of a new beginning for us. Despite Jim's unhappiness about the move, I felt optimistic for the first time in several years. The house was passed on to a nurse friend whose husband was a graduate student and, sadly, I sold my little sturdy Ford Coupe.

Last Trip to the Mountains

We took our last trip that summer to the Skyhomish River with Richard Hugo and his wife, Barbara. Dick loved fishing and he took us to their favorite spot on this beautiful rushing river surrounded by the snow-capped Cascade Mountains. I had never been fishing before and had no intention of doing so then, but I couldn't pass up an opportunity to go to the mountains one last time. Franz and I climbed rocks and we watched Dick fish. He was totally absorbed in throwing out his line and reeling it back in. I don't remember that he caught a fish, but that was not the point. Being quiet, at one with the river, the rocks, and the mountains was the essence of fishing. His wife sat on top of a huge rock with a book that absorbed all her attention. She looked up now and then when Dick reeled in his line, smiled, and said nothing. Apparently, she had been there many times before and was content to return to her book. I remember Barbara as a very beautiful, yet very shy woman, almost skittish, like a wounded puppy. I felt disappointed that we didn't get to know each other. She and Dick seldom came to any of the parties that we attended. They seemed like really down-to-earth people and Jim admired Dick's poetry—they were both in Roethke's workshop—and the fact that he worked in the Lockheed airplane factory.

I thought it odd that Jim admired someone who worked in a factory, because in the past he hated the idea of working in a factory like his father did for fifty years. Yet, Jim told me several times that he wished he could be an ordinary person like a carpenter or a machinist. Ironically, when he went into the Army, he scored very high in mechanics. I believe he worked as a photographer during his time in Japan.

While Dick fished, Jim sat alone against a tall pine tree writing in the notebook he carried with him wherever he went; and Franz played on the edge of the water, sometimes throwing a stone into the river. I sat nearby taking in the scene, and I said my farewells to the beautiful river and the mountains.

Journey to Minneapolis

Early in August 1957, we traveled for two days by train from Seattle to Minneapolis. For the most part, we enjoyed traveling by train. We were relaxed and enjoyed the scenery. Franz could run up and down the isles, and he liked talking to other passengers in our railroad car. At times, Jim would get irritable and sound angry because he *had* to leave Seattle, and I did not respond. I was happy and relieved to be gone from there, and I felt hopeful we could make a fresh start. I made the decision I would not work, and we discussed this together as well as the possibility of my taking night classes during the fall quarter. He seemed agreeable; after all he would be earning enough to meet our needs. I decided it best to find a place to live and get settled before we discussed the more delicate subject of another baby.

Fortunately, we found a furnished upstairs apartment on our first call, and we were invited to dinner by the neighbor who handled the rental because our landlady was out of town. She and her husband were quite cordial and offered to help us in any way we needed them. I was pleased with the friendly and welcoming reception we received by strangers. Hopefully, this was a good sign, and I looked forward to exploring the city with Franz.

Jim's feelings were mixed. Sometimes he was morose and angry about being in Minneapolis; then, his mood would change completely and he would be enthusiastic about the faculty, particularly Allen Tate, John Berryman, and Brom Weber in the English Department, and Bob Ames, Phil Siegleman and Morgan Blum in the Humanities Department who welcomed us and were very pleasant.

195

Something was missing for Jim, though. I could tell he was still pre-occupied and homesick for Seattle and the people he knew there. I suspected that he missed one person in particular, although I didn't know who she was. Once settled, Jim threw himself into teaching, writing poetry, translating Trakl's poetry, and working on completing his dissertation on Dickens.

I, on the other hand, fell in love with Minneapolis, the parks, especially the Minnihaha Parkway, the lakes, the zoo, the Mississippi River, and the sun! After five years of almost daily rain in Seattle, I was ecstatic seeing the sun again; even the winter days, though frigid, were sunny. I thought it was a perfect place for raising children and going to school. I felt "at home" here, for the first time in my life. Within a few months I decided we needed a house, and I went ahead and purchased our first house, a little cottage with a large back yard on Como Avenue, just a couple of miles from the Como Zoo in St. Paul.

I was accustomed, by then, to Jim's complete indifference to any matters that had to do with housekeeping, childcare, buying another car, and paying bills. He turned over all these details of everyday life to me along with his monthly check. I was a willing participant in this arrangement, and I accepted the responsibility willingly. Besides, I needed the stability and the regularity of a patterned life so I could do the things that were important to me.

My plan to reclaim myself was to enroll at the University of Minnesota. In September I began with night courses in English, and by spring semester, I was attending two, then later three daytime classes. I got pregnant late that fall, and for the first few months, Jim and I appeared, to all intents and purposes, a happy couple. He and Franz would meet me after class, and we would go to an ice cream parlor in "Dinky Town," as the area around the University was called, and we had ice cream or hot chocolate as the weather got colder.

ALIENATION

We explored the parks and lakes in Minneapolis on weekends, and attended faculty parties, which were very sedate affairs compared to the parties in Seattle. I was more at ease here, but I could see Jim slowly slipping away and detaching himself. He became more and more distant not only from me, but everyone. He even seemed separate from himself. As I look at our photographs from that time, I can see the growing sadness and the sense of despair in Jim's eyes, and my own uneasiness. No matter what I did, I could not ease his pain, nor mine.

Soon after we moved into our new home, I observed Jim compulsively counting his steps before he entered the house. My uneasiness soon grew into concern and fear of what was happening to him internally. He was not talking very much. The exuberant, humorous person I knew all but disappeared. He went to his classes; he came home, ate dinner, and went to his office in the basement that I had arranged for him with a desk, a chair, and bookshelves from floor to ceiling. Upstairs I could hear him tapping away on his typewriter for hours. He started drinking more than usual. He went from buying bottles of wine to gallons.

In the early months of 1958, he was awarded a $4000 Kenyon Review Grant that permitted him to take leave from teaching during the spring quarter. He worked almost continuously through the spring and summer and completed his dissertation. At that time, he was working on his second book, *Saint Judas* (1959), and he was sinking deeper into a depression and expressing suicidal thoughts whenever we were together. Several times when we were driving, he threatened to jump out of the car. I was frightened. The compulsive step counting, the depression with suicidal thoughts, and the increasing agitation and anger were relieved somewhat by his drinking, but then the rage was released. These were definite signs that his personality had been shattered by the "rejection."

I realized, but not immediately, that the rejection of the position at the university in Seattle was only one of the stressors. I was certain he had someone in Seattle with whom he was corresponding. Then, I realized that my behavior was putting stress and pressure on him: I had decided that I would not work since he was making enough money to support us. I started taking classes, I had bought the house, and I was pregnant. He was writing his dissertation and another book of poems, and in the fall, he had a teaching schedule in the English and the Humanities Departments. I urged him to see a psychiatrist at the Student Health Service. Reluctantly, he started seeing Dr. Lamb.

THE BIRTH OF MARSHALL

Into this atmosphere of turmoil and pain, our second son, Marshall, arrived on July 30, 1958. Jims' psychological boundaries were disintegrating. He was becoming more overtly angry, verbally aggressive, almost paranoid, and full of hatred that he spewed out at Minneapolis and the University. At times, he seemed to be confusing Minneapolis with the Ohio Valley, and he was struggling with the old demons about being forced to work in the mills and factories back there. In the middle of the night, in his drunken and manic state, standing in the doorway of our bedroom, he would wake me up machine-gunning me with incoherent words and phrases that were filled with violence and rage.

"Please, Jim, stop! Let me sleep. You'll wake the children." Nothing stopped him but exhaustion. Finally, he would collapse beside me and pass out. I would lie there listening to his breathing, shaking with my own despair and anger.

During the days or evenings, he would become insistent that I sit with him and listen to music, and listen to him read poetry, his own or whoever he was obsessed with at the moment. He was so absorbed in his own thoughts about poetry that nothing else was real any longer, and he seemed lost and disconnected from our children and me. I often wondered how he managed to teach the next morning when he went to his classes. Somehow, he managed to pull himself together and he met his obligations as a faculty member, but I knew this was not always the case.

In October of 1958, I drove him, with Franz and Marshall who was three months old, to Ann Arbor, Michigan, to meet an old friend, Donald Hall, with whom he had corresponded for years. They had met briefly in August and arranged this meeting when they could enjoy a weekend of football and poetry. The trip was long and difficult. Jim had never learned to drive, and I had to stop and nurse the baby every three hours. Then, quite unexpectedly, our car broke down. Jim was agitated and depressed, and Franz was quiet and absorbed in playing with his toys. Somehow, I found a used car lot and bought another car. We arrived emotionally and physically exhausted. That weekend is a blur in my memory, as is the trip that I made a few weeks later to take Jim to Robert Bly's farm in western Minnesota

BACK TO SEATTLE

The worst time for me was when he left on December 20 to return to Seattle to defend his dissertation. I could not understand why he needed to be gone for almost two weeks when the defense of his dissertation was one day, and I was going to be home alone with a newborn and Franz. I knew he had been corresponding with someone, and frankly, I felt threatened. His devotion to friends in Seattle left me eaten up with jealousy and suspicion. Our nightly conversations on the telephone usually ended in an argument. I don't remember when I felt so abandoned. I needed his help and support, and he was not available for me.

He received his Ph. D. and ten days later he returned from Seattle to a hurt and angry wife. I was not prepared for what happened next. He came home unexpectedly late at night, almost midnight. As soon as he stepped in the door, I knew he was angry. The barrage of words that came at me was loud and incoherent. All I remember were his last words, "I am leaving!" and "I want a divorce!" as he slammed the door after him. I stood there shocked, hurt, and devastated. A clear image crossed my mind: a large lead ball used for smashing buildings had just swung into my life and destroyed everything that I had built for us. I crumpled to the floor sobbing.

I never knew where he went to stay. I suspected someone was helping him, but I didn't question him when he came by a few days later to see the children and pick up some of his clothes and books. I knew I had to go on with my own plans.

James and Libby Wright
with sons Franz and Marshall

DEPRESSION COULDN'T STOP ME

Despite Jim's chaotic and often-psychotic behavior, I registered as a full-time student in the spring quarter, 1959. I was still maintaining the household and caring for the children with the help of a neighbor as babysitter, but a part of me knew the marriage was disintegrating while another part of me still clung to the possibility that Jim would get better or stay. I was afraid to face squarely the severity of Jim's mental status and my own depression. When my registration papers did not arrive a week before classes were due to start, I went to the registrar's office to inquire what was holding up my paperwork.

The man behind the counter looked at a folder with my name on it and was quiet for a few moments. I waited. Then, very gently, he said, "I didn't send your papers because your depression scores on the MMPI were off the chart. In other words, you are too depressed to do the work." (Every student enrolled in the University of Minnesota was given the Minnesota Multiphasic Personality Inventory. The founder of the Inventory was on the faculty of the Psychology Department.)

I stood there gathering my thoughts and finally, with a steady voice and a deep resolve, I said, "I know I'm depressed, but I've been depressed before and that has never stopped me from working or studying. If you will let me in, I'll show you what I can do. If I find that I cannot do the work, I'll come back and withdraw my registration. Please, let me register," I pleaded. He gave me the papers and I went to a table to fill them out. For the first time in months, I felt excited and energized. I never had to drop out. I received As and Bs in my classes, and I was even given a scholarship the next quarter.

Jim returned home shortly afterwards. He never told me where he had gone, and I didn't ask. In the midst of the chaos in our lives he was hospitalized and received electroshock treatments. Sometime in the late spring of 1959, I drove Jim, with the children, to the Bly farm for the second and the last time. I did not feel welcomed by the Blys. They were very involved with Jim and poetry, and I felt like a fifth wheel, unnecessary, and basically I was ignored. Carol Bly and I spoke for a few moments as I kept an eye on Marshall who was walking about in the tall grass in front of their farmhouse. The only comment that I remember hearing her say during our conversation was, "Why don't you divorce him?"

I couldn't believe my ears. Who was this person, whom I had just met, who knew nothing about me or my relationship to Jim, who was telling me to divorce my husband? Couldn't she see how sick he was? Was she blaming me for his illness? I was too distressed to say anything, so I took Franz and Marshall and we walked around the farm and looked at a horse in the pasture.

That night Robert laid a mattress on the floor in his office, which was a separate building from the house and a remodeled chicken coop, where the children and I were to sleep. He, Carol, and Jim continued discussing poetry long into the night. Around midnight, a thundercloud burst and rain poured into the place where we slept through the screened windows. By the time, I could pick up Franz and the baby, I was drenched; and I ran into the living room where they were still absorbed in their conversation.

I stood there shaking more with fury than cold and announced, "I am not going to sleep out there in the rain." I don't think Jim even looked up. Robert brought another mattress and laid it on the floor of the living room without a word. I never set foot on that farm again. After that weekend Jim took the train whenever he wanted to spend time with the Blys.

In addition to the classes I was taking, I started seeing Dr. Lamb at the Student Health Service. I completed the spring quarter with flying colors, but Dr. Lamb was so concerned about my depressed mood that he wanted me hospitalized. He had prescribed a couple of new medications that were on the market (Stelazine and Parnate), but they made me too drowsy and I couldn't keep up with two children. Being hospitalized was impossible, I told him. I didn't have anyone to take care of Franz and Marshall. I couldn't ask my babysitter, and I had no family in the area. I don't think I even told my friends what was happening to us.

If anyone in the English or Humanities Department noticed anything out of the ordinary, they weren't saying anything. They were probably accustomed to extraordinary people, like Ted Roethke and

John Berryman, but I thought Jim was much worse than either of them. I was very concerned that Jim's erratic and hostile behavior might antagonize the faculty, or get him fired. He was missing classes and not attending departmental meetings. I knew he was drinking more heavily than ever before, and I was afraid he was getting emotionally involved with a couple of undergraduate students.

In June (1959), Dr. Lamb recommended electroshock therapy for me on an outpatient basis. He explained that an anesthetic would be administered to reduce the intensity of the convulsions. I could rest there for an hour or so until I woke up; then I would be given lunch and afterwards could go home. I must have been very depressed because I consented to a treatment that had horrified me ten years before when I was a student nurse.

I had six treatments that summer. I can remember, after having lunch, getting into my car and driving around Minneapolis for about an hour before I recognized a familiar landscape and slowly found my way home. My memory for names and events were vague and unclear for months afterwards, but I became calmer. I have a recollection of experiencing shock waves going through my brain in my sleep and waking me up.

In July, Eugene Pugatsch came to see us. He had completed medical school and had been accepted as an intern at the University of Minnesota Hospital. That was an unfortunate time to come to visit us, but he came as often as he could and was very gentle and very supportive of Jim and me. I know he felt badly about what was happening us, and he wanted to help but there was nothing he could do. I was glad that he might be able to talk with Jim and spend some time with him.

One morning later that summer, I had an impulse to go upstairs to the attic. I can't explain what stimulated this unusual urge. I knew there was nothing up there, but I found myself walking up the stairs rather slowly and with some apprehension. Standing on the last step I looked down the empty oblong room. The wood floor was dusty, and there was a cardboard box at the end of the room under the little window. I walked toward the box and knelt down to see what was inside. The box was filled with letters addressed to Jim. I picked up the one on top of the pile and opened it. I read it. Shock waves passed through me. With trembling hands, I put the letter back in the envelope. I walked across the room, down the stairs, and by the time I was in the living room, I forgot the name of the woman who had written all those letters. I never went up to the attic again.

About this same period of time, my youngest sister who was just divorced came to Minneapolis with her son (same age as Franz) to attend the cosmetology college in Minneapolis, so we could support each other. I don't think I ever told her I was depressed or that I was having shock treatments. I don't even remember whether I told Jim. I do remember a couple of times when I completely lost my rational self. Jim was drinking and he was in one of his manic, suicidal, irrational, verbal-bombardment moods when I felt overwhelmed, swallowed up, and lost by his madness. Out of a bottomless pit of pain, I wailed, "Jim, you are suffocating me! I feel like I'm dying inside! You are sucking the life out of me! Stop! I can't bear it any longer!"

For once he heard me. He looked stunned, and he became quiet and stopped the unrelenting, savage violence that poured forth out of his mouth like burning destructive lava from an exploding volcano.

BREAK UP

He moved out of the house a second time and was demanding that I give him a divorce. He came back one more time. When he left the third time, I told him he could not come back again. In the next six months, I applied twice for a divorce, but then rescinded the applications. The second rescission came about after a conference with Jim, our two attorneys, and me. At one point, Jim's attorney was trying to persuade me about some kind of settlement for alimony by saying that I would be reimbursed fairly for "the services" I had provided for Jim while he was in graduate school.

"Services!" I screamed at him. "What do you mean by services? What do you think I was doing there? I was his wife, and I worked to help him through graduate school. I wasn't providing him with 'services!'" Then, I turned to Jim and screamed at him, "You're the one who wants this goddamned divorce! Then you go get it! I'm through trying to help you! And, I don't want a cent from you. I can take care of myself!" And I stomped out of the office with my attorney following me.

I stood outside the office shaking with rage. My attorney tried to calm me. As we walked out of the building, he asked me to consider a small amount for alimony, "If you ask for $25.00 and something happens, we can go back to court and get more. If you take nothing, it will be more difficult later. You should consider the fact that you will be a single parent with two children. If you got sick, you might need something more." As I quieted myself, I became a little more rational. I agreed to only $25.00 for alimony and $175.00 a month for child support.

My attorney tried to convince me to file for the divorce rather than Jim, because of the legal and social implications of divorce at that time. I did not fully realize that divorce was fault-based which meant that the one filing was justified and the other was considered totally responsible for the failure of the marriage. The one who filed would have witnesses to prove his position. Added to the legal fault for the divorce was the social stigma of a failed marriage.

When I refused to file again, he then suggested that I not attend the court hearing. He would be there to represent me. Years later, when I acquired a copy of the divorce papers, I realized how true the lawyer's assessment was. I was accused of everything from "cruel and inhuman conduct" to "wounding the mental feelings of the plaintiff (Jim) and destroying his peace of mind and injuring his health."

Yes, there was that one moment that my mind still wanted to reject when I lost control of myself, when I reacted to something Jim said, and I could feel myself being transformed into a wild beast. The rage in me exploded. I grabbed a steel bar that had broken off of Franz' bicycle and swung it at Jim's head. He pulled away and simultaneously put his left arm in front of his chest. I experienced the strong desire to kill him, to pound him into the ground until he disappeared, and I suddenly came to my senses and realized that I had been pounding his arm with the steel bar. I dropped the bar and ran out of the house sobbing.

Shocked at my own destructive impulse, I froze. The realization that I had the desire to kill and destroy another human being filled me with such horror that my body and mind felt paralyzed. I was numb with agony and disbelief.

Jim's second book, *St. Judas,* was published. He brought me a copy. I looked at it and read some of the poems. "What a dark book, Jim." Then I noticed the dedication. I felt as if he had slapped me in the face. I could have handled the dedication to Philip Timberlake, his teacher, but I was deeply offended by the dedication to his student, Sonjia Urseth. I did not even know her personally, but I knew the implications, "How dare you! How dare you bring this to me!" and I ripped the page out and flung the book at him. He left the house without a word.

He was teaching, giving readings, taking trips to New York and elsewhere, and working on his third book. He stayed away for longer periods of time, and he spent many weekends with the Blys. I called him at his office in the English Department when I thought it was time for him to see his sons. Sometimes I had to plead with him to come and spend time with them or to take Franz to a movie or for an ice cream cone.

After one of his trips to New York, he came by the house to tell me, "Someone I met in New York has offered to pay for me to see a psychoanalyst." He eventually mentioned the man's name; it was Hy Sobiloff. He offhandedly mentioned he had met Anne Sexton at one of the workshops that Hy Sobiloff had given. Years later, I learned about his affair with Anne Sexton when I read Diane Wood Middlebrook's biography of her, but that sordid relationship did not concern me anymore. The Jim I knew and loved died a long time ago.

My focus for the next two years was on classes, caring for my sons, and maintaining our home and my stability. I decided my major would be Nursing Education. Teaching was more gratifying and much less physically stressful than working in a hospital. Again, as in childhood, school became a safety zone, my escape, and my sanctuary. I felt accepted there, and I did what I loved most: learning. This was the culmination of a life-long dream to continue my education in college. In my classrooms the reins were off, and I was free to think, to express thoughts, feelings and ideas, and to share these with other intelligent people. I could be myself, that part of myself that was curious, adventurous, and thrilled with the exploration of and examination of ideas.

At the end of my sophomore year, my adviser, Kathleen Dunlap, called me into her office and asked me if I was interested in a public health grant that was available. It would not only pay for my tuition and books, but I would get a stipend for childcare for the two remaining years. I was surprised and, of course, very delighted with my good fortune.

The other comment that she made was even more astounding: "Have you thought about graduate school?" No, I hadn't. I could barely think of one day at a time and all that had to be done. She smiled and said, "Well, you may want to think about it."

Of course I thought about it! What else could I do? No one, since Miss Willerton, in high school, had encouraged me to think of the possibilities that were available to me. Miss Dunlap and I talked again in my junior year. "Do you really believe that I can do the work of a graduate program?" was my first question, and she responded, "I know you can." Silently, I thought, I wish I were as certain about myself.

She went on to explain, "There are two other programs beside Minnesota that have substantial graduate programs in nursing" (psychiatric nursing was becoming my strong interest). "Minnesota has a program that is developing, but I think you would do well to go to one that is more established and has demonstrated that they have a high-quality program." She knew some of the details of my marital situation that I revealed to her, and I realized she was concerned about me and was offering me an alternative to living under such stressful conditions. Mostly, I appreciated her objectivity and I trusted her perceptions about my options, because I couldn't trust mine anymore.

That day I learned that there were two graduate schools in the western part of the country to apply to: the University of Colorado and the University of California in San Francisco. Very soon afterwards, I applied to both schools. Ironically, the weather in Minnesota was an important factor in my decision to choose California. The winters of 1961 and 1962 were extremely frigid and the snow was piled high on the sidewalks until June. I was so tired of shoveling my driveway to get my car out of the garage or shoveling my car from under snow banks that I decided on the University of California.

There was another, a very significant factor that contributed to my decision to leave Minnesota and continue my education in California. I had one more person to talk with before I made my final decision. I was still very ambivalent about the divorce. I could not accept that Jim's demand for a divorce was a rational decision. How could it be rational when he was so sick? I needed to know whether he was competent to make such a serious decision that would affect not only the two of us, but also the lives of our sons.

I called the psychiatrist to whom Jim had been referred by Hy Sobiloff. Jim mentioned his name to me. Of course the psychiatrist would not see me without Jim's consent. Several weeks went by before I reached Jim, and he in turn gave the psychiatrist his consent. Finally, when I received the appointment, I realized he was not going to tell me anything about Jim's condition. In tears and despair, I pleaded with him, "I need to know whether he will get better. What if he realizes at some point that he made a mistake? I don't know whether to wait for him to recover or to get on with my life. I've applied to two graduate schools, and I'm not certain I should go so far away and take our sons away from him."

I paused and waited while he chose his words with detached deliberateness. He spoke slowly, quietly, "I think you had better get on with your life." I sat there in silence and let his words sink deep into my consciousness. He obviously had no doubts; he did not equivocate. I heard him and I understood. I nodded assent and sadly I got up, thanked him, and left his office. After that meeting, I often wondered whether Jim's first psychiatrist in Wheeling would have given me the same message. Probably, only I wasn't ready to hear what he had to say.

Even though Jim and I were separated and he was pursuing the divorce, we saw each other sporadically at our home whenever he decided or I persuaded him to come and see his sons, and when we attended faculty activities together. We tried to maintain the appearance of normality, although I'm sure the tension and distance between us was obvious to our friends and his colleagues. Jim was not funny or humorous at these affairs. His hostility spilled out inappropriately at me, or others who happened to be in the vicinity of his distress. His identity, personally and professionally as a teacher and a poet, unraveled before my eyes; and I felt as much grief and pain for him as I did for myself. The deepest wound I suffered was Jim's rejection of me and his abandonment of our sons. I could not understand his seeming lack of concern for Marshall and Franz, even if he was absorbed in his poetry and his teaching and he was mentally ill. Now, in retrospect, I can see how hard he was struggling to hold on to the remnants of his identity and his sanity.

His abandonment affected me intensely because I was aware of the psychological impact that the loss of a parent had on children. When Franz was seven, I was so concerned about the signs of depression that he was showing that I took him to a psychologist. She did not think he was clinically depressed but that he was grieving the loss of his father.

In January 1962, Jim came over to ask me to attend the baptism of Robert and Carol Bly's daughter. They asked him to be her godfather. I refused and I was outraged that he would even ask me. "You don't have time to spend with your own sons and you're going to be a godfather for Bly's daughter? Do you have any idea what that means? Besides, why should I go? They didn't want me around. They're not my friends. They're yours. I know they're blaming me for all your problems. So you go. I don't want anything to do with them!" I shouted at him. He left looking dejected and sad and my grief was unbearable.

THE LAST STRAW

Just when I thought I could not handle another trauma, another one happened; no, two more happened. These were the kind of traumas that no one talked about in the 1960s. I never told anyone, except my priest, for two decades. On a wintry evening, perhaps in February or March, I can't remember the date exactly, Jack Miller (*not his real name*) knocked on my door. I had met him once or twice before, but I did not consider him someone who was a friend who would drop in for a visit.

He obviously was drunk. He spoke in a loud voice, his words slurred, and he stumbled over the doorstep when I opened the door. He came in without an invitation from me. I remember saying, "Jim is not here. I think you better go." I didn't understand why he was there. I felt uneasy. The children were sleeping upstairs. I stood by the door and told him to leave. He lunged at me and tried to grab me, but I slipped away, and I pushed him. He stumbled again. Angry now, I said more emphatically, "I want you to leave, and I intend to tell Jim that you were here." I opened the door and stood stiffly as he walked out. Then I locked it immediately.

What is happening? I wondered. Why did he come here? I did call Jim at his office the next day and told him, "Your friend, Jack Miller, was here last night, and I want you to tell him to stay the hell away from me." Jim told me a few days later that they almost had a fist fight, but that didn't stop Jack. He came back. I don't think he was as drunk as he was the first time because I couldn't fight him off. He grabbed me and threw me on the couch. I struggled and I wanted to scream, but I was afraid of waking up my sons. He overpowered me and raped me. Then he left without a word. I was confused. I didn't know what to do or who to call. Then, the question crossed my mind: Did I do something that made him think I was interested in him? No, I knew there was nothing about him that appealed to me. The few times that I saw him, he had been drinking and I thought him loud and obnoxious. Still guilt and doubts gnawed at me. Whatever possessed him to come here and do that? I could not say the word rape. That happened to women by strangers. I did not know that rape occurred between people who knew each other. He was a friend of Jim's! How could he do this to me in my own home?

After that, whenever I saw a particular poem that Jim wrote, I wondered if Jim knew. How could he? I never told him. I had gone to my priest, but I presented it as a sexual problem that I had committed. I didn't tell anyone that I had been raped until twenty years later when I confessed to my therapist. Did Jack also blame me, as the Blys did, for Jim's problems? I wondered if he was one of Jim's friends who testified against me in court. Years later, I heard there were rumors that I was having an affair. No name was mentioned with whom, but I immediately thought Jack Miller probably spread that rumor to justify his actions. Perhaps, he testified for Jim that we had had an affair.

Ironically, Jim wrote that poem in 1962 when he was working on his third book: *The Branch will not Break*, and he dedicated that book to me in my Greek name Eleutheria. Recently, in Jim's book *Above the River*, I found, typed on a yellowed piece of paper, the following note on the dedication for *The Blessing* which he changed to *The Branch Will Not Break*:

> *For Lib*
> *...at the window in Zell am See, when her face*
> *and the evening snow lit the candles*
> *of the Three Kings who came toward us*
> *shining and singing, on the drifted roads*
> *below....*
>
> *(Next, the following line in the original Greek:)*
>
> *"I tell you this: somebody after we are*
> *dead is going to remember us."*
> *(Sappho)*

In the spring of 1962, I put our house up for sale, I repainted the kitchen, and I completed all my class assignments. I planned to take a trip to Ohio to see my family before leaving for California. I had no idea when I would return to the Midwest again. I had not told them about the impending divorce, and I felt it was necessary to explain to them why I was going to California with our sons and without Jim.

One afternoon in May, another visitor dropped by the house to see me. Larry Keller (*not his real name*) was in Minneapolis to give a reading and to see Jim. He said he also wanted to see me, to take me out to dinner, and to talk over old times.

I was surprised that he wanted to spend an evening with me. We had not been close friends. I thought of him as a classmate of Jim's and a fellow poet. When I asked about Sally (*not her real name*), he said they were divorced. For an instant, a wave of sadness passed over his eyes; then he smiled and said, "Do you know any good places to eat?" I did, but first I had to arrange a sitter for Franz and Marshall and change clothes for dinner out.

The evening was pleasant enough, but I thought we were both trying hard to be social and not get into any deep or dark subjects. Oddly, I remember he was very polite. He waited for me to order, and then he ordered the same dinner I did. I thought he lingered over coffee a little longer than was necessary. I had not been out to dinner for a long time, and I felt uneasy after a while. I wanted to get home to my sons. Finally, dinner was over, and I was driving us home. Larry had asked to sleep on the couch. He was very respectful and almost shy about his request, and I consented.

The boys were asleep when we returned to the house, and I paid the babysitter who lived nearby. We were in the kitchen and I was preparing a cup of coffee for him when suddenly he grabbed me, laid me across his lap, and started spanking me. Startled, I tried to jump up, but he held me down very tightly. "What are you doing? Please, let me up." He continued to spank me harder and harder. "This is not funny! Let me go!" I shouted, tearful and upset. "You're hurting me!" I struggled but he did not stop. He picked me up and laid me on the couch in the living room.

Again, I found myself in the same untenable situation I had been in with Jack Miller. My mind could not comprehend what was happening again, or how I got into this predicament. I was raped twice within several months, and yet I could not say those words aloud. I felt like everything that I was holding onto to maintain my self, my identity, my life, was slipping away, and I was drowning. Everything was lost. This was unreal. It could not be happening again. I was having a bad dream, a nightmare.

He let me up when he had finished, and I stumbled up the stairs to bed where I sobbed myself to sleep. I awakened early the next morning. Did I dream what happened? Did it really happen? I put on my robe and walked cautiously down the stairs. I was shocked. He was still there. He was dressed and seemed uncomfortable. He did not look at me. He mumbled, "I'm sorry. I don't know what happened."

All I said was, "Please go." I stood stiffly by the open door as he walked out. I felt shattered. There was nothing left of me. My self disintegrated. The person I was disappeared. Only an empty shell, a skeleton with a thin layer of skin holding me up was all that was left. My whole being had vanished.

Habit and discipline got me through the next couple of months. I made the trip back to the Ohio Valley with my sons. I felt like a mechanical robot... empty... lost... I was just going through the motions of being a person. We returned. Waiting for me was the final divorce decree dated July 11, 1962. James Wright divorced me. This was one of the few decisions Jim had made in our life together, and I was certain he did not make that decision alone.

On July 12, 1962, I graduated with honors from the University of Minnesota, School of Nursing with a Bachelor of Science Degree in Nursing Education. Finally, my dream of completing college had come true. For a graduation present, Jim gave me Soren Kierkegaard's *Works of Love* with the following inscription:

> For Lib, on the day of her graduation,
> with pride in her devotion to some
> things that mean far more to me
> than my own failures and that we both
> loved and clung to a long, long time ago.
> Love,
> Jim
> July 12, 1962

We two lovers who had escaped the Ohio Valley by clinging to each other, who had nurtured, then tormented each other, now found ourselves alone and bereft. I had lost my best friend, my husband, and the father of my two sons. On my graduation day, my pride was consumed with shame; my hopes were lost inside my failures. (Jim and I soon found we could not easily walk away from our

213

bond.) I learned later that he was hospitalized again, soon after our departure from Minneapolis. In September he returned to his teaching position in the English and Humanities Departments where he had taught for the previous five years.

I was accepted for the Graduate Program in Psychiatric/Mental Health Nursing at the University of California, San Francisco. Before leaving Minneapolis, I sold our home and furniture, and I kept the necessary household items that were needed to start over again.

My life was broken. I had no self to speak of. For months I was afraid to look into a mirror for fear no one was there. I was no longer anything exact. I felt dizzy, as though I had separated from my physical self.

We experienced a death—a death of our relationship—and we were forced to mourn alone. Each of us did walk away. We went in different directions. On August 5, 1962, I loaded a U-Haul trailer with toys, household necessities, our camping equipment, and supplies for the journey and hitched it to the back of our 1956 Chevrolet sedan. Early the next morning, rising from the ashes of our life, we headed west with Franz, aged 9, as my "navigator," and Marshall, 4, in the back seat playroom, surrounded by toys and books. Our new life was just beginning.

PART III

JOURNEY WESTWARD

CREATING A WHOLE NEW LIFE

From Minnesota
to California

Life lived soulfully is not without its moments of darkness and periods of foolishness. Dropping the salvation fantasy frees us up to the possibility of self-knowledge and self-acceptance, which are the foundation of soul.
(**Thomas Moore, Care of the Soul**)

My sons and I took seven days to cross the two thousand miles to California from Minnesota. I planned frequent stops for Franz and Marshall to play and swim when we came near a river or lake, and to explore the Badlands, Yellowstone National Park, and Mt. Rushmore. I allowed time for the unexpected or unknown events that were likely to occur.

We intended to do some camping along the way. We spent the first night on a beach at the edge of a river in North Dakota. As soon as I started setting up the three cots, large droplets of rain fell slowly at first; and within minutes, we were deluged by a heavy thundershower. Hurriedly, I stashed the cots in the trunk and we all jumped back into the car to prepare for sleep. The wind blew all night, and I awakened frequently from my place in the front seat of the car to check the water level. I was afraid the water would rise and flood the car.

Early the next morning, before the boys were awake, I set off on the second day of our journey. That day was uneventful, except for the evaporation of the brake fluid as we descended a hill into Wall, South Dakota. After a short rest for the car, the brake fluid re-condensed, and we went on our way.

On the third day, the car stalled on our climb into Yellowstone National Park. A stranger informed me that traveling at such high altitudes required an adjustment of the carburetor. He proceeded to open the hood of the car and made the necessary adjustments. Within minutes we were on our way to visit Old Faithful, the most famous geyser in Yellowstone. As we entered the park, we were entertained, and frightened, by the brown bears that wandered freely on the trails.

As the hours and the miles flew by, the towns we passed through began to look very similar. At times I felt as if I were driving in circles. I felt disoriented and confused. I checked the map, verified the town we were in and the highway route, and I'd reassure myself that I was in the right place. Then, I'd drive on.

I can't remember in what city or state we were in when I had to purchase a new fuel pump and a set of tires. I recall a series of steep hairpin turns coming down a mountain road before coasting into this town. That night for the first time on the trip, we slept in beds in a boarding house.

In the morning, rested and well fed at a small cafe, we picked up our car at the garage and continued our journey westward. Later that day, we visited Mount Rushmore and further on we saw the early efforts of a sculptor with ambitions of carving Crazy Horse out of a huge mountain of rock. For Marshall and Franz, the best part of the whole trip was swimming in the Great Salt Lake.

For me, the most frightening moments of the entire trip occurred on the evening of August 12, as we crossed over the Sierra Mountains from Nevada to California. The sun was setting. The shadows on the road grew darker and broader. Suddenly, I could not see anything except the white line on the edge of the road. I was momentarily blind as I passed into the darkened spaces of the road, and I could see again in the places where the sun was shining through the trees.

"Now, what shall I do?" I asked myself. The edge of the road seemed to drop down thousands of feet into the valley below that was filled with evergreen trees. Stopping on the edge of a mountain did not seem like an appropriate solution because cars were whizzing past me as if I were standing still. In the distance ahead, I saw two men standing beside their parked truck hitchhiking.

"Shall I pick them up?" I wondered. They looked like rough characters.

"Well," I answered myself, "What choice do I have? If I keep

217

driving, we might end up in the chasm below. If I pick them up, I might get raped or murdered."

"Maybe they are decent guys," whispered the ever-trusting part of me as I pulled up behind their truck and stopped. One of the men came toward me. He was tall, slim, about thirty. I asked him, "What's the problem?"

"Our truck broke down," he told me, as he glanced in the back seat, "and we're trying to get a ride into Sacramento for parts."

"I'm going to Sacramento, too," I replied, "but I'm getting sun-blind, and I'm afraid to drive any further on this mountain road. If you drive my sons and me to Sacramento, I'll let you come with us." He accepted my offer and waved to his buddy to come over. The tall one got behind the wheel, and I moved into the middle seat as the other man got in the passenger seat. I felt very vulnerable between them, and I breathed a sigh of relief when my sleeping sons woke up. I explained, "Franz and Marsh, I'm having trouble with my eyes and these nice men are driving us to Sacramento."

For the next hundred miles we chatted and got acquainted with each other. I told them I was divorced recently and heading for San Francisco. I was relieved that we were not going to be murdered and dumped over the mountains. The men were pleasant and polite, even though the driver seemed interested in more than driving us to Sacramento. I was completely depleted. Quietly and gently, I let him know I was not available.

In Sacramento, he drove us directly to a motel with a swimming pool. The boys were thrilled. As soon as we had a room, they were in their bathing suits and in the pool. The men and I had a cup of coffee together while the boys swam. We all laughed when Franz came out of the pool with green hair. Apparently, he had not washed out all the salt in his hair when he swam in Salt Lake. The combination of salt and the chlorine in the swimming pool turned his hair green.

Before the two men left us at the motel that evening to continue their journey, the driver handed me a slip of paper with his name and address written on it. He asked me to send him a postcard from San Francisco when we got settled. I promised I would. I thanked them both for helping us and I said "goodbye."

San Francisco

Windblown and exhausted, we arrived in San Francisco on August 13, 1962. Terrified by the fast traffic and the steep streets, I parked the U-Haul, with the attendant's permission, in a gas station before I proceeded slowly up a precipitous street to Parnassus Avenue where the University of California Medical Center was located. My first stop was the Housing Office to get addresses of flats and apartments. Our first shock as we got out of the car was the drop in temperature from ninety degrees in Sacramento to the forties in the windy coastal area where the University was located, which was steeped in thick fog.

I must have looked lost and forlorn because a young woman came up to me as I looked at the list of rental places that the clerk handed me and said, very gently, "Don't look for anything today. My husband and I will help you find a place tomorrow. You can stay with us tonight." I was speechless and too tired to refuse. I nodded and followed her car to her apartment.

The next morning over breakfast, her husband checked the want ads and found a very reasonably priced apartment for us, $125.00 monthly. By noon that day we had located the lovely furnished place on Douglas Street, just beneath the Twin Peaks where the sun *did* shine. I felt so grateful and fortunate that I had met the young couple. I thanked them profusely for their kindness and thoughtfulness and we said, "Goodbye."

Every day of our journey, the strangers or, as I called them, "angels" who crossed our paths, were very kind and very helpful. After thanking the couple and saying goodbye, I drove back to the gas station to pick up the U-Haul with all our belongings. I picked up a postcard and sent it to the two men who drove us from the mountains to Sacramento. I thanked them both for helping us and said "goodbye and good luck."

My sons and I spent the rest of August in San Francisco getting acquainted with grocery clerks, the gas station attendants on the corner, and some mothers who were at the playground with their children. During the first month in that beautiful hilly city, Bill, who worked in one of the nearby gas stations, replaced the brakes on my car. He very graciously advised me to ease up on my brakes. I was riding them too hard coming down the hills. He smiled and said, "You'll get used to the hills very soon." I nodded doubtfully as I drove off.

Franz, Marsh, and I explored the nearby Castro shopping area, which had a movie theater that only cost a dollar. We took streetcars down Market Street and to Chinatown, and we spent many hours in Golden Gate Park in the planetarium, the aquarium, and the museum. The boys' favorite spots were the beach (when the weather warmed up in September), the zoo, and the neighborhood park where they met other children and where I learned to play volleyball with some adults. For a few weeks before my classes started this was very entertaining, and I had an opportunity to talk and get acquainted with a few of the women in the neighborhood.

As September rapidly approached, I enrolled Franz in the fourth grade at Douglas School and Marshall started attending a preschool on Church Street. My own classes did not start until the end of September. Some of the time alone, I reflected on and reviewed the years that led me to this point in my life—alone in a strange city, a single mother with two sons, and starting life over again. "How am I ever going to make it here?" I wondered anxiously. I felt so alone and so vulnerable, but I wouldn't let myself dwell on my fears and hopelessness. I knew I would be fine as soon as I started graduate school.

I became familiar with Castro Street, which was within walking distance, and the neighborhood seemed like a small town to me. I found most of the services that I needed there: of course, there was a movie theater; and there was a bank where I opened a checking and a savings account, and a small grocery store, and a variety of other shops. The Safeway was only about a mile down Market Street where I did my weekly shopping for groceries.

In the opposite direction, a block or two toward the Twin Peaks, we discovered a Laundromat on one of our walks. Afterwards, every Wednesday evening after dinner, we spent a couple hours there. While I did the laundry, Franz did his homework and Marsh played with his toys on a table nearby. During our early weeks there, I only washed the clothes. Then, I'd drive back to our apartment and carry the basket of wet laundry up to the roof to hang them up there. I very quickly realized that clothes did not dry outside like they did in Minneapolis—where, even in the winter, clothes dried in the crisp dry winters and they came off the lines not only dry but stiff as boards—and they smelled fresh and sweet. In San Francisco the clothes were drenched from the fog and the dampness in the air. Despite my housewifely objections, I resorted to using the dryers at the Laundromat.

Although we settled in and gradually were feeling more at ease in our new home, I still felt very much alone and isolated. One sunny afternoon as I walked up Castro Street, I heard someone calling my name, "Libby, Libby…." I stopped. Surprised and pleased that someone recognized me, I smiled and turned to look behind me. I saw only a small crowd of strangers going about their own business. No one seemed to notice me and they walked around me.

"My God!" Am I going crazy?" I thought with trepidation. "I'm hearing voices!" I stood quietly for a few moments taking deep breaths to quiet myself and find a rational explanation.

Finally I realized, "No, I don't think I'm losing my mind. Probably someone shouted out to a friend, and I thought I heard my name. That's not unusual. I really must be lonely, and I do wish I knew someone to talk with…. Don't worry," I told myself. "In a couple weeks classes will be starting; then you will get to meet quite a few people." Reassured, I took another deep breath and went on my way.

FAMILY ROUTINES

Every weekday Franz, Marsh, and I had breakfast together. I

packed Franz's lunch and he would walk to the Douglas School just a few blocks from our apartment. Then, I drove Marsh to his preschool on Church Street and took him into his classroom where he was greeted warmly by the teachers and students he was getting to know. Afterward, I drove up the hill to Twin Peaks to the library and to my classes. From June through August, Parnassus Avenue and the entire area around the Medical Center were steeped in fog and clouds. The temperature was at least 20 degrees colder on the west side of the Twin Peaks than on the east side where we lived.

The weekends were spent with my sons. On Friday evenings, we usually went out for dinner at a nearby diner, the A & W, which was located just downhill from the Federal Mint Building. They served Papa Burgers, Mama Burgers, and Baby Burgers and the best root beer floats west of the Mississippi. Franz and Marsh always ordered Papa Burgers and I had a Mama Burger, and we all laughed together when our order arrived. They knew they were not "Papa" but they enjoyed pretending, and they ate all of their huge burgers. Afterwards, we went off to the Castro Theater for a movie.

On Saturday mornings we shopped for groceries together. In the afternoon, the boys went to the school playground while I cleaned the apartment; then I would meet them there. I joined a volleyball team to meet some adults in our neighborhood. I was awkward at first, never having played before, but the women were encouraging, and I learned to play hard and enjoy the physical workout. Franz and Marsh played with the children who were there in the park with their parents, or they were on the swings or sliding boards.

Frequently on Sundays, we went to the zoo where we spent hours watching a vast variety of animals, birds, monkeys, and apes. I did a lot of people watching. I was so impressed with numerous ethnic families who were there—people whose origins I could not identify from all over the Pacific and the Eastern World. I enjoyed listening to the different languages and dialects, even if I didn't understand them. I felt at home there in the midst of all those strangers for I was one of them.

We explored Golden Gate Park, attended fascinating shows of the planets and the stars at the planetarium, and we wandered around Fisherman's Wharf and China Town. The first time I went to Fisherman's Wharf, I was amazed at the size of the crabs and the many different kinds of fish buried in the ice in the stalls stretched along the crowded sidewalk for over a block. I stopped at one place and asked if they would send some crabs to Ohio. They did, and I ordered six of the largest crabs to be sent express to my father. A week later, I received a letter telling me that he was absolutely astounded at the size of those crabs. He had never seen any that large before. The ones that came in from the Atlantic were tiny in comparison. I felt so pleased that I had thought to send them and my gift had made my father happy.

In September and October the days were sunny and warm along the coast, and we went to the beach in San Francisco at the end of Geary Street on Sundays to have picnics. The boys played in the sand, built sand castles, and chased each other in the frigid waves.

Later that autumn, Jim called from Minneapolis to say, "I've been invited to give readings in San Francisco and Berkeley, and I'd like to see you and the boys."

"Do you have a place to stay?" I asked knowing the answer would be "No." Without a second thought, I said, "Let me ask my landlady if she will let you stay in the vacant apartment upstairs. A man was living there until a week ago when he moved out." I did ask her and she said, "Yes, he can stay here." When I told Franz and Marshall their Dad was coming after Christmas, they jumped up and down and were noisily very happy.

JIM VISITS

When he did arrive at our door late in December, I was startled by his appearance. He was much thinner than I remembered him being, and he was aloof and distant, almost stiff, when he greeted me. He did have a smile and a warm hug for his sons, thankfully. They were overjoyed to see him, and they clung to him, all three talking at once. I have very vague recollections of those two or three days he was there. I was surprised to realize that I still had some very strong feelings for him and wanted to get close to him, but he maintained his boundaries very well, and I felt shut out again. He obviously was better prepared for our meeting than I was.

I dressed Franz and Marsh in their Sunday best suits and took them to their father's readings. I was aware that I was on the outside of the circle of his admirers where he stood smiling and talking and holding his sons close to him. That was the first time the reality of being the ex-wife hit me. I stood there taking in the scene and thinking, "*I am* the ex-wife," and took a deep breath to calm myself. "I still have a lot of work to do. I have to let go of this love I still feel for him, and the grief. I hope Dr. Gould can help me to heal these wounds," I thought to myself. The pain inside me was excruciating.

When their father left the next day, Franz and Marsh suffered the pain of loss again. They cried together. I joined them putting my arms around them, and I cried softly with them. I knew I had to hold myself together and comfort them. As their crying subsided gradually, I reassured them that we would make it. "We've done very well since we got here. We will be OK again. I promise."

During the next few months, Franz would come home from school and sit alone in the living room while I fixed dinner. By spring, Franz was coming out of grief and depression slowly. Marsh was his usual chatty self playing with his toys and watching TV. In spite of his grief, Franz did well in school. At dinner we each talked about our experiences at school. Marsh talked happily about his activities at preschool. He thought it was very funny that his Mom was going to school. Franz would join us sometimes, or he and Marsh would tease each other.

FRANZ FINDS A FRIEND

In the spring, Franz brought home a friend from school who was older than he; I guessed about two years or so. Afterwards, he shared his thoughts with me, "You know, Mom, I like it here. I have a friend now. I'm good in my studies and I like sports, too. I did real well in the tryouts for baseball." I agreed that those were very fine accomplishments, and I gave him a hug. The pain in my heart eased a notch or two.

Marshall did very well in preschool where his teachers guided him very closely in his activities with the other children. He even developed an ability to lead his classmates through the games they played out of doors. However, the following year in kindergarten, he started showing signs of hyperactivity and distractibility. He seemed unable to stay seated, follow his teacher's directions, or to color within the lines. His teacher was on the verge of suspending him, but I persuaded her to keep him in her class. I was unable to stay home from my own classes for a week or two, and I could not see how effective that would be for Marsh. She kept him in the class for the rest of the year without any serious mishaps.

In the first grade, Marsh had his eyes examined and was found to have astigmatism that required him to be fitted for glasses. That spring Marsh lost three pairs of glasses. Soon afterward he lost his bicycle and his jacket. I was concerned about his distractibility and his inability to hold on to his belongings, but nothing more drastic happened with Marsh in the next couple of years of elementary school. His grades were very good and he played well with the other children in his class. As for me, I was constantly concerned about their growing up without their father being more available to them, and with no other men in their lives. Most of the teachers were women.

At other times I would think, "I had a father and he caused me more fear and pain than any of my friends had to deal with. And, how much fathering was Jim able to do? Not much for Marsh, although he was very close and loving with Franz during his first five years. I don't know how much difference it makes whether a child has a father or not. All I know is Franz is having a hard time, and Marsh has had very little connection with his father. I guess I'll have to wait and see what happens."

WORRIES AS A SINGLE PARENT

Reflecting back to those years as a single parent, I know I was very worried about my sons and the impact the divorce had on them. I was hurt, depressed, and seeing a psychiatrist, and I was concerned that I might not be as attentive to them as they needed. I provided as much stability as possible in their lives, and we had some very happy times together. In fact, Franz told me later those were some of the best times for him. He had a bicycle and went all over the neighborhood, and even downtown on his own. He enjoyed exploring the area alone or spending time with one friend only. I remember suggesting to him that he try to make more than one friend, but he seemed content with one friend at a time.

As time passed I became very concerned about the older boy with whom Franz had developed a friendship. His name was Gary, and he was a tall lanky boy who had a very rough unkempt appearance and who struck me as very needy. His father was a single working parent, and Gary was on his own frequently. He got in trouble with the police, and this frightened me. I did not want Franz being associated with an anti-social boy. He was very vague about the problems Gary was having, and I asked him to stay away from him and to make another friend closer to his own age. Years later, Franz told me that Gary ended up in prison for a very serious crime.

Marsh was a cheerful, seemingly happy little boy who was very energetic and easily distracted. He started one activity and in the middle of some game or other, he would go off to do something else. His preschool teachers were aware of these tendencies and monitored him very closely and helped him to stay focused on whatever he started. However, in kindergarten, his teacher had more children to attend to and she could not give him the individual attention he required.

At six he began the pattern of losing his belongings, particularly in the springtime. In the fall and winter he did very well in school. He was a very bright enthusiastic student. His pattern of distractibility (he would talk when the teacher was presenting the class material, and get up and walk around the room or look out the window) and losing his belongings continued throughout his childhood, adolescence, and adulthood. None of his teachers and the several counselors to whom I took Marsh to be assessed were able to tell me what caused this behavior, (but deep down in my heart, I worried the problems were caused because he did not have a father and/or I was an inadequate mother). Later, when Marshall was seventeen, we learned about manic-depressive illness and attention deficit disorders. By then, and with much therapy, I had let go of my "mother guilt" and was better prepared to cope with Marshall's problems.

Sanctuary

GROWING A NEW SELF

I was born with a love for learning. I wanted nothing more than to be a perpetual student my entire life. I loved most of my teachers because they opened the doors and windows of my mind to different worlds and different kinds of relationships than those I had known in my family and culture. No matter how badly I felt at home, in school I was safe, and I felt understood and accepted. As an adult, whenever I was confronted with a crisis or a major transition, I went to school or I took a workshop where I could think and sort out what was happening in my life.

In late September 1962, there I was back in school again. This time I was in the Graduate School of Nursing. On the first day, I walked toward the registration table for new students and Molly Goldberg greeted me. She was a large, buxom woman with a wonderful welcoming smile, and she introduced herself as one of the faculty members in the Psychiatric/Mental Health Nursing Department. As soon as I looked at her smiling face, I knew I was home again.

I was very much aware that I had unfinished business of my own mental health that needed care. I felt fragile and in much grief over the loss of my marriage, and I needed to heal this loss. In early October, while undergoing the required medical examination, I requested a referral to a psychiatrist. The resident performing the physical was surprised by my request. "You don't look like you need a psychiatrist," was his naïve response. "I know," I replied, "I never do, but please don't make me prove to you that I do. I'd hate to spill my guts all over your nice clean floor." The metaphor worked. I was referred to Dr. Miriam Gould, and within a week she agreed to see me. In our first appointment she arranged my therapy: once a week in the Student Health Service and once a week on a private basis at $25.00 a session.

I was so relieved that I found someone to talk with so readily. I remember Dr. Gould as a dark-haired middle-aged woman with a tendency to bite her nails. "I do, too," I thought to myself. "At least, she doesn't chain smoke as my therapist in Seattle did." She was attentive and sharp. I liked that. "She won't let me off the hook very easily," I observed. I was pleased to start rebuilding my new life, and I didn't want to waste any time.

Dr. Gould and I met twice a week and I poured out my pain and grief in each session. As a Freudian psychotherapist, she did not say very much in our sessions, and I assumed she wanted me to do all the talking and bring up whatever emotions were inside me. One morning she surprised me when she asked, "What do you think about after you leave here?"

"…think about? I don't know that I do much thinking. I feel so very relieved when I leave here, like a big load has been lifted off my shoulders." She did not respond verbally, but she looked at me sternly—at least that was my perception. For a moment, I felt like I had disappointed her so I did start thinking about what was happening in our therapy sessions. I was rather relieved that she wanted me to think and that she wanted me to tell her my thoughts as well as my feelings. I had assumed she only wanted to hear my feelings. In the next few sessions I talked more about my classes and how I was doing in them.

At one point after the first semester ended, I think she was surprised that although I cried very easily, my grades were all "A's." I wondered whether she believed I might not make it in graduate school because I was so depressed. I was so excited that I had made it! I had my own doubts about my abilities to function, but I realized I had never failed in school at any time, no matter how depressed I was. I just would not allow that to happen. And that's what I talked about that day—my devotion to learning.

As I now describe the beginning of my therapy with Dr. Gould, I realize that I was transferring feelings that I had toward my father to her. I could not talk to my father without crying, and I was so completely frozen in my relationship with him that I could not express any thoughts, wants, or needs directly to him. My mother would talk to him for me. I was more aware of my negative transference feelings toward male doctors and rigid nurse supervisors, but I felt trust for Dr. Gould from the beginning and I was relieved to have her as my therapist. Still I felt very vulnerable and completely defenseless, and it's understandable to me now that I would perceive her as a "stern" authority figure even though she was very attentive and accepting.

On Becoming a Clinical Nurse-Specialist

The first time that the entire class of one hundred nurses met with the Dean of the School of Nursing, we were confronted with a challenging piece of information: "We are preparing you for jobs that do not exist—yet. You will have to go out there and make your own jobs." *[The School provided advanced training for medical, public health, and psychiatric—adult and child—nursing.]* "You will have to go out in the medical world and demonstrate that you can function competently as clinical nurse specialists and psychotherapists."

At that time, I was not concerned about jobs or the future. I was focused completely on learning, growing, and healing. That was more than enough for me. I soon realized that I was the only single parent in that entire group of nurses, and I had the added responsibility of raising and providing for all the needs of two young boys. Fortunately, the stipend I received from the National Institute of Mental Health was supplemented by the monthly check from Jim, and the five hundred dollars was sufficient for our needs. I even saved fifty dollars a month for our emergency fund or for a vacation.

As a graduate student in "psych" I learned about psychiatric nursing and doing psychotherapy with severely disturbed hospitalized patients; that was very challenging and exciting at the same time. I had learned to talk with patients who were unreachable when

I was a student nurse before the advent of psychotropic medications. The more difficult part of the training in graduate school was working closely with psychiatrists. I felt ill at ease and awkward at first, but I soon realized these men were there to teach doctors and nurses alike, and they were understanding and kind. Fortunately, because of the work I was doing in my therapy, I was able to make progress in this area of dealing with authority figures during the first year. Eventually, I learned to work closely and collaboratively not only with psychiatrists but other professionals as well—social workers, psychologists, and other allied professionals on mental health teams.

ALTERNATE LEARNING METHODS

In the classroom we learned about the theoretical foundations of establishing a relationship with a patient, and on the psychiatric ward we selected the patient with whom we worked as long as he or she was hospitalized, sometimes for weeks or months. We learned different theories of working with patients: psychodynamics, communication, interpersonal relationships, and group dynamics. We had clinical supervisions three times a week where we reviewed our interactions with our patient.

Janet Bell was my supervisor. She was so gentle and kind that all my pain that I had neatly tucked away in a compartment in my mind would spill out through my tear glands. I think I cried in every session we had together for an entire year, and neither of us allowed the pain to interfere with our work.

I soon realized that my learning style was backwards; that is, I learned intuitively and "with my gut" first. Then I would go to the library to find the principles and theories that explained the work I was doing. Janet was very patient with me, "Yes, your intuition serves you very well in this work, but if you want to use your skills with other patients, you will need to substantiate your interventions with theory." That year under her caring tutoring and objective demeanor I learned to think and problem solve more deliberately with patients and faculty, and my boundaries grew firmer with the trust and acceptance that I experienced in all phases of my learning experiences.

The other important people in my first year as a graduate student were the faculty who taught, guided, and encouraged us through the struggles of learning to observe and interact with patients and becoming more aware of our own behavior, feelings, and thoughts.

In addition to seminars, studying, supervision, writing and presenting papers, we had weekly small group sessions in sociodrama facilitated by Betty Furuta. This format was an adaptation of psychodrama, a psychiatric treatment used with patients as a therapeutic way of enacting their emotions and problems. In this class we reenacted and corrected our interactions with patients. We would start by discussing any difficult interactions that we had had with our patients that week. Then one of us would volunteer to role-play the patient, and the nurse might play herself or someone else would role-play the nurse. This way each of us had an opportunity to play a part and experience the feelings of the patient as well as the nurse. This method was extremely helpful in the development of our own awareness of how our behavior affected others and how each of us was affected by others, whether patients, nurses, or teachers.

Once a week we had sensitivity training facilitated by one of the faculty with a group of fellow students. Molly Goldberg led our group, and together we examined our personal interactions and how we evolved, individually and collectively, with a group of strangers. We learned how we dealt with authority figures and how we developed close relationships with peers and faculty.

All of this experiential learning in addition to my own therapy twice a week made me feel as if I was being turned inside out and examined under a microscope. Sometimes, I felt as though I were dying with grief and pain, and at other times the self-examinations were exhilarating as I overcame my fears, guilt, and grief. As my self-esteem and confidence grew, I was transformed from the fragile depressed woman that I was into one who was giving birth to her new Self! I was feeling more secure and stronger as my wounds healed. The emotions of happiness, empathy, and compassion were stirring inside me as my growing Self evolved. I developed firmer, clearer psychological boundaries. I learned to think and to problem-solve. In my supervisory sessions and the classroom, I learned to substantiate my interventions with clinical and theoretical principles as well as utilizing my well-developed intuitive skills.

During the summer I was required to take a six-week course in Public Health, which I had not had in my basic training. I had a list of families with multiple health issues whom I visited once or twice and assessed any needs or problems. Many of the families that I visited reminded me of my own neighbors back in Ohio who had modest homes that were kept orderly and clean. I don't remember any great problems with the people I visited. Everyone seemed very cordial and grateful to have a nurse visit and ascertain that they were managing their problems well.

The others who were involved in my development as a novice psychotherapist were the four classmates with whom I became fast friends: Selma, Pat, Miriam, and Louise. We spent the time between classes in the cafeteria, laughing at our mistakes and learning together. Selma and Miriam had a tremendous sense of humor, and we supported each other through whatever difficulties arose for each of us. I was good with process notes, which Miriam did not understand. I helped her with clinical processing notes after interviewing a patient, and she helped me to understand statistics, which were easy for her. We became very close and mentored each other.

SECOND YEAR RESIDENCY

On August 31, 1963, I received my Master of Science Degree, and another huge boost in my self-esteem and self-confidence. I received a second grant from NIMH (National Institute of Mental Health) for residency training in psychiatric nursing for the next school year. That fall semester, I pursued my goal of learning family dynamics and family therapy. Betty Furuta agreed to act as my supervisor. As usual she was direct and honest about the work we would do together. She said in our first interview, "I do not know anything about family dynamics, but I do know individual and group dynamics, and we'll work on this project together."

The next hurdle was convincing the psychiatrist who was the Director of the Inpatient units at one of the local hospitals that I was competent to work psychotherapeutically with an entire family. Fortunately, I had had the public health training that summer, and I told him I felt confident that I could handle family situations. After all, nurses had been making home visits for a hundred years. He was still not convinced because he asked me, "Do you think you might have some kind of 'Peeping-Tom Complex' that makes you want to see people in their homes?"

I was taken aback by his question. I couldn't believe such a presumption about my character, but I answered him directly and calmly, "I do not believe I do. I have been reading the literature in Family Dynamics, and I believe this will be a very important movement in psychiatry in the next few years. I have Mrs. Furuta as my supervisor, and I'm sure she will keep a sharp eye on my work, and I am in therapy twice a week."

Although he still may have been skeptical, he gave me permission to select a patient on the ward with the assistance of the ward psychiatrist. The psychiatrist on the unit, Dr. Carlson, to whom I had been assigned as my clinical supervisor, was kind and very accommodating. When he learned that I spoke Greek, he selected a Greek middle-aged woman who had been diagnosed schizophrenic as the patient with whom I would be working. He was sending her home for a couple of months to see how she managed. Her husband and two adult children did not seem to understand how to cope with her, so he wanted me to see her at home and evaluate her adjustment.

Dr. Carlson introduced the patient, Mary Vasilis (*not her real name*), to me and we talked together for a short period of time. I told her I was going to come to her home after she left the hospital, and we would talk together about whatever concerned her. She gave me her address and telephone number, and I arranged to go and see her following Monday.

I arrived at her home promptly at 11:00 a.m. and she seemed pleased to see me. She was home alone. Her husband had decided to go to his work rather than stay and meet me. She said he did not understand her problems, and he just wanted her to get better. Her home was nicely decorated and very neat and clean. She was doing some chore or other whenever I came to see her, and she was troubled by voices in her head. The medications that were prescribed for her did not help in controlling the auditory hallucinations.

Late in November as I drove to her home, I heard the dreadful news of President Kennedy's assassination. I was so shocked I could not believe what I was hearing. When I got to Mary's home, I was still shaken. She was not aware of what had happened, and she seemed more distant and withdrawn that morning. She was not interested in discussing anything, and she stood at the sink cleaning some spinach that she was planning to cook.

That afternoon I reported the worsening of her condition to Dr. Carlson, and he told me that her husband had called to complain that she was not getting better. He decided she had to be taken to the state hospital in Napa for long-term care. I was sad for her, but I had learned that many patients did not get better, especially if they did not have their family's support. The medications we had at that time did not work on relieving the psychotic symptoms; mainly, they kept the patients tranquilized.

My next patient was Bill, a carpenter, who was diagnosed Paranoid Schizophrenic. When I asked whether he would be interested in working with me, he was very enthusiastic. I told him I would visit him in the hospital once a week to talk about his concerns and that I would like to work with his family as well. "Do you think they would be interested?"

He couldn't believe that I was willing to make a home visit to talk with his wife and three teenage daughters. "Do you really mean it? You would go to our home? We've had so many problems lately. They don't understand what I am going through." I agreed to talk with him and his wife when she came to visit him. She, too, was so pleased that someone wanted to help them all to deal with her husband's problems.

I arranged to go to their home every Wednesday evening at 7:00 p.m., and I would continue to see them and Bill until he was released from the hospital. When they could no longer afford the private hospital, Bill was transferred to Napa State Hospital (about forty miles from San Francisco), and I drove there every week to see him.

Our goal for the family was for them to learn how to talk with each other about their concerns and problems without a lot of arguments, and to learn how to listen and accept each one's perspective on different issues.

The following summer when Bill was discharged from the state hospital, I worked with the entire family to accept the changes that had taken place in all of them. As the family was reunited and reconciled with each other, my last task was to help them to let go of their dependence on me. I was deeply touched by the work they did to understand each other and to express their feelings to each other with more understanding and compassion. I felt I had learned as much from the process of family therapy as they had learned from me. I wrote a clinical paper based on my work with Bill and his family for my Psychiatric Nursing Class. Later, this paper was published in 1966, and I called it, *A Therapeutic Relationship with a Patient and Family.*

CAREER TEACHER

In my third year of graduate school, the faculty had arranged to hire a social worker, Ben Handleman, to teach the faculty Family Dynamics and Family Therapy. He had been trained by Virginia Satir, one of the founders of Family Therapy, at the Mental Research Institute in Palo Alto, California. I was invited to participate in the class. By that time, I was becoming a competent clinician and so adept at theorizing and applying principles of intervention that I was recommended for, and received, a Career Teacher Grant from NIMH to develop and practice advanced teaching skills, in addition to my clinical work. I was thrilled that my goal to learn, practice, and teach Family Therapy, along with individual and group therapy, was being realized.

For the next two years after that, I was hired as an instructor in the Undergraduate Nursing Program where I lectured on psychiatric disorders, supervised nursing students in their clinical experiences on a psychiatric unit, and facilitated one or two groups of nursing students in group dynamics. In 1967, I became the first instructor in the Graduate Psychiatric/Mental Health Program to teach Family Therapy with Ben Handelman. This was a perfect way for me to continue learning through teaching family dynamics and family therapy, along with supervising graduate students with individual patients and families.

LIFE OUTSIDE OF ACADEMIA

With time and much care, I began to feel healed and whole. The emotions of life were stirring inside me. As my new Self grew, I left the dark cave of death and failure behind and emerged into a meadow filled with the sunshine of success and fulfillment. Slowly, I came back to life, and for the first time in many years, I looked forward to the future with hope.

I had one more personal task to perform in bringing closure to my old life. One Saturday morning in the spring of 1964, I packed a picnic lunch for my sons and me. I took the gold wedding band out of the dresser drawer where it had lain for three years, and I drove us to the beach. While the boys played in the sand and chased the frigid waves, I walked out on an old wooden pier and stood there for a few moments in silent prayer. Then, I said goodbye to a marriage that had died more than seven years ago. I closed my eyes and flung the ring as far as I could into the forgiving waters. The pain was gone. The will to live was greater than the wish to die. At long last, the energy of life was flowing through my body. I felt the joy of living again.

INTEGRATING MY LOST SELF

The final requirement of the Career Teacher Grant was to attend a two-week residential, basic-encounter group at Lake Arrowhead in the mountains of Southern California. The group leaders were clinical psychologists who had trained with Carl Rogers. Our leader was Dr. Gerald Haigh, and there were eleven women and three men in our group. By the end of the first week following a twelve-hour marathon session, I felt lost, disconnected from myself, and frightened. When I returned to the group for the feedback session at midnight, I was crying and trembling.

"I feel so drained. I feel like I've been on a long journey. I don't know where, and I'm looking for someone to run to… I feel like I'm trying to reconnect with my self. " I spoke in a low, almost inaudible voice interspersed with tears, sighs, and long pauses.

The group gathered closely around me; and Gerald, speaking in a soft kind voice, asked me, "Who are the different people? Who are the different parts of you?"

For the next hour, with the gentle support of the group and Gerald at my side, I searched the dark corners of my psyche to find my mothering Self. I needed to reconnect with my mother and to learn from her how to mother my two sons. This was one of my most severe crises, yet the experience was a significant growth experience for me, and a peak experience for the group. Slowly and tenderly I reconnected with my mother through my memories of her and through my identifying with the women in the group who reminded me of my mother.

As Gerald explained the process to us later, "You offered your pain to the group, and the group reciprocated and offered its healing attention back to you. This enabled you to integrate previously repressed memories with your present identity as a mother and a woman." The group's authentic interactions allowed me to work through my previously unexpressed grief experiences over the loss of my mother, and I was able to assimilate "mother image fragments" into my own identity. This was a most painful yet one of the most fulfilling group experiences of my life. During a period of solitude in the woods, near the end of the second week of the group process, I wrote the following poem:

Thought Fragments

I am
Alone with myself
In the underbrush of my life
Surrounded by the raging
Stillness of the trees.
The sun creeps through
The treetops in the distance.

Pain and joy
Rise to meet the sun.
I think of what has transpired.

2.
I reached for the stars
In the exuberance of my youth.
The stars stretched forth and
Lifted me into the warm brilliance
Of their light.
Gently they sent me back again.
My search for that moment
Has ended here
Where I have crawled through
The depths and caverns of my soul.

3.
I am dark still earth
Soaking the rain of your touch.
Dry leaf curled in yourself.
The blood of life gone from your veins
I feel close to you.

4.
I am the sea spray and the wind
Howling in my ears.
I become the rainbow in the depths
Of the gray green sea.
I am cold in the warmth of your
touch.
I am warm in the chill wind of
Your breath

5.
I am lost.
I stand on the abyss of separation.

Ghost of forgotten memories
Rise to enfold me in their sweet
Bitterness.
I return to the unknown and
Familiar world of noise and bluster.
I am afraid and glad.

Afterthought
The underbrush is not all darkness
and cold.
There is lightness and warmth,
Delicate weeds and soft bird feathers.
Excruciating joy
Of being
I am.

Dr. Haigh published this poem along with excerpts from the midnight session in a book, *Ways of Growth: Approaches to Expanding Awareness.* The title of the article that he wrote was *"The Residential Basic Encounter Group."*

The next poem was written several years later in another group experience when I was a group leader in a weeklong encounter group for nurses.

A Gift to the Sea

In my search for tenderness and love
I uncovered a treasure chest of pain.
I re-experienced the agony
Of bitterness and hate.
Then gently sealed the cover tight.

This morning with chest in hand
I wandered toward the sea.
On my way,

I stopped to watch a squirrel eating.
A twig swung leisurely in the wind
And a thin fine thread of a spider's web
Weaved gently in the sun.

I continued my slow thoughtful
Journey to the sea
And when I stood there with the great
Waves rolling at my feet
I shouted to the sea:
"Here, I have a gift for you
And I want you to take it with you
To do as you will."

A wave with long outstretched
Fingers reached joyfully for my gift
And I watched her toss it for fun
To the wind and the sun.

With empty hands I turned away
Relieved of my treasured burden
I was free once again!

Spring in
San Francisco, 1964

HAIRCUT

That April day was sunny and warm; the sky was clear and blue, not shrouded in the fog as it usually was. I felt light and happy and wanted to run and skip around the block like I used to do on my way to school when I was a child in Martins Ferry, Ohio.

"You're not a child anymore. You're a woman, and next month you're turning thirty-six," scolded the parental voice in my head.

"I know how old I am, and I feel better than I have in years. Why can't I be happy?" my adolescent voice retorted. "I've earned a little joy in my life. I'm almost through with my second year in graduate school, and I've worked very hard for two years! I'm becoming a good therapist, and I feel wonderfully alive for a change. I'm coming out of that dreadful depression, thanks to Dr. Gould, and I want to celebrate. I'm going to get my hair cut!"

Yes, I was thirty-six, but I felt like sixteen for the first time. When I was sixteen years ago, I was in a deep depression from which I didn't emerge until I was in my twenties. Now, I was going to start living again. Only this time I wanted to do it right. I was on my way to the beauty shop near the Haight-Ashbury. I was going to clip off my long, thick black hair. For a change, I wanted short hair.

To be truthful, I was a little nervous. I hadn't had a haircut for over fifteen years, but here I was sitting in a chair, and my hair was lying limp on the floor. I almost cried. The hairdresser was a thin, young, blond woman who styled my hair in a beautiful pageboy. She combed and patted my hair admiring her handy work, and I smiled and nodded when she said, "That style looks so good on you!"

My hands were shaking as I paid my bill. I almost ran out of there because my heart was pounding so hard. I could hardly breathe. "I think I'm having an anxiety attack," I said to myself as I walked fast toward my car, got in, and started the motor. I sat there for a few minutes and breathed deeply to calm myself. "What is this all about? I just got my hair cut, and I'm feeling panicked!" I questioned myself.

Slowly, as I calmed down, I could think again. Was it just the haircut? What else could my reaction be about? "Well, what do you think it's about?" my alter ego whispered in a mischievous tone. "All those feelings stirring you up inside, and there's your sudden interest in the males around the campus. I saw you looking at them," and she laughed.

Yes, it's true. In the last month or so, I felt as if I had just wakened from a long sleep. One day I noticed all the young men in the library and all around the campus. They looked so young! Were they really old enough to be in medical school? I felt so much older, even if I was feeling like a teenager. I was surprised when I heard myself say that word. I had never used that word, "teenager" before, at least, not in relation to myself.

I associated the word teenager with dating. I remembered the kids in high school as they paired off in the junior and senior years, always together, even hugging and kissing each other in the hallway between classes. I avoided looking at them. I think I was slightly embarrassed even though they felt free enough to do that in the open in front of teachers, classmates, and God! Such behavior was forbidden for me. I was even scolded when a Greek neighbor saw me walking down the street with a male classmate.

And here I am daydreaming about dating. I suddenly realized I've never dated! Jim and I never considered ourselves to be on a date. We met somewhere to drink coffee and talked for hours. Even when we were seriously involved, it wasn't dating. "Well," said that impish little voice in my head, "isn't it about time you started thinking about it?"

"I suppose so." I never said this, not even to myself before,

"But.... I don't know how to go about getting a date." After thinking about my dilemma for a few minutes, I had an idea. "I know what I'll do! I'll ask Selma. She's a good friend and she knows San Francisco. She's lived here for years. She will know what single women do for dates!" Suddenly, I felt excited and thrilled with the possibility of a male friend to go out.... on a date! Or just go out to dinner. It was such a long time since I'd talked with a man my age.

I saw Selma the next day in the coffee shop. She was reading and drinking coffee. I sat down across from her and opened my own book. She looked up and smiled. "Hi! How are you today? Are you OK? You look different. Oh, my gosh! You cut your beautiful long hair! What in the world made you do that?" She stared at me with her mouth open as if she wanted to cry.

"I know. I felt the same way yesterday. I'm getting used to it and I think I like it. I know this will sound silly, but I've been wondering about something." I hesitated searching for words. "Well, where do women go in this town when they want to meet men.... or one man, rather?" I think I blushed. I felt warm and uncomfortable.

"Well," said Selma with a smile. "You mean you're getting interested in men. I can hardly believe it. I thought you were immune to men. You hardly notice them."

"Well!" I repeated. "They're so young around here. I have no idea where to go to meet someone my own age. I certainly don't want to go to a bar."

"There are places where singles go to dance; it's a nice place downtown. I'll look it up for you, and there are dating services advertised in the Sunday paper, in the section where the movies are listed."

"Thanks, Selma." I said, "I appreciate your help. I'll check the paper on Sunday. I'll let you know what I think next week. I better run. My Sociology Class will be starting soon. See you!" We both smiled as I headed toward the classroom.

IN SEARCH OF. . .

Many times that spring I shook my head and wondered, "What am I doing?" I felt silly, light-headed, and constantly scanning the environment. I was much more aware of men wherever I went than I had ever been before. "I think I've been a single mother too long, and I'm feeling like a silly adolescent."

I was surprised that I actually could feel like an adolescent at the age of thirty-six. With all the turmoil that was going on in my life and in the world back in the 1940s, I believe I skipped my adolescence. I remember reading a newspaper article about a research study that was done in France with young adults. The study found that these young people had postponed their adolescence, but when the war over, they were going wild trying to catch up with what they had missed. Well, there I was in San Francisco twenty years later, in my second year of graduate school, raising two sons alone, and emotionally I, too, was experiencing myself out of control, free, and happier than I had been in years. What was happening to me? I was searching for something or someone, but who? Finally, the realization dawned on me that I was behaving like my schoolmates in high school and having fantasies of an imaginary mate!

Suddenly, being a single parent scared me and seemed like a bigger task than I had realized. Would I be able to handle two sons alone, as Franz rapidly approached adolescence, and Marshall needed more than I could give him? I could not be mother and father at the same time. I worried that they did not have a father figure in their lives.

After school ended for the year, I thought they should see their dad again. I made arrangements to send them to St. Paul. When Jim was refused tenure at the University of Minnesota in 1964, he was hired at Macalester College. This was my sons' first trip without me. The airlines provided care by the airline hostesses. Upon their return, Franz told me his father was not very well. He was frightened at times when his father was talking to people who were not there and he was drinking heavily. I regretted my decision, and I never sent them again until after Jim's remarriage several years later.

One evening an insurance salesman had arranged an appointment to come to my flat to discuss a life insurance policy with me. I was aware of a part of me observing my behavior and giving me a blow-by-blow description of what I was doing, "Look," I said to my alter ego, "I can't help this. It's hard enough, and I don't need you making it harder for me, so be quiet." As I listened to his spiel about my need for life insurance, I realized I was looking him over and making frequent eye contact.

He was tall, about six feet tall, slim, good-looking, and spoke with a thick German accent. He was talking about insurance, and I was looking into blue eyes and noticing that he had blond hair, and he was about my age or a few years older. I don't think I bought any insurance that evening. I learned his name was Helmut and he *was* German and had been in this country for about ten years. Later, I learned he had served in the German Navy in the U-Boat Division during the war. I couldn't believe that I would allow an ex- Nazi into my home. They had destroyed many of our ships in the battles of the North Atlantic, and there I was getting acquainted with a man who represented a government that I had hated.

Of course, he claimed he was not a Nazi, but a seventeen-year-old young man who was inducted into the Navy and required to serve his country. We had very animated discussions about the war; and as we got to know each other, a warm, friendly relationship developed. I knew I would never marry him, but he was a good conversationalist for a while. As it turned out, he told me that he had a girlfriend in Germany. She bore his son, who was twelve years old, and she was raising him alone.

As a result of our talks (and I must have spoken about my divorce and about being a single mother), he decided to go back to Germany to renew his relationship with the mother of his son. She was waiting for him to decide to marry her. She expected to come to San Francisco and live with him and their son. He had purchased a house in the Sunset District and it was ready and waiting for his family.

Our relationship ended with a warm handshake. I wished him and his family a happy life together. About a year later I saw him in downtown San Francisco with a young blond boy who looked just like him. If Helmut recognized me, he gave no sign. We passed each other without speaking, and I smiled to myself. My first date ended happily for him.

That summer and fall I continued my search. I attended some

meetings of a group called Parents Without Partners and went to a Singles Club. Neither was comfortable for me. Since I was not accustomed to going out alone (and I had no idea how to go about getting a date), I'd find a table where other women were sitting and introduce myself.

They were as nervous as I was, so we developed a little camaraderie among ourselves. When one of us was asked to dance, those at the table cheered her on with smiles and nods. I felt so self-conscious, and I tried very hard not to show it. We were being examined by the men who stood off by themselves or nonchalantly walked by eyeing each one of us slowly.

While we sat there being appraised, an image came to me. I saw a large auction block with men bidding, but instead of bidding for cattle or horses, they were bidding for women – for us. Only here it was a silent auction. A memory was triggered off at one of the dances. This arrangement of men looking over the women reminded me of the discomfort I felt when I was a young girl and I walked past the coffee house and the bowling alley on Hanover Street back home. Those were the places where men gathered to watch the girls pass by. What a terrible ordeal that was for me and for us women at that time!

I thought the men had a much better deal. They could choose anyone who appealed to them, and we sat there and waited to be chosen. How demeaning and outrageous this dating game was! For the first time in my life, I had a momentary appreciation for the arranged marriages that my father had attempted for me. In that situation, I was in control and I didn't even know it!

I did get asked to dance, so I felt encouraged enough to go again. My observing alter ego let me know that I was attracting men from other countries. One was Chinese; another man was from Japan, and one from Italy. There was no question that they wanted more than dancing, and I was not ready to go that far with someone I hardly knew. Beside, I remembered something Dr. Gould told me, "You can say no. You don't have to do everything that a man asks of you!" What an extraordinary thing to say to me—a woman reared to be an obedient, dutiful woman who was taught she had to do whatever her father told her! I had a choice! (I learned this lesson many times in the ensuing years.) I decided to try another tactic. I developed my own profile of the man I wanted to meet, and then I signed up with a dating service. I don't remember the exact details of the profile, but since I was attracting Europeans and other ethnic men, I decided I wanted a man from a middle European country.

A strikingly tall older woman who wore a long high-necked gown and had her gray hair high on top of her head interviewed me. She reminded me of a nineteenth century English woman because she spoke with a New England accent. She was very kind and gentle, and she told me what to expect, "The appropriate gentleman will be given your profile and telephone number, and he is expected to call you and invite you to dinner. He will pick you up and pay for your dinner. "You must remember that you don't have to do anything you don't want to do," and she emphasized the last statement.

She did not explain her use of "appropriate," and I assumed she had her own system of choosing men for each woman. Because meeting men at dances was so stressful, I didn't even think to question her. I realized sometime after the interview that I had placed myself into the same position as I was in at home. Ironically, the matchmaker this time was a woman and not my father.

That year ended with a more civilized approach to the dating scene. I'd get one call a week, and I'd have an opportunity to talk to the man on the telephone and learn a little about him. One was a schoolteacher, and when I told him I had two sons, he opted out of seeing me. I realized that the men had their own expectations, which I did not meet. That was all right with me. I felt relieved that I didn't have to waste a lot of time and energy getting acquainted with someone who wasn't interested in a life that included my two sons.

One of the more engaging people I met was a man from Brazil who was in San Francisco on a Fulbright Scholarship in the field of Law. I thought he might be very intriguing to talk with and reminisce about my own experience with Jim in Vienna, but he had a very different agenda. He was looking for a woman who would want to go back to Brazil to marry him and live with him and his mother on a plantation. I was direct in my response, but not totally honest. I sensed that a divorced woman with two sons was not who he wanted to take home to his mother, so I only told him I was not interested in leaving the country. He seemed disappointed and we went our separate ways. (In retrospect he might not have been disappointed if I had told him the truth.)

After a date with a young stockbroker, I decided to call it quits until after the New Year. In late November he invited me to go to a movie with him and I agreed. I wondered how we would get to know each other in a movie, but to my surprise, I learned all I wanted to know. During the movie he put his arm around my shoulder. At first, I thought he was being friendly and comforting, but in a short while, I realized that his arm was getting heavier and heavier. My mind flashed to the burdensome feelings I had when Jim was so dependent and leaned on me so much. Did I want another man whose needs were so great and heavy? No, I did not. By the time he drove me to my flat that evening, I decided that I did not want to go out with him again. Somehow, I knew he was going to ask, and I very politely said, "Thank you for a pleasant evening, but I don't think I want to go out again." He looked hurt and surprised, and I felt a little sad. I didn't like the feeling that I was rejecting him, but I thought, "Better now than later." I postponed all other dates during December and decided to start again after the New Year. The holidays were for Franz, Marsh, and me.

On January 15, 1965, I had my first date with Miklos Michael Kovacs. Smiling, he came up the flight of stairs to my flat. He was all dressed up in a blue suit with matching tie, polished shoes, and holding a natty hat with a little blue feather on one side. ["Oh, my God, he looks like my father!] He took my hand, which I held out when he announced who he was; and in a flash, he clicked his heels together, bent over, and kissed my hand. I was stunned with disbelief and giggled as he said my name. The image of Nelson Eddy kissing Jeannette MacDonald's hand and then dancing away to the strains of a Viennese waltz flickered before my eyes, and I was swept off my feet and into his red Triumph convertible without another word.

I felt more relaxed and amused than I had been in months. In a thick accent, he told me that he was one of the Hungarian Freedom Fighters who came to the U. S. in 1956 as a refugee. We exchanged little tidbits about ourselves, including that we were both divorced. His next question caught me off guard: "Are you thinking of getting married?" I was so surprised that I haltingly answered, "Well, yes, I guess I am." I looked straight ahead and thought, "He's not wasting any time." In a few moments I felt uneasy that I answered so honestly. Then, the thought occurred to me, "Isn't this what dating is all about?" Aloud I asked, "Where are we going?" He mentioned a restaurant that was unfamiliar to me somewhere in the East Bay around Concord.

After that, we were both quiet until we reached the restaurant. Again, to my amazement, he had made a reservation and a table was ready for us. I looked around the restaurant that was a bustling place with a ballroom, a live band, and couples dancing. The tables were covered with white linen tablecloths, napkins, and place settings for two. In the middle of the table was a majestic candlestick with glistening candlelight. I smiled happily and felt excited to find myself in such a grand place. Miklos was quite at ease as we looked over the menu, which was quite extensive and very expensive. I was hesitant, and he asked if he could order for me. I nodded "Yes. I'm sure whatever you order will be delicious." He ordered Veal Parmesan, salads, and a bottle of wine.

We ate slowly, sipped wine, and danced several times. He was a smooth dancer, and I felt strong hands in the middle of my back as he graciously guided me around the dance hall. I felt breathless and awed by what could be described as a very romantic evening. I was in another world. I had never experienced anything like this ever before. I realized I had never received so much attention from a man before. I don't remember what we talked about, if we did talk; I was floating "on cloud nine," and I do believe I fell in love that night.

Franz (age 12) and Marshall (age 7) Wright
Almost every weekend, Libby took her boys
to Golden Gate Park in San Francisco.
This photo was taken there during the same month
(January 1965) that Libby met Miklos Novacs.

Libby's Three Sons

Franz (b. 3/18/53) and

Marshall (b. 7/30/58)
got a little brother,
Andre (Andy)
Michael Kovacs,
born
September 28, 1966

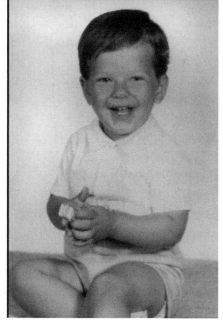

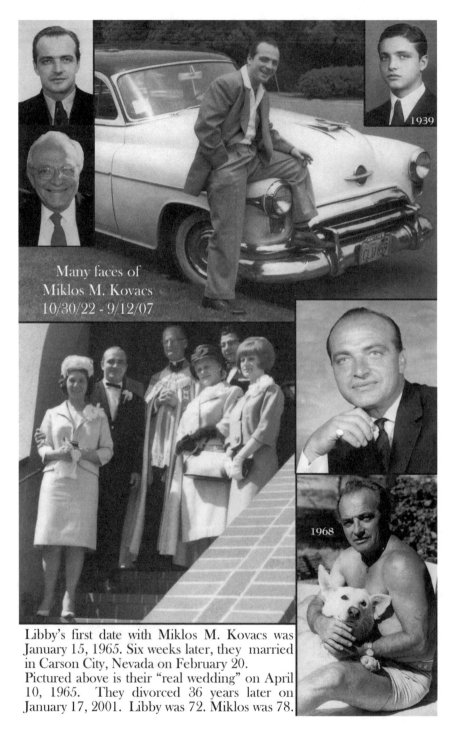

Many faces of
Miklos M. Kovacs
10/30/22 - 9/12/07

1939

1968

Libby's first date with Miklos M. Kovacs was
January 15, 1965. Six weeks later, they married
in Carson City, Nevada on February 20.
Pictured above is their "real wedding" on April
10, 1965. They divorced 36 years later on
January 17, 2001. Libby was 72. Miklos was 78.

During the next month, I was introduced... (and) was very impressed with his mother, Anna, a gracious, white-haired, outgoing, friendly woman who spoke no English and conversed enthusiastically in Hungarian.

Even though I loved her and wanted to be her friend, I knew that she and I would not do well living under one roof...

I'm sure he and his mother preferred that I stay home and raise my own sons, but Anna's coming to live with us was their idea of being helpful to me. Or was it?

Miklos' mother, Anna

Falling in
Love, 1965

Falling in love was a new and thrilling experience. "Head over heels" was the expression used over forty years ago. In the movies during love scenes, the violins built up to a crescendo as the two lovers looked deeply into each other's eyes. Although love scenes in movies were often deeply touching and inspiring, they also made me squirm from embarrassment and discomfort when I was young. Then, I'd shrug and think, "That's Hollywood. They always overdo love relationships." If life was like that, it certainly did not last very long with couples I knew. I don't think I trusted love as it was portrayed by Hollywood because I didn't see love manifested that way in real life.

Yet, there I was years later behaving in exactly the same silly, lovesick way. Now, as I reflect, was it silly or a different kind of experience? As an adolescent I was depressed. I was not allowed to date like my classmates, and I repressed all my emotions. Perhaps, this was my opportunity to experience the fun I never had before.

The following Monday after that exotic Saturday night date, I shook my head in disbelief, "What is happening with me? Am I going crazy? You're a mother, a single parent, for God's sake! Pull yourself together! Think about what you're doing."

"All right! All right!" I responded to the critical voice in my head. "Let me think about what I can do." Then I remembered that I was taking a class in psychoanalytic psychology. Dr. Strasbourg, gray-haired, probably in his sixties, a kind gentle man who worked as an analyst, had graciously agreed to teach a group of psychiatric nurses Freud's theories. He offered us one consultation session if anything came up that was distressing for us during the semester that we needed to discuss with him. That Wednesday I went up to him after class and scheduled an appointment.

His office was located in a beautiful and spacious Victorian house overlooking the San Francisco Bay. The office on the second floor was grand. A very large mahogany desk surrounded by blue velvet winged chairs was on one side of the room and an actual couch on the other. I sat down in one of the chairs across from Dr. Strasbourg and started to talk nervously about my situation. "I'm trying to make sense out of what happened to me on a date…." I began my conversation.

As I look back and see myself as a young woman, I realize that, even then, I was trying to understand a very basic, fundamental, and yes, primitive occurrence. I was always trying to find a rational explanation for whatever happened in my life. Probably because, as a first child in an immigrant family, I felt responsible for understanding events of life in order to explain them to my parents or to fix, correct, change, or do whatever was necessary for me and those around me.

"Dr. Strasburg, can you tell me whether it's normal or acceptable to feel this strongly toward someone I just met and who reminds me of my father – the good side of my father? He's even about the same size and build of my father who was short, about five feet five inches. Miklos is about five feet eight inches. He is strong and husky like my father. He even has hands like my father's. He's a very good dancer like my father…. Mostly my father worked very hard and made a good living for us after the Depression and during World War II. Although my father was depressed and sleep-deprived, he knew how to have a good time at picnics, dances, and parties that were regular events among the Greek people in our community. And my date was a very good dancer."

I felt my face light up as I recalled my father dancing the Sirto, twirling a large white handkerchief, and skimming gracefully over the floor and around the line dancers. The people sitting around the dance floor would applaud and shout, "Yia Sou! Bravo, Paul! Yia Sou!"

Dr. Strasbourg listened as I related the story of my first date with Miklos and how quickly I actually fell in love. "Yes," he nodded, "it's quite common that we fall in love with someone who reminds us of our parents." Did I imagine he said, "Yes, that's quite acceptable? You will get to know each other better as the years go by, and you will see each other as you are, eventually." I never imagined such a response! Or was this what I wanted to hear? At least he didn't say anything negative about such a phenomenon, but I have wondered, both in my personal and in my professional life, about making decisions when we fall in love. One of the most important decisions of our lives is the one to marry and to live with another human being forever after. Frequently, this decision is made when we are unconscious ("in love") and in an altered state of consciousness. How sensible or realistic is this action?

I left Dr. Strasbourg's office feeling reassured and a little more confident. Even if I was a single mother with two young sons, there was nothing wrong with finding a man who knew how to love and be playful and who was so sophisticated. I quickly learned he was adventurous and sometimes reckless.

One night as Mike drove me to my flat, he suddenly was going through every red light on Castro Street. It was around midnight, and fortunately there was no traffic; but I gasped with fear and shouted, "What are you doing?" He laughed and slowed down. He never did anything like that again, but he did love to speed. I learned that he raced his car in rallies, loved motorcycles (as did my father), and played soccer until he was forty.

Still as I have pursued healing and transforming my life, I have given considerable thought to my falling in love and getting married the second time. My actions oftentimes seemed completely out of character for me. I am usually a very thoughtful and reflective person before making decisions about events that could bring about major changes in my life. That one time in 1965, I acted so impulsively that I couldn't believe what I was doing. Even now, forty years later I want to better understand what happened.

I wonder what influenced me to fall in love so quickly? Was it having psychotherapy twice a week for three years in San Francisco, and about three years of therapy in Minneapolis, previously? I revisited my early childhood experiences, and I relived and resolved much of the grief and losses of childhood. Yes, that's a real possibility, resolving the early problems tossed me right into adolescence, and adolescents are impulsive. Maybe, for the first time in my life, I felt normal like other people.

In my classes and seminars, I was making the transformation from a medical-surgical nurse to a psychotherapist. I was hungry to learn as much as I could and I was immersed in the psychological theories and the skills necessary in working with very disturbed patients.

In addition to the regular classes, we had sensitivity training, sociodrama, a variation of psychodrama, and clinical supervision three times a week. All of these activities required intensive introspection and examination of interactions with patients as well as fellow students and faculty. The greatest challenge for me was to be completely open in expressing my thoughts and feelings and explaining the rationale for everything I did. I waded into interactions and revealed all my fears and grief in order to remove the emotional hindrances that interfered with my work, my own healing process, and being an authentic person. If I wanted to protect myself from all the self-disclosures that were very painful, I couldn't. I felt so vulnerable with my fragile boundaries that I literally was in the process of rebuilding (with the support of therapist, teachers, and fellow students) my identity from childhood onward.

Not too surprising, I woke up one morning feeling like an adolescent. I was changing and growing a new self! I was so excited and thrilled that I was no longer depressed and in pain! I did not realize that I had not completed the process of integrating all the changes and understanding, that this was the beginning of a complex developmental process that involved further changes on a biological, intellectual, and psychological levels. I still had a lot of growing to do that would take years.

However, the quest for a mate is a natural biological process; and as an adolescent in my family and culture, I was compelled to repress most of my biological needs, particularly the expression of sexuality and femininity. My priority at that time was to complete high school and avoid "being married off" to a man selected for me by my father.

For the first time in my life, and at the chronological age of thirty-six, (and psychologically sixteen), I was free to find a man who wanted to spend his life with me and, I hoped, wanted to help me raise my two sons. However, I didn't know the first thing about dating. More importantly, I did not know how one decided who the "right" man was. Without my father to make the decision for me, I resorted to the assistance of an elderly woman as a matchmaker, and a psychoanalyst to help me make the judgment for myself. Ultimately, I decided, not through a rational thought process, but like millions of other women on the basis of emotions, fantasies, and infatuation. I "fell in love!" in a whirlwind romance of six weeks! I was wined and dined and danced and gifted with jewelry, and most significantly, I felt special to this man. I had more attention – loving, adoring attention—than I had ever had in my entire life. My intellect and will melted away and I became a malleable, pliable, lovesick Cinderella! Before I came to my senses, I had run off like a girl escaping reality, and we were married!

Now, in my elder years, I am shocked by the audacity of those two adults who did not consider the consequences of their impulsive act. There were two young boys who were not prepared for the enormous change in their lives. They were suddenly excluded from their mother's new life without an explanation. How does a mother explain those actions? I did not realize the impact of what I had done until years later.

As I remember those long-ago days, I can see more clearly the underlying and unconscious reasons that I was attracted to ethnic men at the time I started dating. Their accents attracted me! From my first date with Helmut, who was German, and later there was a Japanese sociologist, a Chinese graduate student, and once an Iraqi and an Iranian. My father spoke with a strong Greek accent. I think that was one of the most familiar qualities that attracted me to Miklos.

As I return to my memory and listen for the sounds of my father's speech I remember him and my mother talking softly with each other in the next room as I fell asleep. I remember their laughter when they were enjoying themselves at a dinner or a dance. I just realized that I believe that Greek is one of the most beautiful and expressive languages I have ever heard. I hear the sounds of pleasure, happiness, and excitement when a group of Greek people are enjoying themselves. When they are angry, sad, or grieving, there is no doubt whatever in the listener's mind what is being expressed. There is such clarity in their expression of emotions that one does not need a translator to understand the words or their meaning. I am intrigued by any accent or language that I hear spoken, whether I know the people or not. I find myself listening to the sounds and feel a pleasant sense of familiarity even when I don't understand what is being said.

Another hidden memory emerged recently when I remembered our first dance. Miklos put his hand on my back in almost the exact spot that my father had placed his hard hand and gently supported me while giving me a bath. I was nine months old at the time.

The most obvious similarity, and the one that was more deeply buried than the others, was the fact that my parents eloped, and we did too!

BEYOND THE WHIRLWIND

In one week I had gone from a very practical, responsible, intelligent, and sensible woman, to a lovesick adolescent. I suddenly felt as if my world had turned upside down and inside out. My reality was no longer steady, stable, and predictable. I was caught in a whirlwind. My emotions were swirling through me out of control with my boundaries melted away. Everything was off balance.

The only thing I could think about and feel was the excitement of seeing Mike again the next evening. (I started calling him Mike—his middle name was Michael—instead of Miklos because his given name sounded too formal.) I went through the motions, performed my tasks, taught my classes, and attended meetings as usual, but everything was unreal and disconnected. I felt happy, light, and airy. In the evenings, I prepared supper as usual while Franz and Marsh played and watched TV in the living room, but I was completely preoccupied with thoughts of Mike.

Even my guide, my alter ego had vanished. No wonder, Freud called falling in love a delusional state. The Greeks of long ago had referred to Eros as a "divine state of madness." I was definitely in an altered state of consciousness, and I did not know how to find my way back to where I had been, and I'm not sure I wanted to go back. This state felt delirious and delicious at the same time.

Mike brought me gifts, we went out two or three times a week, and I didn't even think about how my newly found sense of being was affecting my sons. They were spending more and more evenings with my neighbors, Jean and Sam, who lived in the flat next door. They enjoyed playing monopoly and cards with Franz and Marsh, and Jean encouraged me to "go out and have fun. We'll put the kids to bed. Don't worry; they'll be all right with us."

There was something not quite right about what was happening, but I did not know what to do. I came to my sense of reality once or twice and went to the library and bookstore to find something on children of divorce. I found one article that said that children of divorce did as well in school as children with both parents. I knew that already, but how do I tell them what's happening to me? I couldn't even explain it to myself. I wasn't sure it was appropriate for a mother in her middle-thirties to be dating a man. How would I explain that to Franz and Marsh who both sorely missed their father?

I didn't find any answers anywhere. There was no information about single parents and how to deal with these dilemmas. My friends were happy for me. "It's about time you had some fun," they exclaimed as they approved of my dating and encouraged me to continue. I don't think I could have stopped the relationship if I wanted to; it was moving and developing faster and faster everyday. Yet, deep down, there was an uneasy feeling that came to the surface of my consciousness periodically and I brushed it aside. "I'll deal with that later."

Our Reno
Wedding

On the weekend of Washington's Birthday, February 19, 1965, Mike and I were on our way to Reno, Nevada, to be married. Just six weeks after we had met! We did not tell a soul. We simply said we were going skiing. Of course I had never skied, but I "planned to take lessons."

Since we were both married previously, we were expected to go through a church divorce. Mike had converted to the Episcopal Church, and I wasn't sure what my status was with the Greek Orthodox Church. I expected that they had even more stringent rules about divorce and I did not want to go there. I agreed to go through the process the Episcopalians required with one exception: I did not want an annulment. I had two children that proved I had been married. I chose the other option—the marriage had died. After all, I had spent five years grieving the loss of that marriage. The other factor that prevented our marriage in the church at that time was the beginning of Lent, and marriages were not performed until Palm Sunday when we were scheduled to have a more formal ceremony, and then we could invite our friends.

I learned something about Mike that weekend. He did not like anyone telling him what he could do or when he could do it. We called that an "authority conflict" in social psychology, but at the time, I found it attractive that he was so "assertive and independent." I had noticed a couple of other instances when he defied city regulations and made some structural changes on his house without getting the necessary permits and inspections, but like so many other people "in love," I ignored early signs of later problems. I don't think I questioned, why was he in such a hurry? I learned the answer to that question almost a year later.

* * * * *

Late one night as we prepared for bed, the telephone rang. Mike cheerily answered the phone as he usually did; then he stopped, "Who is this? Oh…" He looked at me, and then quickly looked away.

"Mike, who is it?" I whispered. I was concerned that something unpleasant was happening.

He put his hand over the mouthpiece of the telephone and whispered back, "It's a woman I knew." He looked uncomfortable.

"Well, what does she want?"

"She wants to sue me for not marrying her! She says I promised to marry her. I don't remember that."

Obviously, it was too late now. I was surprised and disappointed, but I was calm and took charge, as I was prone to do. "Let me talk to her." He handed the phone to me, relieved. "I'm Libby," I told her. "I'm sorry you are hurt and upset, but what is it you want?"

She sounded more angry than hurt. "I'm going to sue him!" she exclaimed.

"What good would that do?"

"Well, I'm not going to give him any of the sweaters back that he gave me"

"Of course not; you may keep them." I decided, without conferring with Mike.

Not much more was said. She hung up, and I looked at Mike askance. I didn't want to hear his story. "It's over, I hope?" He nodded, yes, and we never discussed it again. He had lived over forty years before he met me and I was sure there were a few more stories that I would hear about; but right then, I was tired, and I turned over and went to sleep.

* * * * *

So we drove to Nevada from San Francisco. The snow had stopped falling, the roads were cleared, and we had no difficulties until we arrived in Reno near midnight. The courthouse was closed! We learned from a security guard that we could get a marriage license in Carson City. There was no stopping Mike at that point. I preferred staying in Reno and getting a motel room and waiting until morning, but he was determined to plunge forward through snow and mountains. We arrived in Carson City at 4:00 a.m. I was exhausted. I was not accustomed to staying awake all night. By 4:30 we were standing in front of a minister with his wife and a stranger as witnesses. At 5:00 a.m. we were having breakfast in a restaurant celebrating our nuptial. I felt as though I was dying from lack of sleep, and Mike was happy and smiling.

Reality began to slip in through my clouded mind as I awakened later that day. My first impression was of being hung over—no, not from drinking. I get hung over from lack of sleep, even if I get eight hours sleep during the daylight hours. I lay there next to Mike, my husband! I wondered whether I could get up quietly and have a cup of coffee without waking him. He was still sleeping soundly and peacefully. I turned over and gazed at his handsome face. I felt rested and happier than I was last night. How can someone I hardly know bring out so much joy in me? I lay there musing and listening to the silence and fell asleep.

AFTER ELOPING

We drove back from the mountains in Mike's little red Triumph, brimming with warm loving feelings and smiles. We agreed to keep our secret from family and friends and to start planning our "real wedding" in the church on April 10. Thereafter, we would have a third celebration between January 15 and April 10–February 20!

Mike continued to live in his home on Marietta Avenue with his mother who had emigrated from Hungary two years previously. My sons and I stayed in our flat on the corner of 17th and Douglas Streets where we had moved when the owner of our apartment building decided to sell.

During the next month, I was introduced to his mother and his friends, and I introduced him to my sons and my friends at the university. I was very impressed with his mother, Anna, a gracious, white-haired, outgoing, friendly woman who spoke no English and conversed very enthusiastically in Hungarian. She reminded me a little of my grandmother who greeted whomever she met in Greek with a great smile and an out-stretched hand.

Anna immediately volunteered to sew my wedding dress, and she wanted me to go shopping with her to buy the pattern and the material. "How kind and generous of you," I said to her through Mike as my translator, and we agreed I'd pick her up on Saturday and together we would go shopping. I was very pleased with the prospect of becoming friends and possibly developing a mother-daughter relationship. She was so pleasant and enthusiastic, and in spite of the language barrier, we did have a good time shopping for the material for my dress and the pattern. I felt very excited about the possibilities that Franz, Marsh, and I would be part of a family again.

I learned that she was a very experienced seamstress, and Miklos knew a great deal about clothes and styles because he worked in his mother's shop in Budapest when he was an adolescent. Later, Mike told me a little about his father. He was an artist and a civil servant in the government who had been killed by the Russians when they invaded Hungary at the end of the war, and they confiscated their home with all his paintings. Mike believed the paintings had been shipped to Russia.

In the next few weeks, I gathered the basic outlines of Mike's story and his mother's. One of the first events he told me was about the fighting that broke out in Budapest in late October 1956. The Hungarian Communists defied the Russians because they wanted to maintain a national focus, and the Russians' scope was to spread their philosophy and occupation to an international level. Once the rebellion started, other parties joined the fray, and more intense violence broke out. The threat of rebellion brought more Russian troops and tanks into Hungary to subdue the fighting. Diplomats approached the U.S. and the United Nations, but the response was a "hands off" policy. Other events in Egypt at that time took precedence.

Miklos saw the fighting as an opportunity to escape another siege by the Russians. Out of necessity, and in the midst of fighting and chaos that erupted in the streets of Budapest, Miklos became one of the leaders in the Hungarian Revolution of 1956. When he realized the United Nations was not going to intervene and save them from occupation by the Russians, he gathered over a hundred men and women who wanted to get out of the country. Many of the people who went with him, his wife, and friends were people of the upper class and nobility. They knew they had to escape or they would be the first people that the Russian Communists would round up and either kill or imprison. Mike and a group of men broke into the old Hungarian Army armory and took as much ammunition as they could carry and armloads of machine guns to protect themselves from the Communist Patrols. With no more than the clothes on their backs and food for the journey, they fled out of Budapest and headed for the Austrian border —about 125 miles away—and freedom.

They saw Russian soldiers in the distance and kept walking through woods and forests. They avoided being seen until they came closer to the border where they ran into soldiers, but they were able to shoot their way out of the skirmish. Miklos was shot in the upper leg as he ran. When they were safe again, he bandaged his wound as best he could, and they kept moving and shooting back. When they reached the Austrian border, they handed over their guns to the military guards; and Miklos was taken immediately to a hospital in Vienna where his wound was treated.

The group as a whole decided they wanted to go to the United States as refugees. But others went to Switzerland and many others to Australia. In early December, they left for an airfield in New Jersey. There they learned that employees of the San Francisco Chronicle were sponsoring them, but first Miklos decided he would speak at the United Nations against the invasion of his country by the Russians and against the Hungarian Communists. He returned to the air base for a few days. Then they left for San Francisco on or about December 6th (Miklos' name day. Miklos translated in English was Nicholas—St. Nicholas Day).

Later he learned that he had sealed his status as a permanent exile with that speech. For the next thirty-three years, he was labeled *persona non grata*—an enemy of the State—of Hungary.

I was deeply affected by the stories of Miklos and his group's bravery and the suffering they endured in order to be free. I felt a deep emotional connection with Mike as a freedom fighter. I had fought a different kind of battle for my freedom, and I knew both the cost and the benefits. My love and admiration for him grew as I learned more about their travails as a people conquered, first by the Germans, and in 1945 by the Russians. I admired the love they obviously shared with each other and the close community they established in San Francisco, and I wanted to belong there, too.

Mike took me to the Annual Hungarian Spring Ball, and I felt like Cinderella. I felt very special when I was with him, and his friends opened their arms and hearts to me. In spirit they were very much like the Greeks who knew hundreds of years of pain and struggles against foreign invaders. My compassion for my own family and ethnic group grew as I became familiar with the Hungarian culture. They both had the same capacity for suffering and for celebrations. Neither group felt defeated by their ordeals. The United States was a new world and offered them another opportunity for freedom and prosperity. They probably had hidden thoughts of returning to their homeland some day, just like the Greeks.

Church Wedding
and Honeymoon

Surrounded by friends and family, we were married in All Saints Episcopal Church in the Haight-Ashbury on April 10, 1965. I was excited and nervous as I listened to the priest's words, and my voice quivered as I responded, "I do." Mike kissed me and we turned to walk down the aisle again toward the door. We were greeted by smiles, handshakes, hugs, and more kisses. I was overwhelmed and filled with glorious feelings of joy and elation.

We had a small reception at Mike's home where his mother had prepared a luncheon for about twenty people. Pictures were taken, and one of Mike's friends, Joe, had a movie camera. People were talking, laughing, and eating: the whole event seemed exciting, happy, and unreal. I could not believe that I was so happy. Mike was the perfect host – smiling, talking, and serving champagne.

In the midst of the celebration, Mike's mother said something rather shyly, which was unlike her, and someone translated, "I want you to love me."

Surprised and startled by the comment, I replied cheerily, "I do already!" The startling part of this message to me—what I heard—was, "Take care of me." This frightened me and I heard a warning or a threat, "If you don't...be careful."

The familiar sound of this request reminded me of my father saying, "Children are for taking care of your parents...."

"What have I gotten myself into?" my anxious, realistic self whispered in my ear.

Later that afternoon when everyone had left, we changed clothes and went to the home of the secretary of the Psychiatric Nursing Program, Barbara, to pick up Franz and Marsh. I had discussed whether my sons should come to the church wedding with a number of people at school: classmates and instructors. The general consensus was "No, it's probably best that they don't go." I was not sure what to do, and finally I agreed.

We all drove together to Southern California where my sister, Ann, and her husband, Richard, lived with their two daughters, Renee, three years old, and Millie, a year old, and Michael, who was the same age as Franz, twelve, and the only child of Ann's first marriage. I introduced my husband to my sister's family, and we spent a few hours getting acquainted and reacquainted with each other.

Ann and I hadn't seen each other since she remarried, and we met her small daughters for the first time. Franz and Marsh were happy to see their cousin, Michael, again; and I was relieved to see them both smiling. Mike and I went on to Mexico where we planned to stay in Ensenada, a small fishing town and resort, for only three days and head back again.

We had our short but very intense, special time together. The pleasures that flowed through and over us, the happiness that we experienced together can only be described as magical, delirious, and delicious. Time stood still! Nothing mattered. The world around us evaporated. We were alone. We were together, merged in the unreality of an unforgettable love, enveloped in a cloud of love that absorbed us both, two in one, floating in eternity above the earth, without boundaries, without cultural and ethnic accoutrements; we were united and inseparable. We tasted the bliss of the forbidden fruit, the love, the gift that could not be grasped or possessed; we descended slowly, gently, and reluctantly to the world below. We whispered, "Our love will last forever! Nothing and no one will ever separate us."

When we returned to the "real world" our honeymoon continued off and on when we managed to have time alone, but too soon we were caught up in the turmoil of fulfilling responsibilities as professionals, joining two households; and for me, there were the always-present responsibilities of parenting as well as blending Mike into our family, and we into his, with all the adjustments that these new roles entailed.

Mike had never raised children before, but when I saw him with one of his friend's two young children, I was reassured. He was very playful and affectionate with them. They knew him and were very excited to see him again. He laughingly picked up both of them, and they threw their arms around his neck, laughing as he hugged and kissed them. They chattered in Hungarian, and he listened attentively to their conversations. "Please let him be that way with my sons," I prayed. "How wonderful that would be!" I thought to myself. I learned more about his childrearing methods a little later.

House Hunting

One of our first decisions after we returned to San Francisco was that we had to find a bigger house, and we decided to look in the outlying areas rather than in the city. Mike decided he would sell his house because it was too small for all of us, and I agreed to increase my savings in the next two months so we could have a substantial down payment. One of my first questions was, "If you sell your house, where will your mother live?" Even though I loved her and wanted to be her friend, I knew that she and I would not do well living under one roof. I even suggested that we pay for an apartment that she could move into. Mike listened, I thought, but did not respond in any explicit manner one way or the other.

Every Sunday for the next few weeks, Mike and I explored a different area in the East Bay. Oakland and Berkeley seemed too crowded to me, and Mike was interested in going a little further East toward Orinda and Concord, a growing area of suburban towns. Toward the end of April, we went into Walnut Creek, which was located in the middle of that area, and we found a beautiful spacious house with three bedrooms and a swimming pool. I was quite taken by the small hillside behind the house. I could almost see the lovely garden that was going to be there next spring.

I think we both agreed simultaneously to buy this house on San Luis Drive. This was the perfect house for us! It meant that I would be commuting to UC San Francisco—about thirty-nine miles one way—and Mike, to Berkeley, about twenty-two miles. He had applied to the NASA Space Program at UC Berkley and was accepted to work on the Apollo Project. We were both thrilled that he landed such an exciting job.

I couldn't wait to tell Franz and Marsh about the new house. Marsh was excited, especially about the swimming pool, but Franz wanted to stay in San Francisco. He had grown to love the school and the friend he had made, and he enjoyed riding around town on his bicycle. I was concerned about his friend's involvement with the police, and I didn't want Franz getting in trouble with him. I loved San Francisco, but I preferred living in the smaller town where the schools were considered of higher quality.

I admit I was so involved in my relationship with Mike and getting ready to move that I did not realize that Franz was feeling neglected and even abandoned by me. We had always been very close, especially the last seven years. Then, all of a sudden, his mother changed and was not as attentive as previously. Later, I wondered how my involvement with Mike must have felt to him. At the time, I just did not know how to approach the subject with him.

Once the decision about the house and the move was made, then I could spend some time on the weekends with my sons while Mike readied his house to be sold. When he and the boys were together, we all felt uneasy. I wanted the three of them to like each other. I very much wanted us to be a close family, but I realized all of us needed more time to get to know, and to feel, more at ease with each other.

During the next two months, Mike sometimes had dinner with us and stayed the night, but he often stayed in his own home because after work he was involved in removing the bathroom in the basement of his house. He had not gone through the proper procedures of getting the necessary permits to install it, so the inspector forced him to remove the extra bathroom before he could sell it. Of course Mike was frustrated and angry about the regulations that he viewed as the city's intrusion into his rights as a property owner, but he complied and did not have any trouble selling the house.

I remembered when my father had some of the same thoughts when he started running his own trucking business. He would get frustrated because he not only had to have state licenses for his trucks, he had to get interstate permits from the Public Utilities Commission to haul to and from other states. Eventually, he accepted the reality of the situation and stopped "fighting city hall," and Mike would, too, when he realized that laws and regulations were to be obeyed whether he liked them or not.

One evening I had dinner with Mike and his mother. She was a gracious hostess and an excellent cook. One of her women friends dropped in, and we all had dessert together. They had their traditional wine with dinner and a steady stream of Hungarian conversation went on. At one point Anna looked at me, and her tone changed and with a smile she said something that seemed to be directed to me. I looked at Mike for a translation, and the friend was nodding her head and looked a little pensive.

He laughed and said, "Oh, it's nothing. Something she did for me when I was on trial in Hungary."

"Then it must have been important. She looks like it was something she valued," I responded, not wanting to be brushed off.

Her friend answered me: "She said she gave him birth two times; once when she delivered him and once when she saved him from the Communist Court."

"Oh, that sounds very serious. You will have to tell me that story sometime, Mike."

"Yes," he said, "I will tell you that story, but not now. I think we better get home to Franz and Marsh." I thanked Anna for the great dinner, and we left.

That statement by Mike's mother sent another shockwave through me. "What did I get myself into now?" I wondered to myself. "Why did she say that with that smile—or smirk—at this time? Was she telling me something? Like: 'You may be marrying him, but he's mine. I've given him life twice. Can you do that much for him?'"

I tucked my thoughts away. I'd have to see how this story played itself out in our day-to-day life. I did not have to wait long. On June 1st we started moving to our new house in Walnut Creek. A moving company hauled the furniture. I had a few things left in the hall closet.

I was taking some smaller boxes down from the shelf in the closet that I was going to put in my car.

"What's that?" Mike asked.

"Oh. It's a box of letters from Jim, my first husband." I felt uneasy as if I had been caught with a secret.

"Do you want to keep them or should they go in the fireplace?"

That part of my life was over. Burning the letters was a conscious way of ending it for good. The voice in my head said, "Oh, no! What are you thinking? Jim is a famous poet, and these are letters that Franz will want to read someday. They will be valuable someday. They are part of Jim's legacy to Franz and Marsh.

I couldn't concentrate on my thoughts any longer. Mike was waiting for me to hand the box to him. "I guess we can burn them," I said softly….

I can still remember sitting there on the floor holding that box for a few moments; then I handed them to Mike. He placed the box in the middle of the fireplace and lit the letters with his cigarette lighter.

I watched as a huge piece of my life scrambled in bits and pieces of ash up the chimney. I wanted to cry. "What have I done?" I mourned silently.

That was the one regret that has stayed with me throughout the years that followed.

Franz and Marsh were outside waiting for us to come down. Mike went ahead of me, and I locked the door to the flat that was home for two years.

We were all quiet as I drove us through the neighborhood toward the freeway. As we crossed the Bay Bridge, I wondered aloud, "Mike, you haven't mentioned where your mother is going to live? Does she want to stay in San Francisco?"

He didn't say anything for a few moments; then, "I was thinking about that, and since you are working and the boys are going to be home this summer, I thought you might want to have her help you with them and with the housework. She can do the cooking too."

That was not what I wanted to hear. I didn't say anything because I was irritated and wanted to calm down. Finally, I said in a firm clear voice, "I wish you had discussed this matter with me. I'd like to have a say in the decisions that affect me." I stopped before I really "blew my stack," as we used to say in Ohio. Was this what his mother was hinting? "He's not going to leave me behind. He wants me with him." This was my interpretation of her meaning. I was overcome by many mixed feelings.

I felt a deep disappointment and hurt. More so, I felt as if I had lost my place as the special one in Mike's life. His mother was more special! I could never do what she had done for him. For a period of time, I think I was even envious. How can I compete with her? I can't and I won't. I will have my own relationship with him. "Well, I guess the honeymoon is over," I thought to myself.

I was learning that the Hungarian refugees were different from the Greek immigrants: they were better educated than the Greek immigrants who were mostly peasants and fishermen. The Hungarians had left their country to flee from the Russian onslaught and to make a new life in America. Mike's family was upper class and his family associated with royalty. Mike told me, "We never would have emigrated if it hadn't been for the Russian invasion. We were very happy in our country before the war." In some ways they were the same: they came to this country to survive, and like the Greek immigrants, they always looked forward to the day when they would return to their homeland.

The two ethnic groups were similar in that they valued their elders and took care of them, so I should have known that his mother would come to live with us. Sooner or later, I was afraid she would expect me to take care of her. I knew I couldn't do that and work, and I definitely had no intention of quitting my job. More significantly, I felt very threatened. Not only did his mother save his life twice, but now there was the specter of their return to Hungary someday. And what would happen to me—to us?

Early the next morning Mike returned to San Francisco to bring his mother to Walnut Creek. After drinking a cup of coffee, she set about unpacking the boxes and putting dishes in the cupboards. There was a large closet area in the kitchen that I intended to use as a storage space for cleaning supplies and the broom and mop. She started to place pots and pans in that space, and I could feel my irritation turning to anger, then rage. At that moment, I knew I did not want her there arranging my kitchen, but I calmed myself and asked Mike to tell her that was going to be the broom closet. I went out in the backyard to take a deep breath and to think.

My disappointment was strangling me, and I swallowed hard to keep from crying. I knew the arrangement with Anna there was going to be difficult. I had prepared myself for some struggles between Franz and Mike, but I never imagined that I would have to cope with his mother in our house this early in our married life.

"Let's wait and see. She's strong and healthy and she may be of some real help when you're away working," suggested my rational and patient alter ego. "You know what will happen to you if that Greek temper of yours gets turned loose. Let's not make matters worse than they are."

I shifted my focus on the garden. "There are plenty of weeds to pull when I really get up tight," I thought. "There's plenty of space for two or three fruit trees. How about a peach tree? A plum and a cherry tree would be nice, too." So, I distracted myself into a little calmer state.

Now looking back, I can see so clearly how the two different families would clash as soon as we found ourselves in the same house. Mike and his mother were a tight unit with their own culture, language, their deep emotional attachments; and my sons and I were just as tightly connected with our own habits and patterns. I had no idea how the two families could ever become blended.

I tried to be understanding. After all she was older and well set in her ways. I learned that she, too, had been traumatized when Mike was picked up by the secret police and imprisoned. She also was imprisoned for two or three months. "When they took her to prison, her hair was brown. When she came out her hair was all white," Mike related in a soft, matter-of-fact tone of voice. I was horrified. "She has never told us what happened," but he knew what he had gone through and he was not talking either.

He had a deep scar on the right lower side of his abdomen. One night I asked about it. "They took out my appendix," he said with a smile. I looked at him doubtfully. I knew what an appendectomy scar looked like. "No," he admitted. "That's where they kicked me." I asked for no more details. I was sickened by what they suffered. He served his country to come home to that kind of treatment. Such unbelievable cruelty was difficult, if not impossible, to comprehend.

After they arrived in this country and Mike testified at the UN, he was considered a radical anti-communist by the F.B.I. He laughed when he told me the story of how the F.B.I. picked him up in a big black limousine one day when a Soviet Dignitary arrived in San Francisco at the their embassy. He said, "They told me to behave myself and not to go near the embassy. Then they winked at me and let me out on the other side of the car. I didn't make any trouble that time."

Who Makes Breakfast?

On the first Monday morning in June after our move to Walnut Creek, I awakened early intending to fix breakfast for Mike before he went to work. I didn't have to be in my office until later, and I was looking forward to a quiet time together. As I approached the kitchen, I heard Mike and his mother talking quietly. She was drinking coffee as Mike ate his breakfast. The two of them sitting there conversing looked like a familiar cozy scene that, apparently, had been going on for two years, since she arrived in this country.

I sensed there was something wrong with that picture. "I'm supposed to be sitting there talking with him after I had prepared his breakfast," I thought as I walked back toward our bedroom to consider my next move. Although I awakened earlier the next two mornings, Anna was already there preparing Mike's breakfast. I was simmering discontentedly; no, I was very upset and angry! I decided to talk with Mike that evening.

"I know your mother has been fixing you breakfast these past two years that she's been in this country, but don't you think it would be more appropriate for me to do that?"

"Of course, sweetheart," he agreed heartily. "I'll tell her that you want to do that for me."

"No, that's OK. It's silly of me to get upset. If she wants to do that, I don't mind, really." I felt the old shameful jealous feelings that I had as a child when I felt displaced by the birth of my sister, Mary. I realized that once I expressed myself and felt that Mike had heard me, I really did not mind. I was being childish.

Dealing with Anger

All those times at home when I felt no one heard me—when I felt insignificant and invisible—all those feelings of frustration, anger and rage would rise up and I'd feel as if I were choking. As a child, I'd stamp my feet and scream, "I don't care! I don't care!" If my godfather, Mihalis, was there he would take my hand and walk with me, and I would calm down. As an adolescent, I could really lose it and overreact with family members when I felt disregarded and disrespected. Later, in my first marriage, when I felt ignored or taken for granted and when I was betrayed, then all hell broke loose inside me. After many years of therapy, I learned that I did not have to react that way.

Mike helped me to learn to lower my voice, to calm down, mainly because he was so overwhelmed when I confronted him. He would grab his car keys and go for a ride, leaving me to fume. Eventually, I learned or grasped the fact that if I yelled, Mike would leave. If I wanted him to hear me, I had to speak with my normal voice. Even my sons suffered from the traumatic experience of my shouting at them or Mike.

Over the years many women who came for psychotherapy expressed the same pain and anger when they did not feel heard by their spouses, parents, and others.

Customs and Stories

From the beginning of our relationship, I sensed a closeness between Mike and his compatriots of which I had no knowledge and probably never would. I had a similar feeling when I was around my mother and her sister. They had one language that they spoke their entire lives, one culture, customs that they all participated in, and experiences that were unknown to me. I grew up in an environment where almost every household in our neighborhood spoke a different language, came from a different cultural, ethnic, or religious background; and although I felt accepted and loved to a large degree, I felt the outsider most of my life. I became a marginal person as I grew older. Yes, I had close friends and people whom I loved, and they in turn loved me. I enjoyed my position as a participant and an observer, and at the same time, I felt uneasy.

When Mike and I were together, I felt an intimacy I had never known before, and yet there was much that we could not share with each other because of our language barriers, and his reluctance to talk to me about the many painful experiences he had had. He was secretive, non-communicative, very private, and certainly not as open about himself as I have always tried to be. Many times when we were with others, especially his friends, and they were talking Hungarian, joking, teasing each other, and telling stories, I was completely in the dark. Even when someone tried to translate what was going on, I felt even more of a stranger. That's it. I felt like a stranger in a strange land, and I felt disconnected, not an intrinsic part of what was going on around me.

No matter where Mike and his friends met—in their homes or on the street—they all hugged and kissed each other. Joe, one of Mike's closest friends, laughingly told me, "We men had to stop kissing each other on the streets because the Americans looked at us in a strange way." When men and women first met, the custom was for the man to kiss the woman's hand; afterwards the men kissed the women on both cheeks whenever they met. Men kissed men as a part of their greeting, and out of respect particularly with older members of their group; and women did likewise. One of my friends said after meeting Mike, "He is one of the best kissers and huggers I've ever met."

Once, soon after we were married, while we were attending a party with my associates from the University, I saw Mike kissing one of my friends very passionately on the lips. I felt very hurt and jealous. Later, when we were alone, I told him that kind of kissing was not acceptable to me. "Kissing hands and cheeks is one thing; but kissing on the lips is another." Although I felt my position was very provincial, even petty, of me, I wanted to make myself very clear this time. I had had one long and terrible experience with an unfaithful husband. I did not want to have another one.

Mike respected my wishes, when I was present; but I had my doubts about other times. He had a tendency to disappear at gatherings. He was a natural flirt, and his exuberance and enthusiasm for having a good time was irrepressible. Eventually, I overcame my objections because "that's Mike."

I got glimpses of Mike's childhood and adolescence from the short stories he told me of his upbringing. "My older sister, Marta, was a real chatterbox. She talked so much that I didn't speak until I was three," he said with a big smile as he continued, "After the war, she married a man from Ecuador and went to live in his country. She was a racecar driver and was killed in 1952 driving a Lamborghini. I didn't know she was killed until 1956 when I was released from prison." For a few moments, he appeared sad but brightened up immediately to tell me a tale about the times he stayed with his grandparent and was chased by the ducks or he went fishing with Grandpa.

From stories that he told about his grandparents, I sensed that Mike loved them very much. He stayed with them for long periods of time when he was under five. He talked about his grandpa with much pride. "Grandpa had vineyards and he was famous in that part of Hungary for his brandy. Grandma never forgave him for not eating a piece of their wedding cake; he preferred his sausage and bread. Grandpa died on his eightieth birthday after drinking brandy all night with his buddies. I hope someday that's the way I will go, too," smiling as he remembered his beloved grandfather. Thoughtfully and sadly, he would add, "After the war, the Communists took his house and land which he had left to me." Before long I realized that underneath all his enthusiasm and ebullient spirit was a dark river of pain and sadness that he kept well hidden from himself as well as others. I was patient and let his stories tell me about his life before, during, and after the war.

Miklos was expelled from the Gymnasium (a secondary preparatory school for college) because he was kissing a girl when he was fourteen. His parents sent him to another school in a border town across the river from Yugoslavia. At sixteen, he had his first sexual experience with the household maid; and at seventeen, he said he received "a big slap in the face from my father because I went gambling at a casino and won enough money to purchase an Indian Motorcycle the next day. My father was angrier that I had gambled than he was about my buying a motorcycle."

At seventeen, he attended a dance at a club where he saw his father dancing with an unknown woman. He went up to the pair and asked to dance with her. He and his father never spoke about that incident, but he was certain his father was having an affair. "A lot of men have affairs, but it's not such a big deal as it is in this country." He never said whether his mother did too. I suspected she did. She married again after the Russians killed her husband when he tried to fight off a soldier who was raping her. Miklos never mentioned that event again, and I was speechless.

I learned that in Hungary the drinking age started at sixteen, and this was the age of consent in sexual matters, too. There was either no law similar to our Statutory Rape Law, or the law was much less stringent; he wasn't certain. "At sixteen we were considered mature enough to make our own decisions," he announced.

At nineteen when he was attending the University of Budapest, he got involved with an underground movement that was helping Jews escape to Sweden. Miklos and his family were members of the Roman Catholic Church. He became a runner of certificates of Baptism for Jews that were delivered to the ambassador from Sweden who was getting them citizenship in Sweden where they were emigrating. He told me the ambassador's name was Raoul Wallenberg, who was later captured by the Russians and sent to a Russian prison where he disappeared. Mike spent time in the same prison years later.

Miklos completed two years at the University, and in 1941 he was inducted into the Hungarian Army. He was trained as a driver of a tank and promoted to lieutenant. When the Germans invaded Hungary that year, they took control of the Hungarian Army, and the Panzer Division was the first to be sent to the Russian Front, specifically to Leningrad where the fighting was vicious and merciless and the weather was brutally frigid. The Russians pushed the German and Hungarian troops back toward Eastern Europe.

After all the soldiers in Miklos' tank were killed, he saw an opportunity to escape. He took off in his tank and headed toward Poland until it ran out of gas. Abandoning his tank, he walked through frozen fields and deserted villages until he saw a motorcycle parked by a barn. Without any hesitation, he drove off on the motorcycle as far as the Polish Border. The details of how he went from Poland, along Ukraine, and from there to the Hungarian Border were scant.

My questions, such as, "What did you eat?" "How did you travel over those frozen miles?" "Where did you rest or sleep?" "Did anyone help you?" remained unanswered for the rest of our marriage. At times when I was curious and I'd ask for details, he would not respond. Often I encouraged him to write down whatever details he could remember; and he tried several times, but did not complete anything.

Unfortunately, when he finally reached the Hungarian Border, Russian soldiers met him there. I can only imagine how horribly disappointed and devastated he must have felt—to have evaded the Russians in their own country and across all those long frigid miles— only to be captured so close to home! "How dreadful!" I thought, and I felt like crying from the pure frustration that he must have felt. The worst was yet to come.

Miklos must have hoped that he would be imprisoned in Hungary, but there was only more misfortune in his future: he and hundreds of other Hungarian prisoners of war were shipped off to Siberia in railroad boxcars. For two years, they worked as slave labor in railroad factories on very little food. When he and others were released in 1946, Miklos weighed ninety pounds.

He returned to Budapest where his mother and stepfather lived in an apartment, and he stayed with them to recuperate. When he regained some strength, he thought about returning to the University to complete his studies in Engineering. He took walks to the University where he freely discussed his experiences as a war prisoner in Siberia, how they were worked from morning to night every day and were starved. "Look at me! I'm an example of the Soviet Paradise of Siberia! Do you believe all their propaganda about freedom and democracy?"

Unbeknown to Miklos, the freedom of speech policy of Sanctuary that had existed on University grounds had been eliminated, and he was being observed by Secret Police and allowed to talk for about a month. One night after midnight a group of policemen broke into the apartment where he was staying and hauled him off to prison.

He was imprisoned and placed in isolation. He was beaten and tortured, and he refused to give them what they wanted to hear— that he was a traitor to his country. Eventually, he and other young men who had returned from the Russian Front and Siberia were placed on trial as traitors. These trials, and those in Russia, were called at that time "Stalin's Show Trials." Miklos was sentenced to be hanged, and some of the men he knew were actually hanged.

Miklos was kept in isolation for a year waiting for his sentence to be carried out. He did not know that his mother had sold many of her belongings, expensive rugs, fur coat, jewelry, and whatever else that she could sell, to get enough money to bribe a Russian officer to testify on her son's behalf. Somehow she accomplished this seemingly impossible feat, and Miklos' sentence was reduced to life in prison.

He and many others were imprisoned in the coal mines in Eastern Hungary. For nine years those men who had served in the army and previously had attended the University worked in the coal mines and studied under the guidance of professors from the mining engineering departments of the University of Budapest. They earned their degrees in Mining Engineering and worked as slaves. Miklos earned two mining engineering degrees. In time, the political positions of the government eased up on imprisoning Hungarian soldiers, and Miklos was released in late 1955, along with many others.

Once I asked him, "What gave you the strength to survive in prison?" He answered, "I read Dostoyevsky's *Crime and Punishment*, and I knew I was not guilty. I had nothing to confess."

Because the ex-prisoners refused to identify themselves as Communists, they were unable to find jobs in the cities and towns where they lived. Some returned to work in their former prisons, the coal mines, but Miklos refused. Living freely was not easy. Miklos was extremely suspicious and very paranoid about being observed and followed when he returned to Budapest. He could not work, and he stayed in his mother's apartment. After several months of rest and care, he recovered enough that he could think about re-establishing relationships with old friends. He married a woman he had known before the war.

The political situation was changing, and by October 1956, the Revolution that was brewing exploded on the streets of Budapest. Finally, Miklos saw his opportunity for real freedom, and he and his friends planned their escape to Austria, and ultimately, to the United States.

TWO WOMEN IN ONE HOUSE

For the most part, those first three months in Walnut Creek were peaceful. Franz and Marsh were adapting better than I expected. The swimming pool was great recreation for us. We all loved swimming. Marshall was learning to swim and a quick study, so our afternoons and weekends were spent in the backyard around the pool. I had my first opportunity in many years to do some gardening. Pulling weeds and getting the ground ready for planting was a joy and a great way to relax.

Mike was not the least bit interested in pulling weeds. He enjoyed lying in the sun and dozing. His skin turned bronze every summer. As a result of those terrible years in Siberia and the mines, he became a sun worshipper during the long summer months in California.

Anna, Mike's mother, seemed content for most of that summer. Then, my sons' behaviors started to irritate her. Toward the end of August, she didn't like that they did not ask permission to get juice or cokes out of the refrigerator. Of course, she couldn't tell me, so she complained to Mike as soon as he got home from work.

I'd get home about an hour later, and I learned to distinguish when they were chatting and when she was complaining. The only times I asked for a translation was when I thought she was complaining. At first, Mike shrugged and said, "Nothing is wrong. She just wants the boys to ask her to go to the refrigerator."

"Well, I am sorry if she is offended," and I could feel my anger rising to my throat. "I've always allowed them to help themselves when they wanted to eat or drink something, especially if I wasn't home. Do you think you can help her to understand that I was a single parent and they learned to take care of their own needs? I don't want my kids hassled because they want to help themselves."

I don't think she approved of my childrearing practices, but she accommodated as much as she was able. Franz and Marsh were not accustomed to the Hungarian cuisine, and they had their complaints, too. I reminded Mike and his mother that we had grown up in this country, not according to the Hungarian culture, custom, and social structure; and she shouldn't expect my kids to kiss her hand and to always ask permission to do what they knew how to do. I don't think this went over very well. She continued to complain about one thing or another almost every evening at dinner until I had my fill. I was beginning to feel excluded in my own home, and I was becoming more and more resentful.

I'm certain that Mike had his own feelings of disappointment. I probably was not adjusting as he had hoped. He probably would have been very pleased had I learned his language. I did learn words and phrases, but I did not have the energy to learn such a difficult language. I was busy with my own work, commuting, and coming home to an upset mother-in-law, husband, and children. The environment of our home was becoming more and more unpleasant. In fact, coming home was damned stressful.

I did not realize until many years later that I did not want to learn their language. I was afraid of being trapped again by adapting more to their wants and needs. I did not want to become a Hungarian lady like his mother. Stubbornly or defiantly, I wanted to be myself. I had fought so hard with my own family to find my own identity, I was not about to give it up and conform to another set of expectations.

One night when Mike and I were alone, after everyone else had gone to bed, he asked, "How long do you think you are going to continue working?"

I was so taken aback by his question that I stammered, "What? Did you just ask me to quit my job? Why? Why? Did I ask you to quit your job when we got married?" I tried to calm myself for a few minutes. Then, slowly and clearly, I asked, "Do you know that I spent seven years in school? Four at the University of Minnesota, while I was going through a dreadful divorce and raising two children alone, and then three years here at UC. I'm getting my first job as an instructor in September. This is what I worked for all these years—so I could teach—and you want me to quit?" I sat there looking at him and shaking my head, "My God! Do you know what you are asking?" He was startled by my outburst and outrage. He did not respond (I learned that this was his typical response – no response), but my position about working was clear. We had not had time, really, to talk about my career. I'm sure he and his mother preferred that I stay home and raise my own sons, but Anna's coming to live with us was their idea of being helpful to me. Or was it? Mike decided he wanted his mother to come and live with us when I explicitly said, "No, I'd rather pay for her to live in an apartment in San Francisco where she would be close to her friends. And… she could come and visit us."

One day late in August, I came into the kitchen in time to hear his mother speaking rapidly. She was obviously upset. Irritated I asked Mike, "Now, what is she upset about?" When she heard my voice rising, she got up and walked rapidly to her room.

"Oh, no, you are not going to do that," I thought. I went to her room, opened the door and said to her sternly, "You are coming out whether you like it or not. We have a problem, and I want to straighten it out." I took her by the arm, and pointed the way to the kitchen. She started to scream and she looked frightened.

I spoke slowly, controlling my anger, and I asked Mike to translate. "I know it is difficult for the two of you to be living with young children who are not particularly well-behaved according to your standards, but you both will have to understand; they've been without a father here for three years and in Minneapolis for four years." I paused for Mike to talk with his mother. She looked hurt and angry but she said nothing.

"I don't want to hurt you, but we have to do something about all the complaints that you have almost everyday. Do you understand?" I said. I could feel my throat getting tighter, and my mouth was dry. "The complaints have to stop!"

She would not look at me and she gave no response. She made a short comment to Mike in Hungarian, got up, and fled to her room. He did not translate her comment, and we sat there in silence.

"Mike, do you want me and my kids to move out? Is that what she wants? I can do that, but I can't handle her filling your ears with… I don't know what to do. Will you talk to me?" He shrugged his shoulders and replied, "She's an old woman and she does not understand what the boys say and they don't understand her."

"I know, and I don't want to put you in the middle, but I'm tired of her constantly complaining. So you talk to her and find out what she wants to do about this situation, or I can take my sons and move back to San Francisco."

The next morning was Sunday, and we were getting ready to go to church. "Is your mother coming out of her room today?" I asked. Mike looked at me and responded, "She packed and left early this morning to take a bus to San Francisco. She's going to stay with a friend for a few days."

"She walked all the way to the bus station? That's about a mile! Well, I'm sorry, but maybe that's the best for her. What did she want me to do with my kids?" He never answered me at that time.

A week later Anna called to say she found a job with the help of her friend. She was working as a housekeeper and cook for a wealthy couple in Piedmont, in the hills overlooking Oakland. "I think that's wonderful. Is she happy there?" I exclaimed with great relief.

Mike and I went to see her on the following Saturday and she was truly happy. She was in her element: a big house, a very support-ive lady-of-the-house who loved Anna's cooking, and she received many accolades from guests (from twelve to twenty-four) who came to dinner on special occasions.

She was very pleased with her new home. She gave us a tour of the kitchen and the upstairs. She could hardly contain her enthusi-asm for having the opportunity to live in such wealthy surroundings. She lived and worked there for seven years. In doing so, she collected enough Social Security and a state retirement benefit to live inde-pendently until she was eighty-two.

Now that I can look back without all the emotional entanglements of blending two families, I can see more clearly what some of the difficulties were. She and Mike focused on her relationship with the boys "not understanding her and she did not understand them." Her issue, and probably Mike's too, was that she did not understand me, and I did not understand her. More importantly, she was the grand dame and she was expecting me to learn from her the proper customs and etiquette of being her son's wife! Was that the reason for her coming to live with us? Was she there to teach me how to become a good and proper Hungarian wife?

Having It All: Love and Work at the Same Time

I remembered that day in my Sociology Class—when I reacted to the professor's statement that we were all middle class. "Middle class? Who me? I am not middle class. I came out of the working class, and that's what I will always be!" I exclaimed. Professor Strausmann quietly and with a smile replied, "No, you're not. Not if you are attending the University of California. That makes you middle class."

I drew a deep breath and said, "I'll have to think about that." A friend from Seattle who came to see me in San Francisco, while attending a conference, picked me up for dinner one evening and said with a big smile, "I knew I'd find you in a working-class neighborhood." I laughed, "Well, it comes naturally, doesn't it?

I learned a lot about life in that industrial ghetto in Ohio that I called home for the first twenty-three years of my life. Love and work were the most important things in life, as Freud reminded me when I was in graduate school. Love was mostly associated with pain and suffering in my mind, and work with joyfulness. Work was fulfilling, exciting, and rewarding. Yes, there were difficulties in work, too. In my early years as a nurse, I did not understand the politics of nursing. Change was not tolerated, and I loved to learn and to make changes. I lost my job as a Head Nurse when I tried to make changes without consulting the Director of Nursing. I learned from that experience: just because I was sent to a workshop on improving nursing, that did not mean that changes were acceptable in the actual hospital setting. During graduate school and afterwards, I was better able to handle issues and problems with people at work. Obviously, I did better at work than I ever did at home where I often felt overwhelmed, confused, and frustrated. I couldn't make sense of many of our family interactions.

In Walnut Creek I clung to the happy moments. I didn't want to believe the undercurrent that I felt in the midst of what seemed to me our nice, middle-class life. "They (middle class people) didn't have explosions of anger, did they?" Yes, I'm afraid they—we—did.

Many more years would pass before I realized that one purpose of marriage was to resolve the "unfinished business" of the past. We all bring our baggage from home into our marriages: we bring our histories, our unresolved issues and conflicts with our parents, siblings, and others into the marriage in order to relive and rework them with our spouse/partner and free ourselves from the past so we can continue our growth and development as adults. In living through this difficult process we find our true selves.

Once Anna was settled and happy in her new home, we all relaxed and established our own routines and patterns of living together. Mike loved to cook, which was a great relief for me, and I cleaned up afterwards. We did everything together, especially on the weekends when we shopped for groceries and new furniture that was necessary for a bigger house. The boys started making friends with the neighborhood children, and the public school that they attended was within walking distance.

We had a very active social life: parties at our house where Hungarians and "Psych" people from the University mingled or we attended Hungarian parties and dances in San Francisco. On weekends we would all go on drives to the Bay Area or to Clearlake where Mike wanted to buy a piece of land on which he could later build a house. We had similar goals, and we worked well together in saving our money in order to accomplish them. We all attended the Episcopal Church on Sundays, and we both were very pleased and excited about the work we were doing and our life style. There was much to talk about when Mike and I were together. Yes, we were happy for the most part. I don't think I ever felt as contented as I was in the early years of our marriage. I even started yearning for another child.

When I realized I was pregnant, we were absolutely thrilled. One of the first comments Mike made was, "Now that you are pregnant, are you going to stop working?"

I was not as surprised as I had been the first time he asked me to quit my job. I looked at him and said very patiently, "Mike, being pregnant is not an illness. I do not have to stop working until I'm ready. Besides, I'm teaching nurses; I am not doing heavy physical labor. I love my work and I will not quit."

I worked until I was eight and a half months pregnant. Andy

was two weeks late, so we had a whole month to wait for him. During that month, Mike would take me for rides in our car on the bumpiest roads he could find. We wanted to bring on my labor as early as possible. But our baby did not budge until he was ready.

OUR SON, ANDY

Our son, Andre Michael, who was always "Andy", was born on September 28, 1966 at 9:40 a.m. At thirty-eight years of age, my labor and delivery were very difficult. Yet, I experienced the most awesome feeling. From the first moment I held my infant son, he was completely separate from me. He was a beautiful, happy, and sturdy little boy. Mike received a traffic ticket for speeding from Berkeley to the hospital in Walnut Creek. He was so excited he handed a cigar to the policeman who gave him the ticket.

On October 10, Andy and I started commuting to San Francisco where I worked half time that year. I took Andy with me twice a week for about six weeks. I found a babysitter about a block from my office, and I would go there between classes to nurse him. After a few weeks, he started waking up on the way home and cried until I stopped and nursed him on the side of the freeway. I was not comfortable with our arrangement at that point and decided to get a sitter closer to home.

Andy thrived in our family. Franz learned to hold and feed him his bottle. Marsh laughed and played with him, and they had a great time together when we bought a little jumping seat for him. Seemingly, without much effort on our part, he learned to walk and talk and he got potty trained by following his brothers to the bathroom. By the age of two, he was such a confident child that he knew exactly what he wanted in terms of toys, food, and music—he sang along with the singers on the radio, and by three he could sing most of the popular songs. He was physically well coordinated and could whiz down the hills of Walnut Creek on his scooter with some of the older boys. As he grew, he made friends with old and young alike.

We bought a house in Clearlake Oaks where we spent summer vacations and had a getaway place when we needed to escape from the busyness of our lives. Andy became friends with an older couple who lived nearby, and they took him boating and fishing with them. Mike liked motorized "toys" and collected a couple motorcycles, a boat, and a truck to haul the boat. By the time he was eight, Andy had his own motorcycle that he rode around the streets near our summer home. Marsh broke his arm attempting to jump over a dry creek bed on his motorcycle. Franz was off in his own solitude.

THE LATE SIXTIES

Still, for all the activity and good times, I was aware of a dark undercurrent that flowed through our lives. The late sixties were turbulent times, and living in the Bay Area, we found ourselves in the middle of the turmoil that changes bring: civil rights and anti-war (Viet Nam) marches, changes in dress, hippies and drugs. I was marching in San Francisco, and Mike in Berkeley got swept up with some of the Berkeley-type activities. I was shocked when he took me to a party one Friday evening, and I found myself in a smoke-filled room with bodies stretched out in chairs, couches, and floor in a state of somnolence.

I whispered to Mike as I headed for the door, "What kind of party is this? They all look like they've passed out!" He smiled awkwardly, "It's a "pot" party."

"You mean marijuana!" I almost shouted. "Why did you bring me here? What are you doing around kids like these? Are you smoking that stuff?"

I was thoroughly disgusted. I could not believe that he would do such a thing. I wanted to go home.

Yes, Mike was willing to do whatever everyone else was doing. He just didn't want to miss out on anything. Yes, I know he missed his entire young adult years, but does that make it right to do whatever he pleases without concern for anyone else? I was thinking of my sons. What if they see him smoking pot? I wouldn't put it past him to smoke out on the patio. No, I can't have that.

Sometime later, I did find a bag of pot in our bathroom, and I flushed it down the toilet. I didn't say anything at first, but some changes started happening in our family. Franz started letting his hair grow. He refused to wear the slacks that Mike had bought for him. He wanted to wear blue jeans like all the other kids his age. I tried to persuade him; then I insisted that he wear his regular clothes. Finally when nothing worked, and out of complete frustration, I'd yell at him, "Do as you please, but you can't stay home from school." Blue jeans were for after school and weekends. Slowly the transformation took place but not before a maelstrom hit our family full force.

How Could He?

Franz' hair grew longer and longer each week until, at fourteen, his hair was down to his shoulders. I adjusted, but Mike did not. In fact, he got angrier and angrier. One day he looked at Franz, muttered, and his face changed into a dark growling monster before my eyes. Franz refused to get a haircut. Mike, enraged at Franz's defiance, went to the closet and pulled a pair of scissors from my sewing basket! He was heading straight for Franz who was standing in the kitchen looking downcast and uncertain. He looked up and instantly started running through the house with Mike right behind him.

I saw the scissors and started shouting at Mike, "Don't, Mike, let him go. Stop that!" Mike grabbed Franz by the arm, then pulled him down on the floor and held him down with his left leg and knee. He went for his hair. Mike was holding a handful of hair with his left hand, Franz kicking and struggling to get away, but Mike, the stronger and heavier one had Franz pinned to the floor. He began hacking at the hair in his hand; then Franz went limp and was sobbing. I was screaming and pulling at Mike's right arm and hand trying to get the scissors away from him. Finally, he got up, threw the scissors on the floor swearing in Hungarian, and went outside to have a cigarette. I remembered momentarily when he told me how his father slapped him for gambling, but I don't remember exactly what happened after Mike attacked Franz.

Did I hold my terrorized son and reassure him? Did I sit on the floor beside him, crying with him? Or, did I follow Mike outside to scream at him some more. How could he attack a child in such a horribly mean and destructive way? This was not the gentle, fun-loving Mike whom I loved. Where did that rage come from? I actually did not remember that scene for many, many years until Franz told me what happened. I believe I dissociated emotionally. I completely blanked out; I was so shocked, hurt, and frightened again.

I may have been reliving my own terror when I was twelve and my father saw me riding a bicycle. He had forbidden me to ride bicycles. "I am not raising you so you can go out there and get yourself killed," he told me in his stern voice. "Do you understand me?" Downcast and afraid, I nodded, "Yes."

I could feel my fear rising up my back before I actually saw him coming after me. I dropped the bicycle in the street and ran for our house. I was screaming and crying as I ran into the house and to my mother. I was behind her, holding on to her for dear life. My father's enraged face looked like death itself coming after me. I knew he was going to kill me or, at the very least, I would get beaten.

My mother, with her arms outstretched and her hands pushing against my father's chest, trying to hold him back and crying out to him, "Stop! Stop!" in a loud voice that I had not heard before. Perhaps he did want to kill me for disobeying him, but my mother saved me. Did Mike want to kill my son for his defiance and disrespect? "Oh, God, how could this happen again?"

Even my grandfather had chased his son, my father, when he was eighteen. My father, a sailor, was going up the gangplank of the ship on which he was shipping out, and he turned to see his angry father coming after him. He panicked, ran, and stumbled over some ropes and fell into the hold. He was hospitalized for three months while recovering from numerous fractured bones. As a child, my father suffered physical abuse by his father, neglect, and hunger. At the age of eight, he was put to work as a sponge diver. He must have been terrified, diving without equipment and only with a rope around his waist and the other end of the rope tied to a rock. When he found the sponge, he would untie the rope and swim up to the surface.

CHALLENGES ON THE HOME FRONT

I was in my sixties when I finally learned that I suffered from Post-traumatic

Stress Disorder, as my dad did and probably his father, too. Miklos' experiences on the Russian Front, in Siberia, and in prison were unbelievably traumatic. He was definitely a candidate for PTSD. As he aged, he developed full-blown symptoms in the late 1980s and through the 1990s (depression, irritability, nightmares, flashbacks, over-reaction to sudden noises). Research indicated that World War II veterans were likely to show signs of PTSD late in life with physical and mental deterioration.

My sons were already vulnerable to the genetic disorder of Bipolar Illness. Added to that was the grief over losing their father at very young ages, Mike's periodic rages and paranoia were terrifying and very traumatic for them. Marshall suffered Mike's anger, especially if he could not eat a particular food, like liver or an unusual Hungarian dish. Mike became so enraged one evening when Marsh refused to eat his dinner that he took his plate with food on it and flung it at him. Marsh moved his head and the plate missed his head as it sped by him.

I immediately jumped between the two of them, shouting at Mike to stop. I knew how he felt about food being wasted after being starved for so many years, but his emotional reactions were so excessive that I blamed his mother's leaving for his rage. "Your mother chose to leave. I know you blame me, but you have to take control of your anger. I won't have you attacking them in this horrible way! Do you hear me?" He would leave. Later, I would go where he was sitting, smoking, and drinking a glass of wine. When he was calmer, we could talk, but his anger would go deep inside him where I could feel it simmering.

"Mike, this cannot go on. I went through all that anger with my father, and I do not want my kids to go through that. Do you understand?" Yes, he did, and gradually he did stop, but his need to be in control was turned on me.

With Mike, fierce outbursts occurred about every three or four months the first two years. They were sandwiched in between calm, more relaxed periods when we went camping, spent pleasant weekends at Clearlake Oaks fishing, swimming, and boating. In winter, Mike and I went skiing. Sometimes he took Franz with him, and as soon as Andy was five, he was learning how to maneuver the slopes. After the haircutting episode, I told Mike, when he had calmed down, that he should not take responsibility for my sons. They were my responsibility, and I would take care of them as I had done before we were married.

Although he abided by my wishes, he was not happy with the arrangement. Instead of outbursts directed at Franz or Marsh, he turned his dissatisfaction and anger on me. If he was going to explode, I preferred that he do it with me; but I did not realize until much later that our battles which were fought with loud voices were very frightening and traumatic for Franz and Marsh (were they reliving the earlier screams of their father and me?). Later Franz told me he was afraid that we might kill each other.

Once when I got angry with his mother and criticized her, he slapped me across my face. At the time, we were driving from Clearlake to Sacramento. Franz and Marsh were in the back seat cringing and holding each other. I screamed at him to let me out of the car. I walked down the road so I could think. After a while, I came back to the car, got in, and said in a stern, angry voice, "You will never do that again or I will call the police." We drove home without another word spoken.

One evening, after we spent an evening with a group of his Hungarian friends, he brought up a subject that was being discussed by one of the couples. Their daughter was thirteen, and she was starting "to talk back," and they decided to send her back to Hungary to live with the wife's mother for a year or so. "She will attend school over there where the children are more disciplined than they are here," explained the girl's mother.

"Yes," I thought to myself, "and that will free you up to play your own games." The couples in Mike's group of compatriots had the tendency to play "musical beds," and I made it explicitly clear later on that those activities were completely unacceptable to me. "Don't get any ideas that you want to play around like that. I will not tolerate it. And don't get any ideas that I will send my sons to relatives. I don't know my relatives in Greece, and my father would certainly not be willing to raise two boys at his age. Neither would I ask my siblings. They have their own children. My sons are mine and I will raise them. They are not your responsibility."

I knew by the look on his face when he was angry and resentful about something Franz and Marsh did, but I talked him into calming down, and then I would talk to my sons. Since he would not talk about his anger, I was never sure what the boys had done or whether he was upset with me. I knew that my assertiveness bothered him. He was probably hurt because I did not support him in his methods of disciplining the boys, and I didn't support his mother when she wanted to control my sons, and me, too. I wondered how disappointed and disillusioned he was. Unfortunately, he would not acknowledge his feelings, so I had no idea what was going on inside him.

Franz was very depressed during the eighth grade and his grades dropped. I offered to take him to a counselor, but he refused to go. He did much better in high school. He played the trumpet in the school band. He and Lisa, his close friend, were frequently together, and he did extremely well academically. He attended the University of California, Berkeley, in his senior year in a special program for advanced students. When he learned to drive, Mike gave him the Triumph to drive to school. In spite of all his successes, he was moody, depressed, and angry. He would not talk to me either.

One afternoon, I heard him sobbing in his room. I went in, sat by him, and said, "Franz, what is it? What's happened? Are you all right?"

Between sobs and with a deep sadness, he said, "I just realized that the magic of childhood is over."

"Oh, Franz," I cried out. What could I possibly say to comfort him? I sat with him quietly filled with my own sadness.

I tried to get all of us into family therapy after one of Mike's explosions, but I was not successful. He went with me for one or two sessions; then he would drop out. Since I had "the problems," he had no need to go; so when I needed to talk to someone, I found my own therapist.

The photo albums from that time are filled with happy faces, children around the swimming pool, Anna appearing contented when she visited us, and Mike playing with the white German shepherd puppy, Heidi, that he bought for himself. He was very loving and caring with her, and I often wished he could be that good with my sons.

Franz and Marsh were "my sons," and Andy was "our son." We never became a blended family, nor did we become an integrated extended family with mother-in-law as the matriarch of our family.

Although our arrangement worked for longer and longer periods of time, there was the underlying clash of cultures manifested in periodic episodes of distancing, dissension, and dissonance.

I had my own difficulties growing up in a patriarchal culture, and I was not about to allow myself to be dominated by a matriarch whose word was law. I have no doubts that Mike expected me to be the pleasant, conforming, accepting wife and daughter-in-law who would bring her sons under control and make them obedient children who behaved properly and respectfully toward their elders. From my perspective, they were well behaved, respectful, assertive, and more spontaneous than children brought up in a more homogenous society and culture. They were deeply wounded children, as were all the adults in our family (and Mike's).

I remembered how hard my father struggled with me to make me conform to his standards and customs, and I resisted his efforts most of my life at home. Afterwards, I still resisted rigid rules in hospitals or anywhere else where I worked. I was not about to impose those kinds of rules on my children. I wanted them each to be their own unique person, and they were.

Unfortunately, I had neglected to spell out my philosophy of life to Mike. My freedom and that of my children to become the persons we were intended to be was uppermost in my sense of values. I assumed he would have the same values as me, given his experiences with authoritarian governments, similar to my growing up with an authoritarian father. I believe we did understand each other on an individual and couple basis when we were alone and away from the influence of his friends and mother.

In the family context, we were very different. He obviously loved his mother, and they had a close, understanding relationship. I, on the other hand, took a strong stance about being in charge of my own life whether I was in a family or a group. Our perceptions of reality were very, very different. I wanted them (he and his mother) to accept us as imperfect as we were, and I was willing to abide by and accept as much of their culture as I could manage, but I would not be transformed into a Hungarian when I already had such a difficult time being a Greek woman.

CLARIFYING PROFESSIONAL BOUNDARIES

I also established very clear boundaries around my professional life in those early years. I made my decisions about working, attending conferences, and doing workshops. These activities were for my professional development, and I did not ask permission to attend. I always let Mike know when I would be going and when I would return.

There was one other time when he got extremely angry with me and acted out one last time in a destructive way. I had been invited by the coordinator of Continuing Education to facilitate one of the sensitivity groups for nurses in a project she was developing called Building Community in Hospitals. This project, which extended over a two-year period of time (1970-1972), was to meet four times a year at the Conference Center at Asilomar on the Monterey Coast. The participants were nurses of all levels from staff nurses to supervisors and administrators. I was thrilled to be invited and to work with three well-known psychologists who were experts in the field of Group Dynamics in large organizations.

Of course, I informed Mike when I would be going. I sent a memo to Dr. Langsley describing the program, and he agreed that this was a great opportunity and learning experience for me. When the day arrived and I was due to leave, Mike insisted that I stay home that weekend. "Mike, I talked with you about this. I made a commitment and I am going. They can't find a substitute for me at this late date!" He appeared very glum and resentful. All of a sudden he flung the coffee cup he was holding in his hand. As it sailed by my head it lacerated my scalp. "What is wrong with you?" I shouted as I put a towel on my bleeding head.

I drove myself to the emergency room, and the doctor sewed several stitches to close the wound (I lied to the doctor. I said, "I slipped on the driveway and hit my head." I was sure he did not believe me.) I left later that afternoon for the four-hour drive to Asilomar.

We never had any more discussions about my professional activities. Although after that incident he seemed accepting on the surface, I had uneasy feelings about what was unspoken. Since he would not

talk with me, I let the subject drop. There were no further alterca-
tions. (I wondered how he would get back at me.)

Disappointment and Disillusionment

*During the first stage of marriage, commonly called Romance or Honeymoon,
both individuals open aspects of themselves that were not available before; then, each
can see the huge potentials for giving and receiving love. However, when our expectations of each other stretch beyond the boundaries of who we are, then disappointment and disillusion are inevitable. As a marriage therapist, I consider this response
to be the beginning of the transition to the second phase of marital development.*

I was aware of problematic behavior patterns very early in our
relationship, but I admittedly was so "love sick" or "crazy" that I
would not let myself think about what was happening. I had never
met a man who was so attentive and entertaining, and who knew how
to have fun in life! More than fun, he loved life and freedom—his
freedom. I loved the aspects of his personality that were romantic,
sophisticated, and exciting. I wanted to hold on to this image of who
Miklos was, his own person, because these were my deepest desires
for myself—to have my own identity and to be free of all shackles
that smacked of patriarchal controls. My impression was that he was
a highly intelligent, creative, and complex person who would not be
threatened by a woman who was intelligent, competent, and capable
in her own career.

In the beginning I saw him as one of the most well rounded persons I had ever known. Yet, I saw momentary flickers of behaviors
and actions that did not fit my image. He defied social rules, as if he
were entitled to make his own rules of life: running red lights and add-
ing a bathroom without the required permits. On a personal level he
did not hear, or did not want to hear, my request that his mother stay
in San Francisco. He decided to bring her to live with us two months
after we married, as if to say to me, "That's how it is going to be." He
tried to convince me it was for my benefit that she was coming.

I ignored my own reactions of hurt and disappointment and I
tried to comply with the situation even though I knew that arrange-

ment would not work for us. I had two sons who needed my help in making the necessary adjustments with a stepfather and a new home. They already had experienced some major changes and traumas, and I did not need or want a mother-in-law in the middle of our family to add to the complexities that were ahead of us.

I saw the potential in Mike for fathering or being friends with my sons. Here, I was very mistaken. This was my greatest, and lasting, disappointment. Later, when I learned that he had fathered two other children—one son, long ago in Hungary who grew up to become an active member of the Communist Party. The second was in San Francisco with a Hispanic woman. He met her once after she had the baby, and he recognized his blue eyes in the little girl. He never accepted responsibility for either one.

I suppose the Hungarian men, like the Greek men, never considered "illegitimate" children as theirs. The women were completely responsible, and they were considered disreputable as well. Apparently, he did not have to abide by his promises to women, as I learned a year after our marriage.

On some level, I believed that the woman who called threatening to sue him for not marrying her was being truthful. Was that the reason we eloped so quickly? Was this his way of getting out of a difficult situation? I felt uneasy. I could not admit I felt used and manipulated.

Yes, he was a warm, loving, accepting person, but his caring nature was very selective and possessive. Very often I felt he wanted me all to himself and resented that Franz and Marshall needed me. I was terribly disappointed that he could not express any understanding or empathy for my two sons, but yet he expected them to conform to his image of who they were or ought to be. I believe he expected the same from me: conformity and obedience; and most of all, he wanted me under his control all the time.

There was no doubt how he felt about our son, Andy. He was "the apple of his eye." They did everything together from bathing and swimming, riding the motorcycle and the boat, changing the oil in the car, and working together at whatever needed repair about the house. Andy obviously followed in his father's footsteps. He was an entrepreneur at eight when he started his neighborhood business of cleaning the neighbor's garages, mowing lawns, and later selling newspapers in order to save enough for a bicycle and a waterbed.

Our conflicts continued over Franz and Marshall. I could not face the fact that Mike was incapable of accepting my sons on a friendship level, much less on the parenting level. I could not face another relationship that was traumatic for my sons…. and I failed to protect them adequately. Neither could I face another divorce and single motherhood with three children. I chose to live in a family divided which was familiar to me. One, a small nuclear family, moderately happy, and the other with my sons and me, filled with the underlying tensions, stressors, and pain that were not resolvable. I made another mistake.

The seeds of our discontents had been planted early in our lives in our individual families and cultures, and we both relived our own conflicts in our marriage—unknowingly and unanticipated at the time we met. Miklos thought he found a nice European-grown woman who would slip into the role of wife who followed the rules of husband-in-charge and who would allow herself to become a trophy wife to show off and compete with the other wives in terms of fancy dresses, jewelry, and furs.

Of course, I was flattered to be given all those gifts until I realized what they really meant. In exchange for these "prizes," I would have to give up my hard-earned freedom of choice, my individuality and independence, and my identity that was forming and in process. The price was too high, and intuitively I reacted to the expectation that I had to conform to his ethnic standards and customs without any consideration for my values. That was too close to my own upbringing, which Mike learned about soon enough. Slowly and after some fierce arguments I could finally verbalize that I did not want to be treated like a "showpiece porcelain doll." Perhaps that was the beginning of the end of our relationship.

My hopes and expectations were that I had finally found a man who was strong enough to accept me as I was and who would provide the space and patience in our relationship for my growth and his. Yes, I expected him, me, and us to change, because he adapted very well to the American culture, or at least to some aspects of it, and I saw the potential for the five of us to become one family.

If we could work together as a partnership, which we did when it came to saving money, buying property, and financially expanding our base so we could travel, then we could do more growing together. However, Mike was not interested, nor did he know how, when I expected him to talk with me, to open himself on a deeper level and in more intimate interactions. I hoped that we could really get to know each other. I believed to be truly known by another, not only sexually, but also psychologically and spiritually, was the ultimate love between two people. I realized he was not ready to do the hard work of confronting his painful experiences of the past; and without mutual consent, I did not feel safe to share my own unfinished business. I decided to wait and see which direction we would take.

PERSONAL GROWTH AS A WAY OF LIFE

By our seventh year I had to settle the conflict within myself. I knew I had to continue growing and developing as a professional, and, after all my insisting, I thought we had come to an understanding that I would be in charge of my professional life and my sons. (Later, I would realize that Mike's lack of response to any position I took did not mean assent.) My other dilemma was whether to continue my own growth process. I knew I still had a great deal of psychological work to do in order to continue resolving my family issues and my development from adolescence to adulthood. I was very aware I had not completed growing my intended or True Self. Mike seemed content with himself and who he was, and I realized if I insisted in going in my own direction, our marriage was at risk, especially if I changed beyond his capacity to accept me. I decided this was a chance I had to take. My personal development was essential to me, even if Mike did not understand or want to participate.

I could not stop my own growth by will alone. I discovered the process was normal and natural and once I started I could not go back. I did not want to go back. I achieved my adolescence at the age of thirty-six and this meant that I had years of catching up with myself as an adult. Who was I as an adult? Would I have married so impulsively if I had been an adult and had a clearer sense of the direction my life was taking? Yes, I wanted to learn how to share my life with someone who accepted me and who was willing to struggle together with our pasts in order to achieve the kind of family we wanted together, someone who was willing to talk with me and we could really get to know each other, someone who would discuss problems and conflicts and was willing to make decisions together. I wanted a close loving relationship and a family. Thus far, I did not have the skills or the tools to achieve my personhood without constantly having to assert myself and fight for my values and beliefs, which was not effective. I was tired of fighting to be myself, but I would do so until I learned better ways.

In my work, I had to know who I was so as not to entangle my issues with those of my clients, students, and other professionals with whom I collaborated. At home, the better I knew my Self, the better I could keep from getting embroiled in my own and Mike's past family matters. In retrospect his explosiveness may have been early signs that the pain from his war wounds were rising up in reaction to feelings of loss and disappointment. Like many immigrants, refugees experience unresolved grief over the loss of homeland, family, friends, and life style. Perhaps, his disappointment in me as a wife had contributed to his emotional reactions. Eventually, these signs and symptoms would demand some kind of reckoning.

In 1974 a psychologist who was willing to work with me on a long-term basis accepted me into therapy, and I began another journey into self-discovery. This path which I called, "facing the reality of my life to the utmost of my ability and capacity" was not one for the meek or indecisive parts of me. Such a journey required every ounce of patience, discipline, perseverance, persistence, and faith that I could muster and commit to the therapeutic process. The surprising element in this journey was that I ran right into the undeveloped and unacknowledged spiritual self and God within me. There were some aspects to this trip within that were inspiring as well as terrifying at first, and ultimately where I found peace and another kind of love that was beyond anything I ever dreamed possible.

When I insisted on being in charge of my sons and my professional life, I could feel Mike's distancing, withdrawal, and rage. I saw aspects of him that were terrifying and incomprehensible, especially, when he turned his brutal, vindictiveness first on Franz and Marshall, then on me. I think I must have regressed into a dissociative state the first time he attacked Franz because I could not remember later what happened. I froze and later reacted with my own anger and rage. In retrospect, I can see now that his extreme reaction evoked an earlier defensive position that I used to protect myself against my father. I had to suppress and repress my negative perceptions of Mike in order to continue living in that environment because I could not bear to experience another loss of my family, and I did not believe that I could survive the pain another time.

On his part, Mike had to save face with his mother and his friends, because he could not control his wife. He protected himself by maintaining his self-centeredness, and what I called his cockiness, through his heavy drinking, his betrayals, and unfaithfulness.

You the reader may suggest that I chose my professional life over my marriage and my family and so it might seem. My view was that I wanted to live my whole life, not just play different roles in different situations. Yes, I was a mother and a wife, and I wanted to be the best that I knew how to be. I realized that my early development had left me with obstacles that had to be overcome if I was to become the person God intended me to be. Those personal, psychological, and mental blocks and obstructions interfered with my professional life as well as my personal life, so they had to be dealt with.

Fortunately, or unfortunately, psychological issues cannot be removed surgically. They must be confronted, changed, and integrated on mental, psychic, and spiritual levels that require a conscious willingness to enter into the dark side of our personalities and transform the self into the True Self. Some people call the self that evolved in a family, culture, and society the false self, the persona, or the mask; but I call it the protective self that aided me in surviving all those external influences.

This journey is unknown to people who are unwilling to take that first step. I was willing to do whatever it took to become what Sidney Jourard called "the transparent self." I did not want to continue hiding or being hyper vigilant about preserving as much of my own identity as I had achieved. I knew I had to get back into psychotherapy and whatever other means were necessary to continue growing.

Changes
and Transitions

MY PROFESSIONAL LIFE

Professionally, from 1965 to 1970, I was becoming a competent instructor and clinician. However, there were no clinical experiences provided in my work as an instructor. I found that as a teacher of a clinical practice, I needed to participate in some kind of clinical experience for my own continued learning. Clinical practice and teaching went hand in hand.

So I went out in the community to find places where I could practice my skills. I found two opportunities to work as a volunteer in the Veterans' Hospital and with the VISTA Program (Volunteers in Service to America), which was similar to the Peace Corps, only volunteers worked in this country instead of overseas. In the hospital, I joined a psychiatrist as a co-therapist in working with a group for schizophrenic men who were learning to interact with each other. In the second, I was assigned to make home visits with two Black women who lived in Hunters' Point—an area that was a ghetto at the time. The Vista Program was housed in a legal office. The attorneys handled the legal problems of their clients, and I was to handle the mental health problems.

The women I saw were having multiple problems in living in addition to mental and emotional problems. One of the women I visited was severely depressed; she had two troubled children, no husband, and was on welfare. Another woman had relational issues with husband and boyfriend. She pulled a knife from her bosom that she carried with her at all times to protect herself.

These experiences, along with teaching Family Therapy to graduate nurses, conducting sensitivity training with undergraduates, and supervising both levels of nurses were very rewarding and fulfilling work. I was doing the work that I'd always dreamed of doing, but I knew this job was not going to last.

University policy required permanent faculty to have doctorate degrees. Instructors were expected to stay on the faculty no more than five to seven years; then they were to move on to other jobs or to further education. Thus, every summer I spent time visiting hospitals in an effort to find a position as a Psychiatric Clinical Specialist.

Just as we had been promised when we entered the program, there were no jobs to be found in the Bay Area. Not only were there no jobs, there was nothing like a job description for a clinical nurse to work in outpatient mental health clinics. I discovered that social workers were monitoring patient's medications rather than nurses.

I found one psychiatrist who was in charge of a county out-patient clinic who was willing to let me work as a volunteer one evening a week for a year, interviewing patients in crisis; and he would consider writing a job description for the Civil Service Personnel Board. I'm sure he must have run into quite a bit of resistance with the Nursing Administrators because at the end of my term, he apologized that he had not been able to get the job description into the Personnel Office.

Fortunately, in the spring of 1970, Dr. Dan Adelman, the Social Psychologist who taught Group Dynamics in the Nursing Department, informed me of a job opening for a Mental Health Nurse Consultant in the Sacramento Mental Health Program. I called immediately and set up an appointment with Dr. Donald Langsley, the Director of the County Mental Health Program, who had actually written and had a job description accepted by the Civil Service Personnel Board. When I asked him how he managed to do that without the consent of the Nursing Administrator, he admitted he had asked her to do it; but after waiting two years she had not written a job description, and so he wrote one of his own. This meant that I was an employee of the Mental Health Department and not the Nursing Department.

This arrangement was a blessing for several reasons: I did not have to work under the rigid direction of a Nursing Director who resented nurses with degrees. She told me she resented that I came into the system through "the back door," that is, I applied for the job in Mental Health and not in the Nursing Department. She let me know in no uncertain terms that she did not approve of my attitude: "You came across too strong in our first meeting." She expected loyalty, not independence or assertiveness. And, I thought I was being on my very best behavior that day.

Fortunately, Dr. Langsley (author of a research study on Crisis Intervention with Families) was my boss, and he gave me a job description that was comprehensive, to put it mildly: I was to teach the inpatient nurses how to work in the community and in out-patient clinics; I was to recruit at least six more Masters level nurses! (I could hardly believe my ears. Here was a psychiatrist who wanted more nurses on board! How exciting!) I was to act as consultant to nurses in other psychiatric hospitals and to other professionals in community agencies in the county. Since I had been trained in family dynamics and therapy, I was to teach these subjects to the members of the interdisciplinary teams that consisted of psychiatrists, psychologists, social workers, nurses, and psychiatric technicians; and I was to supervise nursing, human services, and other students who were in the program.

When he completed telling me his description of my job, I could hardly contain my excitement. It was a perfect job for me, and although I thought this project would take me years to accomplish, I asked for one other consideration. Since I was a licensed family therapist (as of 1967) and I worked privately two evenings a week, I wanted his permission to do four hours a week of family therapy. He agreed without blinking an eye. Best of all, I was to report to him once a month on my progress, and he gave me free reign to organize my schedule and my work in the best way I knew how.

"And by the way," he added, "you will be on the Administrative Team and your wages are a thousand dollars a month." I was flabbergasted. That's unbelievable! That was two hundred dollars more than I was making at the University! And I had an office of my own!

I was overwhelmed and I took a deep breath and said, "Thank you, so much." Although Sacramento was about seventy-five miles from Walnut Creek, the traffic was so light that I traveled the distance in less than an hour and a half, whereas, the commute to and from San Francisco, only thirty-nine miles, took me two hours, and on Fridays, three hours!

Actually, I completed the goals of my job in four years: I recruited five nurses with Master's Degrees. Four nurses were assigned to one of the three mental health teams, the crisis clinic, and one went to the inpatient unit. In the next few years we hired additional nurses with degrees who worked in outpatient clinics and inpatient settings, and who consulted with schools. My consultation work covered private psychiatric units, public health nursing, and a variety of other public agencies. Occasionally, I even drove back to the Bay Area where I consulted with nurses in a couple of hospitals outside of Sacramento. The best part of this position for me was I was a CHANGE AGENT in all senses of those words, and I had the complete support of my director to do what I thought best for each situation!

Two years later, the University of California, Davis, Psychiatric Department of the Medical School, took over the administration of the County Program. Dr. Langsley submitted my name to the Dean and the Chair of the Department, and I received the appointment of Assistant Clinical Professor of Psychiatry. I was so surprised and honored to be the first nurse to receive that title that I immediately wrote a letter to my father who had retired to Tarpon Springs, Florida.

My hope was that he would finally acknowledge my accomplishments. His response was an acknowledgement of sorts: "At least you didn't disgrace me." I smiled when I received his letter. All those years when I yearned for his approval, and now that I had it, it didn't matter any more. I was pleased and happy with what I had done, and that meant more to me. I thanked my father and asked if Mike and I, and Andy, could come to visit him and my stepmother, Irene. I had not seen him for ten years.

VACATION IN FLORIDA

We drove across the southern states to Florida in August 1972 in miserably humid weather. We dropped Marsh off in Texas where he had been invited to spend a few weeks on his teacher's (Mr. Ashford) ranch. He would return to Walnut Creek by bus.

My father seemed more content than I remembered him, and Irene catered to him. She seemed very happy. Dad had retired from his trucking business in the late 1960s and moved to Tarpon Springs, a haven for former sponge divers from Kalymnos. He was so pleased to meet Mike that he took him around to the coffee houses to introduce him to all his countrymen, and they spent the first day together. We all spent the next few days at the beach on the Gulf of Mexico. Finally, my father was happy about something I had done. I married a man he could respect and admire.

A week later we were on our way up the East Coast to Sterling, Virginia, where we stayed with my sister, Mary, her husband, Gusty, and their two adopted grown children and two grandchildren. Mary worked in a government office in Washington, and Gusty was a lively, happy-go-lucky hairdresser who loved cooking a big Greek dinner for all of us. We stayed a couple days and went on to Ohio to meet my brother and his family. Everybody accepted and loved Mike and Andy.

The journey back to California was long and hot, and we were very happy to be home again. Marsh arrived a few days later looking very depressed. The last week in Texas, he was in a car accident. He was taken to a nearby hospital and examined by a doctor who gave him a clean bill of health. Another boy in the group had dived off a bridge into a river with many rocks. He broke his neck and died a few days later. I was very upset that I allowed Marsh to talk me into letting him go to Texas rather than coming with us. Years later, he told me what actually happened: "Mr. Ashford gave me some "speed" and allowed me to drive one of his cars. I was going too fast and flipped over. My head hurt, but I was OK."

MORE CHANGES AND NEW DIRECTIONS

Later that year, Mike was laid off from the Space Program. Many engineers were laid off in the early 1970s. I believe the cause of the lay-offs was the cutting back of federal funds. All the stressors in my life—good and bad—triggered off my own cycle of depression. As I have done every decade since I was twenty-five, I re-started therapy which helped me stay on an even keel with work and my problems at home.

Mike and I talked about his options, which were not optimistic. Jobs in other space programs were affected by budget cuts, or if there were jobs, they were too far to commute. "You know, there's one thing I've always wanted to do," he said to me one morning over breakfast. "What's that?" I asked. "I've always wanted a coffee shop where people could come and sit and read the paper or play chess—just like they do in Hungary and many other European cities."

"I think that's fine, Mike. I don't think I'll be much help, but I have a good job that will support us while you start this coffee shop. Perhaps there's a small restaurant for sale. Have you checked the papers?" He did think about this possibility and did his research, and within a couple of months, he found a small café for sale in Orinda, just ten miles or so west on the freeway. He was more excited than he had been for some time.

He worked with the owner for a period of time until he felt confident enough to take over, and when he did, he was the cook and manager. He had a couple of waitresses, and they served breakfast and lunch. Later, he introduced dinners and served Hungarian cuisine. He broke even the first year. The second year was a little bit stronger financially, but basically my paycheck covered our household expenses.

I don't remember when I began noticing some changes in Mike's behavior. He seemed more sprightly, excited, even cheerful, and gay. For a long time, he seemed tired and overworked. I thought he was beginning to realize that restaurant work was not easy, but he would not consider selling it. Now, his mood was up and I didn't know what was going on. He left unexpectedly one evening to return to the café. I felt very suspicious, so I decided to follow him. He may have noticed me behind him. When he got on the freeway, he started speeding. I tried to keep up with him, but I was not comfortable driving so fast. I slowed down. "He's heading for the café. I'll get there in plenty of time… for what? What am I going to find?" I wondered.

As soon as I walked into his place, I saw him in the booth close to the kitchen. A young waitress was sitting opposite him. I didn't recognize her. "She must be new," I thought and went to the booth and sat next to him. "Was this why you were driving so fast? You couldn't wait to come here to see her?"

I looked over at her, but she continued to count the pile of money in front of her, her eyes focused on what she was doing. Mike was counting dollars and change. He didn't greet me with his usual, "Hi, Honey!" He continued counting money, as if I wasn't there. He never responded, he never argued, and he never admitted any wrongdoing; because I learned over time, he believed, "What you don't know won't hurt you."

"I understand what's going on, now. I'll see you later when we can talk." I stood up and walked out slowly. I was shaking with hurt and anger.

I didn't want to make a scene. There were a few customers finishing their dinner. A couple of men in one of the middle booths were playing chess. My thoughts were crashing in my head. "He got his wish to own a café; and the girl was not too unexpected, was she? After all that's what his father did. Now, he's reenacting scenes from his father's life. This must be one of their customs too; or is this the way he gets even with me?"

While driving home, I tried to calm myself. Tears poured down my cheeks. "What am I going to do? I'm not going to drive a hundred and fifty miles a day and come home to this. I've got to see if I can find a place to move into that's close to work. I'm not going to stay here any longer. What am I going to do with Marsh and Andy? They can come to Sacramento with me."

During the following week in Sacramento, I asked several of the office workers if they knew of an apartment for rent near the Medical Center. One of the administrators had seen a *For Rent* sign in an upstairs apartment on the next block. On my lunch hour, I walked over to check it out. There was a telephone number to call and I did so. Yes, the one-bedroom would be available in a month. I asked the manager to hold it for me, and I mailed the deposit.

I went home that evening prepared to tell Mike I would be leaving. He still denied he was having an affair. "Mike, you can deny all you want. I trust my eyes and my intuition. You have been more distant recently, and now you're acting like an adolescent on his first date. I'm not going to stay here as long as you're seeing that girl. She can't be much over twenty-two. Aren't you a bit old for her?"

Again, he gave me the silent treatment. I was hurt, but this time I was not devastated. I could think and I was fairly calm. I talked to Marsh and Andy and simply told them that I was very tired of commuting every day, and "I'm thinking of staying in Sacramento and coming home on Wednesday evenings and on the weekend every other week. Do you want to come and stay with me and go to school there?"

Neither of them wanted to move to Sacramento. I hired a young man, Lee, from the Community College, to look after Andy in exchange for his room and board. He was Chinese and obviously knew how to handle my son. Lee became like a big brother for Andy. They went bowling on the weekends, and Andy learned to cook and eat a lot of rice. Eventually, I did take Marshall to Sacramento and enrolled him in a private school.

Not commuting every day was a great relief. I actually walked to work in just a few minutes. And living alone was heavenly. I brought my bicycle and went riding after work. I had time to read, and one of my first activities was to write a paper on Death and Dying for a conference at Columbia University. I had been consulting with the staff nurses on a couple of wards at the Medical Center on the impact of dying patients on nurses who cared for them, and I was making rounds with one of the Chaplains who visited dying patients. This was an interest of mine. In Graduate School, I had written a research paper on the literature on death and dying—this was not a popular subject at that time and the grade I received was a "B" because the instructor thought the topic was not that relevant to nursing.

When Elizabeth Kübler-Ross published her book in the early

1970s on "Death and Dying" and began training medical students and giving workshops, the subject caught on like wildfire and swept through hospitals all over the country. All of sudden the subject became very relevant, and I was on the frontlines starting bereavement groups, giving workshops, and writing papers and giving speeches on the subject. One of my papers was accepted for publication in a book called, *The Nurse as Caregiver for the Terminally Patient and His Family (1976)*.

My work was going extremely well. With personal psychotherapy and a series of Rolfing (deep tissue) Massages, my depression lifted, and I was not exhausted from commuting everyday. In fact, my relationship with Mike improved. I went home on Wednesday evenings and we took turns driving to Sacramento and Walnut Creek. We started dating again, and Andy enjoyed being with us. We were a family again!

A life-long student, Libby not only graduated from high school, something she had to fight for to break tradition in her family, but she went on to nursing school, then college and graduate school. Libby graduated with honors from the University of Minnesota, School of Nursing with a Bachelor of Science Degree in Nursing Education on July 12, 1962. She received her Master of Science Degree on August 31, 1963 in Psychiatric/Mental Health Nursing followed by two post-graduate years of further study and practice in Psychiatric Nursing and Teaching. She was awarded her Ph.D. on November 5, 1982 at the age of 54 (above photo) in Marriage and Family Therapy, from the California Graduate School of Marriage and Family Therapy.

Liberty Kovacs is the most inspiring person I have ever known... her life—as teacher, therapist, and writer—is an embodiment of self-sacrifice, triumph over adversity, and the never-ending quest to lessen rather than contribute to the suffering of other human beings. – **Franz Wright**

Sacramento

After a year, I asked Mike whether he wanted to move to Sacramento. He needed time to think about it. All of his friends were in the Bay Area. Our house would be sold, and we would settle in Sacramento where he could find another job. I think the most difficult part of the decision was selling his café – and letting go of the girlfriend. Yes, she was in the background and I did not pressure him. I simply told him, "I will not come back to Walnut Creek to live. I'm staying here. I've got a great job, and I'm sure you will be able to find a job here, but it's your choice."

He thought about my proposal for six months. He finally decided to sell his business and our house and buy one in Sacramento. In fact, he bought two other pieces of property (duplexes) that he could rent and use as investments for his retirement. He got a job at McClelland Air Force Base. The affair went on a few more months, until he received a bouquet of roses for his birthday. "That's it! Either this stops or you can leave!" He called her and ended the relationship.

I was more angry than humiliated by his juvenile escapade, but I realized during the year that I could live very well without him. I meant it when I said he had a choice about returning. I didn't want him to come back unless he was ready to let go of the girl, of course; but he had to let go of his connections with his Hungarian cohorts; he had to move further away from his mother, sell his business, and our house. These were serious considerations for him, and he had to choose.

Later, he told me that he came back because Andy asked him, "When are we going to live with Mommy again?" He would do anything for his son, but I knew he would not return if he didn't have some feelings for me, too. Despite the betrayal, I still loved him. More importantly, he gave me something more valuable—reluctantly, to be sure—he had accepted that my work was important to me, and I could still be his wife. I knew I would always be Andy's mother, just as I was Franz's and Marshall's, no matter what happened to the marriage. Our relationship was very significant for me. I felt a sense of stability and security that I had not experienced before. And, I knew from my experience that I could live a very productive and happy life alone, if and when we came to that point again. In fact, I knew I could take care of myself no matter what happened.

He told me once that he could never live with a woman he did not love, and I believed him. I knew when he stopped being affectionate and loving, the relationship would be over. In the meanwhile, Andy was not going to have a broken home, and my commitment to my older sons was as strong as ever. I realized that I had reached the first level of adulthood! I was living my life and our life together, with all the difficulties, problems, and struggles that marriage entails, and it had its rewards and pleasures as well. I was content with that.

A Successful Program

By 1976 our program, now the UCD Mental Health Service, gained national recognition as one of the best mental health programs in the country. The crisis clinic went from five hundred hours of crisis work a month to eight hundred hours by the end of the decade. We did thousands of hours of outpatient clinical work, and we met our goal of keeping hospitalizations to a minimum.

Our philosophy was to treat individuals and families in the community as soon as possible to prevent the need for long-term expensive hospitalizations. Only those patients who were a danger to self and others and the gravely disabled were hospitalized, and then only for seventy-two hours. If there was little or no improvement, patients were held for another fourteen days.

Patients who had been hospitalized for years in State Hospitals were being released to communities programs like ours for care. Unfortunately, the more successful we were, the more the politicians started cutting our funds on the national and state levels.

When there was no hope of retaining the programs we had developed, the leaders of our program started moving to other states. Dr. Langley moved to Cincinnati, Ohio. Several clinicians followed him there. By 1978, I had applied and been accepted at the California Graduate School of Marriage and Family Therapy for doctoral work. I attended on a part-time basis the first year. I stayed one more year in the Mental Health Program, and after resigning the most exciting job I had ever had, I began attending classes on a full-time basis.

I've always regretted that the great program we had was slowly dismantled to meet political goals rather than the needs of the people. Most of us who worked in this program went into private practice and continued to do the work we had been so well trained to do.

Father and
Sons

In 1967 Jim Wright remarried, and that fall he and his bride, Anne, came to San Francisco. He wanted his wife to meet Franz and Marsh and to spend a day or two together. The boys were so excited and nervous about seeing their Dad again. They hadn't seen him for three years.

Mike drove us to San Francisco and the gathering was very cordial. I was happy to see Jim again, and he looked much better than the last time I had seen him. He seemed a little uneasy but so very happy when he saw his sons again, and he greeted them with a big bear hug. I was so relieved that they would have their Dad in their lives again. Thereafter, they spent the week after Christmas in New York, and they had great vacations with Jim and Anne during the summer months in different places: Vienna, Paris, Montreal, and Hawaii

FRANZ, MY OLDEST SON

Franz graduated from high school in June 1971, with quite a few honors in German and English. He was chosen as an exchange student to Belgium. He took his pain and his depression with him. I hoped that the change in environments might help him to come out of the dark mood that seemed to envelop him. I had a couple of my therapist friends talk with him a few times, and they thought he was grieving and missing his father.

His surrogate family in Belgium took him on a vacation to a resort on the Adriatic Sea. While there, Franz began having panic attacks. He developed a severe fear that something was going to happen to his father, and he had to go back and see him. After a month, the Belgian family decided that he should return to the States. He flew directly to New York and stayed with his father and Anne for about a month before returning to California.

He had applied and was accepted to start in the winter quarter at Oberlin College in Ohio. In January 1972, he flew back to Ohio to begin classes. Later, I learned that he had met a girl named Camille in Belgium, and she, too, was attending Oberlin. The relationship did not last. She was intent on marrying and Franz was not ready to take that step.

Although we went to visit him the following summer, neither Mike nor Franz were at ease with each other so we did not stay long. We went on to Columbus to visit my brother, Tony, and his family. Franz came back to California a couple of times, but he always seemed anxious to return to Ohio. I thought it rather paradoxical that Franz was so enamored of a place that both his father and I had fled from almost two decades before.

Franz became addicted to alcohol and drugs at Oberlin, and he graduated in 1977. I went back for his graduation and joined Jim and Anne who were there that weekend. Franz was excited and rather exuberant that weekend, and he seemed very pleased that we were there with him. I was a little troubled by his behavior, which seemed more aggressive and agitated than I had ever seen him before. I had suspected that he was using drugs, but I said nothing to him at that time. I hoped it was a transient fad that would fade away.

After graduation he went east to New York and from there to Boston to be near his Dad and where he could write poetry. I encouraged him to think about graduate school, but he decided he wanted to work on his own writing. He started publishing his poetry while he was at Oberlin.

Franz wrote me a note dated December 31, 1979, informing me that his dad was very ill and was scheduled to have surgery the following week. He said, "I've spoken with him: his courage and his will to go on with his own work gives me a lot of hope. I have to admit, though; it's hard for me to shake off a growing sense of futility and hopelessness. Knowing my own tendencies, I try to combat them…."

He was at his dad's side throughout his hospitalization during the next three months. He was quite devastated when his father died of throat cancer on March 25, 1980, a week after Franz' twenty-seventh birthday. Jim was only fifty-two years old.

His father's death was another huge loss for Franz. Like many adult children whose parent(s) die at a young age, Franz retained a sense of impending doom as he approached his late forties and fifties. He was convinced he would not live past fifty-two. For the next decade or so, he went through some hellish experiences. He sought psychotherapy and medical treatments for the bipolar and panic episodes that he suffered frequently as well as attending meetings at Alcoholics Anonymous.

He married Elizabeth Oehlkers in early October 1999 and converted to Roman Catholicism. He continued writing his poetry throughout the years, and he was awarded the Pulitzer Prize in 2004. He and his father are the first father and son poets to win that prestigious award. Franz and I have reconciled and we are friends again.

The day before his fifty-second birthday, March 17, 2005, he sent me the following Email:

> Dear Mom:
>
> How strange to think that tomorrow I will turn the age Dad was when he got sick and died. As you can imagine, this has been producing some rather dark feelings all week.
>
> On the other hand when I woke up this morning and practically laughed out loud at the incredible mysteriousness of the following fact: that while my birth must, without question, and for better or worse, have been one of the most glaringly memorable days of your life, I myself have no recollection of it whatsoever!!! Don't you find that funny?
>
> I am thinking of you with much love.
> Franz

I was deeply touched. Franz has overcome and transcended much pain and torment, and he is excited and thankful to be alive and to be living a very full life. I, too, am deeply grateful for my son and his joy.

MARSHALL, MY MIDDLE SON

As Marshall left for school early in September 1965, he turned and said, "Mom, I promise I'll turn over a new leaf. I'll reform this year." I was surprised by such a thoughtful statement from my happy-go-lucky son. What did my precious seven-year old son know about reforming? I wondered. I was so touched by his serious intention. "That's wonderful, Marsh. Have a great first day at school!"

He really tried hard and he did do very well—from September to February—his grades were all As and Bs and he was a happy child. Then something happened. He became restless, inattentive, distracted, talking constantly. He spent most of the spring months in the principal's office. Mr. Jeffers was a short, balding man who had worked with children for two decades. He smiled when I went to discuss Marshall's behavior. He would laugh and reassure me: "He's a fine young man. He just has Spring Fever."

I was not comforted. I would ask my colleagues about Marsh, and no one seemed to think there was anything seriously wrong. "But why does he behave this way every spring? Is there such a thing as Spring Fever?" Not even the Child Psychiatric people had any answers. Of course, I turned on myself and questioned, "What am I doing wrong?"

[There were no psychiatric diagnostic categories, such as Attention Deficit Disorder at that time; nor, theoretically, did the professionals believe that children suffered from depression or manic depressive illness (later changed to Bipolar) at least, not until the mid-1970s when studies started coming out in the medical journals and books confirming that these major affective disorders did occur in children and adolescents].

When Mike turned his anger on Franz and Marsh, I was very

protective of my sons and I forbade Mike from hitting them. I know my taking "their side" angered him, and he could not understand my position that he was not to use physical punishment. This was incomprehensible to him, and it took him a while to realize I meant it. After all, his father slapped him a few times and he was able to handle it, plus all the other physical abuse he suffered in prison and in the mines.

Whenever I disagreed with him, particularly about managing my sons, he would mumble under his breath that I was his "enemy." "No, I am not your enemy," I'd reply. "I just disagree with you on the way you treat my sons. Don't you understand how hurtful that is for them?"

When Marshall completed the sixth grade I decided to send him to a private school where there were fewer students and the teachers would have more time to be attentive to Marsh's needs. I talked with Mike about my decision, but spending the extra money on a private school did not please him. I insisted and found a small private school in Danville, about ten miles to the south of Walnut Creek. Again, Marsh did very well during the first half of the year; but by spring, he was "acting up" again.

There were a couple of teachers who did spend more time with Marshall, but nothing seemed to change until the cycle subsided during the summer months. Then, suddenly, his behavior got worse. He came home one evening acting very giddy, laughing and talking inappropriately. "Marsh, have you been drinking?" He shook his head "No." "Then, tell me what is wrong with you?" He laughed and went running out of the house.

The next day I took him to the Mental Health Clinic in Martinez where I had worked for a year as a volunteer. The counselor who interviewed Marsh smiled when he came out of his office and said, "He's using a little marijuana. It won't hurt him and it seems to calm him down."

I couldn't believe my ears. "I'm a nurse and I don't believe that children should experiment with such drugs. We don't know what it does to them." Apparently he thought I was overreacting and overprotective, because he said something like, "Well, kids are using different kinds of drugs these days. They're OK."

I felt frantic and helpless at times because I could do nothing to stop what was happening to Marshall. He seemed to be out of control to me, and I had no idea where the drugs were coming from. (Many years later, Marsh told me that one of his teachers "turned me on to speed and pot!") He could not manage high school, and I placed him in another private school in Sacramento where I learned that more drugs were available there as well. Even some of the teachers were using "pot" during breaks.

By the time Marshall was seventeen, he was getting more aggressive. One day, he attacked Mike in our backyard and had him in a stranglehold. I tried pulling his arm, but he was stronger than I was. Feeling desperate and afraid he might kill Mike, I grabbed a broom and hit him on his back. He finally let go and ran out of the yard. Mike was out of breath, but he was all right and very angry.

I called my nurse friend, Polly, who was working at the Sutter Memorial Hospital and asked whether he could be hospitalized there. I knew Dr Margolis who worked there with adolescents, and I wanted him to examine Marshall and tell me how he could be treated. I was terrified at the possibility that he would be diagnosed schizophrenic, but I had him hospitalized. I had to know what was wrong with him so he could be treated, finally.

Dr. Margolis had a social worker interview me to get a thorough family history of Marsh since birth as well as family background, my history of depression and my family's, as well as similar information about his father's illness, alcoholism, hospitalizations, and his background. Then, I had an interview with the doctor several days later. With the information that I gave him, he diagnosed Marshall with manic depression and a drug-induced psychosis.

He prescribed Lithium, a natural salt medication that stabilized Marsh's mood. After two weeks in the hospital, Dr. Margolis transferred him to a residential treatment program for adolescents where he stayed for six months. From there he went to a group home for boys where he could continue his convalescence.

He attended high school during this period of time and was able to graduate while he lived in that home. I visited him every Saturday, and he seemed to do very well there for about a year and a half. When he was ready to be released, Mike decided he did not want Marsh living with us. I understood that he was afraid of another attack; but more than fear, I felt he was deeply resentful of my son. I continued to explain to him why Marsh behaved the way he did, but Mike was impervious to my explanations. He could not comprehend the concept of mental illness. He could not understand that his judgmental and moralistic attitude had affected Marsh (and Franz) in a negative way. All he would say was, "Marshall cannot live here anymore."

Because he was a "consumer" of the mental health services, Marsh was placed in a Board and Care facility where his medications were given to him daily. This was the beginning of Marshall's career as a mental health patient and a drug addict that has lasted his entire adult life. He had numerous hospitalizations over the years, always as a result of stopping his medications and continuing to use/abuse a variety of stimulants combined with marijuana. There were periods of times when Marsh was clean and sober.

I stayed in his life and we spent time together once week for years. That was our time and we did a variety of activities together. We went to movies, had lunch or dinner together, and sometimes went shopping. On special holidays, he spent the day with our entire family. On his birthday, I generally made or bought a large cake and delivered it to the home where he was living at the time. For presents, I bought him whatever items of clothing he needed. I stopped purchasing things that could be sold for drugs.

One of our most enjoyable activities was taking drives together. There was one birthday we spent on the beach in Marin County and flew kites. In the fall he enjoyed going up to Apple Hill near Placerville where we went from farm to farm and enjoyed the different goodies that were sold, especially apple pie or strudel and ice cream.

Several years ago on an autumn Friday afternoon, I drove Marsh from Sacramento southwest on Route 84 toward San Jose. The day was bright, warm, cloudless, and my forty-three-year old hippie son was sitting beside me quietly enjoying the scenery that we had not seen for several years. As we climbed the hill toward Altamont Pass, windmills appeared on the horizon. Thousands of huge metallic birds were spinning their wings and collecting the earth's energy into nearby generators. We smiled at each other as we remembered seeing the windmills for the first time years ago when we lived in Walnut Creek. I didn't have a camera, but I mentally clicked a picture of those wonderful birds as they collected the wind.

This was a trip that I had not planned with great enthusiasm. Marsh wanted to go to a concert given by Bob Dylan, one of his adolescent idols, and he wanted me (his mother of all people!) to go with him. Reluctantly, I consented. I suspected that this would be my first, and last, concert of this kind. The musician was over sixty years old, and I was a decade plus older than him. "Besides," I thought mistakenly, "his music was not as loud as some I have been avoiding for the last two decades."

We arrived at the San Jose Arena in plenty of time. I had ordered our tickets several weeks before and was to pick them up at 6:00 p.m. With a couple of hours to spend waiting, we went across the street to a children's park decorated for Halloween with scarecrows and ghosts. We sat on a park bench and watched children climbing on ropes and sliding down multicolored boards. Several times we walked around the pleasant little park. Time passed very slowly, and I very deliberately put myself in a quiet, slow-paced frame of mind, and waited.

Eventually, we picked up the tickets, ate a picnic lunch that I had packed that morning, and were standing in line when a slim young man came toward us. He was carrying a huge sign on two poles in the shape of a cross, and it was strapped around his waist. In large red letters, the sign proclaimed Christ had died to save all sinners. Needless to say, he got needled by others who were standing in line waiting, trying to be patient and looking forward to the music.

"Get away. We're just here to have a good time," shouted one of the men behind us. Of course, this was what the young man with the sign was waiting for, and he started the sermon that he must have practiced many times. He called us all "pagans" and "sinners" and the cross talk became more vociferous on both sides. A video camera with sound would have been more effective than a camera or my memory to record the sermon and the responses, since I can't remember all that was said.

Marsh and I tried to ignore the commotion, and before long the line was moving toward the door and our seats. I was so happy that I had paid the extra money for seats; otherwise we would have been down on the floor with hundreds of others milling around. The picture I have in my mind was of a thousand people gathering on the floor of the arena; some sat; most stood in the spot that they chose as theirs. There was a respectful air about the way people placed themselves. Excitement and anticipation was growing, but still in a muted, controlled fashion until the musicians gathered on stage. Then, in unison all the voices rose to greet and welcome Bob Dylan and his accompanists: two other singers with guitars, a bass player, and a drummer. Bob Dylan, white-haired, dressed in a cream-colored tight outfit, sang in his familiar raspy, incoherent voice for the next two and a half hours. I did not understand a word he sang, but, thankfully, the rhythm was catchy enough to keep my feet tapping and hands swaying in time to the music.

Here's the scene that kept me occupied during those two and a half hours: the stage had a backdrop of thick curtains that changed colors as the lighting was focused on them. They changed from blue to gold, to green and red, to purple. Then, right behind the musicians there must have been huge vats of incense that filled the stage with smoke and exotic smells. I wondered if that was done to cover the smell of marijuana that I noticed was growing stronger as the hours wore on. Then, there were those thousand or so bodies that moved in rhythmic waves, singly at first, then in groups, and eventually the whole group was weaving and waving and shouting as one body and one voice.

As I watched, I felt as if I were observing a pagan ritual. Even those around us in the seats grew more rhythmical and would rise to their feet as if to some secret signal that I had missed. The sounds and movement of the audience became more and more ecstatic in response to the musicians who became more and more exhilarated by the sounds they produced until the whole arena was in a euphoric, rapturous, and elated altered state of consciousness.

After the concert, we left the auditorium and walked to the parking lot, and I wondered if my ears would ever be normal again.

Marsh was very happy. We had a three-hour drive home ahead of us and, despite the loud music, I was very pleased that we had spent the day together. I loved being close to Marsh.

He continued to live in board and care facilities; and once for a period of four years an older couple invited him to live with them. They had an empty trailer on their property and he could have a place of his own. They cared for him and looked after him like he was their son until they had to move out of state. They have stayed in touch with Marsh over the years. That was the most stability that he had for over a decade. Afterwards, he managed to stay in the board and care homes for longer periods of time.

In early 1980, when I learned from Franz that his father was dying, I asked Marsh if he wanted to see his father. He did. He hadn't seen his father since he was sixteen, and he wanted to talk with him. He felt bad that he had written his father a very angry letter and exclaimed, "You are not my father! You have never cared for me!" He wanted to ask his father to forgive him. I sent him to New York and asked Franz to look after him. He was not permitted to see his father; and he returned dejected, very sad, and deeply wounded. His father rejected him, again—first at birth; then his father refused to see him when he was dying.

Over the next three decades, he became a habitual user of street drugs. He learned that he could not use medications mixed with street drugs so he would discontinue his medications. Then, he would become psychotic and very aggressive under the influence of methamphetamines and "crack."

In 1983 I filed a restraining order against him for his aggressiveness toward Mike and me. One afternoon he came to our home and with a crowbar smashed all the windows in the house plus mirrors and the television. He immediately went to the Crisis Clinic and had himself admitted to the psychiatric ward.

Despite all his drug use over the years, he miraculously was jailed only twice in the 1980s; and that was because he violated our restraining order and I had him arrested. He spent several weeks in jail and came out asking me to get him some help. I paid for his psychotherapy treatments with a social worker who saw Marsh regularly in individual therapy, along with a psychiatrist who prescribed his medications. Marsh attended sessions sporadically because he saw no need for therapy.

Over the years, he was hospitalized numerous times. He had many mental health helpers, attended several recovery programs, and was in a number of outpatient mental health programs. In the late 1980s and 1990s, Dual Diagnosis Programs were developed where mental health problems and addictions were treated simultaneously, but by the 2000s the professionals decided that these programs were not working. Now, the mental health programs will not treat addiction problems, and the alcohol and drug rehabilitation programs will not work with the mentally ill. Marshall has been shuffled from one to another, neither working for him.

Not until he decided that he could no longer pursue this lifestyle or he would die that he finally, in 2005, decided to stay clean and to attend meetings at Narcotics Anonymous. Like many other addicts, he attempted many times before to stop and always returned to using drugs. Death is the Great Motivator for many who succeed in changing and transforming their lives.

I pray everyday that Franz and Marsh will continue on their paths to recovery. Marshall and I are now learning how to live more peaceably with each other. It's not easy, but both of us want to build a new relationship with each other, and he wants to be free of drugs. This is the first time he has chosen a Sponsor. I believe his commitment is strong, and I say many prayers for both Franz and Marsh.

Stability
for a Change

Our family life was fairly stable with the three of us. Mike worked the day shift, I was working in the Crisis Clinic and teaching family therapy to the interdisciplinary staff, plus I opened a small private practice one evening a week. Andy was a good student and had a very active after-school life. He enjoyed his friends so much that he decided in the third grade that rather than becoming an "A" student, he preferred developing his friendship activities and he did not mind the "Bs and Cs" as much as I did.

I was very perturbed because I knew he was bright, and just a little more effort on his part and he would be at the head of his class. Andy was not interested in being that ambitious, and I accepted his decision finally when he did not respond to encouragement, bribes, or coercion. He had chores after school, and he developed his own neighborhood grass-cutting and garage-cleaning business. By twelve, he was waking up at 5:30 a.m. to deliver newspapers to earn money for his special needs, like a waterbed.

A little later, I was working in one of the area clinics and was considering returning to graduate school for my Ph.D. Mike and I discussed this possibility and I thought about it for about a year. The funds for Mental Health were being cut, and I knew the program would not last the way it was for very much longer. Mike agreed that he would support me when I wasn't working full-time. I was developing my private practice, and I was frightened at the thought of not having a regular salary. I decided that if I was eventually going to work full-time in private practice, I'd better be more prepared than I was.

In September 1978, I started attending the California Graduate School of Marriage and Family Therapy on a half-time basis. I was commuting again one afternoon a week. As usual for me, I was thrilled to be back in school again. This was my home, my sanctuary, and my joy. No matter what else was going on in my life, those hours of class were my happiest days.

With deep sadness and grief, I resigned my position in the UCD Mental Health Program in August 1979, and I registered as a full-time student at the California Graduate School. This meant that I would be commuting to the Bay Area twice a week again, but this was not as bad as driving that distance five times a week, and I was not working full-time. I was building my practice, and I earned enough money to pay for my tuition and books. I was working through my grief over giving up the best job I ever had. Deep within me, I missed my great position.

I immersed myself in my studies. I was familiar with much of the family therapy literature, and I found the classes very exciting. More importantly, there was the very real possibility that I would get the assistance I needed to develop a dissertation on a subject I had been researching on my own for about five years: the developmental process of the marital relationship. I was very intent on finding a theory that explained how the stages of intimate relationships evolved.

After working with families for ten years, I came to the conclusion that I needed to understand the marriage relationship better if children were to develop in a healthy environment. When children were the "identified patients," I started focusing on the couple's relationship. Once I determined where the problems lay, especially in the communication systems with families of origin, then the child "was unhooked" from the parents' issues and helped to stay out of the middle of the marriage. Of course, this was a complex process that took me years to unravel; but slowly, I began seeing relationships between the couples' difficulties and the families they came from.

Sometimes I was able to track one problem in the marriage through several past generations of their extended families. This was very exciting, particularly the suggestion that the problems in the marriage resulted from the couple's "unfinished business" with their parents and family of origin.

The idea that marriage progressed in stages evolved from observing certain patterns that occurred with my clients in the 1970s. The divorce rate had skyrocketed to fifty percent from sixteen percent in the previous decades. The couples were struggling with issues of dependence and independence, usually between the fifth and seventh year. I did some small informal studies of my private clients and those whom I was seeing in the Mental Health Program. I wanted to see if there was any relationship with the problems they were having and the number of years that the couples were married.

My studies indicated that the mean number of years that my clients were married were between 7.2 and 7.5 years. The national average was 7.5 years. The idea that the "seven-year-itch" might be more than a humorous colloquialism began to take hold and evolved into the idea that perhaps marriages, like groups, children, and families, developed in stages.

To my great consternation, there was no such theory to be found in the U.C. Berkeley Library where I went to do my research. I found bits and pieces of research by family sociologists about the first year of marriage, but little or nothing on the later stages. There was a small literature on family development, and stages of growth and change were outlined, as well as in childhood and adolescence; but there was nothing substantial in marriage development. That was to be my project for the next three years.

My Father
is Dying

Late in May 1979, I received a telephone call from my stepmother, Irene, in Florida. "Your father is critically ill with colon cancer. If you want to see him alive, I think you better come right away." As quickly as possible, I made arrangements to be absent from my classes and flew to Tampa. From the airfield, I took a cab to my father's home address. The cab driver had difficulty finding the place and was surprised that the address was in a primarily black neighborhood. I wasn't that surprised. My father loved our black neighbors as much as I did, and most of the truck drivers that he hired were black.

The evening was warm as I walked up the porch steps to the screen door and knocked. The other door was open and I could see into the living room. I waited for Irene to come and let me in. When she saw me she was beaming with smiles and told me, "I'm so happy you're here." I gave her a hug and walked in. My father was lying on a couch to my left. I turned toward him, and he said, "Irene, who is this?"

Surprised, she answered, "Paul, it's your daughter, Liberty." He stared at me for the longest time, not recognizing me. I went over and sat in a chair beside him, "How are you, Dad?" I asked softly. I knew his mind was clouded with pain medications, and that's probably why he didn't recognize me; but even so, I felt a deep sense of pleasure that he didn't know me right away. I said to myself, "What a gift you've given me, Dad! By not recognizing me, you have validated my growth and the changes I've made! I could never see completely what I had done, but if my father doesn't know me, then I

have changed! Thank you for the best gift you have ever given me!"
I smiled at him wordlessly.

The next day while Dad was sleeping, Irene and I went out for
a walk. I asked her about funeral arrangements, and she looked
startled, "I couldn't do that. He might get better," she exclaimed.
Although she called me because she was fearful that he might be dying, she was in denial when she saw him talking and smiling a little.

"I'm sorry, Irene. I don't want to upset you, but while I'm here,
why don't you let me help you make the arrangements. I don't know
how much time he has, but when he does go, you're going to be
upset and grieving, and I don't think that's the best time to make arrangements. What do you think?" She agreed, and we walked to the
nearest funeral home. We made arrangements for him to be buried
in Martins Ferry, according to his wishes, which he had told to Irene.
She was quiet afterwards, and I saw her give a sigh of relief.

Later that day, I called my siblings, Mary, Tony, Ann, and Jack,
and said to each of them, "If you want to see Dad before he dies, I
think you ought to come very soon. I'm guessing, but I think he has
six weeks." In fact, he lived seven weeks. Before he died, Irene had
one request of him, "Please marry me in church or by a priest here
at home." He consented after twenty-five years of being married in
a civil service. The priest did come to their home and married them
a week before he died.

Dad was flown back to Martins Ferry where we had a memorial
service for him in the Greek Orthodox Church that we all attended
throughout the time we lived there; and I believe we were all married there, except Jack who was married in Wisconsin. Most of us
went to different parts of the country (only Tony lived nearby in Columbus, Ohio); we left to get away from the Valley and our father.

Remarkably, we all gathered in the funeral home, in the church,
and at the cemetery to say our last goodbyes to one of the strongest,
most stubborn, and determined men I had ever known. Relatives,
neighbors, and old friends—those who had survived him—all came
to pay their respects. We had a very happy reunion, and we buried
my dad next to my mother. Irene had hopes of being buried on the
other side of dad. After all those years, my parents were together

again. Several times when I have gone back "home," I always go back and visit them, too. I feel happy when I am there with the two of them side by side again. Irene still lives in Tarpon Springs near her two daughters and their families. We exchange Christmas cards every year.

Life Goes On

When I returned to Sacramento, I continued my life and my schooling. I was rather surprised that I did not feel grief-stricken over the loss of my father. I felt more reconciled. I felt more at peace with him than I had at any other time. I was accepted. I returned to my work on synthesizing a theory of marital development from five theories and from clinical practice, with a great deal of help from the faculty who were on my committee. In the summer, 1982, just before I was scheduled to defend my dissertation in October and graduate in November, I became emotionally blocked for six weeks. I could not think nor write a clear sentence in my dissertation. My mind was going around in circles. I became anxious, very frightened, and felt frozen inside.

Finally, I called my chairperson, Karen Saeger, Ph.D., just about the same time I received a note from her asking me, "What's going on? Come in and see me." I wondered how she knew I was having a hard time, and I was grateful that she was so thoughtful. I burst into tears as soon as I saw her and tried to explain what was happening to me. As if she hadn't heard me, she started calling me Dr. Kovacs. That terrified me because I could not believe that I would ever be able to function again or to complete the work I had started. "WHY are you doing that?" I almost shouted at her. Because, Dr. Kovacs, I think you will be just fine and you will finish on time."

I left uncertain I could do anything more. I never understood what purpose her response served, until I had a dream two nights later. I was at a podium in a classroom and was taking my dissertation out of a satchel to present to the class, but it was all in disarray. I was having trouble sorting the pages in order. I started to feel frantic; and I looked up at the class, and there in the last seat in the first row sat my father! He was smiling at me and nodding "Yes" to me! He was finally giving me permission to continue my work.

Karen knew my story, that my father had not believed that I needed a high school education, much less college or graduate school. My repressed fear of failure and my fear that I was disobeying my father surfaced in the middle of the analysis of the statistics. I was not as confident with statistics, and I had to hire a statistician to help me with the analyses. I believed that the dream of my father giving me permission was really Dr. Saeger telling me that she believed I could do it and I would become "Dr. Kovacs." Even so, I still hold on to that warm, quiet feeling deep inside that my father *was* giving me permission and forgiving me.

With great relief and disbelief, I woke up that morning and started writing, fast and furiously, to complete the research section of my dissertation. I outlined the six stages of marriage and the basic tasks of marriage, and I wrote and interpreted the statistical results in the next month.

When I defended my dissertation, I reported that the time or the number of years married was not a significant factor in the stages of marriage, because many people got stuck in the Power (third) stage as well as in the Separation-Individuation stage (fourth). In fact, couples could be stuck in any stage for a number of years, in any marriage, if the tasks of each stage were not completed. Dr. Joan Druckman, another member of my committee, believed the tasks of marriage were more important than the length of time married. Karen, Joan, and Dr. Russell Di Barttolo, the Director of Dissertation Research congratulated and praised me for producing a "heuristic piece of work."

Like much of the research that is done, there is always more to be investigated. Since I started working on the dissertation, I've spent twenty-five years continuing to explore the theory with couples in therapy as well as the tasks of marriage that must be completed for a marriage to grow and develop. Although more research and writings have been published on marriage and relationships in the last two decades than ever before, there still remains a great deal of work to be done by the next generation of clinicians and researchers.

ANDY, MY YOUNGEST SON
ADOLESCENCE (1980-1984)

Adolescence is a difficult time for many parents, particularly if parents have unresolved issues that have not been recognized. This was true of Mike and me. Mike seemed to want to avoid participating in this part of his son's life by accepting TDY (temporary duty) assignments that took him out of the state, and I decided I needed more fun in my life. There certainly was a big lack of fun in my own adolescence. In late spring in 1980, I went white water rafting with two of my classmates. Even though I was working on the statistical part of my dissertation that summer when Andy was fourteen, I was available when problems happened.

Marshall was grieving the death of his father; his drug use had intensified that spring; and he was hospitalized for several weeks in the summer. Andy was doing his own experimenting or doing something mischievous. One of the most expensive and troublesome incidents that Andy presented to me was one that he accomplished with his two buddies, the Cisneros brothers. One bright summer day when the three teenagers were bored, they decided to practice shooting the B-B gun (one of the boys received for his birthday) out of his bedroom window. They each took turns shooting holes in a large window in the building across the street. Of course, they never considered the consequences.

From the angle of the holes made by the B-Bs, the police quickly deduced that the shots came from the upper bedroom of the home where Andy's friends lived. The next day a policeman delivered a warrant for $2400.00. Andy sheepishly told me about the escapade and said, "My share of the bill is $800. Are you going to pay for it?"

"Yes, I guess we will have to pay for it, but you're going to repay us by doing chores for the rest of the year," was my response. He repaid us by washing windows and the cars, cutting the lawn, and cleaning the garage; and he never did anything like that again. Of course, he found other problems to get into.

Andy's experimenting with drugs got him involved in selling. He couldn't resist an opportunity to make money, but he didn't know that he was crossing into dangerous territory. One day I received a call threatening Andy's life. I told the man at the other end of the line very emphatically, "I will call the police if anything happens to Andy. So you stay the hell away from my son." Our house was burglarized a week later, and I did call the police. Andy usually was a very levelheaded boy, and he was very aware of the problems that Marsh was having with drugs. By the time he was a high school senior, he realized he was in deeper than he intended or could manage. I think he was frightened of not being able to get out of the drug scene. I know I was scared out of my wits for him.

Before he graduated from high school and without discussing this matter with us, he went downtown to the recruiting offices and questioned the officers from the four services and picked up all the literature he could find. Sometime later he came home and announced to me, "I've decided to join the Navy."

I was shocked. I never dreamed he would think of going into the service. "That's quite a decision, Andy. What made you decide on the Navy?" I asked. I had been hoping he would choose to go to one of the community colleges in our area.

"I've been looking at some of my friends who are using drugs, and they seem very stuck. I think if I go away, I can break the ties I have with those guys."

"Sounds like a wise decision, Andy," I said. "I'm proud of you for working out your problem. Your dad and I will certainly be at your graduation. How long is your enlistment?"

"Three years." Andy looked very pleased with his decision, and I was relieved that we had survived his high school years.

As long as we didn't talk about "your sons" or "your mother," we did well together...

When the three of us were together, we were at ease and very congenial. We enjoyed being together and not having to be active and doing all the time.

Andy

Miklos, Libby, & Andy

Father & Son: Miklos & Andy Kovacs

Andy, Kaye & Amanda (b. 1989)

Andy & Kaye

Kaye   Andy Jr. — A.J. (b. 1991)   Amanda

Nεw
Mεxico

DESERT JOURNEY (1980)

For two months in late spring of Andy's freshman year in high school, Mike was away. He had volunteered to go on TDY, (temporary duty away from McClelland Air Force Base) to renovate F-111 fighter planes with electronic equipment. He was very excited that he would be doing some very highly specialized work that he didn't get to do in his regular job, and he expected that the extra money would be helpful with my graduate school expenses.

I thought this was the worst time for him to be away from home, when I needed his support with Andy; but I agreed that the job sounded very important, and "Andy and I can come to New Mexico sometime in June for a short vacation. We've never been to that state before."

In the middle of June, Andy and I headed for Clovis, New Mexico. I had no idea how long we would take to get there, but I called Mike and let him know we were on our way. I'm comfortable around areas where there are bodies of water, rivers or lakes, but I'm very uneasy in desert territories. All I could see when we got into Arizona were vast areas of sand and cactus scattered in the dust.

On the evening of our third day we reached Albuquerque where I had planned to stay overnight; but the temperatures were cooler at night and we decided the drive would be more pleasant. After dinner we drove straight through all night. We reached Clovis early in the morning. Mike had given me directions to the townhouse he had rented, and we arrived at his door around four o'clock. I knocked and rang the doorbell, but we had no response. Several times we called, "Mike!" "Dad!" I was about to throw a small stone at the upstairs window, and I was wondering where we could go for a couple of hours if he didn't wake up. After what seemed a long time, we heard his sleepy voice coming toward the door. "OK, OK, I'm coming."

"Dad!" called Andy as he opened the door. He was so happy to see his father that he gave Mike a big hug. He missed him terribly when he was gone. Mike hugged and kissed both of us. We were both happy to be there. I was exhausted. I don't know which was more difficult: driving by day when the sun and the sands were so hot or at night through the desert that was totally black when the only light shining was from the faraway stars. We crawled into bed finally and fell soundly asleep. There were two bedrooms upstairs, so Andy had a room to himself instead of the couch as he was anticipating.

I awakened to the smell of coffee brewing and Mike preparing brunch. It was past noontime on Sunday. We all had the day to rest, lounge around, and be together again. I liked the spacious townhouse that was very comfortable and was provided very inexpensively by the Air Force. Mike answered Andy's questions about the work he was doing, and he told us about the town which was "dry;" so in the evenings, he and the other workers from Sacramento drove across the border to Lubbock, Texas, to get their liquid refreshments.

When the three of us were together, we were at ease and very congenial. We enjoyed being together and not having to be active and doing all the time. Mike was very warm and affectionate, and more relaxed than he had been for a long time. The stress of having Marsh in our lives was very irritating to him, and I'm sure he resented the energy I put into dealing with him. I said very little about Marsh or Franz when Mike was around. I thought he resented me for not sending them away or giving up on them. He contemptuously called them "drug addicts" when he was angry, and I was certain that he resented that I had not been more accepting of his mother. We did not discuss our resentments when we were together. I still felt the barrier between us that we were unable to resolve.

As long as we didn't talk about "your sons," or "your mother," we did well together. In retrospect the lack of resolution of these problems in our lives eroded our love for each other and fragmented our relationship. I was sharply aware when we were at Hungarian functions that I felt disconnected from Mike no matter how friendly we were with each other. I never felt that I could bridge the gap that separated me from his countrymen/women, especially when they talked in Hungarian, or told their "in-jokes" and they all laughed, except for me. If one tried to translate, the joke never came off very well in English. I was the stranger, even in my own home, when the gatherings were at our house or at Clear Lake. I'm sure if I had chosen to be more social with them, drank more, and learned their language things might have been different. I'm just as certain if I had given up my work, my freedom, and my life, everything would have been very different --- and I would have been dead inside.

When Mike went to parties with my friends and colleagues from the Mental Health Service, I could feel his discomfort when we were talking "shop" and he did not understand our laughter and "in-jokes." Although he was very sociable and outgoing, I was sure that he was feeling uneasy.

Marriage is difficult in the best of circumstances. When there are broad cultural and ethnic differences, the difficulties seem magnified and impassable. Yet, when the three of us were together at home or at Clear Lake, when we were fishing, or swimming in the middle of the lake, or water skiing, we definitely belonged together. We enjoyed being with each other and our love felt true and real, and each of us was our own person—individual, unique, and strong. I'd forget for the time being that there were other times when we were distant, or angry, and disconnected.

The same can be said about Franz, Marsh, and me. We were our own unit, yet each of us different, unique, and very intense. Even in anger toward each other, we permitted each to be his/her own person – separate, yet together. I realized that the feuds that divided my family of origin did not help me to overcome the barriers in my own marriage. Of course, Mike and his family had their issues, which were never discussed.

One summer weekend when the Mental Health Department was having a party on a boat going down the Sacramento River, I overheard Mike talking sarcastically about me to one of my co-workers. He really got nasty a couple of times, and I looked at him startled and hurt. He had never spoken about me like that in public ever before. (I suppose he could have been saying mean-spirited things about me with his Hungarian friends, and I never would have understood.)

I took him aside and said quietly to him, "What are you so angry about? If you're pissed of at me, tell me when we get home; but I want you to stop being so disrespectful to me here." He walked off to the bar. I wondered whether he was drinking more than I realized; but even when drunk, he had never been so insulting. If he was feeling ill at ease around people who were my friends and colleagues, he didn't say a word to me. Who knows what was bothering him? He didn't say a word on the drive home because he had passed out.

In any case, in New Mexico, we had a very restful week. I read, Andy watched re-runs of M.A.S.H., and we walked around Clovis while Mike worked. In the evenings we went out to dinner and came back to the townhouse for a little T.V. before bedtime. On Saturday we went to a picnic in the afternoon where we met other people from Sacramento who were on Mike's work team.

The picnic was in a very nice park and, as we entered, we could smell steaks and chicken being barbecued. Mike took us around and introduced Andy and me to his co-workers. Everyone was very cordial and friendly, except one person. She looked at me with a surprised side-glance, and then looked away very quickly. She mumbled, "How do you do?" and walked away rapidly.

When we arrived at 4:00 a.m. a week ago and Mike took so long to answer the door, the thought flickered through my tired brain, "I wonder, is someone with him? I don't remember that he's such a sound sleeper." I started to imagine a scene: two of them asleep. Suddenly, Mike hears our voices. He wakes up quickly, she slips something on, and he takes her down the stairway and lets her out of the back door.

When I looked into that woman's eyes at the picnic, and she looked startled, then quickly glanced away, my suspicions were aroused. My antennae blinked, "Oh, oh." I smiled to myself. He's a tricky one, isn't he? He came all this way to have an affair so I wouldn't confront him again. He could not handle confrontations. He felt overwhelmed whenever I asked him to consider a problem or an issue with me. Oddly, I wasn't angry. I hoped I was wrong. I didn't say anything to Mike then or anytime after that. I wasn't surprised. I think I was expecting something like this, and I was almost indifferent. I met a woman back in the 1960s who told me, rather nonchalantly, "I know my husband sees other women, but as long as he comes home to me, I don't mind." I suppose that can be called maturity and maybe I'm getting there slowly.

Andy and I left the next day to cross the desert on our way home. All I wanted was to go home where I could think and clear my head. I tucked away the thought about the woman, and I didn't consider that he was having an affair until he went on the next TDY to Idaho a year later. I was very certain then that I was not mistaken.

Andy did not want to leave his father. I told him that I was afraid to cross that desert alone, and I wanted him with me. I was not honest with Andy. I was apprehensive about driving through the desert alone, but I was more afraid that he would realize what his father was doing.

Before we left, I packed the ice chest with ice, water, and some soft drinks. I placed a couple of towels in the chest so we could keep cool while driving. The road was long and meandered through the desert. All I could see in every direction was sand and cactus. In the faraway distance I could see red stone mountains and jagged rocks. There were no houses or gas stations visible ahead. What would I do if I ran out of gas? The sign at the last station said that it was the last one for three hundred miles. Fortunately, my Volkswagen could go that far on a tank of gas. I became more concerned that the desert heat was dissolving the tires. Every so often a piece of tire flew off and landed in the middle of the road. "Damn." I thought. "They must be recaps."

Every time the tire flew off, my heart jumped a beat, and I gasped. At first, we had two-hundred miles more to go then, one-hundred, now it was fifty, and I prayed that enough of the tires would remain to get us to the next town where I could buy a new set of tires. Andy was there in the passenger seat moping because he wanted to stay with his dad. I was irritated and angry with his dad for doing such a stupid thing. Andy had a cold towel wrapped around his head, too. He was drinking a coke and complaining about the heat.

I wanted to leave Andy with him because Mike had more influence at this time in our son's life. I thought it would have been better to let him stay than coming home and having to deal with drug dealers. Mike did not believe me when I told him Andy was getting mixed up with drugs. Usually Mike would have insisted on keeping Andy with him, but he didn't this time. So I was right! I resented that he considered that woman more important than letting his son stay with him. Andy was not listening to me, and I was not able to manage him as well as I used to when he was younger.

Finally, on the horizon, some buildings appeared, and I took a deep breath and sighed with relief. The tire shop was right there on the edge of town. I left the car with one repairman who promised to change the tires and have the car ready in an hour. Andy and I went across the street to the small café to have lunch.

Awakening the Past

Since March 25, 1980, when James Wright died of throat cancer, I gave four extensive interviews in person to three biographers and to a graduate student: the first with Larry Smith (1985-1986) who produced the video tape, *James Wright's Ohio*. He and I collaborated on a paper about my life with Jim. The paper was called *Years of Travail*. Although Larry submitted it to several journals, the article was not published. However, much of that material has been integrated into this book.

In 1989 Saundra Maley interviewed me several times over the telephone. She was working on her dissertation on Jim's early poetry that was published as *Solitary Apprenticeship James Wright and German Poetry* (1996). Peter Stitt, the first official biographer of James Wright, interviewed me for several hours in my office (1991). Later, in June 2001, Jonathan Blunk spent almost an entire afternoon reviewing my life with Jim.

Each interview took several hours, and each one re-opened wounds that I had worked very hard in psychotherapy to resolve and heal. The interviewers were all very kind and respectful, and I'm afraid I may have surprised and startled them by the intensity of my emotions. I was surprised by my own responses, which told me there was still some unfinished business that I needed to complete. In telling and retelling my story, I participated in the reactivation of bittersweet memories by revealing the common, ordinary, and the intimate details of my relationship with Jim (he was always "Jim" to me, never James).

But were my wounds completely healed? I thought so until I was interviewed and remembered and revisited memories that were best left buried. Afterwards, I realized that whenever I looked at my son, Marshall, I recognized the familiar features, expressions, gestures, and gait of his father. Every time I looked into his troubled face and saw the burdens of his illness and his shattered life, I remembered. When my sons experienced their own cyclical episodes of depression, mania, and phobias, I remembered. And when they descended into their own particular chaotic hell of rage and fury brought on by their own memories as well as the effects of drugs and alcohol, I was there again. Over the years, when Franz called drowning in fear, hatred, and despair, I remembered.

Why does anyone want to tell her story, especially one that ended so painfully and destructively? To bring closure is the common response, but what does that mean? Our marriage ended over forty years ago and I moved on. The havoc that occurred in my first marriage and the devastating divorce that followed became strong motivating factors in my choice of graduate study at the University of California in San Francisco. My goals at that time were to study family theory and family therapy in addition to the regular program of individual and group therapy. I wanted to learn as much as I could about what happened to me in my family of origin, as well as in my marriage to Jim.

I made a new life for myself as a professional clinical nurse psychotherapist and a marriage and family therapist. In my position as a mental health consultant – "Change Agent" – I used the skills I learned in making changes in the care and treatment of psychiatric patients in hospitals and in nursing practice. For almost a decade this was my focus and highlight of my work as a nurse. I married again in 1965 and had another son, Andy. Even so, I felt compelled to return to the "unfinished business of the past" where I left shards of my life, and I needed to reclaim those pieces and integrate them into my life. I will not be whole until I complete this task.

Emotionally
Distant (1983–1988)

Our marriage changed more and more over time. I was aware from the very beginning of red flags—danger signals—and I was aware that I made choices that endangered our relationship. I learned from reading, teaching, doing family therapy, and from experience that when one partner is growing and the other stays in the same emotional place and digs in his or her heels and refuses to compromise, the tension, which comes from each one pulling the relationship in a different direction, will ultimately polarize the marriage and pull it apart.

We both took positions and became unbending. Yet we both went on as if we were united in the direction that we wanted our marriage to go. I had fought long and hard in my family of origin to gain my freedom, my education, and my identity that I wanted and needed; and I had paid a high price for it. I would not let go of all that I had fought for and conform to Mike's cultural expectations.

He had fought destructive foes and almost lost his life for his country, his freedom, and his identity. I think we both understood the other. We both tried to meet each other with some degree of cooperation, but our marriage could not be sustained through the many struggles.

Mike accepted, and supported as much as he could, my work and educational choices. He knew what I did was extremely important to me. I know he had great difficulty accepting my first two sons. I would not consider giving them up or sending them away. That was utterly impossible and incomprehensible to me. He was unable to contain his resentment that I did not "listen" to him, and my sons suffered from his retaliation.

Another sore point for him was my inability to accept his mother as the Matriarch of the family. His love and loyalty to her ran very deep. I understood this; yet I did not feel the same sense of loyalty to her that he expected of me.

There was one other factor that I did not consider significant until the later years of our marriage. In a patriarchal society the man must maintain control of his wife (and female children) in order not to lose face in the company of his male friends and associates. Because of my lack of conformity and obedience, especially when I refused to return to Hungary after my first trip, I made it difficult for him to maintain the façade of power over me for his friends and his extended family in Hungary. Mike let me know that his relatives wondered why I did not travel with him, even though I had very explicitly explained to him that I did not like the way he treated me when I was there, and I could not spend three weeks or more where no one spoke English. Besides, I had discovered a recreation that was more meaningful and great fun, too—I looked forward to river rafting every summer.

Although I attended many social activities with Mike, I played none of the party games that were common among his country-men/women. I was not flirtatious, nor was I interested in switching partners. I had a low tolerance for alcohol and for staying up all night. Frequently, before midnight I would leave quietly for home and bed. After the first few years, I insisted that we take two cars to parties so I could slip away when I was tired. I'm afraid that because of my independence, Mike may have had to take a lot of teasing and joking from friends and relatives.

I knew early on that we were different, with different perspectives of life and marriage, and certainly different values. The winter of 1983 offered us an opportunity to be together for a week. I wanted to attend a conference on Family Therapy in New Orleans, and I suggested that he come with me for a short vacation in a warmer cli-mate. The arthritis in his hands, legs, and back was becoming more painful, and the winters were becoming more difficult for him. He agreed the trip might give him some relief.

In the afternoons and evenings when we were together, the distance between us was palpable. We had little to talk about. Our interactions were mostly chitchat, then silences. "How sad," I thought, "that we should come to this. I have clients who are practically in the same place, and I can give them hope through the work that we do together. They want to be there, and they want to learn how to talk, work, and play more effectively with each other. I can find help for us, but I know Mike will say, "I don't have any problems; you're the one with the problems."

Obviously, marriage requires both people working and making the necessary changes together, but that was not our situation. Mike was content with his views of a traditional marriage; and I was the one who expected something different that he could not even imagine, no matter how much I tried to discuss my thoughts with him. Yes, I saw the early signs of our differences, but I was not willing to deal with another divorce with three children. I clung to the idea that he was flexible and we could work on life problems together. I was mistaken. He, apparently, perceived me as more pliable and easily swayed by his suave and sophisticated ways, and he was wrong, too. We were there in a beautiful city, with magnificent restaurants and the wonderful sounds of jazz and blues, and we might as well have been a thousand miles apart.

Disability Retirement for Mike

When we returned home, he went back to work to face a situation that had become intolerable for him. His arthritic hands would swell, especially when he used power tools. Unable to do his assignments, he was required to report to the nurse in the Health Clinic who declared him unable to work, and he would be sent home. After a few months, he went to the Personnel Office to request a transfer to another area. He had worked as a designer of instruments in one of his previous jobs, and he had other skills as a mechanical and electronics technician, but no transfer was forthcoming.

Serendipitously, I attended a workshop on the subject of Workmen's Compensation that spring. This was a required continuing education class for Marriage and Family Therapists who were newly qualified to treat clients who were covered under the State Disability Act. When I came home, I immediately told Mike, "I learned today that you qualify for Federal Workmen's Compensation. First thing Monday morning, you must go to the Personnel Office and put in your application. I'm surprised that no one, not the nurse or your supervisor, advised you that you might be eligible. There are signs that are required to be posted in the work places so that all workers should know about this benefit."

He did follow up on my suggestion and was told to see his physician and get his recommendation about his ability to continue working. Soon afterwards, he was laid off and given temporary Workman's Compensation. After two years, he was placed on permanent disability with full compensation until the end of his life.

As another part of his retirement, I suggested that he develop a hobby or join some of the Fraternal Organizations in the community. Mike remembered his father had been a member of the Shriners. He joined the Free Masons. A year later, he advanced to the Scottish Rite, and a year after that, to the Shriners.

He became very active in their regular meetings, and he volunteered as a Greeter. There he could be his charming, sophisticated, and gracious self. He was very popular, and I joined him for dinners and dances that were held frequently. The money that they collected from these and many other similar events all over the state went toward the building of the new Shriners Children's Hospital in Sacramento. One of my more favorite activities was volunteering for the clinics where children were evaluated to determine the degree of their disabilities or handicaps that resulted from severe burns.

MY WORK BEGINS AGAIN

In late 1982, after the completion of my dissertation and graduation, my focus and energy was directed on building my private practice for couples, individuals, and families. I was amazed with the changes that occurred in my field of work. Previously, the main people who came in for counseling and therapy were women. If they were married, my policy was to see the husband at least one time. The men came reluctantly and the problems were considered the women's concern.

Then, almost overnight, not only did the men come with their wives; they frequently called and made the first appointment. I accepted every couple who called and, before long, I was working four twelve-hour days. I was seeing couples of all types who were having relationship issues they wanted to discuss: married, unmarried, remarried, co-habiting, and gay and lesbian couples. I even did a few business partnerships. In addition to my clinical work, I started teaching classes for couples once a month at one of the community learning facilities.

One of the most exciting aspects to my work was that the couples understood my theoretical framework: most of the problems that couples have are the result of growing up in different families where each learned their family's communication system. The goal that we worked toward was to redesign their marriage with a communication system that they developed through their interactions. Blaming each other was an exercise in futility. They each practiced talking, problem solving, and resolving conflicts together until they could express themselves openly and honestly; and especially, they each could ask for his/her individual wants and needs. They designed fun activities together, and they could express their own style of affection, love, and forgiveness.

Many married couples came in threatening or preparing for a divorce. I designed a structured trial separation that permitted the two to separate and deal with finances, children, and their relationship on an ongoing basis from three to twelve months. They each came to see me for an individual therapy session and on the third week I saw the two of them together. The therapy sessions were focused on helping each one to make the changes he or she was willing to make. Then they would discuss their issues and negotiate the changes they wanted to make together.

After a few years, the divorce rate for clients who came with that purpose in mind started declining until my records indicated one couple dissolved their marriage in one year—whether I saw 125 new clients a year or fifty. This record was still strong and firm until I retired (2005). Over the years, I dropped my working days from four a week to three, and, finally, in preparation for my retirement, I was down to working only two days a week.

During the summer months, I'd take a month off and Mike and I would travel in Europe, or spend long, lazy days at Clear Lake swimming and boating. By the middle 1980s, Mike was becoming very homesick. Many of his friends made yearly trips to their homeland, but Mike was not able to get the necessary visa. Once he wrote to the President of Hungary, whom he knew as a fellow inmate in prison, to get permission to go back home. He wrote back and suggested the Mike "stay where you are." He started getting depressed and preoccupied, scheming different ways that he could get into the country. He considered using false identification papers and passports, and he suggested that I go to Hungary and take Andy with me.

I refused. I thought it was too dangerous for him or us under any circumstances. Of course, I understood his need to return to see his relatives who were still alive and to see his country again, but the consequences if he got caught—prison or death—was too high a price to pay. At about that time his mother was diagnosed with late-onset Alzheimer's. We moved her to an apartment nearby. Later she was placed in a seniors' residence, and finally into a nursing home. Mike saw her several times a week, and we had her over for Sunday dinner until she was incapacitated.

ANDY AND THE NAVY

Andy went off to the Navy in the spring of 1985. We attended his graduation from Boot Camp in San Diego. He looked very strong and very healthy. He did very well. The one question I had for him was, "How did you handle all the yelling that they do with new recruits?" He smiled and said, "They don't know me so that's not me they're screaming at. I just let it pass." I was pleased and very proud of him. He had such a clear sense of his self-esteem and his identity; our son was a confident, self-assured, and happy young man.

He was assigned to the *S. S. Iowa* in Virginia Beach. After training exercises at sea, the ship was sent to the Indian Ocean and Andy was gone over a year. Wherever he went he made friends and had a lot of fun. He signed up for hazardous duties in order to make extra money. He was enthusiastic about how much he had learned in the few months that he was in the Navy: "I've learned more in six months than I did in four years in high school!" And, more importantly for me, he broke loose from his drug-using "friends."

At the end of their year abroad, he returned to Virginia. The first person he called was his father, "Hi, Dad, I'm back! Guess what? Our Captain says we can invite our fathers to come on board with us for a week while we do exercises. Can you come? Great! And, Dad, would you bring me my car? I want to drive cross-country when I get discharged…. OK?" Mike was just as excited as Andy. He drove across country and flew back to Sacramento after a very exciting week at sea. From the pictures he brought from his sea voyage, it was obvious that the two of them had a marvelous time.

TOW TRUCKING AND MARRIAGE

Andy took a month off after his discharge (1988) from the Navy to reconnect with some of his friends and to decide what kind of work he was going to do. He was not interested in college, and like many of the men on my side of the family, he turned to trucking—tow trucking. He worked for a small company for three months and decided he wanted his own tow-trucking business. He asked us to help him buy a business that was for sale.

Even though he was only twenty-three, we both had faith in him and knew he would accomplish whatever he set out to do. And he did. Within another year, he met Kaye, a very beautiful, exuberant, and energetic young woman. They moved into a house together, and a year later they married and had a lovely daughter, Amanda (1989). Two years later (1991) their son, A.J (for Andy, Jr.) arrived—the "spitting image" of his father.

Kaye joined Andy in his business as bookkeeper, secretary, and general helpmate. Andy, in turn, became the "chief cook and bottle washer" at home. He loved cooking and playing with their children. They all four do everything together and are devoted to each other. Of course, they have had challenges to deal with and both have struggled and worked through their issues together. Kaye's widowed mother, Sally, had a stroke in the early 1990s and she came to live with them.

Although both worked very hard on their expanding business, they also found time for recreation and fun: Andy, with his Harley Davidson motorcycle, joined a group of men who take periodic trips throughout California and neighboring states. He is also a very active Rotarian and a member of the Tow-Truck Association. Kaye always loved horses and has two that she rides and trains for shows. Amanda is excellent in school and loves raising small animals for her 4-H class. AJ, of course, is following in his dad's footsteps: he has his own motorcycle and when he's not in school, he is going on calls with his dad. Andy has converted to Roman Catholicism, and their two children have been confirmed.

Return of the
Exile (1989)

In 1988 the Iron Curtain was torn down in Eastern Europe. Mike was one of the first in line for a passport and visa. In June 1989, he and other exiles returned home, and they were given a hero's welcome. He was so excited about being back in his homeland that he called me after a couple weeks and asked exuberantly, "Honey! Send me another thousand dollars. I want to stay another month! I can't believe what's happening. All of Budapest is out on the streets, and they're celebrating their freedom and the return of the Freedom Fighters who fought against the communists. They're calling us heroes! Can you believe it?" I sent him the money.

When Mike left in the middle of June, I was flooded with feelings of loss and grief. I felt as if he had died and left me. I knew I was over-reacting when I realized I was re-experiencing my old fears of abandonment and rejection. "He is only on a trip, visiting his family for the first time in over three decades," I reassured myself. Another part of me responded, "Yes, but what if he wants to stay there? You know he only came to this country because he was a refugee. He never intended to emigrate and leave Hungary."

I felt I had lost him. He was never coming back! He didn't. Yes, physically, he returned, and he brought home the sick, wounded Miklos. The other Miklos, the irrepressible, fun-loving, friendly Mike never returned. He was different, more preoccupied, not always present, and disconnected. And then there was the party.

TWENTY-FIFTH ANNIVERSARY

April 10, 1990, was our twenty-fifth anniversary. He wanted to throw a big party not only to celebrate our marriage, but also to celebrate his reunion with his family in Hungary after a thirty-three-year exile. At that time, his cousin, John, with his wife, Velma, were visiting us. This was a great opportunity to observe both extraordinary events in our lives.

That special occasion was filled with the joyful laughter and conversations of Hungarian friends who had come from San Francisco to rejoice with Mike and his relatives. Some of my friends were there; and my sister, Ann, and her husband, Richard, had driven up from Southern California to share our celebration.

We had plenty of food; and Mike, in his irrepressible exuberant way, was serving the champagne. He glowed with happiness. The whole house seemed to be bubbling with light and chatter. As I looked around, I felt pleased that everything was going so well. Mike came up to me and gave me a hug and a kiss. I smiled at him and felt quiet and content as I stood beside my friend, Polly, and listened as she talked with my sister, Ann. They met for the first time that evening and were getting acquainted.

Suddenly, I felt as if I were standing outside of the activities looking in. I was no longer involved in what was happening. I felt alone and puzzled. Then I heard a voice say clearly and distinctly, "The marriage is over."

Startled, I looked around to see who had said such a thing. No one else seemed to notice. They were absorbed in their conversations. "Where did *that* come from?" I asked myself. "What a ridiculous thought! I can't imagine where that came from. I was feeling so good a few minutes ago. Mike seems very happy. What's happening to me?" I tried to shake myself free of this strange occurrence.

Slowly, I returned to the party. The dark thought hovered over me as I struggled to regain my equilibrium and enter into the conversation that Polly was having with my sister. I couldn't shake the thought. I walked from room to room nodding and smiling mechanically to those who noticed me. I came to the kitchen and did what I usually do when I'm anxious or upset. I started "puttering" —washing dishes, wiping the counter, anything I could do to keep my hands busy and calm my mind. I knew I had to prepare myself. A big change was coming. I didn't know what kind of change, but something big was ahead for me.

The Big Change

"You are my enemy!" The first time I heard those words, I was shocked. Then I thought he must have made a wrong translation from Hungarian to English. Perhaps he meant that he resented my disagreeing with him about punishing my sons, and that I would take responsibility for them. When he said those same words again, I had to consider them more seriously.

I concluded that he really meant, "If you value your sons more than me, then you are my enemy!" Perhaps, he was implying that he equated stepchildren with illegitimate children who were not considered as valuable as a child of a marriage. If he meant this, then I had to be concerned.

The third possible meaning came out of the situation with his mother when he brought her to live with us soon after we were married. I believed that his mother was capable of taking care of herself, and I did not want to be responsible for her when she was in good health. Later, I came to see that he assumed because I was not willing to care for his mother that I then would not take care of him. I realized much later that he did not distinguish between care of a healthy person and care of a person who was unable to care for herself because of illness.

I believe I did demonstrate that I would take care of him and I did. I realized that Mike's and his mother's thinking about illness and death was wrapped in a web of superstition. Many immigrants, including my parents and relatives, were frightened of doctors and hospitals because they were associated with "a place where people go to die."

Thus, every time I insisted that he go see a doctor, or I would take him to the clinic myself, he believed I was trying to "get rid" of him; therefore, I was his enemy. He spoke these words another time when I suggested that we have a will made. We were in our fifties at the time, and the medical and legal professions were recommending end-of-life preparations.

I'm one who does not let important events left to chance. I decided it was time for us to take care of those matters. I asked Mike if we could both go to see an attorney to have our will done. This time he was horrified and asked, "Are you trying to get rid of me?"

"No, I am not. I simply want to make these preparations in advance, not just for you, but for me, too." He was not assured. Finally, I said, "How about if I go alone and do one for myself, and if I am not struck dead by a bolt of lightning, then you can go too. He agreed that I should go alone, but he didn't want to go with me later. He agreed to let me get a will in his name and bring it to him to sign. That's as far as he would go.

A year or so later, as I explored end-of-life preparations further, I learned that a family trust is more effective if I wanted to include my adult children, Franz and Marshall. Of course, this idea angered him, but I did not change my mind nor did I argue with him any further. As his condition declined with each return from Hungary and he was approaching his seventies, I suggested the time had come for a long-term care policy for both of us.

He became alarmed and more paranoid. He was convinced that I was making plans to get rid of him. I decided he could think what he wanted, but I did not believe in leaving these arrangements for our children to manage. I did not make an issue of any further arrangements nor did I ask him to participate. I made the arrangements for both of us. By then, I'm sure he was convinced that I was planning some evil scheme to do away with him.

I was surprised that he continued to return home from Hungary. I believe his paranoia became more and more intense after each of his visits back there. During his second trip, he went to the mines where he was imprisoned and requested copies of his records while he was imprisoned there. Of course there were no records. They had been destroyed. The next year, he went to a government office to apply for his mother's retirement benefits, but they were no longer available. Finally, he was reinstated as a citizen of Hungary and was issued a new passport. Now, he had dual citizenship—Hungarian and American.

After his yearly visits in the mid 1990s, he returned home seriously depressed and ill. In 1993 and 1994 he developed pneumonia. In 1995 he came back so depressed that I requested that our doctor put him on an anti-depressant. He gave Mike a prescription; and he would take the medication at home, but when he returned to Hungary, he stopped taking them. In 1996, he complained one evening about an episode of temporary blindness. The next morning I rushed him to the urgent care clinic. The doctor diagnosed his problem as TIA's, that is, temporary ischemic activity or mini strokes, and they were causing the temporary blindness. He was scheduled for an immediate angioplasty to reopen his clogged carotid arteries.

After the angioplasty, the doctor told him, "You're a lucky man. You could have had a stroke if your wife didn't get you here when she did." He had been having symptoms of temporary blindness for over a year and a half before he finally told me. Afterwards, he told his friends at the coffee shop where he went every morning and to Kaye, our daughter-in-law, that I had saved his life.

Three Sisters

Ann   Libby   Mary

Front Row: Libby, Libby's sister Mary (Mihelarakis),
Cally Kardules (Tony's wife)
Back Row: Barbara & Libby's brother Jack Kardules, Gusty
Mihelarakis (Mary's husband), & Libby's brother Tony

Challenges
(1990s)

Those years were full of pain, fear, and anger. When one's life starts coming apart at the seams, all hell breaks loose. There are options, or on a more elemental level, survival mechanisms: fight, flight, or regression. All three were happening, and all at the same time in my family. I spent much of this time in fear and grief, although the rest of my life at work, church, and play were still on track.

In the 1990s decade my family, nuclear and extended, were in crises and major transitions. There were tragic deaths: my youngest brother, Jack, at the age of fifty, died of lymphoma in 1993; my middle brother, Tony, retired in 1991 at the age of sixty, died four years later of lung cancer. There were deaths of elders: Aunt Maria and Aunt Helen, in Greece, of heart disease and cancer respectively. My mother-in-law, Anna Gilicze, died of complications resulting from Alzheimer's disease in 1994 at the age of 96.

Franz and Marshal were having periodic and very difficult crises resulting from alcohol and drug abuse as well as the underlying bipolar illness. They experienced abandonment as a result of Jim divorcing me, and then my marriage to a man that, out of his own frustrations and wounds, became violent and abusive toward them. Franz was in psychotherapy for about four years in the early 1980s and again in the 1990s and became aware of his early losses, grief, and painful experiences with Mike; and he released his anger and rage toward me. He struggled to understand what occurred between his father and me, and for a time blamed me for everything. Gradually, as he reached a more stable and objective perspective, he was more accepting and forgiving. Although his verbal attacks were extremely painful for me, at that time, I knew that if I were patient he would get past this struggle through the recovery process and reach a more balanced view of what happened to his parents. And he did.

My two sisters and I were going through our marital crises at about the same time, and we each dealt with them in our own individual way. The one common expression of pain that was typical for the three of us was our explosive anger. I realized that our reactions were extreme and characteristic of a long familial pattern. Mary and Gusty were threatening divorce and separated for a short time; then they reconciled. Ann arranged to have an intervention with Richard and the rest of their family, and he agreed to go into an alcohol treatment program. Recovery is a lifelong process, and gradually they were together again and they still have their ups and downs.

I was in psychotherapy for, at least, three to five years every decade of my life since I was twenty-five. In the '90s, I was in therapy for the entire ten years. In addition, I had been having (since 1984) massages from Tara, a highly skilled and well-trained massage therapist in a variety of Eastern practices, and I went through another series of Rolfing massages, a three-year stint with acupuncture, and two years of group therapy followed by two years of art therapy. Most of these treatments and healing practices overlapped each other. At one time, I was doing three of these a month. My approach to healing my own wounds and fears was multi-dimensional. I worked on all levels of body, mind, and spirit toward becoming a free, fully integrated, and whole person. I am still growing and changing because I believe that life is an ongoing process of growth and development from birth to death, the last stage of life, and God is the Ultimate Healer. Perhaps, we are never completely whole and healed. Even in my late 70s, I still run into an obstacle deeply hidden in my psyche.

In 1994, after an absence of twenty years, at which time I was exploring Eastern Religions, I returned to an Episcopal Church, Trinity Cathedral Church, in Sacramento. I felt a deep need to reconnect with my Christian roots. I found a place of freedom, acceptance, love, and peace that included a diverse congregation who were interested in finding God in their lives. At last, I was home and on a solid foundation. I had all the support and love I needed to get me through my hellish experiences.

The premonition that I experienced on our twenty-fifth wedding anniversary was accurate. Our marriage was dying slowly. Mike's first open statement was made a week after he returned from Hungary in the summer of '92: "I've decided that we will not have sex any more." I was stunned. "How dare you! You can't make a decision like that without talking to me about it! Who is she? Did you find someone in Hungary?"

"That's your imagination again," he replied sarcastically.

"No, it's not my imagination. I've always known when you were having affairs. I met one of your women friends in Clovis, and there was another one in Idaho. Did you think that by leaving the state, I wouldn't know? I know you've been sleeping around in Hungary, too. Is it Ellen's sister? You told me you were staying in her apartment."

"You have an active fantasy life," he repeated. After a few minutes of silence, he started complaining, "You didn't listen to me. You wouldn't do what I wanted you to do, just like you didn't listen to your father either." He was becoming more upset, "I want someone who will take care of me." Then, he switched to attacking my sons referring them as "your drug-addict sons."

There it was! The truth was finally coming out of his mouth! For the first time he admitted his expectations of me. He expected me to be an obedient child-wife! Like his mother, of course, and that was what he expected of a wife—of me! He was no different than my father who expected me to be an obedient daughter and marry a man of his choice—and the second time, I did. My father liked and approved of Mike as my husband. Neither culture expected women to think, to be responsible, or to have an identity of their own. They were only good for raising children and taking care of their husbands.

Whatever I wanted didn't count. His needs (and his mother's) were of the utmost importance. As a woman in her mid-sixties, I was supposed to fall into the roles that they expected of me, first of all, that of caretaker. Of course, I wanted to believe that they were more sophisticated and more accepting of a woman's individuality, but I was mistaken. In a small area in our personal lives, we connected, when we were a family of three. Everything else was an illusion. I had never been accepted; I knew that. A close friend of Mike's said to me when our divorce was in process, "We were never friends. You were Miklos' wife. That's all." The truth was coming out in little bits and pieces!

As he aged his (unspoken) expectation was that I would stay home and care for him; but there I was, when he went on disability retirement, suggesting to him that he join a social club and/or develop a hobby. I was busy building my private practice and working twelve-hour days. He must have been really hurt and disappointed. No wonder he was so depressed and sick every winter. That was exactly how his mother handled her hurt and disappointment. She would stop eating, get very weak, and call her son to come and take care of her, that is, feed her. She would get strong again for a period of time, and the cycle would start again. Until her final days at ninety-six, when she was so ill and there was no likelihood of recovery, Mike with deep sadness made the decision to discontinue the intravenous feedings. She died ten days later in November 1994.

In the next six years, his health declined steadily. During the winter months, he was in constant pain with arthritis throughout his body. He could hardly walk. He refused to have a hip replacement. His drinking and cigarette smoking increased. He could hardly breathe because of emphysema, chronic bronchitis, and heart congestion.

I thought I was taking care of him by taking him to the doctors, getting his prescriptions, and having food available for him. Now, I can see that he literally wanted me there beside him to feed him and nurture him like a child. In my experience as a nurse, I believed that people should be encouraged to be self-sufficient as long as they were able, not infantilize them by doing everything for them. I did not do what I thought was inappropriate. This was one way that I contributed to the death of our marriage. In fact, every thing that I wanted in my life contributed to the death of our relationship!

Miraculously, every spring, his health improved and he could make plans for his next trip to Hungary where he spent whole days in the hot springs, which were considered healing. Not only the Hungarians but also many other Europeans believed in the healing qualities of the springs and pools, because they were filled with people from all over Eastern and Western Europe.

I traveled to Hungary in 1991 to spend a couple of weeks with him, but I realized again that I did not belong there. One afternoon he was taking me on a trolley to a special café that he enjoyed. I expected him to pay my fare but he had a pass and I did not have any change. When the conductor asked for the fare, I looked at Mike to pay and he acted as if he did not know me. I was embarrassed and mortified. The conductor shook his head and said in Hungarian something about "Americans who come here for free rides."

I got off at the next stop. Mike followed me. I was furious, "How dare you treat me like that. Why didn't you pay for me?" He mumbled something that made no sense to me. "I am never coming here again. You can come and do what you have to do, but I am not coming again. And I don't care what you tell your relatives!" I spent the rest of the afternoon trying to calm myself.

The following summer, he returned to Hungary, accompanied by Ellen, the wife of a close friend, who had a sister in Budapest with a spare room in her apartment. Her husband had died the past year. I knew Ellen and her husband did not like me because I was trying to restrict Mike's drinking, which I knew was a futile act on my part; and they believed that wine was healthy for him, even when he passed out from drinking. However, I never dreamed they were so malicious as to set up my husband with her sister. They probably thought he would be better off with a Hungarian woman, and they arranged for him to stay in her vacant bedroom. I'm sure his monthly disability check had something to do with this arrangement. Upon his return that year, he asked me to withdraw $20,000 from our investments so he could buy an apartment building in Budapest.

I refused because I did not trust his judgment, and I thought some relative, or Ellen and her sister, were taking advantage of him. Of course, that made him angrier and more determined to push me out of his life. I was getting a very distinct impression that he wanted me to move out of the house and out of his life. He had someone else he wanted to bring in my place. One day I said to him, "Mike I know you want me to move out of our house, but I am telling you very clearly, I have no intention of moving out. Any time you want to move, the door is open. If you want to go back to Budapest and live there, we can get a simple divorce and you can take your share and live very well over there. I'm sure you will find a nice Hungarian woman who would be willing to take care of you, and you could provide for her extremely well, too." He did not respond.

In the fall of 1998, he made up a story of having a Shriners' meeting in San Francisco. He did not give me any return time, and he did not come home for two days. I called the Shriners' Office, and they told me they had no meetings scheduled. I contacted a friend of his who had coffee with Mike every morning when he was in town and asked if he knew where Mike might be. He seemed reluctant at first, but when I said, "Is he by any chance visiting his friends in Concord (Ellen who introduced her sister to Mike)?"

He was surprised that I knew that much. He answered, "Well, yes. He went to San Francisco to pick up her sister at the airport." I thanked him, and called the telephone in Concord. "Hello, Ellen, may I speak to Miklos?" She hung up on me. I waited, and as I expected, Mike came walking in about two hours later. He had a very cocky walk ("Like a rooster," I thought) and a big smile.

"Well, you're finally home. Did you have a good meeting?" I asked in a very sarcastic, controlled voice and he nodded, "Yes." "That's good. Now you can pack your suitcases and move to Concord, because you are not staying here any longer."

The smile disappeared from his face, "What are you talking about?"

"Mike, don't play games with me. I know you went to the San Francisco Airport to pick up your girlfriend, Ellen's sister, so you can go back there, *because you are not staying here any longer,*" I answered emphatically.

"Why didn't you tell me what you were doing? I suspected you were having affairs over there, and you told me it was my imagination. I don't sit around and imagine things like that. I knew from your lies, and the way you have been pushing me away these last ten years since you went back to Hungary, and even before that. I told you I would not move out so you could bring her here! Why didn't you tell me?"

"I thought what you don't know won't hurt you, and I guess I was a coward," he said sheepishly.

"You may be a coward, but I think you wanted to play your stupid sneaky games. Please, just get your things and leave." He did with no further words. He filed for divorce in late December 1998, and it was finalized, January 17, 2001, two days after the anniversary of our first meeting thirty-six years ago.

When he returned in 2003, he decided he could no longer make the long journey to Hungary again. On the previous two return flights, he had gotten on the wrong planes and went to Seattle instead of San Francisco. He realized that he was incapacitated and could not live alone. As Mike grew more and more fragile and disabled, Andy and Kaye agreed that he could not be left alone. Within a year, they sold Mike's condo and built a small cottage on their property for his dad. Andy and Kaye and their children are looking after him as well as Kaye's mother who was incapacitated by strokes. All four have become excellent caretakers of parents and grandparents. They are living examples of a loving family. Am I proud of and happy for them? Oh, yes. I certainly am. I am also very sad and have some guilt that I am not the one taking care of him.

A Current Ran
Throughout Decades

HOOKED ON RIVERS (1980–1998)

I knew the moment I saw the Klamath River in June 1980 that I was hooked on whitewater river rafting. At the time I was a fifty-two-year old wife, mother, psychotherapist, and a graduate student working on my doctoral dissertation and attending classes. In fact, it was just before the Intensive Family Dynamics Seminar that I overheard two of my classmates, Donna and Pat, talking about going river rafting. Excitedly, I interrupted their conversation, "Did you say you're going river rafting?"

Donna, slim, athletic, with short-cropped brown hair looked surprised, "Yes, we're signed up to go three weeks from Friday. Why? Are you interested?"

"Yes, I am. For the last few years, I've been collecting brochures sent by different rafting companies, but I've been too frightened to go alone. Which company are you going with?

"The Turtle River rafting Company out of Mt. Shasta, and it's an all-women's trip," replied Pat. "Would you like to go? I can call and find out if they have room for one more person." Pat, a divorced mother of two teenaged sons was more experienced than I when it came to camping and wilderness experiences.

"I can't tell you how much I would love to go, but I'm also scared to death of rivers and fascinated by them at the same time. Would you call, please? I really want to try it, even if it scares the hell out of me." I needed some recreation in my life. That's one thing I did learn from Mike—fun was important to balance one's life. He enjoyed parties, dancing, and drinking, and I loved camping and hiking, but I hadn't done any for a long time.

The following week, Pat announced, "You're in. I made a reservation for you with Turtle River. You can come."

For the next two weeks, I prepared for the river-rafting trip by gathering together such items as a sleeping bag and pad, wool socks, cap, sweaters and pants, as well as shorts and a swimming suit. Even though it was late spring, we had to be prepared for hot, cold, and rainy weather. (I didn't realize until later that wool keeps you warm even if the water is freezing.) The Klamath is considered a warm-water river of about sixty-eight degrees. All the other rivers that I rafted over the years were cold and some were extremely cold, like the Tetchanchini, a glacial river in Alaska, where we floated beside icebergs; and the Colorado, which was thirty-nine degrees Fahrenheit even when the temperature was a hundred degrees in the canyon. But I'm getting ahead of myself. Let me get back to the Klamath.

We arrived early Friday morning at Happy Camp, a small crowded sandy beach on the Lower Klamath which is the "put in" for the different rafting companies, and we immediately spotted four large rubber rafts with "Turtle River" marked on them. Pat, Donna, and I introduced ourselves to the guides and to the other rafters who were milling around. When all sixteen women had arrived, we were called together by Louise, one of the guides, and a very attractive, tanned young woman in her early twenties with thick blond hair braided and wrapped around her head.

"OK, ladies, gather around and I'll show how to pack your bags. See those black rubber bags over there by the oars and lifejackets? You will put all your things in one of those bags. Each bag is labeled with a California River. Remember which one is yours. You'll have it for the whole trip. Also pick out a lifejacket that fits snugly and that will be yours for the whole trip."

My bag was named "Eel." Louise demonstrated how to pack, and she went off to finish loading her boat. She returned later, checked our bags for air pockets and made sure they were tightly sealed. "You don't want to get to camp tonight with a bagful of wet clothes," she cautioned us.

Since I was a beginner, I had to pack and re-pack my belongings repeatedly until there were no air pockets left in the rubber bag. Every piece of clothing had to rolled and fitted tightly into the bag. Then, the top of the rubber bag was folded over two or three times, and with my knee pressing on top of the bag I squeezed out all the air. We could only take the essentials: just clothes and tennis shoes (or sandals or rubber booties) that were needed on the river and spares to change in the evening. Sleeping bags were placed in even larger rubber bags, and valuables were placed in metal ammo boxes. A day bag was available for clothes that were peeled off as the day got warmer. Such things as sunscreen were placed on the sides of the rafts along with water bottles that were easily available and absolutely essential to prevent sunburn and dehydration.

One of the constant reminders on river trips was "Drink plenty of water." An extra gallon was carried on each raft. The guides were very watchful and adamant about this mandate. Our well-being and enjoyment was their primary concern.

Everything was packed on the boats and tied down with straps that were buckled tightly so that nothing would be lost—even if the raft capsized. When I say "everything" was strapped down, I mean chests filled with food for seven meals for twenty people, cooking utensils, dishes and tableware, gas stoves, folding tables and chairs, and two large rectangular metal containers lined with plastic bags that were used as toilets. Yes, there was a toilet seat, too.

Whatever could not be burned in the campfire at night had to be carried out, and that included garbage, cans, bottles, and other disposables, and the excrement collected throughout the trip. Everyone took part in loading and unloading the boats. We were responsible for packing our rubber bags, putting our sleep gear in proper bags, helping to set up camp in the evening, and taking it down in the morning. We also took turns helping to prepare meals.

Finally, we were ready to start the trip down the river. We picked a boat and a place to sit. On paddle boats everyone paddled. On dories, only the guide rowed. Usually, there were four to six paddlers in each raft. The guide in the back paddled and also used her paddle as a rudder. The two in front set the pace, and we all followed the guide's instructions. That meant that we had to respond quickly, so the first thing we did when we got into the raft was practice right turns, left turns, back paddle, and dig in! We also were taught what to do if we "wrap," that is, when the boat hit a rock in such a way that the pressure of the river wrapped the boat around the rock and held it there like a magnet; and how to get out from under the boat if it capsized. Finally, "If you fall out of the boat and are caught in the current, don't panic and don't try to swim. Turn on your back with your feet straight ahead and flow with the river. (Having your feet facing straight ahead was a way of protecting yourself from the rocks.) The current will take you down river and as soon as you see an area to land or hold on to, head for it. We will pick you up!"

Once the lessons were over, we were on our way. Excitement and anticipation was high. My focus was concentrated on holding the paddle firmly, keeping rhythm with the front paddlers, and most importantly, staying in the boat. Gradually, I relaxed and let myself look around.

The mountain, the trees, the birds, and the river were beautiful and so peaceful. The only sounds we heard were warbling birds and the water splashing on the sides of the boats. I enjoyed observing the guides in all the boats. I was absolutely thrilled with the skillfulness and styles of each of the women. Marguerite, the lead guide, was a quiet, thoughtful woman in her early thirties with sad eyes and long brown hair. Later I learned that nine months out of the year Marguerite worked as a physical therapist, and during the summers she guided on rivers in Northern California and Oregon. Beside the Klamath, she worked on the Salmon, Scott, Owyhee, and Rogue.

Louise, Beth, and Maggie, the other three guides, also appeared at ease, yet also alert and observant of the subtle changes in the currents and flow of the river. They all exuded a quiet confidence and self-assuredness and an air of deep inner calmness. These characteristics intrigued me, and I wanted to learn more about them and their lives on the river.

Louise and Beth were college students in religious and environmental studies, respectively. Maggie lived in Weed, California and taught elementary school. After training with the Turtle River Rafting Company, they each had several years experience working as guides during the summer months.

Suddenly, the current changed... it became swifter. Ahead we heard a thunderous rumble. As we turned the bend, we saw the rapid ahead and we were heading right for the middle of it. "Right turn!" shouted Maggie our guide. "Back paddle!"

The boat was heading for the rapids backward! My heart was pounding. I gripped the paddle tightly and pushed vigorously against the rushing water. Quickly, the raft turned and was suspended right over the swirling chaotic rapid. "Now, dig in! Dig in!" Yelled Maggie. We were paddling hard and fast. "Keep digging!" As I dug in, I looked squarely in the face of a river that seemed determined to swamp our boat. I put my head down, closed my mouth to keep from swallowing river water, and continued to paddle urgently and intensely. Wave after wave covered us, and after a seeming eternity, we were out of the rapid. A spontaneous shout of pleasure and relief came out of all of us, and the "old timers"—the more experienced rafters—held their paddles in the air and shouted again. Now, I'm laughing and I feel the joy and pleasure of survival. We made it!

Rivers are very forgiving and even playful. How rapidly we found ourselves on a gentle and smooth span that became a mirror. The two women in the front of the raft started bailing water out of the boat. Bailing became routine after each rapid, and we all took turns. (With the development of self-bailing rafts, this task became unnecessary a few years later.)

After the excitement of running a rapid, we stopped paddling and shared our fears and perceptions with each other. "For a second there I thought we were going down backwards!" "I felt like I was falling out, but I didn't! Paddling keeps you in the boat! That's amazing!" The anxious laughter and talking went on and on. Gradually, a quiet calm came over everyone.

Between rapids we got acquainted with each other and with the surrounding environment. We learned the names of rapids—Rattlesnake, Dragon's Tooth, Swillup, and Guide's Nemesis—and we watched the birds swooping over trees, flitting over water and catching bugs in mid-air, and we learned their names: Osprey, Bald Eagle, Great Blue Heron, and Merganser.

At noon the guides spotted a small beach and we stopped for lunch. Suddenly a folding table appeared, and within minutes, the guides were slicing cheese, tomatoes, onions, pickles, and laying out all kinds of meats for sandwiches. Fruit, cookies, and lemonade were also available. It seemed like hours since our last meal, and I realized I was famished. We peeled off life jackets, sweaters, and boots and found shady or sunny spots to sit and relax. I ate my first meal on the river. Everything tasted delicious. On a river ordinary food tastes like gourmet meals, and the spread that was laid out so casually quickly disappeared. I've been impressed by the quality of the meals pre-pared on rivers. Many of the guides are actually gourmet cooks.

After lunch, we put on life jackets, climbed into our boats, and ran a few more rapids. Since it had been a long day for all of us, we made camp early. As soon as the boats landed, we all pitched in and helped unload all the supplies and equipment; then, we each went off in our own directions to find a camping site for the night. Some of us came back to the beach and assisted the guides in setting up the kitchen, pre-pared snacks, or helped with the preparation of dinner. Others went hiking or settled on their sleeping bags to read or take a nap.

The guide responsible for setting up the toilet went out scouting for a secluded and scenic spot facing the river. A roll of toilet paper placed on a rock in a highly visible place signaled the location and availability of the lavatory. When the paper was gone, a waiting line formed at a respectable distance. A bucket of water and a bottle of liquid soap nearby reminded us to "wash your hands" before return-ing to camp.

With the necessities taken care of, I went off to make a home-away-from-home in a wooded area. I laid my sleeping gear (or set up my tent) between two or three trees or bushes and close enough to the river that I would not have to carry my bags such a long distance in the morning. The trees or bushes gave me a place to hang my wet clothes and tennis shoes to dry. Some spread out and formed indi-vidual campsites at the distant end of the beach. The guides usually gathered together after a run to relax and discuss the events of the day and to plan for the next day. One of my favorite activities on a river was gathering branches and dead logs and assisting the guide in charge of building the campfire.

Before long, as our hunger pangs increased and the smell of cooking food beckoned us, we all gathered around the fire to review the day's run and listen to the guides tell their stories and experiences on the rivers. We got better acquainted with each other. We were women from different areas of the San Francisco Bay Area and other regions of northern California. As it turned out in most groups, some of us were married, with or without children, single or divorced and working in different professional areas. We were different in many ways and still we found areas of commonality as well. Before long a small community of river rafters formed.

Night descended. Stars filled the sky. Yawns reminded us that it had been a long day. Saying goodnight, and with the aid of the campfire and our flashlights, each woman made her way to her sleeping bag. There were the stragglers: Janet, Delores and Betty – the night people – who cannot bear to leave the campfire at nightfall, and they sat and talked quietly for another hour or so. Eventually, the camp was still and everyone, including the creepy-crawly insects and animals, were asleep.

The rising sun and the smell of coffee wakened me. I am a morning person and an early riser anyway, but on the river my urge to move on was very strong. I was dressed, washed, teeth brushed, and black bag packed before most of the others were out of their sleeping bags. We had a leisurely breakfast. Dishes were rinsed in water with Clorox, then washed in a bucket of hot soapy water, rinsed in hot water, and placed in nets to dry.

Each of the guides had her specific task for the day. The work was done efficiently and quietly, whether it was breaking camp; packing the food, utensils, and the kitchen equipment; putting out the fire, or hauling the toilet to the beach. As they completed one task, each went to her boat and packed on her share of the supplies and baggage. The rafters broke their own camps, packed black bags, and brought their gear to the beach where they helped load the boats.

The biggest decision we had to make in the morning was,

"Which guide am I riding with today?" The tradition on rivers was to ride in a different raft everyday. This way the guides and rafters got to know each other better. I believe there were other reasons for wanting to get familiar with everyone on the trip, at least for me there were. Here we were—twenty women in the wilderness with no telephone or radios. If anything happened, I wanted to know who I could count on if I needed help.

Generally, I have been very impressed with the people who enjoy the wilderness; they were cooperative, self-sufficient and friendly, and they were protective of the environment. The guides were helpful, supportive, and encouraging. They wanted each of us to enjoy our stay on the river, and they seemed intent on serving our needs in every way possible. They also wanted us to have the best and the safest rafting experience that they could provide without exposing us to unnecessary risks and dangers; for this I was deeply grateful. Some of the rafters radiated toward like-minded and formed little groups within the larger group. By the end of a trip, some had become good friends. Probably, the rest of us would never see each other again. We would go our separate ways to live our separate lives, but here on the river, we were together—synchronous when we were paddling and in harmony with each other and with nature for a short time.

The time on the river was one of discovery about each other and ourselves. I learned that I needed and wanted periods of solitude. As a busy wife, mother, and professional, I didn't realize how much I needed my own space and time until I went to the river. Although I found rafting the rapids thrilling, it wasn't the danger or the excitement that called me. I discovered more peace and freedom in that brief weekend than I'd had in years, and I wanted more. I wanted moments to think, to contemplate, and to just let go of the drivenness in my life. I wanted to feel life at its most basic, at its fullest, and in the present.

So I fell in love with the river, and before I knew what was happening, thoughts and plans started running wildly through my mind. "I don't want to go back. I want to stay here and make my home here on the river. I wondered, "What do I have to do to learn to guide? If I were twenty years younger, I would chuck it all and become a river guide. Give up graduate school…. forget the dissertation… what about my family? They're not going to leave to come out here in the wilderness."

The pragmatic part of me soon took over and said, "Look, you've worked hard all of your life to get where you are. You can't give up everything. Beside, you're over fifty. How long do you think you would last on the river?"

By the end of the weekend, I had come to my senses enough to realize that I did not have to give up everything. I could do both. I could do the white-water rafting on weekends and during the summer vacation and I could keep my family intact and continue graduate school and do my work. After all Marguerite, the lead guide, was single and in her thirties, and she worked as a physical therapist during the year and took off during the summers to work as a guide.

Later that weekend I learned that, as much as she loved rafting and guiding, Marguerite was giving them up to go back East and work full time. She was a woman of few words, and she was giving up something she loved without explanations or excuses. I didn't learn the story behind such a drastic move, and I felt very sad and disappointed for her. As for me, I began planning my next rafting trip.

For the next eighteen summers, I went white-water rafting for a weekend, then for five days, then for two weeks. I came back to the Klamath River a few more times, and I even did the swimming rapid with Marguerite's help. She wrapped her strong left arm around my shoulder, and we surfed around a twelve-foot boulder at the edge of the rapid. The next time I did it alone.

Louise, the other guide from the first trip who had the blond braided hair was there also. We hiked up a mountain stream for about a mile in search of the Ukonom Falls, a double waterfall that was considered sacred by the Native Americans. In some places along the way, the freezing water was so deep that we had to swim. When we finally reached the falls, we all stood in awe of the magnificence before us. A sparkling dark blue pool, surrounded by trees and moss at the foot of the falls, gave them the appearance of an icon. Louise reached the falls first and sat beside then in a Lotus position. With her eyes closed and her long blond hair flowing down to her waist, she looked like a goddess. We sat reverently in the moss and absorbed the stillness and spray of this sacred space. None of us spoke for a long time.

Something was happening to me on the rivers—something beyond words—something I had experienced on rare occasions in spiritual places: a deep sense of peace and inner stillness enveloped me, and I knew I would be back. For many years I stayed away from the church of my childhood. Throughout those years I searched silently for a spiritual connection through various forms of meditations. Here on the river I felt closer to a spiritual presence than anywhere else. I discovered another reason for rafting.

I not only rafted the Lower Klamath again, but also the Upper and the Middle sections that were technically more difficult—class IV and V, rather than III. The currents were stronger, the rapids deeper, and the rocks bigger. I made another decision on one of these rivers: I would practice and develop my skills and stamina on the smaller rivers until I felt ready to do the big one. Then, I would promote myself to do the most challenging river of all—the Colorado.

When I did the Owyhee River in the Oregon desert in 1983, I knew I had to do the Colorado, but that would take much more preparation. The Owyhee River is small and a difficult river—very narrow and surrounded on both sides by cliffs and canyons—full of big rocks, chutes and steep rapids. This splendid river is called the miniature Colorado, and it can only be rafted in the spring when the water flow is at its highest. After June the river dries up.

On the second day on the Owyhee, an unexpected incident occurred: Steve, the guide on our boat, lost his balance and fell in just as we were coming around a sharp bend in the river into a narrow gorge. We were paddling very hard and heading for the canyon wall. When we didn't get the next call from Steve, I looked back and he wasn't there.

"Now, what?" I thought as the canyon wall loomed ahead. Another boat was nearby, and I called out to David, the lead guide, "David! Tell us what to do!" "Left turn!" he yelled back, and we responded in time to skim past the canyon wall. One of the other boats picked up Steve, and within minutes he was back in our boat giving

1993
Tetshinshini River
Alaska

1995 - Coruk River
in Turkey

Hooked on Rivers
(1980 - 1998)
(age 52 - 70)

The **big one** - the Colorado River, here for her 61st birthday in 1989. She also rafted the Colorado River again when she turned 70 in 1998.

The rivers helped Liberty, as the Irish would say, make her soul.
- Franz Schneider

us directions again. That was really a close shave, and we were so relieved to have Steve in the boat again that we didn't even tease him about falling out.

The next day, we stopped on a bleached white sandy beach to have lunch and to explore a cave that was just above the beach. The cave, huge and deep, was under water in the winter. We saw signs of where the river level dropped on the sides of trees lining the beach. After lunch we climbed up the sandy bank and entered the cave; it was dark, damp, and deep, spreading broadly into the far walls of the mountain. I felt a cold chill come over me. I stood there for a moment feeling apprehensive, nervous, and scared. "I do not want to be here," I thought and turned around and went back to the beach where I waited for the others to return.

Around two o'clock, we were back in our rafts ready to do another two or three hours of rafting before stopping for camp, but as soon as we got out on the river, a big wind came up quite unexpectedly. Rowing was difficult and the guides were concerned we would tip over, so we headed for the nearest beach a few miles down river. As soon as we unloaded the boats, the wind died down.

We had plenty of time before dinner, and a few of us women decided to find a place in the river to take a bath and wash our hair. As I dried my hair, I looked up bending my neck back to see the top of the canyon. The steep rugged rock at the very top of the cliff looked down at me, and as I stared at it, I saw a huge eagle with beady eyes and a sharp beak staring back at me. "Oh, God! I'm seeing things. It must be the heat and the wind," I assured myself. I looked around the camp. The guides were talking or resting in one of the rafts. The other women were sunbathing on the beach and no one else seemed concerned about the eagle. I knew it was a rock, but it looked like an eagle to me. I couldn't take my eyes off it. I could feel its eyes staring intently at me, and I could see its sharp beak.

At that moment David passed by and I said, "David isn't that an interesting crag up there at the top of the cliff. Does it appear like an eagle to you?"

He laughed as he looked from the rock back to me, "Are you hallucinating, Libby?"

I laughed with him, "No, I'm not prone to hallucinations. It may be an illusion though." I continued to look. I started to feel perplexed and uneasy, yet fascinated. When we were in the cave, I felt the chill of something evil there and left. Now, I'm seeing an eagle in the rock staring at me. What does it mean? No one else seemed interested so I walked away, still puzzled.

Three days later, when we came out of the river, we learned that three weeks earlier three people had drowned and were found in the cave. They were not wearing life jackets and they had been drinking.

During the next fifteen years, I rafted some of the wildest rivers in the western states including the middle fork of the Salmon, the Snake River, the Tetchinchini in Alaska, and the Colorado twice —the first time on my sixtieth birthday and the second on my seventieth. After the Owyhee my rafting trips became pilgrimages. Once a friend asked me why I liked river rafting so much and without thinking I said, "That's the only place where I can find God." My answer astonished me more than her. I had not articulated my secret yearnings to anyone, not even myself.

"Is once a year enough? Why don't you bring God into your life here outside the rivers?" Her questions surprised me, and I did think about what she asked. I realized that being on the rivers awakened the spiritual aspect of me that was well hidden from my conscious mind. This awakening was stimulated the first time on the Klamath River when we swam to the Ukonom Waterfall.

There was something special about every river and I felt as if I were absorbing God's peace and love from the atmosphere and the beautiful natural environment that surrounded us. Happily, my experiences were affirmed when I discovered a quotation from Meister Eckhart: "God is a great underground river that no one can dam up and no one can stop."

THE COLORADO RIVER

The Colorado River was absolutely enthralling and overwhelming—just trying to comprehend that the multi-layered and multi-colored canyons had been there for millions of years and were continuing to evolve was mind-boggling.

About a week into the trip we were floating down the Colorado River. The breeze was whistling through the canyon and ruffling the smooth water into gay riffles. Our guide and six of us passengers were resting and quiet after plunging through one of the huge rapids that made this river famous.

Around the bend we saw a sand bar and a large flat rock protruding over the river like an enormous diving board. The guides of the four boats navigated toward the left side of the river, and one said nonchalantly, "We'll stop here for lunch and those of you who want to use the 'diving board' overhead may do so while we put the food out on the table."

"That looks so dangerous," I thought to myself. "I hope whoever dives off is a powerful swimmer. The current is very strong, even when the river is smooth." Silently, I wished I had the strength and the courage to dive off, but I knew I couldn't go against such a deep and heavy current. Within moments we landed, and immediately we began unloading the tables and the food containers in preparation for lunch.

The youngest members of our group were a brother and sister-pair of adolescents with more energy than common sense who were clambering up the rocks and the canyon and reached the diving board before us older ones were out of the boat. "Come on, Dad," Jimmy shouted to his father, "this is great! You can do it with us. We'll all jump off together!" Their father, Charlie, a husky man, somewhat overweight, gave a sigh and climbed up the wall of the canyon. I was sitting under a tree in the shade, and I held my breath as the three took each other's hands, counted to three and, with a running jump they plunged into the depths of the river.

I held my breath and waited for them to come back up. They did, after what seemed a long, long time. They sprung up through the brown waters, out of breath and exuberant. Others followed—shouting and diving and going up, over and over and over again.

After a while I lay down to rest, and immediately I fell asleep. In my dream I, too, climbed blithely up the canyon rocks and stood on the edge of the platform looking down into the dark waters. I took a deep breath, stretched my arms over my head, rose up on my toes, and dived deep into the muddy waters. Suddenly, I was going deeper, below the fast current of the brown water into an area of the river that was aqua blue in color and into a gentler current.

I swam effortlessly through layers of blue water and reached another level of the river that was clear and light as air. I landed on a sandy beach at the bottom of the river and walked toward a cave that invited me to enter. I walked slowly into the cave and I realized I was in a sacred place. There before me, against the wall was a flat stone altar held up by two large rocks with a large candle burning in the center. I stood there in awe and reverence before an altar.

I awakened to the call for lunch. I was still filled with wonder. I had not forgotten the episode with the eagle. All these experiences at different times over the years were awesome. They must mean something, but what was the significance?

Yes, in my elder years I felt the need for a more spiritual life, but I was reluctant to return to the church of my childhood. I had a similar awesome experience as a young child standing in church beside my grandmother, overwhelmed by the chanting, the candles, and the smell of incense. I discerned a deep sense of the mysterious and faithfully I attended church until my middle thirties. When I finally left thoroughly disillusioned with my life and the church, I had no idea where to go from there.

For many years I explored different spiritual paths – Eastern and Western. In 1994, when my life was thoroughly fragmented, I found my way (with God's help) to Trinity Cathedral Church on Christmas Eve. I had been searching for a place where I could belong, where I could continue to learn and grow spiritually, and where I could contribute and share my own skills and knowledge.

As soon as I walked through the door, I felt something significant was happening. Christ's birth was being celebrated and everyone—clergy and laity—all were participating in the celebration and joyfulness, and I wanted to be part of the celebration and this community.

I felt welcomed and accepted. I was given the gift of time to find my own comfort zone and to gain the sense of belonging, of being a part of something meaningful. There were many opportunities to participate and to serve the community. Thankfully, I was home at last.

On the rivers, I rediscovered a connection with a spiritual mystery. One day, much later, I searched for the meaning of the eagle in the Bible. In a passage in Isaiah (40:28-31), God spoke of his concern for his people. He is faithful and does not desert us. He waits for us!

Have you not known? Have you not heard?
The Lord is the everlasting God, the Creator
of the ends of the earth.
He does not grow faint or grow weary;
His understanding is unsearchable.
He gives power to the faint,
and strengthens the powerless.
. . . .
But those who wait for the Lord
Shall renew their strength,
They shall mount up with wings
Like eagles,
They shall run and not be weary,
They shall walk and not faint.

In July 1998, I returned from my second rafting trip on the Colorado River. This was my seventieth year, and I had promised myself ten years before that I would return to celebrate this birthday in the Grand Canyon and the Colorado River. I wrote this letter at the end of the trip to say goodbye to the canyon and the river:

And there you were in your awesome splendor waiting for me. You were as magnificent as I remembered you. Your size was overwhelming—one canyon on top and behind another—huge as coliseums and stadiums. The shapes and sizes varied in their vastness. Sometimes I saw Gothic Cathedrals with intricate spires; in another place I saw classical temples – one was named Zeus' Temple. As I gazed at monstrous rocks, I saw gargoyles, elves, and saintly faces.

During the day your colors were soft pastels until the setting sun's rays magnified your canyons into deep oranges and reds and purples. Suddenly, the canyon walls changed into tapestries hanging from the sky with paintings and etchings that only God could have sketched there.

Your cold water numbs our feet in less than a minute, and your dark green and brown waters change from smooth mirrors and playful riffles into loud rumblings of waves and chaotic rapids that seem to want to pull us out of our boats and toss us about like little rubber toys. But the guides know the river and they listen to the currents and humbly follow your directions. They flow onto the smooth tongue and descend into the deep plunges of the rapids. Huge waves toss us hither and yon sometimes playfully, sometimes with vigorous backhanded slaps that push us against baggage or onto the floor of the raft. "Hold on!" shouts the guide. "Lean into the waves! If you stand against the water, the waves will push you over!"

I learned again to flow with you, River, and to respect you. If I surrender and trust you, you will fill me with your glory, beauty, and love. Sometimes we flowed silently down your smooth currents and listened to the sounds of the canyon. You and the wind whispered secrets to each other—two billion years of timelessness together, connected and at one with each other. I wanted to be a part of that connectedness. I came to join in the whispering, and I gave you my gifts of trust and love so you would let me into your secret world.

You and the canyon filled me with your colors and your ancient layers of red rock, granite, and shale. You let me taste the timelessness of eternity, and for a brief moment you lowered the veil of time and space and let me glimpse God's face.

A New Century

APRIL 2001–SPRING CLEANING

THIS IS WHAT WAS LEFT WHEN HE WAS GONE: his tools, his knee-high boots, a movie camera, and dozens of knick-knacks.

The tools were neatly arranged in drawers, on hooks, and on shelves. Every time I went in the garage to go someplace in my car, they were staring at me, constant reminders of the pain of failure and loss.

That spring, three years after he left, the camellias blossomed early and the air was warming up, and I was struck by the spring-cleaning bug that hits me every year about the same time. I suddenly got this strong urge to clean the garage and get rid of all the things I did not need or want any longer.

I checked with a couple of neighbors about a place to take or sell used tools, and I offered them whatever they could use. Someone mentioned a second-hand dealer on Broadway, and I called him to inquire whether he was interested in buying used tools. He was! My neighbor, Warren, cautioned me that they were worth at least two hundred dollars.

Cheerfully, I loaded three boxes with all kinds of tools and in-struments and took them to the store on Broadway. I laid them care-fully in an area that the store manager pointed to, and I waited for him to complete his business with another customer. To pass the time, I walked around the barn-like space and looked at all kinds of things new and used that covered every inch of wall and floor space. Eventually, he came over and scrutinized my three boxes and in a very matter-of-fact manner said, "Two-hundred dollars." In a similar matter-of-fact response, I said, "Thank you, I'll take it." With the money in hand, I went out the door with a big smile on my face. There was no bickering or bartering or argument. Just like that I made two hundred dollars! The easiest money I ever made.

I was so encouraged by my success that I decided to sell the movie camera that had been in the closet for about twenty years and never used. I found a camera shop on H Street that took used cameras on consignment. I would get paid when someone bought the camera. About three weeks later, I had a call from a clerk who told me that the camera had been sold and I could come and pick up my money. A little later I was there picking up fifty dollars for a camera that had never been used. For a few minutes, I understood why people liked having yard sales and going to antique shops. I felt very good knowing that someone had found value in an old movie camera.

The following spring when I was going through the house and garage getting rid of broken and no-longer-useful objects, I saw those old dusty boots on the basement stairs. I put them out on the street for the city pick-up the next morning, but I think a homeless person took them before the truck got there. They had been worn after every heavy rainfall to clear the storm drains on our street that flooded after rainstorms. Our neighbors and we would be out on the street, ritualistically, clearing the storm drains of leaves and other debris to avoid the overflow from coming into our yards and homes. Hopefully, the man who picked them up made good use of them.

Last week I became aware of all the knick-knacks that he left and that were still on the shelves all over the house—in the kitchen and breakfast nook, in the dining room, and in the bathroom. As I looked them over, I decided, I can have a yard sale later on or pass them on to our daughter-in-law who likes collecting all sorts of odds and ends. But the old memories no longer hurt, so I think I'll leave the knick-knacks where they are for a while longer.

Reunion Trip "Home"

On May 4, 2001, I was on a flight from Sacramento to Cleveland, Ohio. Jean and her husband, George, were waiting for me when the plane landed. All my questions about recognizing them melted away as soon as I saw the older couple huddled anxiously at the top of the passageway closely observing the faces as they passed by. As soon as I saw them, I smiled broadly and went toward them with outstretched arms.

"I know you!" I said to Jean as I gave her a big hug. "You haven't changed that much!" Then I gave George a hug, too. He grinned and said, "Hi, Lib. It's been a long time."

"I'll say it has been a long time. Can you believe it? Fifty years! And we're all a little grayer." We laughed and talked our way to the Baggage Claims and from there to the parking lot and to the drive from Cleveland to Cuyahoga Falls where they lived.

They had invited me to come two days early so we could spend time together getting reacquainted before the reunion. Jean and I had been roommates during the last year and a half in Nursing School. I'd forgotten how close we were. In our senior year, she came to me to tell me she might be pregnant. We both knew what that meant. In those days nursing students were not permitted to be married. She and George had eloped at the end of the first year, and I was the only one who knew their secret.

We both were very anxious for the rest of that week. A couple of days later, we passed each other on the medical ward where we were stationed. She leaned close to me and whispered, "It's OK. I'm not pregnant!" I breathed a big sigh of relief, nodded, and went on about my duties.

Jean revealed another secret to me that reunion weekend. She was diagnosed with beginning symptoms of Parkinson's disease. *Oh, God, not her, too. I had a friend back in Sacramento who had just received the same diagnosis.*

Her main concern was whether George could take care of her. From there we went on to other subjects. Jean was not one to spend a lot of time moping or feeling sorry for herself. She was a very pragmatic, down-to-earth person who took what life gave her with a quiet, matter-of-fact acceptance. She and George had a deep faith that had sustained them since their early days together.

Later that day when we went for a walk, she told me that George was writing a book about his wartime experiences for their grandchildren. He fought in the bloody Battle of the Bulge during World War II. After a long pause, she sighed, "He came out of that war with a chest full of medals and a promise to God that if he came out alive, he would go to church every Sunday." Then Jean said quietly, "He and one other man were the only survivors in their platoon."

After another long silence, she went on talking as we had done years ago, "I didn't tell you in my letters that I had a breakdown last year." After a while, she explained that she had suffered a deep depression two years after her mother's death. Probably the diagnosis of Parkinson's had set off fears of aging and the anticipation of years of increasing helplessness. "I'm not sure I'll be able to depend on George's ability to take care of me as he has done over fifty years. He's older than I am, and it's a big worry for me."

We walked without speaking again for a long time. Feeling helpless myself, I tried to be reassuring. "You've been together a long time, Jean. You'll find a way to deal with this. You both have a strong faith and you have each other." Words were so useless at times like these, so I then decided to be quiet.

The next morning I woke up in their home and was swept up in their routine. Breakfast consisted of cooked cereal, orange juice, and tea. Afterwards they sat together in their family room reading the morning paper aloud to each other. When one found an article on the environment that was of interest to both of them, Jean clipped out the article and put it on the desk. Later that day, George would write another letter to the editor. This was their main pastime—writing articles and letters to the editor.

"How comfortable they are with each other," I thought, just slightly envious. I wondered if I had ever felt so at ease in my own marriage, which was in the process of dissolution. I didn't think so. Divorce was not a topic we discussed on this weekend. Not relevant at this time. Neither of us brought it up.

On Saturday, George drove us to the Enterprise Rental where I picked up a car I had requested weeks earlier. After the reunion I planned to stay in Martins Ferry to visit my old neighborhood and spend the day with my childhood friend, Estelle.

I examined the spotless car with the salesman and happily signed the papers. In a few minutes we were on our way. Jean came with me so we would have a little more time to talk, and George drove ahead of us at 55 miles per hour in the 55-mile zone, and 65 miles per hour in the 65-mile zone. At first, I was impatient. I wanted to pass him up and drive my usual ten miles over the speed limit. Then I decided to relax and follow him at his pace. We had all day, and it was only three and a half hours to our destination, a hotel in St. Clairsville where the out-of-towners were to meet in the afternoon of the reunion.

From Cuyahoga Falls we drove past Akron, New Philadelphia, rolling deep green hills, and forests of slim swaying birch and poplar trees. I have never seen those shades of green and smoky blues and purples in the distant hills anywhere else in the world. There is no other place where those "Green Walls" can be found.

Like clockwork, George stopped periodically at rest stops so we could take short walks to relax tightened muscles and stiff backs. Then, on we went for another hour or so toward our rendezvous with class-mates from a nursing class I had not seen for fifty years. "How will I recognize them?" I wondered. I remembered their younger faces, which were imprinted in my mind.

After 150 miles of non-stressful driving (how different from the California freeways!), we arrived at the Hampton Inn and settled in for the day and night. Later that afternoon, Jean and I went for a walk still engrossed in renewing and reviewing the intervening years of our long-ago friendship. At one point Jean turned to me and said, "You know, you are a remarkable woman, Lib. I can't believe you did all the things you've done, all those degrees, and the work you've done, teaching, consulting, and writing. I'm amazed. I had two daughters, and I could barely get my CE (Continuing Educa-tion) Units for my license. How did you do it?"

"I'm driven, I suppose, but seriously, I've thought about this for a lot of years. At first, I thought I was just very determined to go to school. I loved school and learning, and I did not want to get mar-ried for the sake of producing children. I wanted to have a choice about my life and what I did. Now, at this stage in my life, I believe that it was God who has guided me all these years. I have no other explanation. How else could I have persisted? It's been difficult, especially when my marriage to Jim came apart. That hurt my sons so badly. Then, marrying Mike made matters worse for them; but he was a good father for Andy. I know I should have left, but I couldn't bear to be a single parent again. I thought I could change things, but I've learned the hard way. I can't change anyone but myself. That's hard enough."

From a distance Jean saw three women approaching the entrance of the Inn and called out, "Agnes, Louise, Martha!" They stopped, looked at us through squinting eyes, and then one pointed a finger and walked in our direction. They recognized us. I did not, for the life of me, find the faces I remembered.

Slowly, the eyes, the smiles, and the voices of these women resonated and matched the remembered faces and expressions locked away in my memory. It was strange how some of our features remain the same while wrapped in wrinkles brought on by the strains and stresses of the years. Hugs and kisses revived the warmth of our remembered bonds. Agnes was the only one who was still as slim as she had been in our student days.

Later, I recognized the tight hugs of Millie and Jane! These were the ones I had been closest to so long ago: Jean and Agnes, Jane, and Millie as we went through the "Baptism of Fire" together. That's what we called our nurses training. When we were all together talking and laughing, I recalled the shrill female voices vibrating through the halls of that old dormitory we called home for three years.

As I dressed that evening in preparation for the dinner and meeting the other classmates, I felt the stirrings of excitement and anticipation. There were twelve of us coming together (out of nineteen who had graduated) after fifty years. I learned that three had died already: Sara Lou, Evelyn, and Marie. I felt sad that they were gone. Ella Mae was in Australia; Dora Smith's husband was very ill, and she could not leave him; and Ann didn't say why she wasn't coming. I did not remember that Beverly had been expelled four months before graduation because she announced she was pregnant. "She usually comes to our reunions," Jean told me, "but she decided not to come to this one." I felt the regrets that she must have experienced for missing the graduation after putting in all that time and hard work. The old rules were so unbending and so unfair!

At dinner our class of 1951 was placed at the head table. The nurses from previous and later classes were at tables in front of ours. Those who had ordered chicken dinners were served first; and after a long while, fish was served to those of us who had requested fish.

The singer for the program was a fourteen year old with a lovely, fresh soprano voice singing songs from the 1940s and a few hymns. Her proud father introduced her by telling us that she was "a fragile diabetic who had survived many ordeals with the help and care of loving nurses, doctors, and God."

Then, quite unexpectedly, I was invited to the podium to address the group and tell them where I had been since graduation. "How do I condense fifty years into ten minutes?" I wondered. To calm myself and give myself time to think, I laughingly started with the obvious, "Yes, it's been a long time since I fled Martins Ferry to see the world and to discover who I was. Martins Ferry was the motivating force that propelled me into the future...I was blessed over the years. I wanted to see how much I could accomplish, and I always seemed to be in the right place at the right time...I found my niche in mental health where the doors opened wide for me and I went through." I ended my little spiel with, "It's great to be back. Thank you." Afterwards, I couldn't remember what I said. I felt strange being the only one asked to speak. I wanted to hear from my classmates, and what they had done. Jean told me that Millie was married to an attorney, and she went back to college and received her Bachelor's Degree. All the others worked in hospitals for years. Jean had worked in a psychiatric hospital. Staff nursing was something I knew I couldn't do all those years. That's really hard physical work that I didn't want to do.

After dinner we dispersed and eight of us headed back to the Hampton Inn for more talk, laughter, and sharing of experiences. I was surprised to learn that Jane, who graduated with us, never practiced nursing. She became a well-known artist in Ohio Valley, and she married like all of us did. The only difference among us was that they had stayed married to their spouses; and all, except me, had stayed in Ohio. I was in the process of a second divorce, but we did not talk about that. I was both grateful and uneasy; I felt a little like the prodigal daughter returned.

The next morning I headed for Martins Ferry, a short ten-mile drive over familiar terrain that had not changed very much in fifty years, except for the freeway that ran through the green hills and along the river. I found my childhood friend's home with no problem. Estelle's parents and mine had been best friends. We grew up together, and whenever I came to Martins Ferry I looked her up. This was my last trip back.

This was a happy reunion, too! I didn't remember ever feeling so happy on my visits to Martins Ferry. There was a time when I would leave after a couple of days because I would get physically ill. Now, I wanted to spend the day with Estelle, driving around town and seeing all the places that were so alive in my memory.

She still had that shy smile that added a shade of fragility to her gentleness, and she spoke as quietly as ever. Her husband had died of a sudden heart attack two years ago, and she continued running the store that she and her mother had managed for years. Both of her parents were gone. She had considered moving to St. Louis where her sister lived with her family, but she had met a man recently and their friendship was developing. "I want us to take the time and really get to know each other," she confided. "I don't want to do anything hasty." That sounded like a wise plan, and I encouraged her to do that.

We were at the bottom of Hanover Street where it met First Street, and I stopped the car. I wanted to take a picture of a sign recently installed that read,

WELCOME TO MARTINS FERRY
THE EARLIEST SETTLEMENT IN OHIO

Just a block to the north was the place where Carlisle Street had been. Now the entire area that had been my neighborhood for twenty years was a solid mass of warehouses for miles down that familiar road. Even the blast furnace was gone. I stood there in silence remembering the children's voices that had played on that street. I said, "Goodbye," one last time.

A few blocks up Hanover Street, to the corner of Fifth Street near the library, was another new sign: **The James Wright Place.** This was the town's way of honoring one of her most famous poets. An annual festival has been held in the Martins Ferry Library since Jim died in 1980. Poets come from all over the country to read poetry and honor him. I was touched, and I took a picture of the street sign to share with my son, Marshall.

We drove past Fourth Street to admire the new buildings that gave the uptown a brighter look, and down to the area where the Central School no longer stood. In its place was the sparkling glass façade of the new bank in town. That was a sad sight for me. I loved that old brick schoolhouse that had been there for decades. I said another silent, "Goodbye," to what had been.

Then we drove up the hill to the top of the cemetery where both of my parents are buried and overlook the entire Ohio Valley. At first, all I could see were the graves of our neighbors from the Bottom and the Clarks Addition: there were the Kotellas's and Mr. Vrotsos, and others. Then, there were Mom and Dad side by side again; after all that pain and turmoil, they were together. It was a bittersweet reunion for them and me. Estelle was sad that her parents had chosen a different graveyard. "This is where they really belong," she whispered.

Quietly, we drove down the hill into the Valley again. I was so aware of how different the town was from what I remembered. The air was clean and bright. The hills, no longer gray-green from the smoke and soot of steel mills, were their natural green, and the sun was visible! "You know, Estelle, Martins Ferry is a very pretty town, now that it's been cleaned up." She agreed, "I love to look at the view of the river and the Wheeling Bridge that I can see from my back porch. I sit out there and look at that scene every day."

Later, that evening over dinner, Estelle revealed that she had had several miscarriages and she almost died with the last one. I felt so sad for her. How painful that must have been. Then, her father had a stroke and was an invalid for fifteen years, and her mother and brother had taken care of him. The nursing home for a year was "so bad." Why does life have to be so difficult?

The next morning, we embraced warmly and tightly. "You are my family, now, Estelle. I have no one left in Martins Ferry." Finally, I felt close and connected to someone in the Ohio Valley. I felt grateful for the time we had together. I came home and found I belonged. For the first time in my life, I finally felt resolved and at peace with my family, my background, and my hometown.

The last part of my journey was a brief stop near Columbus to see my sister-in-law, Cally, who had been married to my brother, Tony, for over forty years. He died in September 1995, and she was making a new life for herself as a single woman. She was enjoying her condo; she was happy with her involvement with Weight Watchers, who had helped her lose over seventy pounds; and she was very active with the Art council. She was very excited and enthusiastic about finding another religious home in the Pentecostal Church.

It was Sunday when I arrived, and customary for her three sons and their wives and children to drop in at Cally's for Sunday dinner. When my nephew Michael (Ann's oldest son) and his wife learned that I was there, they also came along for the celebration. This was the ultimate Greek family reunion: loud talking, much laughter, good food, and getting acquainted with young additions to the family. I felt the joy of our togetherness, and I savored this new experience.

When the house was empty and quiet again, we two solitary women could sit and share meaningful moments of our lives: how she missed Tony and wished they could have shared their retirement years together. I spoke a little about my marriage dissolving. "This was a long time coming, about eight years," I told her. "I knew a change was coming. I'm so happy I found a new church home too. I think God led me to this church because it's been perfect for me. I'm learning a lot about religion and its history, and I've got such good supportive friends. Most important I feel accepted and I belong there!"

"We're both making new lives for ourselves, and that's good,"

Cally commented.

The next morning at Tony's grave, I cried because I still missed him, and I said goodbye to him too. My journey home was filled with the poignancy of sadness and joy. On September 11, 2001, Cally was diagnosed with Acute Myelin Leukemia, and she died six weeks later, on October 26th. Another loss and another goodbye! I learned again how precious and fragile life is, and I'm thankful for brief connections.

CONNECTING THE DOTS—DECEMBER 10, 2003

Today I wrote a paper on anger for my writing class, and it practically wrote itself. I realize again that out of painful experiences I learn much about myself. I can sink to the depths of depression, and out of that experience I learn compassion and love. I also can see clearly how strong and healthy I am. I looked over the list of tests and examinations that I've had over the last three years, and something popped up: I lost four relationships in 2000. In addition to my personal losses and grief, there was the terrible destruction of the Towers in New York.

I remember the morning of 9/11. I was driving to my acupuncturist for treatments, and when I heard the news on the radio, I went into shock. I felt numb. I believe I dissociated from myself as the dreadful reports poured over the radio and later on TV. I was horrified again, just as I was during World War II when I heard news broadcasts on the radio and watched the News in the movies. I felt the same shock when I read about our soldiers being killed in the Pacific and on the European Fronts, and later when I saw pictures of piles of skeletal bodies and live ones, too, when the concentration camps were opened. I believe that I suffered Post-Traumatic Stress Disorder in the past and the wounds were reopened in the present.

In the first three years of the new millennium, I suffered four losses. On January 17, 2001, two days after the anniversary of our meeting, our marriage was dissolved, after thirty-five years. My sister, Ann, rejected me; I can't remember why that time. A good friend broke off our relationship because she couldn't handle my anger toward Mike and his friends. (Now, I realize that was her problem more than mine.) Then, after a six-week illness Cally (my sister-in-law) died suddenly of acute myelin leukemia. She was diagnosed on 9/11.

My grief and pain became manifested somatically at first, which was very unusual for me. Over the next three years, I had a series of physical ailments: severe knee pains, a plugged Eustachian tube in my right ear, and I had some bleeding from my bladder. The bleeding required a biopsy, a Cystoscopy, an IVP (kidney tests), and an ultrasound. They revealed nothing.

In December 2001, I developed sciatica and I could hardly walk for a month. In early January 2002, headaches started coming on sporadically that entire year. In the fall I developed TMJ. I had a tube inserted in my ear on December 19, 2002, and it was replaced with a permanent one in June 2003. While I was on vacation in August 2003, I fell and broke my left upper arm. I never had a broken bone as a child, and here I was in my old age breaking my arm! How strange that I would have all these ailments when I was perfectly healthy, but all that pain and grief got converted into physical pain—to get my attention? At the same time, I was in therapy. By the end of 2003, I felt whole again, as if God had "knitted me together" (Psalm 139:12).

ANGELS IN MY PATH—FEBRUARY 29, 2004

During the past three years, I have passed through some of the darkest nights of my life. I experienced grief, fear, helplessness, and terror. At the worst of these times, I felt as though I was dying and called out to God. One night as I lay in my bed sobbing, I felt a presence near me. I thought I saw a very tall, cloaked figure standing over me. Suddenly I felt a stillness and a quietness pass through me. I turned over and slept soundly until morning.

Now, I remember several other experiences of God's presence, but I never called the presence "God" before. I always thought of those experiences as intuition, or "my guardian angel." Over the years I have spent much time reading, studying, thinking, reflecting, and meditating about how God is working in my life. I have developed a stronger belief in God than ever before. As a result of this belief, in addition to therapy and spiritual direction, I have concluded that God has been guiding me throughout my life. There is no other explanation.

Day after day, this experience of wholeness and healing has persisted. I have clarity of mind that I never had before. I know who I am. I feel detached from family members and adult children; yet, I feel more compassion for them than ever before. I have no need "to fix" them. I know I can't heal them. Only God heals us through other people. I know God is working with them too. Recently, I've done some of the best work professionally that I've ever done. I hear myself saying things that surprise me.

The greatest lesson I've learned is that God creates us, guides us, and puts people (angels) on our paths to nurture and heal us. If we allow ourselves to be open to His Presence, He will work through us to heal others.

Only Father and Son to both win the Poetry Pulitzer Prize
1972: **Collected Poems** by James Wright
2004: **Walking to Martha's Vineyard** by Franz Wright

Bookcover from Amazon.com

James Wright at 33 in
1960, the year he won
the Ohioana Book
Award for Saint Judas.

James Wright, 1972

James Arlington Wright was born December 13, 1927
in Martins Ferry, Ohio.
He died of cancer on March 25, 1980 in New York City.
Married to Liberty Kardules from 1953, they divorced in 1962.
He married Edith Anne Crunk in 1967.
All of his personal archives are at
Wesleyan University in Middletown, Connecticut.

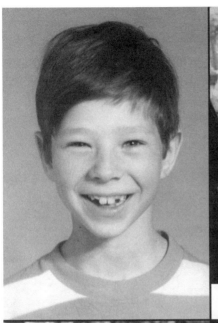

OBERLIN COLLEGE
Graduation - May 29, 1977

Libby's oldest son,
Franz Wright, was born in
Vienna, Austria
on March 18, 1953.

At age 46, Franz married
Elizabeth Oehlkers on
October 2, 1999.

Libby's second son, Marshall Wright, was born in Minneapolis, Minnesota.

Into this atmosphere of turmoil and pain, our second son, Marshall, arrived on July 30, 1958.

Reflections About
Franz and Marshall

FRANZ

This year has been one of reconciliation with Franz and Marshall. Franz has achieved six years of sobriety. He has been attending Mass every morning and AA meetings twice a day, sometimes more. His anger has been more controlled, but it still flares up in an instant if I make the wrong remark, typically which has to do with my ex-husband, Miklos. Franz' contempt and rage that I stayed as long as I did was as potent as ever. He accused me of not protecting him from his stepfather. He said he forgave me, but I felt more scorned than forgiven.

Even so, I felt something in him changing ever so slightly. I was careful in my talks with him. As long as I kept the subject on the "here and now" we managed to have a small conversation. I missed our talks of long ago when he talked about school, friends, the love of his life, and the poem or book that he was writing at the time. I knew he would call when something was happening in his life. I waited and he would call when he was having a poem published in the New Yorker, or when he was getting a book of poems ready for a publisher.

There were the long silences when he was using drugs and the screams for help when he "hit bottom," or when he was so panicked he could not leave his apartment for weeks and months. He stopped coming home to visit. He did not consider Sacramento "home" and he was afraid to fly. He left for college when we were living in Walnut Creek. I

403

made trips to see him when there was a conference in Boston or when I wanted to see him, but I did not feel welcomed. He did the best he could to contain his anger, but it slipped out at some point before I left.

Marshall and I were invited to his wedding when he married Elizabeth Oehlkers on October 2, 1999. These last five years have been the best and the most difficult years of his life. He has worked very hard to heal his life. He converted to Roman Catholicism. He has a trusted and loved companion and wife in Elizabeth, and he attends AA meetings faithfully. These are now his family and he belongs there. This year he spent the winter semester teaching at the University of Arkansas, and he was awarded the Pulitzer Prize in Poetry. He and Jim are said to be the first father and son to win this prestigious award.

By writing about my life and my family, I have come to an understanding that we have all survived some really horrible and appalling situations. I've learned that hatred destroys lives, and forgiveness means letting go of hatred and fear and learning how to go on living with love, acceptance, and generosity in our hearts. Only this can stop violence whenever it occurs in our environment. I'm deeply grateful that Franz and I are good friends again.

MARSHALL

A Mother's Lament

".....knowing that suffering produces endurance, and endurance produce character, and character produces hope, and hope does not disappoint us...."
(Romans 5:3-5)

After many programs (mental health and substance abuse) and many relapses, Marshall is moving forward again into another place that promises help in both of these difficult areas. He is optimistic that this time he will find healing and peace of mind. He left me last night with a kiss and a hug and a big smile on his face as he waved goodbye. Silently, I said a prayer for him.

404

I woke up at midnight in so much pain I could hardly breathe—another night terror. They are coming more frequently for some reason. "You know very well why they're coming again," scolded the voice in my head that part of me that observes my weaker, vulnerable self and gives me objective reports of what is happening in my life.

Marshall was going to be forty-five in two months, and I had hoped and prayed that he would be much further along in his recovery after two years in the program for chronically mentally ill individuals who also used drugs and alcohol. He was using again. Crank or crack—I can't tell the difference—in addition to all the high-powered medications for the bipolar condition that drives him to the edge of psychosis every year between February and the end of May.

Marshall's illness is cyclical. During the first half of the year he has experienced manic episodes since he was a toddler. Then when June came around, he was his good-natured, humorous self again. He was a year old the first time he climbed a five-foot gate in the backyard of our home on Como Avenue in Minneapolis and disappeared. Finally, a woman three blocks away came out of her yard and asked, "Are you looking for this little boy? I saw him wandering up the street a while ago and brought him here where he would be safe."

That was the first time. I stopped taking him shopping with me when he was two because no matter where we went and I kept a watchful eye on him, or how tightly I held his hand, he could vanish in an instant. Once in the Union Railway Station in Chicago, he disappeared and as I searched and called him, I heard my name announced on the loudspeaker, "Mrs. Wright, would you please go to the Information Booth? Your son says you are lost and he is waiting for you!" He was three at that time

His mood cycles continued. When he was in kindergarten, his teacher was ready to expel him because he could not sit still or color within the lines. In elementary school, he spent more time in the principal's office than in the classroom because he had "spring fever." He talked incessantly, he was unable to sit still, and occasionally, he did something malicious, like the time he sprayed the bathroom floor at school with "I hate Mr. Hammond!" (his fifth grade teacher).

He was a bright student who got A's and B's during the fall semester every year. Then after January, his life became disorganized and out of control again, and he couldn't keep track of time or belongings. He lost his prescription glasses, toys, clothes, and bicycles and continued to do so throughout adolescence and into adulthood.

My night terrors appeared that year from January until the end of May. My mind was screaming, "Marsh is going to kill himself if he keeps this up! The combination of medications and street drugs will blow his brains out and either kill him or leave him paralyzed!" This dreadful fear that overwhelmed me at night and left me limp resulted from the stark realization that I was helpless and powerless to do anything to change his situation, to save him. I learned months later that Marsh discontinued his medications for a few days when he started feeling the cravings for drugs.

I knew that I could do nothing to stop him. I'd known it for years, yet my fears drove me to find help. By June, when Marshall's mood stabilized again and my night terrors subsided, I could think more clearly and I continued the work of letting go of him that was necessary for me if I were going to find any peace in this lifetime.

I didn't know much about instincts, but if there were such forces in humans, I know I was driven by something beyond reason that told me, "He's your son. You wanted him, gave birth to him, and you're responsible. You've got to save him. He will die if you don't!" My rational mind gave me a different message, "Let go. You know you can't stop him. You have done everything you can to help him." Yet, I persisted. And his addiction drove him to find drugs.

I searched my psyche and my soul to find a way to detach from my fears for him. Everyone told me I must. I knew I had to. In my efforts to detach from this terrible need to rescue him, I hit my own bottom. I faced not only the terror of losing Marsh, but I went down to the bottom and looked at my own black pit – my fear of abandonment, despair, and emptiness. I prayed for hope and I prayed that God would guide Marsh. How many times had I turned him over to God? How many times had I taken him to drug, alcohol, and mental health programs?

How many times had Marsh come to my door, despite my pleas that he stay away from me when he was using drugs? I could not bear to look at his sunburned unshaven face, his eyes desperate with pain, his incoherence and, at times, his anger and rage and paranoia. I knew he came to me for comfort and solace. I was empty. I had nothing left to give. The more he rambled and searched for words to describe his own horrors, the more I felt frozen, unable to respond. My grief was overwhelming. I was drowning. How could I help him?

One day in late May, he pulled out of himself one clear statement—or partial statement—that came out of a myriad of disconnected words and phrases including, "I want to smash faces." My heart was torn to pieces as I listened to him struggling to make sense, to explain what happens to him. Then after a moment of silence, he said quietly and clearly, "We have endured more suffering than was... what? Normal? Acceptable? Necessary?" We sat in silence together.

Then the terrible guilt rose to his lips and mournfully he expressed his sadness that he carried for so many years that he had not written to his father when he was fifteen when his father was still alive. "I told him not to write to me until I sorted things out and he never did." That was the first time I heard an expectant note in his voice. Was he waiting for his father to write to him after he told Jim, "You're not my father! You never cared for me!"

Suddenly, I remembered another lucid moment when I asked Marsh, "Why do you always run away from me?" His response was clear and soft-spoken, "What makes you think I was running away from you? Maybe, I was looking for someone else." I was startled by the clarity and certainty of his words, and I remembered Marsh running after his father and crying desperately, "Daddy! Daddy!" Jim walked away without turning back. I picked up my sobbing son in my arms and took him into the house, and told him Daddy would come back later as he continued to sob and cling to me. Jim did not come back. He only came because I pleaded with him to come and see his sons.

After that, Marshall found men in the neighborhood to whom he would attach himself. He followed the gas-meter man while he read the meter in our basement, and he waited for the postman to deliver our mail. During the summer he was two, Marshall sat with the men who repaired Como Avenue, while they ate their lunch under the tree in our front yard.

These last two years as he reached middle age, I realized Marsh reminded me constantly of the man who was his father. He looked more like Jim as he aged. They have the same physical build. Marsh has his round face, his impish, smiling eyes, and his long, tapered fingers made for playing a piano or a guitar, or writing poetry, or catching a football. One day as I watched him running, I was astounded by the memory of his father running exactly the same way on the balls and toes of his feet.

June through January, Marsh reverted to his sweet, gentle nature, the same as that of his father. Then, he played his guitar and sang and he read, and he loved life again. Later in February his manic cycle kicked in and, like his father, his demonic side rose up and poured dreadful, ugly words out his mouth. In my memory I returned to the many nights when Jim, in his drunken, manic states, stood at the foot of my bed in the middle of the night machine-gunning me with incoherent words and phrases, and with a violent rage.

"Please, Jim, stop! Let me sleep! You'll wake the children." I pleaded. Nothing stopped him except exhaustion. Finally, he collapsed beside me and passed out. I lay there listening to his breathing, shaking in my own despair and anger. The chasm between us had grown wider and deeper after we arrived in Minneapolis. "How can I reach him when he's like this? I cried silently in utter helplessness.

I am haunted by James Wright who was incarnated in the body of my son, Marshall. No matter what I tried to do in my day-to-day life, the present got swallowed up by the churning storm that was pushing me back into the past. I had no choice at that time but to return to the years when Jim and I were together. The fragments of unfinished grief and unhealed wounds were pulling me back and demanding that I revisit whatever I left undone.

I must go back through all that devastation and reclaim those pieces. Believe me I would give anything not to go back there. I thought I resolved that life years ago. I spent years in therapy working through the pain of that relationship. I let it go a long time ago. I made a new life for myself, and I do not want to go there. I want to go forward with my life, not backwards. I thought I would be free to pursue my many interests, the new friendships, and the new life I was making for myself as a single woman on the fringe of old age. I'm seventy-five, and the years ahead seem very short compared to the three-fourths of my life that has been spent already. This year I have felt more vulnerable, more exhausted, and less able to cope than I have in years.

I've disengaged from my emotional entanglements with my family. I've let go of everyone for whom I felt responsible and had to rescue from the dysfunctions that pursued us through the generations. Now, a year later, Marsh and I have reached an understanding that I cannot continue to rescue him. I love him, and I'll support anything that will help him to quit using drugs, but he must move in that direction and want to save himself.

Yet, I'm not free. Marsh, reminds me of Jim.

There's also Franz. He shut me out of his life for many years. He accused me of not protecting him, of staying with a man who caused him such "humiliation and terror.... I forgive you both, but I also despise you both... I could never allow any child to suffer what you and Dad allowed."

Those were devastating words directed at me. I cannot defend myself against such a barrage of hatred from my own son, my beloved Franz who used to tell his friends that I was his best friend. There is no defense. I know how much he and Marsh suffered with grief and pain when they lost their father. I did not protect them adequately against a stepfather who went off the edge into his own black pit.

During the last five years, Franz has confronted his own demons and struggled through the pain and horrors of the recovery process, and he is succeeding day by day. He has succeeded in transcending all the rage and hatred that separated us for many years. He has found his Self, he has forgiven me, and we are experiencing what he calls, "the oldest and most enduring friendship, the one that I share with you, not to mention my love for you as my mother."

FORTY YEARS HAVE PASSED

Over forty years have passed since the end of my relationship with Jim. My going back there was necessary if I am to find a deeper sense of resolution, healing, and integration of the past and to weave it into the fabric of my whole life.

Writing this book
is my way of expressing empathy
for two innocents who set out in search of their freedom
and their true identities
and ended up destroying their relationship
and almost destroyed each other.

Out of the ashes of their life together,
grew two even more extraordinary human beings.

I want to acknowledge our two lives
that evolved out of that unspeakable disaster,
and I must acknowledge the pain and suffering
that has haunted the lives of our two sons.
I pray for forgiveness and peace of mind for all of us.

In the early months of 2005, Marshal asked to come home to work on his recovery. He promised to stop using drugs and to attend Narcotics Anonymous (NA) everyday. These were my conditions for living at home. He was ready to accept my demands in order to come home to recuperate and heal. Of course, he "slipped" three times. Each time he returned to his NA group. This year he stopped counting the days and months free of drugs. Quietly, he is looking forward to the end of this year as the year to celebrate his recovery. He is growing, progressing slowly, and living his life one day at a time.

Most importantly for me, I get another opportunity to provide a home for Marshall and to give him the sense of security and belonging that he missed out on because of his mental illness and his drug abuse. He is working hard and facing his life. I am proud of him. He attends NA and I am thankful that we have this opportunity to make up for lost years.

IT WOULD HAVE BEEN—FEBRUARY 20, 2005

In the middle of the liturgy, after the congregation wished each other, "the Peace of the Lord be with you," Canon Carey came out in front of the altar and welcomed our interim Dean. He also welcomed all newcomers who had not been there before. Then, he called all those who had a Thanksgiving or a celebration of any kind to come forward. There was a six-year old little girl announcing her birthday, and a woman was thankful to have reached her thirty-sixth year today. One of our priests and her husband were thankful for their fifty-fourth wedding anniversary, and applause broke out from those of us in the pews. Another couple was celebrating their twenty-fifth anniversary, and the last couple, their tenth.

As I sat there smiling and applauding, the thought suddenly occurred to me that today was the day that Mike and I were married in Carson City forty years ago! At least, today would have been our anniversary if Mike had not filed for divorce seven years ago. Has it been that long already? Then, my mind spun off in another direction: how many years has it been since Jim and I were married? From 1952 to today… and we were married on February 10! That was fifty-three years ago! Well, they were both over. There was no way to celebrate or recognize the impact that the endings of marriages have on spouses, or children, and families. No one in my family has ever spoken the word "divorce" since they occurred. It's as if they never happened.

I felt a little sad as I sat there thinking about what might have been a special day. I also remembered feeling a deep sadness that I did not have the opportunity to complete the whole process of marriage, "until death do us part." I've regretted that Andy and Kaye now have the responsibility of caring for the frail, weak man who used to be my husband. "I'm very sad they are doing the difficult work of caring for him. That was the work I had expected to do." I thought with a deep sigh. "I think I really wanted to see this marriage to the end.... come to think of it—I did. The marriage died first, and I grieved for lost years before he left.

I remember thinking, "I'm not leaving. I left once, but I'm not going this time. If you want to go, you are free to do so. The door is open. All you have to do is walk out." And I waited him out. Finally, he filed for divorce on December 30, 1998, at the age of seventy-six. "How sad that he chose to regress than face the end of his life as bravely as he did his twenties and thirties," I thought.

I had such hopes for his potential to grow and transcend his losses and wounds. He chose the more predictable path. Rather than grieve and heal the dreadful injuries he suffered, he chose to go back to his past to recapture his lost youth and found, like we all do, that youth does not exist any longer. Thomas Wolfe said it a long time ago, "You can't go home again."

I started over again, and I've done very well as a single woman of seventy-six. How many times have I started over again? This makes six times. Not bad for one lifetime, and I've still got a way to go.

EASING INTO RETIREMENT—AUGUST 1, 2005

For the past decade I have pondered, considered, and always rejected the notion that I had to retire. "I'm not ready," I said at sixty-eight. There was still too much work to do. As a marriage therapist I didn't think I would ever run out of clients. When I cut back to two days a week and to a limit of ten clients, I still had weeks when I was seeing my limit and sometimes more.

My other argument for continuing to work was: I'm healthy and in good shape physically, mentally, and spiritually. I seldom felt tired after working all day. I felt invigorated. I had time for other interests and for volunteering at church, and I was never bored.

At the age of 69 I decided to start taking my social security, which meant that taxes had to be paid since I continued working. I think I paid higher taxes then than when I was working full-time, or at least it seemed that way.

As I moved into my 70s, my aged husband confronted me with a request for a divorce. Now, I felt working was a necessity for a while longer. I was even more stunned when I was faced with several clients —couples—who were in the midst of their own struggles and were considering divorce. This was a common problem for therapist, but this time I felt as if I was being tested. I'm going through a divorce and I'm expected to help others do the same thing! Tightening my own boundaries to keep my own pain in check was a lesson in discipline, which was necessary in keeping my issues separate from those of my clients.

Of course, I was not as relaxed as previous times. After seeing five to eight clients a day, I was so tired I didn't think I could hold out much longer. Then my caseload would drop to three or four and I felt better. I went along this way for three years. My work sustained me and kept me focused on my clients. Only one couple divorced during the time I was going through my own divorce. There were five or six others who decided against divorce.

I was envious that I could help those couples to reach a more understanding and loving relationship, while I was watching my own being dismantled. That made my work even more valuable for me. I was doing something for others that I could not achieve for myself. Yes, there were therapists who could have helped my spouse and me if he were willing, but he was not interested in working on our marriage, not even after so many years.

At times I felt angry and outraged that he had betrayed me for reasons that did not make sense at our ages, and of course I was terribly hurt and deeply misunderstood. The irony of our situation was that I was preparing for and making end-of-life arrangements for both of us, but because Mike was superstitious, he reacted by becoming paranoid and suspicious of my motives. He accused me of trying to get rid of him. Surprised at his response, I replied, "I did not make arrangements only for you; I made the same arrangements for me too." He was not reassured. I think he used that to justify his actions and to file for divorce.

In the midst of my turmoil and pain, something unusual started happening to me. I had this strong urge to write something more than journals and diaries. I had been collecting stories, immigration papers, and all kind of information about my families of origin. I wanted to complete a long paper on our family history that I had started writing several years ago but never completed. I wanted to give the book to my sons, siblings, nieces and nephews and to my two grandchildren. As usual when I think of something I want to do, I start doing the necessary paperwork right away.

I went over to the State University and signed up for an English class in writing. Five of us were over 50 years of age and 15 were college seniors. I was shocked to realize I had not been in an English class for over forty years! The students look so young, but they knew more about writing than I did. I relaxed. I wasn't there for the grade, and I learned as much from the students as I did from the professor who was quite competent. And I got a B+ as a final grade!

The class was so exciting that I decided to take my writing more seriously. This was a wonderful avocation. I didn't have to think about retiring because I could do both: my work and my writing. Unfortunately, I could not continue in the English class because more seniors, who were required to take the class, signed up the next semester and there was no room for us older "seniors."

I was disappointed that I couldn't get into the writing class, but I was taking a spiritual writing class at our church every Thursday evening, so I focused on that for a few semesters. One day one of my friends, who was interested in writing, asked if I wanted to take a weekly writing class. Of course, I did.

I've been in this writing class for three years. I not only completed the family story, I've written two more parts which altogether make a book. Now, what does all this have to do with RETIREMENT? Slowly and steadily, my focus has turned in a different direction. In the past year, I realized that I could call myself a writer. That's a full-time job in and of itself!

In the past year I assisted another writer, Donna Wade, as her collaborator, to rewrite her story, *I Wanted a Baby and He Didn't*, into a self-help book. And she had a publisher! In the midst of helping her, I thought, "I can write that book on marriage that I've postponed for a long time." Yes, I could. I had all my lectures, articles, and a bunch of miscellaneous writings that I had saved. I found a young woman who called herself a copywriter and editor, and she was interested in helping me to put a book together. I signed a contract with Allison

Shaw and we agreed to meet on a regular basis compiling and organizing my material into a book.

Working on the marriage book took me a step closer toward retirement. More people would have access to my style of working with couples. I didn't have to do the actual work anymore! Now, I am ready to consider leaving my private practice. Two other factors contributed to this decision. For the first time in my entire career, I have not had a call from a new client in ninety days! My caseload has dropped to seven clients, all of whom I've been seeing for two or three years, and I do believe that God is telling me something: "It's time for you to let go."

On June 20, 2005, I decided to put a new message on my answering machine: "This is Libby Kovacs. I am in the process of retiring from my private practice. I will not be taking any new clients. Please call one of the following therapists for an appointment..."

I am feeling quite content and at peace with my life. I loved my work and I gave it my best efforts. I have a new vocation developing and I feel whole and true to myself. When everything falls into place, I know I am making the right move. My lease expires on August 1st which is the 57th anniversary of the day I left home to start a career as a nurse. I feel I have come full circle. I have completed all of my goals and then some, and my life is taking a new and very different direction.

WHAT'S THIS ALL ABOUT?—OCTOBER 22, 2006

Yesterday, I woke up thinking, "I've been rejected! I've been betrayed! I've been found to be unworthy." Yes, I know all that. It's been happening my entire life. These feelings started when I was born. So, is this why I've been falling? I've worked all that out in my therapies. Why is it coming back again? What have I overlooked?

I must start looking at these falls and find out what they mean. I think I'll call the psychiatrist I saw once a few years ago with Mike. I want someone who doesn't know me to look over these events and see what he comes up with. Then, I'll go back to my therapist. I took off a few months from therapy in May, but it's probably time to go back now.

The first wound that I suffered started at my birth when my father jokingly said, "It's a girl! Send her back! No, better still, throw her out the window!" This was the big joke I grew up with—my father laughing and slapping his leg as he told this story over and over to his friends. As I grew, I sometimes couldn't tell whether he was joking or not. It felt real to me, and I felt hurt and rejected.

As I got older, I enjoyed playing out of doors. Roller-skating was my favorite activity, but I also loved to jump rope and playing quiet games like Chinese checkers. My father was definite that sled riding and bicycles were forbidden. Of course, I was tempted to try each of these; and whenever I did, I'd get scared and freeze. The first time I rode a bicycle I could feel my father's presence behind me. I looked and there he was coming after me. I dropped the bicycle on the street and ran. I knew I was in for a good whipping!

I was terrified when I saw him come into the house and he started to take his belt off. I screamed and hid behind my mother. She tried to reason with him, but he was not listening. "I am not raising her so she can get killed by a car," he yelled at me behind my mother. She put both hands on his chest, and said, "Alright, Paul. This was the first time and she won't do it again." She looked at me, "Do you hear your father? You are not to ride any bicycles." She took Dad out in the kitchen and made him a cup of coffee. I went out on the front porch and sat on the swing. I thought about what happened.

A couple of years passed before I was tempted again. This time I was in the park and I asked a friend if I could ride his bike. He let me, and as I rode down the slope behind the swimming pool, I suddenly saw this car coming toward me. I froze. I couldn't remember how to put the brakes on! I veered off to the left to avoid the car, but I found myself going over a wall that I ran the bicycle into. My friend jumped over the wall, and said, "Oh, my God Lib, are you all right?" I was stunned and quite shaken. "My face hurts," I moaned. I knew my face was scraped. "Now," I thought fearfully. "Dad is going to kill me!"

Thankfully, my mother intervened again. She talked to my father. I stayed in my room with a book whenever dad was home for the next three days. I finally came out of hiding. He looked at my face sternly and shook his head as if to say, "You see what happens when you don't listen?" I don't believe I rode a bike again until I had my own children and taught them how to ride their bicycles and I bought one for myself.

The next time I disobeyed my father, I was a young adult in nurses training. I had a day off and I had gone to Jim's farm. It was January and it had snowed. Jim brought out his sled, and I thought, "Oh, no. I can't do that." But I did and, lo and behold, I froze and I ran into a post where I hit my head. Jim was so frightened. He ran and helped me up. "Are you OK, Lib?" his voice quivering.

"Yes, I think so, but I think I'm going to have a headache and probably a black eye." Yes, I certainly did. The X-Ray of my head was negative for injuries. The next day I was on duty in the Pediatrics Ward. There was a little boy with his arm in a sling. I pointed to my head and eye, "Were you sled riding too?" With a big grin on his face, he nodded "yes."

I'm still not certain what this has to do with my falling, but I have a feeling these past incidents are at the root of my present problem. When I think of falling, I see a chasm of emptiness that represents over fifty years of work history—my entire adult life. I know I can't fill that hole by over-extending myself, so I've decided to withdraw from some activities in the next month or so. I want to focus on my spiritual life; and, yes, I will see the neurologist when I have an appointment.

I'm Afraid to Go for a Walk—November 2006

Now, in November 2006, I have had several unusual and startling experiences: I have fallen three times since July. The last time was two weeks ago. I was taking a walk and suddenly, without any provocation, I was falling. I heard the right side of my forehead hit the sidewalk, and my glasses were sliding on the cement. Immediately, blood was flowing from the wound. I was lying face down and on the verge of tears, and I heard a child's voice in my head crying, "Mom, help me!"

I picked myself up slowly. I put my hand to my forehead and found it was covered with blood. I walked home slowly, puzzled and

417

worried. "I don't understand what is happening to me," I thought. "What is happening to me?" I'm walking in my neighborhood and all of a sudden, without any warning—and I did not trip or lose my balance—it's as if, in a moment, I am in an altered state of consciousness and I'm aware I am falling and I can't stop myself.

The third fall lacerated my forehead and required four stitches by a doctor in the emergency room. Again, all the tests (blood panel, heart monitor, echogram, and Cat Scan) were all normal. "This is very mysterious," my doctor said pensively. He's even more puzzled than I am. His next suggestion was, "I'll refer you to a neurologist."

I'm thinking (and I believe my doctor is too), "Is this a conversion again?" This "mystery" is affecting my life. I'm becoming hyper vigilant again. I'm afraid to go for a walk. I don't want something worse to happen—a concussion or fractured skull! God forbid!

Whip it
Into Shape

Yesterday, I shipped my entire manuscript to a "manuscript coach" to shape it and prepare it for publication. As soon as I sent it, I felt the last part was unfinished, fragmented. I suggested in the letter I wrote to him that he "whip it into shape."

Why am I not surprised that I woke up this morning with a severe head cold? I can't remember the last time I was so sick. I remember reading somewhere that an author always got sick when she finished a writing project. Is it possible that writing about all that pain in my life is what is keeping me so healthy?

Yes, very likely, because I made my peace with Dad. Whenever I dream or think about him, he has a smile on his face. I remembered yesterday that he cried out for his Mother when he was dying. I wish he could have shown us his more sensitive side when we were young. I know. He couldn't then, but I am certain that God has helped him to overcome his particular obstacles and to become the person (or spirit) that he was intended to be—even after death.

Then, writing those two articles this past summer left me with a strong sense of love and compassion for Jim. I've forgiven Miklos, too. Given his background and the traditions of his ethnic culture, he did what he was destined to do. I learned a great deal from both marriages: one important point was that when expectations and reality do not fit together, then there's trouble ahead. I always used what I learned in my work. I was able to help most couples who came to my office to work out their problems together, and my divorce rate was one a year. One couple a year would go through a dissolution process, and they did so with much less dissension and anger. One couple a year got divorced out of hundreds, no, several thousand couples with whom I worked over the last twenty-five years, and I could not get Mike to work with me to save our marriage.

We all do our best. Sometimes we succeed and sometimes we fail. I'm grateful for my life. I lived it as well as I knew how and I fulfilled all my dreams, and more. Now, I must let go of the past and stay with the present. This transition called RETIREMENT was easier and smoother than all the others that I experienced. I do believe that I was so accustomed to painful and difficult changes throughout my life; and when it wasn't, my mind and body reacted in this peculiar manner—falling down. I usually come through crises or changes just fine. Everything will be just fine, and I will have the opportunity to celebrate!

My life journey was focused on using the gifts God has given me in a purposeful and meaningful manner, and I believe I fulfilled that aspiration through my devotion to my family and to the work I did with thousands of hurting and wounded individuals, couples, and families. I believe I've learned to live my life as honestly and as authentically as I know how, with much help and guidance from the Source of all that is real and true; and thankfully, I am becoming the person God intended me to be. I will bring this book to a close with the quotation from T. S. Elliot:

> *We shall not cease from exploration*
> *And the end of all our exploring*
> *Will be to arrive where we started*
> *And know the place for the first time.*

Finale
January 2008

Following an enjoyable weekend with her three daughters and their children, Sally Reese, my daughter's-in-law mother, died quietly of another stroke on August 15, 2007. Less than a month later Miklos M. Kovacs died on September 12, 2007.

On December 22, 2007, I received a telephone call from my niece, Irene, telling me her mother—my sister Mary—died of cancer.

May God give them all peace and rest.

TRUE STORIES OF COURAGE AND INSPIRATION

> *Call in your order for fast service and quantity discounts!*
> **(541) 347- 9882**

OR order on-line at **www.rdrpublishers.com** *using PayPal.*
OR order by FAX at **(541) 347-9883** *OR by mail:*
Make a copy of this form; enclose payment information:
Robert D. Reed Publishers
1380 Face Rock Drive, Bandon, OR 97411

Name _____

Address _____

City_____ State_____ Zip_____

Phone:Fax:Cell: _____

E-Mail: _____

Payment by check /_/ or credit card /_/ *(All major credit cards are accepted.)*

Name on card _____

Card Number _____

Exp. Date _____ Last 3-Digit number on back of card: _____

	Quantity	Total Amount
Liberty's Quest by Liberty Kovacs $29.95	_____	_____
Fragments of a Forgotten People by Henry Fast $15.95	_____	_____
***Yalla! (Let's Go)* A Wandering Jew Survives Palestine, Cuba, Jamaica and America** by Alejandro Moden $24.95	_____	_____
The Quander Quality:* The True Story of *A Black Trailblazing Diabetic by James W. Quander & Rohulamin Quander $24.95	_____	_____
Silent Screams from the Hamptons by Christa Jan Ryan $14.95	_____	_____

Quantity of books ordered: _____Total amount for books: _____

Shipping is $3.50 1st book + $1 for each additional book: Plus postage: _____

FINAL TOTAL: _____